WORLD ISSUES *IN THE GLOBAL COMMUNITY*

APRIL 3RD SCARLETT MARKS

GO TO MID-TERM MARKS

WORLD ISSUES

IN THE GLOBAL COMMUNITY

Robert Harshman

Christine Hannell

WILEY

John Wiley & Sons

Toronto   New York   Chichester   Brisbane   Singapore

Canadian Cataloguing in Publication Data

Harshman, Robert
  World issues in the global community

For use in secondary schools.
Includes index.
ISBN 0-471-79692-1

1. Anthropo-geography. 2. Social problems.
I. Hannell, Christine. II. Title.

GF43.H37 1989   910   C88-094857-4

Editor: Lorraine Fairley

Copy Editor: Lisa Stacey

Designer: Blair Kerrigan/Glyphics

Assembly: Melissa Nelson/Glyphics

Artist: Jim Loates

Typesetter: Jay Tee Graphics Limited

Printer: The Bryant Press Limited

Cover Photo: T. Grill/Miller Comstock Inc.

Printed and bound in Canada
10 9 8 7 6 5 4 3 2 1

Contents

Part II
Geopolitical Issues of the World   76

3
Geopolitics

Part III
Human and Economic Issues of the World

Acknowledgements

In writing a book such as this, there are inevitably a number of people who play a vital role in reviewing and editing as well as supplying information and photographs. We would like to thank Judith Walker and the librarians at McMaster University for their invaluable assistance with the research for this book. In addition, we want to thank those who assisted us at the Population Reference Bureau in Washington, D.C. We would also like to thank the following reviewers for their invaluable advice:

Ronald Carswell, University of Calgary, Calgary, Alberta

David George, Medicine Hat Junior Senior High School, Medicine Hat, Alberta

Fred Headon, Maples Collegiate, Winnipeg, Manitoba

Ronald Hynes, Roman Catholic School Board for St. John's, St. John's, Newfoundland

Donald Lloyd, Sir Sandford Fleming Secondary School, Willowdale, Ontario

Clifford Oliver, Board of Education for the City of London, London, Ontario

Thomas Runk, Lindsay High School, Lindsay, Ontario

Ian Wright, The Board of Education for the City of Etobicoke, Etobicoke, Ontario

In the area of supplying photos, we want to thank Bob Haskett for giving us access to the wealth of pictures he has. These photos have added an exciting dimension to our text. We also would like to thank Lorraine Fairley, Elizabeth McCurdy, Rena Leibovitch and the rest of the editorial staff at John Wiley and Sons for their encouragement and support.

Rob Harshman
Christine Hannell

To The Student

Famine, debt, pollution, over-population, wars, terrorism, and disease are topics which are constantly in the news. Living as we do in a wealthy and peaceful nation, few of us have experienced the desperation that is so common in many other nations. We may become involved in fundraising activities, but often we do not fully understand the causes of the problem, nor do we have a voice in how the money or gifts collected are to be used.

In your final years in school, you are preparing yourself for a major change. Whatever your chosen field, it is important that you have certain skills and an understanding of the complex interrelationships that exist between people, the various components of the environment, the way in which we use the world's resources, and the influence exerted by politics and the legacy of past events.

Each of us spends the first part of our lives in situations over which sometimes have little or no control. As we gain wisdom through a combination of experience and education, our ability and opportunities to influence what happens in the world increase. The fields of study, employment, and voluntary activities through which this can be achieved are limitless. You probably are aware of the high-profile activities of modern entertainers, large international organizations, and emergency relief efforts. All of these play an important role in alleviating difficult international situations or conditions.

We must also recognize the importance of the efforts of individuals and small groups. Donations of time and money, whether for activities at home or in other countries, do have a significant impact. On many occasions in this book, you will read about the benefits which resulted from the efforts of a single person, or a small group of people. Activities which bring people from different backgrounds, cultures, politics, and religions together have been beneficial to all those concerned. Through such activities we can gain a different perspective and appreciation for each other which replaces the fear, suspicion, and prejudice fostered by separation and ignorance.

As you proceed through this course, your ability to use statistics, graphs, and maps should improve, as should your research and writing skills. Hopefully, you will be able to recognize the mistakes that others have made when trying to help needy nations, and see how you might act or react if you were in their situation. You should also begin to appreciate the complexity of factors which have produced some of the situations you will have to make decisions on in the future, and the real challenges involved in making improvements.

Be constantly on the watch for bias. Bias involves a subjective viewpoint. As this book is written by people with feelings, beliefs, and perspectives of their own, it is possible that some bias has crept in, even though every effort has been made to eliminate it and present several points of view. Many other sources of information make no attempt to eliminate bias. Often, such sources are intended to sway your opinion without giving arguments on various sides which would enable you to come to a well-informed personal opinion. If you can, try to find out about the people and organizations producing the information that you use. What are their qualifications? Do you know of any particular interest or political perspective that they may be promoting? Is the information that they are using reliable and being interpreted correctly?

Do not give up on the world. Sometimes a problem may seem insoluble, but there is a solution. Sometimes the solution is elusive, at other times expensive and time consuming, but there is a workable solution nonetheless. You can take heart, for example, from how well the environment has recovered when pollution controls are implemented. All is not ''doom and gloom,'' but we must learn how to treat this earth more gently, so that it can recover and sustain life for millions of years to come.

To The Teacher

Organizing and teaching a course in World Issues is a privilege that brings with it considerable responsibility. All of us are aware that there are a multitude of pressures which threaten the well-being and perhaps even the survival of future generations. This situation results from the complex interaction of many factors, including geopolitics, increased expectations, and technological change. These, in turn, have led to the increasingly apparent deterioration of the environment, the desperate living conditions faced by billions of people, and military activities and tensions that occur worldwide.

Students taking this course will range from those who have already developed a deep interest and concern for what they observe or learn through other media, to those who are only concerned about achieving the necessary qualifications to equip them for the next part of their lives. Whatever their motivation, this course offers a unique opportunity for us to enable students to learn about the world and its people. By the end of the course, the students should be able to analyze and evaluate current world problems so that they are better equipped to draw conclusions and contribute to future solutions to these problems.

Obviously, these kinds of expectations are very demanding of the teacher. We are aware that what is observed in the world today is the result of many complex interacting factors. We also know that the world is changing very rapidly, and that it is very important for students to learn how to make use of the resources to which they have access, so that they can keep up with these changes, both now and in the future. In order to contribute to an improved world, students will need to be able to assess situations, and come up with reasonable and creative solutions in light of the successes and failure of the past.

This book was written to provide the teacher with the basis for achieving these goals. At frequent intervals throughout the text, students are asked questions which promote the development of reasoning, evaluation, and creative thinking skills. In the opening chapter, students are introduced to one of the methods which can be used to organize their approach to, and presentation of, research assignments. This method, called the inquiry approach, can be applied to large or small assignments. Student will find relevant independent study questions listed at the end of each chapter, or they can devise topics related to their own interests.

Determining which topics should be included was difficult. There are the obvious worldwide issues such as nuclear war, or the depletion of the ozone layer, but there are many local situations occurring in many parts of the world, such as hunger, international debt, and human rights violations. All of these provide suitable World Issues topics for study.

Following the introductory chapter, the book continues with a study of the variations in the quality of life for the world's peoples. When we think about world issues, the one predominant consideration is the

conditions under which people live, and this is the perspective which we have chosen to start with.

The two subsequent chapters, on geopolitics and industrialization, explain some of the major factors that have contributed to the current world situation. The problems of hunger and population are dealt with next. They have been left to a later part of the book because we believe they are more a result than a cause of many of the world's problems.

Chapter 7 deals with the growing environmental problems facing us today. Not only have we been poisoning our environment, with the consequent threat to our health, but we threaten all forms of life, living things which have as much right to a secure future as we do. Issues of resource depletion, reserves, and alternatives are discussed in Chapter 8. In the final chapter, students are challenged to develop a personal perspective of the world today. They are again reminded that individual efforts can make a difference, and how important it is that each of us understands the dynamic forces that have contributed to various situations.

One factor which we will see changing over the next few decades is the emergence of economic strength in many Pacific Rim countries. It is anticipated that, as the power of these countries increases, the quality of life of their peoples will improve. Other economies may deteriorate, bringing problems and challenges to citizens in such areas as North America and Europe. Adjustments will be necessary to ameliorate the

detrimental effects of such changes. Planning will require the energy of informed people, such as the students in your courses.

Certain parts of the world have so many problems that concerted efforts by people from those countries, in close collaboration with workers from more fortunate nations, will have to continue for many years into the future. We will need well educated experts who have the necessary concern and overall comprehension of the situation to make the best possible use of all the available resources. Again, some of your students could find themselves in that position in the future.

This book provides you with a valuable resource to give students the background that they need. We suggest very strongly, however, that you supplement it with other sources of information and experiences. These could include current events and commentaries as reported in newspapers, magazines, and on television. Personal contacts with people from other nations and cultures are extremely beneficial in overcoming prejudice and in understanding how peoples in other parts of the world live. Our four "Living with the Issues" accounts, found at the ends of Chapters 1, 2, 5, and 9, provide students with a valuable personal glimpse into the lives of people in other cultures.

As the teacher of this course, you will be opening your own eyes as well as those of your students. We hope that you will enjoy the experience and will reap the rewards which come from a worthwhile endeavour.

Part I

World Overview and Quality of Life

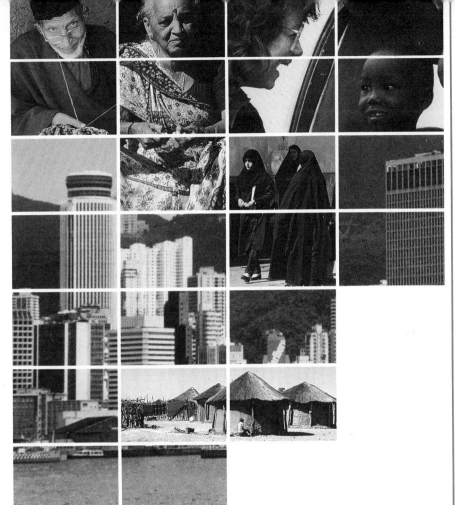

By the end of this chapter, you should be able to:

- recognize the general physical and cultural patterns of the world;
- identify some of the chief characteristics of a modern nation;
- identify some of the major issues which face the world;
- display an understanding of the five worlds; and
- use the inquiry method as a research tool.

1

An Overview of the World

The World Today in All Its Variety

A glance at the front page of a daily newspaper gives some indication of the tremendous variety of events which are taking place somewhere on the surface of the earth on any given day. It is important not to be overwhelmed by the enormity of the world, but to look for patterns and relationships that help us to understand the significance of events and issues.

The following scenes give a hint of the infinite complexity of human affairs. Each scene is based on eyewitness accounts or news reports and is like a snapshot of life taken in a particular part of the world today.

. . . The Sultan of Brunei, the richest person in the world, likes to entertain on a lavish scale. On this particular night, he is host to 1500 political and business leaders. After the banquet is over, the guests are entertained on one of his yachts or in one of the formal gardens that surround the palace.

. . . The traffic and the crowds in downtown Buenos Aires are great, so some of the thousands of "street kids" get lost in the hustle and bustle. Abandoned by their parents, these children live permanently on the streets. One young boy, Andre, shines shoes for 10 cents; his hands seem to be permanently blackened. It's 10 p.m. Andre has fallen asleep in the doorway of an abandoned factory.

Gate to the old city in Fez, Morocco

Rice fields in Bali, Indonesia

. . . Observers in Rwanda report that 35 000 refugees have crossed the border from Burundi to escape the slaughter which has resulted from intense rivalry between the Huki and Tutsi tribes. At least 5000 people have been killed.

. . . An earthquake in remote areas of the Himalayan foothills of Nepal and India has killed at least 650 people and injured many more. Communications in the area are very primitive, and rescue efforts are hampered by blocked roads, railroads which have sunk into the mud, and swollen rivers.

. . . On the night of Tuesday, August 23, 1988, 3000 people were evacuated from their homes in a Montreal suburb. Fire in a nearby chemical warehouse was releasing dangerous PCBs into the atmosphere. The immediate and long-term effects on the evacuees' health are not known, but PCBs are believed to cause brain, nerve, liver, and skin disorders, and possibly cancer.

. . . A small group of medical researchers at the University of Toronto spent many months searching for a genetic clue to the condition known as the Down Syndrome. Whenever they appeared to have reached success, they hit a new roadblock in their research. In March 1988, however, it was different. They came upon a genetic marker which could be the first step in solving the riddle of how to prevent this condition

Questions

1. In two or three sentences, write down your reactions to the scenarios you have just read.

2. (a) Set three questions on these scenarios for another student to answer. Two of the three questions should refer to more than one of the scenarios.

   (b) Answer the questions another student has set for you.

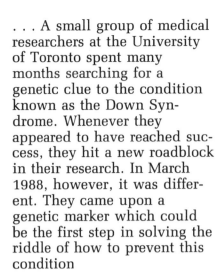

Clockwise from top left, a coffee bar in rural Cameroon; a former head hunter in the highlands of Papua, New Guinea; three girls from a prosperous family at the Taj Mahal, Agra, India; this woman begs for a living in Hong Kong

Introduction

Despite the complexity of the many issues which face the world today, it is important not to be overwhelmed by the issues, but to separate them and then analyze each one in turn. In this way, you can attempt to understand in part some of the forces at work today in the world and the impact which they are having on people and the environment. In this chapter, we will begin to examine a number of key issues which the world faces and how these issues interact with each other.

Major Issues in the World Today

As we have already discovered, there are many issues which face us in the world; there is also considerable debate as to which of these issues are most pressing. The relative importance of issues varies according to our backgrounds, interests, and personal interpretations. For some people, the issue of hunger is the most crucial one for the future of the world, while others believe that the arms race overshadows every other issue.

Question

3. (a) List in order the ten issues which you believe are most likely to affect the future of the world. Give reasons for your selections.

    (b) What does this list reveal about your priorities and your view of the world?

The new stealth bomber is almost invisible to radar. What effect would this have on Soviet defences?

The Five Worlds

Geographers have applied the process of synthesis in a number of different areas of concern. **Synthesis** involves using information from a variety of sources as conclusions are drawn and theories are developed. One of the areas of research is the division of the world into groupings or blocs of countries based on their social, economic, or political nature. The world today is commonly divided into three worlds: the **First World**, which refers to the highly industrialized democracies of the western world such as Canada and the United States; the **Second World**, which is the communist bloc and includes countries such as the USSR, China, and Yugoslavia; and the **Third World**, which includes all the other countries. This division into only three worlds has presented a few difficulties, for it groups together wealthy oil-producing countries such as Saudi Arabia and very poor countries such as Ethiopia. As a result, a different system with five categories has been developed to take into account the great diversity within the developing world. Figure 1.1 illustrates the five worlds.

Although the division into five worlds is based on generalizations for each country, it provides an overview of the world and some of the patterns which are present. Countries within each of the "worlds" have certain characteristics in common with other countries in that category.

Based upon the perspective of the highly industrialized countries, the main criterion for the division of the world into five categories is the degree of industrialization as well as the general standard of living of individual countries. The cultural development of a country is not considered.

The **First World** comprises countries which are highly industrialized and affluent, and in which there are systems of public education and extensive government programs for those who are poor. Most of these countries are democracies. Great Britain, Canada, the United States, and Japan all belong to the First World.

The **Second World** includes communist countries which have strong government control over almost all aspects of life and in which the government regulates the economy closely. There is little political freedom. There is a wide economic variation within this world, from the poverty of a country such as Vietnam or China to the affluence of the Soviet Union. The unifying feature among all these countries is that their governments are communist.

The **Third World** refers to those countries of the developing world which are relatively affluent. Although there may be poverty within each of these countries, there is substantial progress being made from an economic standpoint. Industrialization has taken root, or wealth has been derived from exploitation of natural resources such as oil or minerals. Brazil,

A view of downtown Moscow, the capital of the USSR

Figure 1.1
The Five Worlds

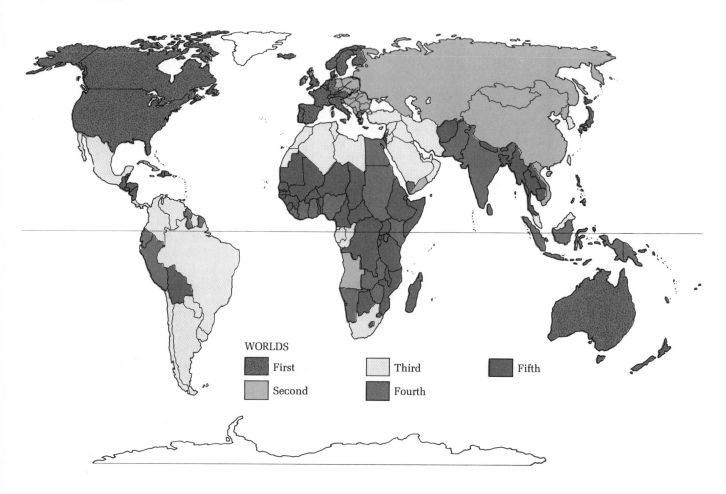

WORLDS

First

Second

Third

Fourth

Fifth

South Korea, Taiwan, Singapore, Kuwait, Colombia, and Venezuela are part of the Third World.

Countries of the **Fourth World** are less affluent than those of the Third World, but have the potential for solid economic growth. Although they have widespread poverty today, they often have rich stores of natural resources and, with time and technology, they might yet have an opportunity to escape this poverty. Countries such as Indonesia, India, Pakistan, Peru, Kenya, Nigeria, and the Philippines fall into this category.

The **Fifth World** is made up of the poorest countries of the world. These countries often have very few known natural resources and little industry. The standard of living is very low, most of the people have minimal education or none at all, and there is little sign that these countries can escape poverty in the near future. Bangladesh, Haiti, Ethiopia, and Chad belong to the Fifth World.

Although these five worlds are referred to in literature and statistical analysis in these terms, for our purposes in this book, the Third,

Fourth and Fifth Worlds will be referred to as **lesser developed countries (LDCs)** or the **developing world**. Those countries which are highly industrialized will be referred to as the **developed world**.

Questions

4. (a) From the Appendix at the back of this book, select as much information as you can which helps to describe each of the five worlds. For example, what statistics appear to define those countries in the Fifth World?

   (b) What difficulties did you encounter as you attempted to define the different worlds in part (a)?

Left, a traditional home in Tanzania on the slopes of Mt. Kilimanjaro; above, highrises in Calgary, Alberta

5. (a) Examine Figure 1.1 which shows the location of the five worlds. Describe the general location of each one.

   (b) What continent appears to contain the greatest number of Fifth World countries? Suggest reasons that might help to explain this distribution pattern.

   (c) Using your atlas as a guide, identify those countries which are in the Third World because of the exploitation of important raw materials such as oil.

   (d) What relationship might there be between the location of the countries of the five worlds and the pattern of trading routes, the movement of capital, and the flow of information around the world?

The Role of Geography

Geography centres on the study of the earth's surface and the forces, both human and natural, which shape that surface. The interrelationships among the various forces active on the earth's surface are also important for geographers to consider.

An example will help you focus on the role of geography in dealing with world issues. Whether you listed "Hunger," "Food," or "Food Supply," as a pressing issue, it is likely that this is one of the problems uppermost in your mind. Many organizations exist, such as the **Food and Agricultural Organization (FAO)**, whose aim is to conquer hunger and to supply desperate people with immediate and long-term help. Taking the FAO as an example, let us suppose that an aid group has been flown to the stricken region of Niger, in Africa. The group members have been asked to study the situation in as much detail as possible. In preparation, they have consulted with other experts to familiarize themselves with the following:

- the background and traditional ways of life of the people of the area (history, anthropology, sociology);
- the climate and soils of the region and the crops that have been traditionally grown there, as well as those which might be introduced (soil science, climatology, meteorology, agriculture);
- health problems and possible solutions (medicine, pharmacology);
- trading routes, sources of products sold in the region as well as markets for products produced in the region (economics, transportation, marketing, etc.); and
- government policies, wars or armed conflicts that have affected the region (politics, geopolitics, military planning, etc.).

The inquiries made ahead of time have to be followed by studies made first-hand upon arrival in Niger. These combined studies must tap many different sources of information if the experts are to produce recommendations. This type of synthesis will be applied to issues dealt with in this book to help you achieve a fuller understanding of the world around you.

Geography also involves the use of practical skills such as graphing and mapping. These skills help geographers to develop syntheses as well as to illustrate the results of their research. Mapping, for example, illustrates the spatial distribution of certain phenomena across the surface of the earth. As one begins to examine the reasons behind the distribution, one discovers more about the world itself.

Questions

6. How does the geographical approach to the world help in understanding issues to do with the environment or land use?

7. What difficulties can you foresee in attempting to draw upon a wide variety of different pieces of information in order to study a problem or a region?

In approaching any study of world issues, it is important to have a genuine concern for people who face difficult circumstances, yet at the same time use principles of scientific investigation to uncover relevant facts that relate to what is being studied. Although the industrialized world has a standard of living which is the highest in the world, there are still many issues which we have not dealt with adequately, and we should be careful not to impose our values on people in the developing world. Solutions to problems will not be fully accepted by anyone anywhere if they are forced on the population. Instead, it is important to promote self-help projects wherever possible. Whether the problem is hunger, soil erosion, or pollution control, people will accept solutions if they are encouraged to seek them out themselves.

Even though the issues which will be dealt with are complex, it is important not to dismiss any issue as being too difficult to explore or as having no possible solution. The inquiry model which is discussed later in this chapter is a valuable tool in helping to solve problems such as those raised in this book.

The issues discussed in these pages have been selected because they are of major significance for the world as a whole. Although some of the issues, such as hunger, appear not to touch certain regions, their impact is widely felt. As the countries of the world become more and more interdependent, a problem in one part of the world has significant repercussions elsewhere.

Other issues, such as environmental degradation, have worldwide implications. Pollution knows no borders, and such developments as ozone depletion are touching the lives of everyone on the planet.

True education involves not only knowledge but also a change of attitude. Merely knowing about pollution, for example, has little effect, but acting out of concern because of the knowledge you have is the truly significant result of education. This book will challenge you to think about some of the key issues of our time and to respond to them as well.

The Physical World

Each country of the world is the product of the interaction of physical and human systems. Despite great human ingenuity, the physical world still dominates human activity. Each physical landscape is itself the product of various forces inter-acting with one another. In order to understand these physical systems, examine Figures 1.2, 1.3, 1.4, and 1.5.

Pollution knows no borders. This coal-fired power plant in the Soviet Union contributes to acid rain problems there.

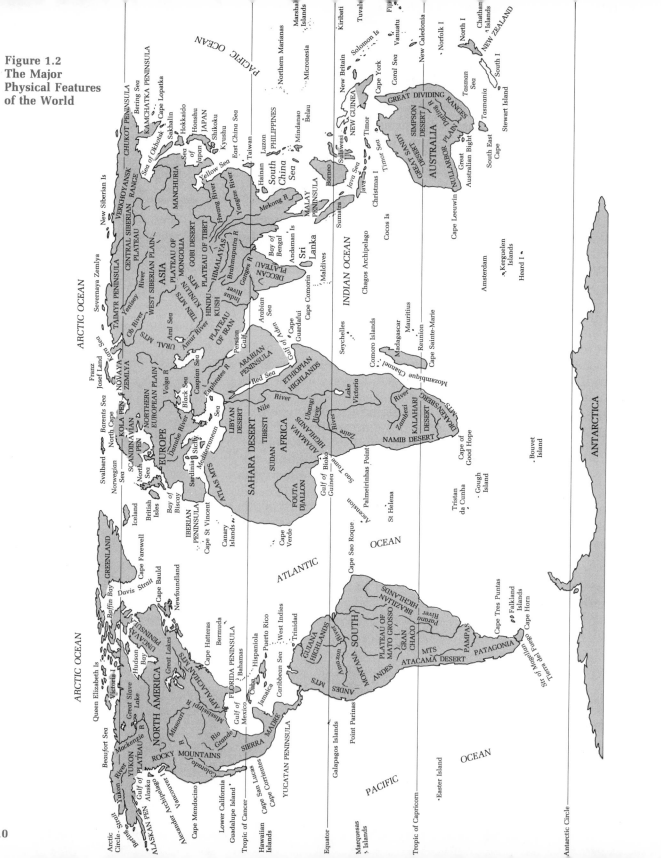

**Figure 1.2
The Major
Physical Features
of the World**

10

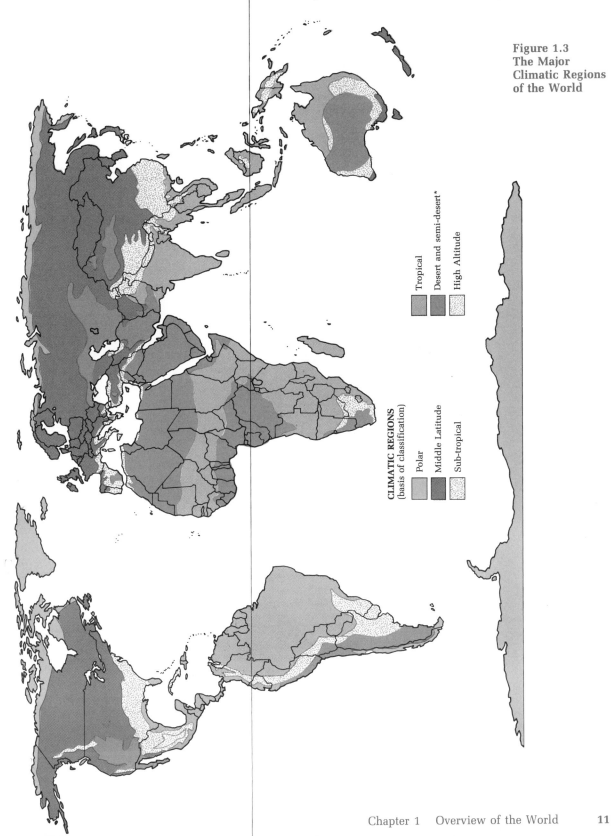

Figure 1.3
The Major
Climatic Regions
of the World

CLIMATIC REGIONS
(basis of classification)

Polar

Middle Latitude

Sub-tropical

Tropical

Desert and semi-desert*

High Altitude

Figure 1.4
World Vegetation
Zones

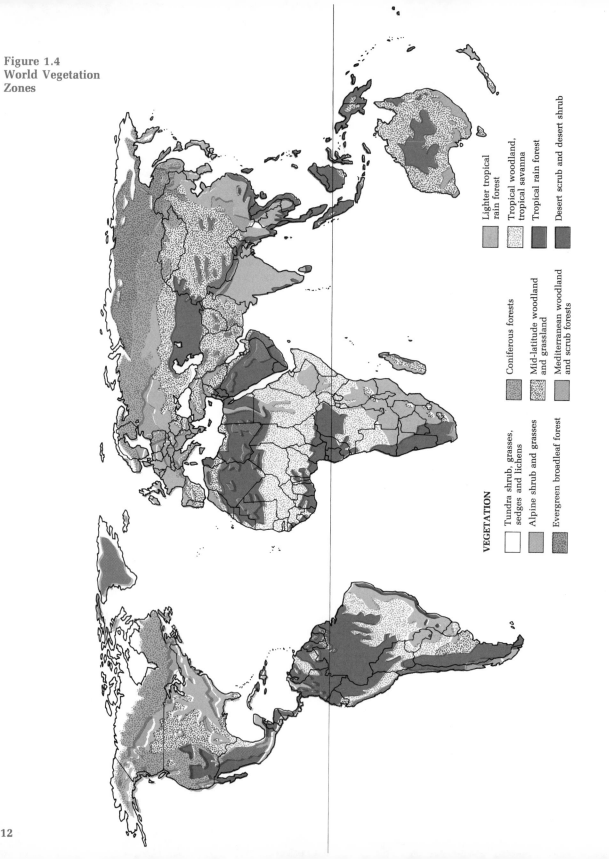

VEGETATION

Tundra shrub, grasses,
sedges and lichens

Alpine shrub and grasses

Evergreen broadleaf forest

Coniferous forests

Mid-latitude woodland
and grassland

Mediterranean woodland
and scrub forests

Lighter tropical
rain forest

Tropical woodland,
tropical savanna

Tropical rain forest

Desert scrub and desert shrub

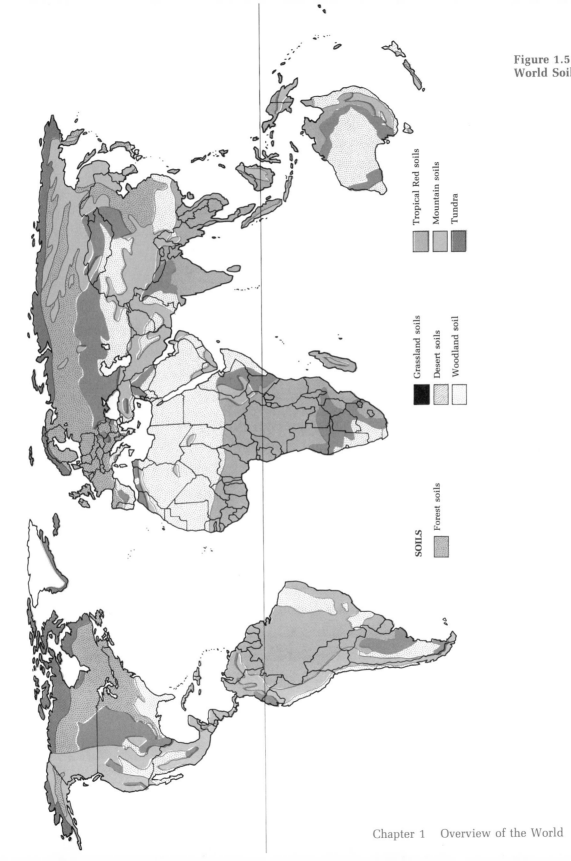

Figure 1.5
World Soil Zones

Tropical Red soils

Mountain soils

Tundra

Grassland soils

Desert soils

Woodland soil

SOILS

Forest soils

Questions

8. (a) Examine Figure 1.2, showing the major physical regions of the world. Describe five major patterns which you can see on this map.

   (b) Based on the map of the physical features only, list those regions of the world which are inhospitable to human habitation, giving reasons.

9. (a) Compare Figures 1.2 and 1.3. What relationship is there between these two maps? Explain your reasoning carefully.

   (b) What relationship appears to exist between the physical features and climate of a region and the vegetation found there?

10. (a) Describe the importance of the soils to the prosperity of a region.

    (b) How can the climate and vegetation of a region affect its soils?

11. Examine the four maps once again and then answer the following questions.

    (a) Explain what makes a region of the world hospitable to human settlement.

    (b) Explain what makes a region of the world inhospitable to human settlement.

    (c) Using a blank base map of the world, develop a map to show where the hospitable and inhospitable regions of the world are. Be aware of the fact that you will have to make generalizations, thus leaving out some details in constructing your map.

    (d) Which areas of the developing world are inhospitable? How has this fact affected their economic progress?

    (e) Some regions of the developing world invite human settlement. Explain in general terms how it is possible for a region like this to still be poor.

12. Suggest reasons to explain why a country such as Canada, which is mostly inhospitable to settlement, is a highly industrialized country. In order to answer this question, you will have to include a wide variety of factors and draw upon your general knowledge of Canada.

Right, street scene in Kano, Nigeria; far right, a temple in downtown Tokyo, Japan

What Is a Nation?

We live in a world dominated by the interests of nations, from tiny micro-states to giant macro-states. The modern nation had its origin in Europe close to 400 years ago, although the concept of the nation-state reaches back into ancient times. Today, the

nation has become the dominant political unit in our world. A **nation** is a political entity which has sovereign political control over a piece of territory. It attempts to control, regulate, or influence the economic, political, and social life of the people living in the area under its control.

A nation may be composed of people who have a common culture, language, or religion as in Japan, for example, or Luxemburg. Yet, in other cases, nations as they develop come to include a variety of ethnic groups, for political or other reasons. Nigeria, for instance, was created by colonial powers who combined a number of different tribal groups. Inherent in the geographic design of Nigeria were tribes with widely different cultures and therefore with the potential for conflict with one another. Latent intertribal conflicts erupted into civil war in the early 1970s in the Biafra region of Nigeria. The damage done by that conflict has taken many years to heal.

Regardless of the origin of nations, national governments are today the structures which manage the people and the resources of the world. Despite attempts to develop a world government which would have power over all the national governments on earth, the power and national pride associated with the modern nations have

prevented a truly international government from coming into being. Some nations have been dogged with corruption and poor management, while others have benefitted from the wise management of their people and land. The results of government management are most clearly seen in the standard of living of its people or the vitality of its cultural life.

The headlines of our newspapers are filled with details of the conflicts between large nations. The very large nations of the world have resulted from the drawing together of different states or nations in order to create a larger entity. The Soviet Union is the product of expansion to control a number of smaller republics or ethnic homelands. The result has been the creation of the largest nation in the world, greater in land area than most of the largest empires of history. Such a country is sometimes referred to as a macro-state.

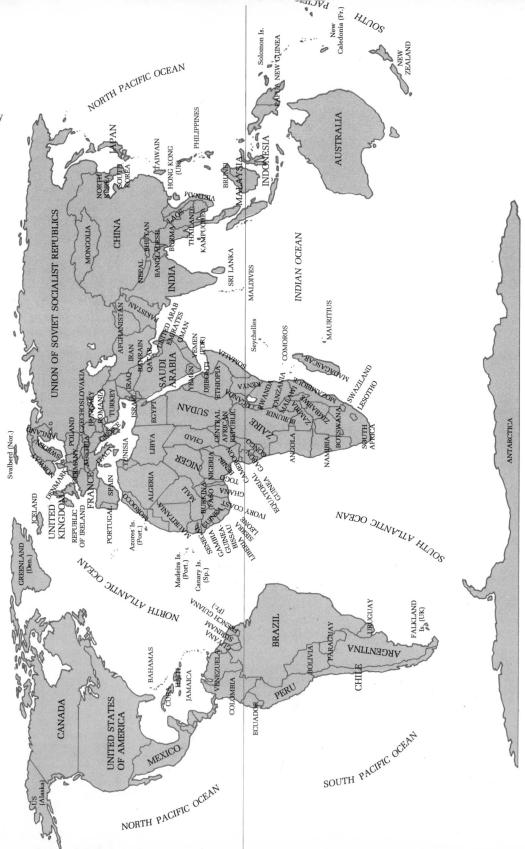

Figure 1.6
A world map showing the major nations. Note the variety of sizes and shapes of the nations.

By contrast, another trend is occurring and that is the development of very small nations, with only a small amount of territory and an equally small population. Grenada in the Caribbean Sea and the Comoro Islands in the Indian Ocean are two examples of very small nations which are sometimes referred to as micro-states.

Throughout this book, you will discover that the national governments of the world are extremely important, and that many contemporary events or changes are moulded by them.

Questions

13. Select five micro-states from the Appendix found at the back of the text.

    (a) Briefly describe the geographic and economic nature of each one of the nations you have selected.

    (b) What advantages can you see in a country's small size?

    (c) What difficulties would a micro-state face in trying to develop economically and survive politically?

14. Using an atlas, select three very large nations which would fit the category of macro-state.

    (a) What advantages would such a country have over a smaller nation, from the point of view of resources, both natural and human, and general economic development?

    (b) What types of conflicts could easily develop between the large and small nations of the world on account of difference in size and therefore point of view?

15. Collect five magazines or newspapers covering world news.

    (a) Identify four nations experiencing severe problems which could threaten their existence.

    (b) For each of the nations which you have selected, try to identify the forces, both internal and external, which are affecting them. These might include a civil war, racial or religious strife, or even occupation by a foreign army.

    (c) What experiences do these countries have in common with each other?

    (d) What general conclusions can be drawn from your limited case studies that can be applied to the future of modern nations in general?

Singapore is a major Asian business centre and port. Is it an example of a micro-state or a macro-state?

Human Culture

Although the physical environment influences the way in which people use the surface of the earth, human culture plays an important role as well. **Culture**, or the way of life of a person or group of people, consists of language, religion, music, art, sport, education, government, work, dress, food, and customs. Although two different groups of people may be challenged by the same natural environment, their cultural differences will strongly influence how they modify that environment. A small village on the northern plains of China, for example, is in sharp contrast to a similarly sized village in Saskatchewan. Clearly, the human landscape is largely a reflection of the culture of the people who live there.

Left, a street scene in Jaipur, India; right, an elderly woman in rural India

Above, a small village in Botswana. Notice the house being built; right, the commercial centre of Hong Kong

18

Agripina, a Poor Mother in Chile

Agripina is a young Indian woman who lives in a **barrio** or poor urban settlement on the edge of Santiago, Chile. At 29 years of age, she has four children and is the sole supporter of her family. She was forced to move to the city because she could not make a living in the countryside working on a rich farmer's land. She makes barely enough money to feed herself and her children by selling trinkets on the streets of the city and doing odd jobs that come her way.

The local self-help Women's Club meets regularly and has been a source of support for Agripina. Although she was baptized Roman Catholic, she rarely attends church and usually works 16 h a day, seven days a week. Her home is a small house built out of corrugated metal and cardboard about 5 km from the centre of town.

Question

16. (a) Briefly review Agripina's culture.

(b) How is your culture different from hers?

(c) What are Agripina's priorities in life? Explain your answer.

(d) What choices or options does she have for the future? Be sure to explain the factors that limit her choices.

(e) How will Chile be affected in the future by the management of its human resources such as Agripina and her family?

An Inquiry Model — A Research Tool

Throughout this course, you will have a number of opportunities to carry out research. When you are researching issues which are complex or which you do not fully understand, it is important to have a model or series of steps to follow. This model of inquiry is a useful tool in research, for its helps you make sure that your investigation is thorough and logical.

Step I *Focus and identify*
Define the problem or issue with which you are dealing. Research the background of the issue, and clarify the major concerns.

Step II *Organize*
Decide on an approach to the issue which you feel will help you deal with it. You might want to ask a question or propose a thesis which you could attempt to answer through your research.

Step III *Plan*
Locate the sources of information which you could use for your research. Make sure that your sources are reliable and up-to-date.

Step IV *Record*
Carry out the research, being careful to record all the information you collect in an easy-to-use format.

Step V *Evaluate*
Sift through the information you have collected and discard any which is inappropriate. Using your other data, try to determine any interrelationships that might exist. Attempt to analyze the thesis which you proposed in Step II. Propose an answer to the problem with which you have been dealing.

Step VI *Come to a conclusion*
Evaluate the solution which you have proposed in Step V and determine to what extent the problem has been solved.

Step VII *Apply and communicate*
Is there more research to be done, and can the conclusions be applied to other situations? Communicate the results of your research to those who are interested in what you have done. Be sure that your writing is clear and coherent.

In order to more fully understand how the Inquiry Model works, let us use the model to help solve a problem. Refer back to the illustration used earlier in the chapter and suppose you are part of the aid group hired by the FAO to travel to Niger to investigate the rural poverty in that country.

Step I
When you first arrive in Niger, it is important to become oriented to the country and its conditions. What do you perceive to be the most pressing issues that face the country? In the process of answering this question, you will likely travel to some of the rural areas and talk to a number of people to try to get a feeling for the country. You want to be careful to remain open-minded in ascertaining the issues to be faced. After some investigation and consultation, you determine that one of the major issues is low crop production and inadequate storage facilities for harvested crops.

Step II
Now that you have identified the general area that you want to research, you must organize an approach which will help produce meaningful solutions. You might propose a question such as, "What simple changes can be introduced which will help farmers increase crop yields and improve storage techniques?"

Step III

In your planning stage, you identify the sources you will consult in order to solve some of the problems you have identified. Visits to farms achieving high crop yields as well as to those areas with serious problems with crop production would be essential to your research. In addition, you plan to draw in research from other countries where similar problems have been overcome.

Step IV

As you carry out your research, you record all your information logically so that you can refer to it later. You make two lists of your observations. One records signs of progress in farming output and food storage and the other includes the failures, as well as those areas of Niger which are suffering most from low crop production. Similarly with the interviews carried out, the information which you glean is organized into categories according to the content.

Step V

As you evaluate the data that you have brought together, you notice that in villages where there are self-help groups for farmers, the production of crops is much greater. You also notice that the use of manure in the fields as well as the limited use of chemical fertilizers will

raise crop productivity. In certain projects, fast-growing and hardy trees are planted as windbreaks to reduce the loss of soil through wind erosion. Your research has also revealed that several foreign aid projects sponsored by countries in the developed world have been abandoned. One such project was a large-scale irrigation project using diesel pumps to move water to the fields.

Some of the success stories in Niger have parallels in other countries of Africa with similar conditions, such as Kenya and northern Nigeria, as well as Burkina Faso. The techniques used in Niger are clearly not isolated instances of advancing technology.

Step VI

After collecting your information from across the country of Niger, you are able to come up with a number of conclusions. Foreign aid programs, no matter how well-intentioned, will not function adequately if forced on the people of Niger from those outside the country without adequate evaluation of their suitability. By way of contrast, self-help groups for farmers are highly successful when the initiative for change comes from the farmers themselves. Likewise, simple technologies have a greater appeal to the average farmer in Niger than those which are complex. Your main proposal is

for the FAO to sponsor the establishment of a large number of farming self-help groups across the country and to provide training for the leaders so that new technology can be spread more quickly and efficiently.

Step VII

As you come to the end of your research, there are a number of questions which remain unanswered. For example, what would be the impact of additional government-sponsored research stations in the rural areas of the country? Should more foreign aid agencies from the developed world be encouraged to come to Niger, or should the government administer the rural improvement programs?

The results of such research should be reported to the FAO as well as to the government of Niger. Informed decision making at every level depends upon carefully conducted research.

Conclusion

In this chapter, we have taken several broad overviews of the world to see some of the key global patterns of both physical and human geography. It is within this general context that the studies in the remainder of the book will be placed. No study of human activity can be understood in isolation, and so it is important to refer back to these general geographic patterns as you proceed through the book. We have also discussed the inquiry model as a valuable research tool. It, too, will be useful as you read further in this book, for it will allow you to analyze and understand more clearly what is to come.

Vocabulary

synthesis
Food and Agricultural Organization (FAO)
First World
Second World
Third World (two definitons)
Fourth World
Fifth World
developed world
developing world
lesser developed country (LDC)
nation
culture

Right, an Indian family in Peru; far right, women in traditional dress in Isfahan, Iran; above, which of the five worlds do you think this textile worker lives in?

Independent Study

1. Select three issues which you believe are of major importance for the world as a whole. Collect a newspaper and magazine file of articles relating to these issues. Search out a minimum of five articles for each issue.

   (a) Draft a two-page summary of the articles for each of the issues that you have selected. Discuss the nature of each issue and any recent developments.

   (b) Based upon the articles and summaries with which you have worked, describe what impact these issues might have on the average Canadian and on the world as a whole, both now and in the future.

2. Select four different inhospitable environments from around the world. Identify at least one human group within each. For each human group, research and discuss the specific nature of their environment, problems which they face in trying to live there, their current lifestyle, and changes which are being brought about by the impact of modern technology and ways of life.

3. Select two countries, one from the First World and one from the Fifth World. Research each country and prepare a report that includes a discussion of the following topics:

   - a brief history of the economic and political development of the two countries, making reference to such factors as the impact of colonialism as well as to the current political leadership

   - the nature of the current political leadership

   - the major cultural differences between the two countries

   - a comparison of their natural resources and their industrial bases

   - a comparison of their standards of living, including possible reasons for any differences you find.

4. Select an issue you have become aware of in your community, and apply the Inquiry Model to it. Follow the seven steps closely. Be sure to recognize that this model is not an answer in itself, but provides a method for investigation and proposing possible solutions.

5. Natural disasters occur throughout the world. Examples of these would include earthquakes, tornadoes, floods, and hurricanes. However, the impact of such disasters, and the response to them, varies greatly from one nation to another.

   (a) Select a country in the developing world which has recently experienced a natural disaster.

   (b) Compare the impact of that disaster on the country you selected with how Canada would have been affected by a similar event?

   (c) Write a short essay to evaluate the factors which have influenced the severity of the disasters and their human toll. Consider such things as population density, emergency seminars, etc.

Helena te Bokkel

Working in Kenya

During a summer vacation, Helena te Bokkel, 25, decided to go to Kenya on a short-term mission project. At that time, Helena had almost completed her Master's degree at Fuller Theological Seminary at Pasadena, California. She was the only Canadian among the 30 students who were involved in the two separate work projects to be undertaken.

In one village, Theraka, the first group of students built a stone church for the local pastor. There was a small village school where basic subjects were taught in English, which was the language of government. Several of the students had an opportunity to do some teaching in the school. The village was near a river which provided water for drinking, cooking, washing clothes, and bathing.

In the mountainside village of Meru, the second group of students were busy building a fence around the hospital compound, painting various buildings, sewing curtains, teaching in the nursing school, and helping to improve nutrition and knowledge of what constitutes a healthy diet.

The greatest benefit that Helena brought back to North America with her was an appreciation for an "event and relationship" culture, as opposed to the "task-oriented" culture of North America. She considers that there are many aspects of the Kenyans' more easy-going way of life which we might well incorporate into our own.

To illustrate what Helena means by an "event and relationship" culture, she relates this story.

"As Steve, one of the visiting students, was good with machinery, his first job was to mend the small gas-powered lawn mower used to take care of the hospital grounds. The delighted groundskeeper went to borrow a jeep so that they could take the mower to the nearest garage, where they could find the necessary wrenches. After half an hour of waiting, the jeep arrived, and Steve loaded the mower into it. The groundskeeper drove them about 250 metres to the garage.

Helena te Bokkel and Steve with two Masai children

"Steve unloaded the mower in front of the garage. A few passers-by started to congregate. Steve asked for a wrench which he proceeded to use. He then needed a smaller wrench, which the garage owner supplied. By now, the number of onlookers was growing, and many interested faces closely scrutinized his work. Steve went to reach for the first wrench again, only to find that it had been put away. Some progress had been made, and then all the local people decided that it was time for a break at the local tea shop where they had chi which is a strong sweet tea, and a snack which was like a chunk of fried bread.

"After the break, they returned, and Steve continued to dismantle the mower, discovering a minor problem that required repair. Everyone then declared that it was lunchtime.

"Each time they walked through the streets, they would gather more and more attention, and a larger and larger crowd. They became the subject of great interest, and the greatest source of entertainment.

"They returned to the garage, and by the time Steve had finished taking the mower apart, it was lunchtime.

"When they returned from lunch, Steve found that someone had graciously put all of the parts together. As Steve had not yet done the small repair, he had to dimantle the whole thing again. He found it difficult to see what he was doing with eight heads bent over his work, and 12 hands trying to help.

"He finally put it all back together, and needed some gas to prime it. One man volunteered to get gas and soon returned empty handed. Steve thought that he had not made himself clear, so he pointed at the machine and said again, 'I need some gas, I need some gas!' The man nodded, bent over the machine and allowed a trickle of gasoline to drain from his mouth into the mower.

"A repair job that might have taken half an hour to do had taken the whole day. But the whole town had had a wonderful day of entertainment. It was a great excuse for getting together and for fellowship. Their philosophy was, 'Let's get together, have fun, and enjoy each other.' "

Questions

1. In Canada, as in many other industrialized nations, much emphasis is placed on the efficient use of time.
   (a) Relate what would most likely have occurred had a lawn mower needed repair in Canada.
   (b) Why do you think that time is considered to be so valuable in our culture? Is this justified, in your opinion? Give reasons for your answer.

2. (a) What benefits and/or problems would result if we were to adopt an "event and relationship" approach to life?
   (b) What benefits and/or problems would result if the Kenyans in the story related above were to become more "task oriented"?
   (c) Summarize your opinions concerning the value of each culture's approach to work.

2

The Quality of Life

Contrast in the Quality of Life in Canada and Peru

"Several years ago, I was waiting in the airport in Lima, Peru, for a friend to arrive from Santiago, Chile. As I sat there, a boy named Luis came and sat beside me. In broken English, he asked my name and what I was doing at the airport. After I told him, he began to tell me about his life. He came to the airport to talk to tourists and to learn English, for this was the language he needed to get ahead. As it turned out, his family lived in a small shack near the airport, under the flight path of the jets. There were 11 children in his family and none of them had the chance to go to school. Both his mother and father worked, but they could never earn enough to feed the whole family, so the children learned to fend for themselves.

"Luis did not think he could get much of a job when he grew older, but he did not want to turn to a life of crime.

His goal was to make friends with some English-speaking traveller who would take him to the USA, because he knew that everyone in America was wealthy, so he could have a 'real' future there. He would not mind leaving his family, and said that he would be good and would not be any trouble.

"Luis then asked the question that has stayed in my mind ever since. 'Senor, why couldn't you take me home with you?' This was certainly a tough enough question, but Luis followed it with another. 'Why is it that you are able to fly back home, go to school, sleep in clean sheets, and have lots of money, but I'm not?' My mumbled answer, that it was not possible for me to take him home, was no answer at all."[1]

Questions

1. How would you have answered Luis' two questions?

2. (a) If you were in Luis' position, how would you feel about leaving your family behind, if you were able to go to North America?

   (b) Do you believe that Luis has a moral obligation to remain with his family? Justify your answer.

   (c) What ethical obligation do you think we as Canadians have to people in other parts of the world who are less fortunate than we are?

3. What important point was Luis making that applies to anyone in the world?

A shanty town behind railway tracks in Lima, Peru. Approximately eight people live in each house.

Introduction

Our exposure to information via pervasive mass media sources brings us news of events, conditions, and issues at home and abroad. There are few people who can remain completely ignorant of the horrors of mass starvation or the poor living conditions of many of the world's people. Those who have been fortunate enough to travel to other nations may have observed these phenomena for themselves. Even within our own country, we can see a great variety of lifestyles, and we should be aware of the many inequalities that exist.

This chapter will give you some insight into the disparity in lifestyles experienced by the world's peoples, and will attempt to explain the causes of this disparity. You will be introduced to issues that affect people directly, such as health care services, the treatment of minority groups, and people's attitudes toward women. You will also read about the major problem of Third World debt and the consequences for the people. The work of some large and small foreign aid organizations will be described and you will have an opportunity to evaluate their efforts and offer your own suggestions for improvement.

This is the key chapter in a book on world issues; hence, it comes before everything except the introduction. What is so very important is how people live. Are they comfortable, adequately fed and housed? Do they have an opportunity to develop and use their skills? Are they treated fairly? What is being done for those who lack basic necessities, and what can we learn from past efforts to help them?

A study of the material in this chapter, however, is only the beginning. The other chapters which follow will help you to grasp the interrelationship between history, politics, population, food, geography, and the environment. The study of those chapters will make the content of this one more understandable in the context of a complex world which is home to so many.

The North and South — The Haves and The Have-nots

"At the end of three decades of international action devoted to development, the result is that, by 1985, there is likely to be an increase of $50 per capita in the annual incomes of the poorest group over 1965 incomes, compared with an increase of $3900 per capita for those of the richest."

CN Tower, Toronto

Some facts to ponder:

- The **World Bank**, which is a United Nations agency administering foreign aid, calculated in 1987 that if the rich nations would invest $12.5 billion in the poorer nations over ten years, the basic needs of the people could be met.

- Each year, people in the rich nations spend about $100 billion on alcohol.

- Americans spend more on cosmetics per year than the total budgets of all the African states that have gained independence since World War II.

- On average, per citizen, the United States uses 100 times as much energy for industry, home use, and transportation as any one of the poorer nations.

Above, poor housing in Bangkok, Thailand; below, what Asian city could this street scene be from?

Left, a town in Chad, Africa

Table 2.1
Contrasts in
Living Conditions
in Canada and
Sri Lanka 1981

	Canada		Sri Lanka	
	Urban	Rural	Urban	Rural
Percentage of housing units with access to piped water	99.8	97.5	46.5	10.9
Percentage of housing units with access to toilets and latrines	99.6	96.9	80.2	63.4
Average number of people per room	0.5	0.5	2.1	2.3

Questions

4. Design a poster that incorporates the information included in "Some Facts to Ponder." Your poster should have an eye-catching title and design.

5. How might a display of posters such as the one you have constructed influence people's attitudes?

6. (a) Do you believe that a change in attitude by Canadians and other people of the more developed world could effectively "narrow the gap" between the quality of life in different nations? Explain your answer.

   (b) In your opinion, what are the most effective approaches when trying to accomplish social change in another country? Consider the merits of foreign advisors, experts, and investment, as well as training citizens of the country being helped. Justify your answers.

Left, residential housing in a Canadian city; below, a farming community in the Philippines

Many people use the terms **North** and **South** to refer to parts of the world with a great disparity in their standards of living. These labels signify that most of the countries with a high standard of living are in the northern hemisphere, while those with a low standard of living are in the southern hemisphere. Australia and New Zealand are the exceptions, being included with the richer North. That is because the differences between "North" and "South" stem from disparity in development or, in other words, industrialization. To speak of a North-South division is to speak of the way the majority of people live within a hemisphere. Within each country there are variations in the standard of living because of differences in income and opportunity.

Figure 2.1
The North-South Split

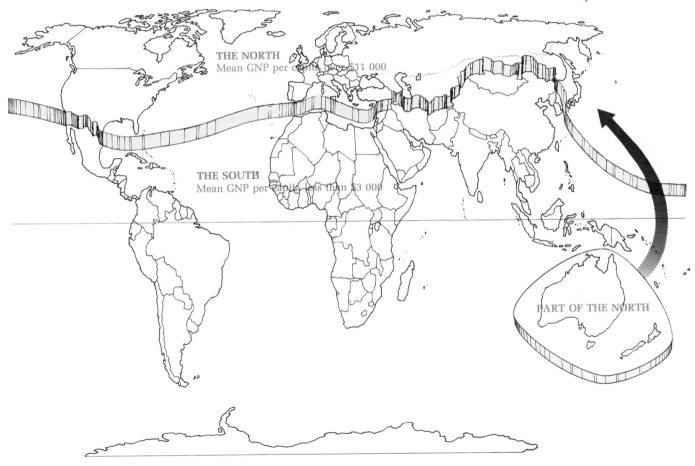

THE NORTH
Mean GNP per capita over $11 000

THE SOUTH
Mean GNP per capita less than $3 000

PART OF THE NORTH

Problems of Growing Urban Areas

It is anticipated that, by the end of this century, over one-half of the world's population will live in urban areas. **Urbanization** is taking place all over the world, but in the South, the rate of growth of the urban population is so great that vast **shanty towns**, **barrios**, or **favelas** are developing around all major cities. Seventy-five percent of the population of Ibadan, Nigeria, and 67 percent of the people in Calcutta, India, live as squatters. The shanty towns they live in consist of shacks of corrugated iron or even of cardboard and packing cases. They have no piped water or proper sewage disposal, and sometimes there are no roads between the shacks. Health services, educational facilities, and employment opportunities are very limited. It is difficult for us to imagine that this life is better than the one they left in the surrounding countryside, but in general this is true. At least now the people are closer to the possibility of employment and to health and other services. However, most burgeoning cities of the southern hemisphere are unable to cope with the needs of their people, and some cities do not even attempt to improve living conditions because they fear that this would encourage others to flock there. Certain governments have actually bulldozed the hovels to force squatters to leave.

Housing on the outskirts of Dacca, Bangladesh

Table 2.2
Urban Share of
Total Population
in Selected
Regions, 1950,
1986 and
Projected to 2000

REGION	1950	1986 (percent)	2000
North America	64	74	78
Europe	56	73	79
Soviet Union	39	71	74
East Asia	43	70	79
Latin America	41	65	77
Oceania	61	65	73
China	12	32	40
Africa	15	30	42
South Asia	15	24	35

Questions

7. (a) Describe and explain your reaction when you hear that people's homes are being bulldozed.

   (b) What arguments could be made in defence of this action?

8. (a) Plot the figures for urban population shown in Table 2.2 as a series of lines superimposed on one graph.

   (b) Using the position and slope of each line as an indicator, group the nations according to the level of urbanization in 1950, the projected level of urbanization in 2000, and the rate of urbanization between 1950 and 2000.

   (c) List the circumstances which brought about the differences that you have observed in part (b).

9. Explain why it is so difficult for a less developed nation to cope with rapid urbanization.

Cities of the northern hemisphere have their problems, too. While in the South the poor areas are located around the outskirts of a city, it is the older, inner core of most cities of the North which usually houses the poorest inhabitants. The residents of inner-city areas may not be short of the basic necessities, thanks to social programs, but they are affected by an environment in which violent crimes, loneliness, and drug addiction are common. Urban renewal is often accomplished by demolishing these areas and replacing them with modern apartment buildings and office complexes.

Bogota, Colombia

Questions

10. (a) What would be your reaction to the demolition of a decaying area of the city with which you are most familiar?

(b) In what ways does urban renewal in cities of richer nations parallel destruction of shanty towns in poorer nations? What, if anything, should be done to help the people who are losing their homes?

A homeless person near Times Square, New York City

The Information Gap

The possession of information is a valuable asset. It is characteristic of advantaged people in our society that they have access to information that leads them to better jobs and financial success. A parallel can be made between this sort of "edge" in private lives and the advantage developed countries have over the underdeveloped ones in access to information connected to the world's money markets and trade secrets. Information on such diverse topics as resource inventory, agricultural productivity, stock market activity, and military manoeuvres is readily available to those who have the necessary training, equipment, and connections. Education is the basic tool enabling people to gain access to, and evaluate, information available from libraries, newspapers, radio, and television.

The ability to control the flow of information gives some nations a significant advantage. The North controls the vast majority of satellites that are in *geostationary orbit*. A satellite in **geostationary orbit** stays at one point above the earth's surface and can communicate with half the world, although usually it is in touch with a smaller area. There is a limit to the number of satellites and radio frequencies that can be used, allowing little opportunity for future developments by nations of the South.

Nations of the North are in a position to ascertain information about the affairs of nations of the South, often without the latter's knowledge, and to use it to their own advantage. Information can be repressed and manipulated to suit the needs of those who possess it. Southern nations are usually dependent on the advanced technology of the North when they use remote sensing from satellites. Thus, if they were conducting a minerals inventory of their nation, the information would come into the hands of a foreign nation first.

In order to control the amount of information that can be obtained by a country such as the United States, some nations have incorporated restrictions to safeguard their interests. For example, Brazil has laws that prevent local subsidiaries of multinational corporations from linking by satellite to their headquarters. Similarly, Canada has restrictions on bank information flowing into the United States.

Question

11. Consider the advantage that access to information gives to a coffee importing company, an international mining company, a newspaper, a military strategist, a government, or an individual politician. Make up an example or relate an actual incident to illustrate your point in each case.

The Haves and The Have-nots

The economic well-being of the countries of the world varies widely. Certain statistics, such as those listed in the Appendix, can be used to analyze and illustrate these variations.

Questions

12. Choose five kinds of statistics from those listed in the Appendix that you believe best indicate the differences between the "have" and "have-not" countries. Justify your choice in each case.

13. Using your chosen statistics, select a graphing technique which illustrates the contrast in conditions between a more developed and a less developed nation. Include a short summary of your observations with your graphs.

The Technology Gap

Research and development are the keys to a nation's progress. Well over 90 percent of such activity throughout the whole world takes place in the more developed nations, and more than 80 percent of patents granted by less developed nations go to foreigners or multinationals. The cost of technology imported by Third World nations exceeds the development aid which they receive. Often this technical help proves to be unsuitable for local conditions, resulting in diminished returns. For example, the building of the High Aswan Dam has caused a reduction rather than an increase in agricultural productivity in Egypt. Further, it has necessitated increased use of fertilizer.

Questions

14. In what ways would a lesser developed nation benefit from having its own strong base in industrial and scientific research and development?

15. Why should lesser developed nations not be forced to rely on research and development controlled by wealthier nations?

16. How could the nations of the more developed world help the lesser developed nations start their own programs of research and development?

The High Aswan Dam, Egypt, with Lake Nasser on the right

Diseases

The kinds of diseases that concern us in our everyday lives are very different from those causing despair in the less developed nations. Here in Canada, many older people are concerned with diseases of the circulatory system which are often attributed to a rich diet and cause nearly one-third of all deaths in the more developed nations. Cancer, the causes of which are not clear, is also a major killer, being responsible for 15 percent of deaths. In addition, increasing numbers of people are developing allergic reactions to environmental stimulants, and many children have respiratory problems.

In the lesser developed nations, one-half of all deaths are due to infectious, respiratory, and parasitic diseases. These cause only one-tenth of the deaths in the more developed world, but used to be much more prevalent. Diseases such as measles, whooping cough, and mumps were customary childhood experiences. More serious diseases such as diphtheria, tuberculosis, and polio were quite common but, as with many other diseases, these have been almost eliminated through widespread immunization programs.

Health and disease concern us all. In the more developed nations, adequate care is usually readily available and is often subsidized by the state or covered by insurance. Many diseases are controlled by immunization programs and the availability of water free of disease-carrying organisms. In the lesser developed nations, medical facilities are few and usually poorly equipped. Obtaining medical assistance may require walking for days to a village clinic, especially in rural areas.

Apart from the diseases that kill, there are many others that make life miserable and completely sap the victims' energy, reducing their ability to contribute to the community in which they live. Worms and other parasites affect at least two billion people. Another devastating condition is diarrhea. There can be many causes, most often related to polluted drinking water. Five million children died in 1987 from the effects of dehydration due to diarrhea. Oral Rehydration Therapy (ORT) provides a simple, inexpensive treatment. You will find more details on page 43 of this chapter and in Chapter 5.

Table 2.3
The Six Major
Diseases of the
Developing World

Measles is contracted by 67 million children in poor countries annually; of these, 2 million die. Serious complications develop in one-third of the cases.

Diphtheria causes death in one in ten children who contract it. Complications can be serious.

Whooping cough causes 600 000 deaths each year, and serious complications for survivors.

Neonatal tetanus kills 800 000 newborns a year.

Polio causes paralysis and deformity. About 260 000 children are affected each year.

Tuberculosis afflicts 2 billion children under the age of five each year. One out of two will die if the disease spreads to the brain.

NOTE: Some of the complications referred to above include blindness, heart damage, damage to the nervous system, paralysis, pneumonia, encephalitis, coma, and convulsions.

Table 2.4 lists reported cases of malaria and cholera, two **water-related diseases**, in which some part of the life cycle of the disease depends on water. As can be seen from these figures, information is not complete. For example, the World Health Organization estimated that there were about 98 million Africans suffering from malaria in 1981, but there were only 7.9 million cases reported in the

Table 2.4
Malaria and Cholera Incidence, 1979-84

	Reported Malaria Cases						Reported Cholera Cases					
	1979	1980	1981	1982	1983	1984	1979	1980	1981	1982	1983	1984
AFRICA												
Algeria	73	36	67	71	41	32	2,513	1,075	X	X	218	45
Angola	522,385	797,688	X	X	X	X	X	X	X	X	X	X
Benin	122,405	131,909	142,872	X	X	X	X	3	2	3	X	1
Botswana	5,954	2,773	X	X	X	X	X	X	X	X	X	X
Burkina Faso	317,533	211,661	326,183	X	X	X	X	X	X	X	X	2,191
Burundi	94,049	79,181	X	X	X	X	915	2,039	582	351	477	180
Cameroon	X	X	X	X	X	X	16	229	243	5	55	392
Cape Verde	621	213	X	X	X	X	X	X	X	X	X	X
Central African Rep	167,346	X	X	X	X	X	X	X	X	X	X	X
Chad	X	X	X	X	X	X	X	X	X	X	X	X
Comoros	X	X	X	X	X	X	X	X	X	X	X	X
Congo	147,521	X	X	X	X	X	X	X	X	X	X	X
Cote d'Ivoire	349,046	X	X	X	X	X	3	X	X	34	X	X
Djibouti	123	69	640	X	X	X	X	X	X	X	X	X
Egypt	474	X	X	423	198	194	X	X	X	X	X	X
Equatorial Guinea	X	X	X	X	X	X	X	X	X	X	X	125
Ethiopia	31,658	X	X	X	X	X	X	X	X	X	X	X
Gabon	16,776	X	X	X	X	X	5	X	7	X	X	X
Gambia	51,993	70,119	X	X	X	X	X	X	X	X	X	X
Ghana	X	X	X	X	X	X	1,783	260	581	1,784	14,160	1,015
Guinea	23,086	X	X	X	X	X	X	X	X	X	X	X
Guinea-Bissau	160,931	148,142	161,496	X	X	X	X	X	X	X	X	X
Kenya	437,660	X	X	X	X	X	1,070	2,808	2,424	3,498	1,049	14
Lesotho	X	X	X	X	X	X	X	X	X	X	X	X
Liberia	X	201,946	X	X	X	X	438	2,690	1,582	670	183	17
Libya	134	106	1,473	X	129	117	X	X	X	X	X	X
Madagascar	302,336	X	X	X	X	X	X	X	X	X	X	X
Malawi	23,237	X	30,234	X	X	X	X	X	261	X	513	X
Mali	180,176	149,308	X	X	X	X	X	X	X	X	X	1,795
Mauritania	X	X	X	X	X	X	X	X	X	X	X	492
Mauritius	128	470	607	X	X	X	X	X	X	X	X	X
Morocco	397	360	98	62	75	318	X	X	X	X	X	X
Mozambique	X	X	X	X	X	X	4,564	1,212	1,753	2,301	10,334	521
Niger	384,029	X	X	X	X	X	X	X	7	X	X	3,788
Nigeria	1,021,331	1,171,071	X	X	X	X	293	139	305	186	171	1,667
Rwanda	137,047	123,882	X	X	X	X	5	30	24	97	54	161
Senegal	508,010	X	498,895	X	X	X	103	X	428	X	X	712
Sierra Leone	79,991	X	X	X	X	X	X	X	X	X	X	X
Somalia	11,343	X	X	X	X	X	X	X	X	X	X	X
South Africa	2,007	1,059	X	X	X	X	2	859	4,180	11,968	4,715	1,182

	Reported Malaria Cases						Reported Cholera Cases					
	1979	1980	1981	1982	1983	1984	1979	1980	1981	1982	1983	1984
Sudan	X	2,925,407	X	X	X	X	845	17	X	X	X	X
Swaziland	X	X	X	X	X	X	X	X	238	538	X	X
Tanzania, United Rep	X	X	X	X	X	X	2,559	5,196	4,241	4,071	1,816	2,600
Togo	294,561	X	X	X	X	X	X	X	X	X	X	X
Tunisia	6	7	1	X	X	X	X	X	X	X	X	X
Uganda	20,305	X	70,520	X	X	X	X	1,539	X	190	X	X
Zaire	317,533	X	X	X	X	X	5,515	1,051	2,379	10,328	2,977	162
Zamba	10,580	X	X	X	X	X	165	57	14	1,403	X	X
Zimbabwe	3,807	14,587	X	X	X	X	X	X	X	X	X	X

NORTH & CENTRAL AMERICA

Barbados	2	1	1	X	X	X	0	0	0	0	0	0
Canada	X	631	538	X	X	X	0	3	0	0	2	0
Costa Rica	307	376	168	110	245	569	0	0	0	0	0	0
Cuba	295	307	573	X	X	X	0	0	0	0	0	0
Dominican Rep	3,080	4,780	3,596	4,654	3,801	2,370	0	0	0	0	0	0
El Salvador	77,976	95,835	93,187	86,202	65,377	66,874	0	0	0	0	0	0
Guatemala	69,039	62,657	67,994	77,375	64,024	74,132	0	0	0	0	0	0
Haiti	41,252	53,478	46,703	65,354	53,954	54,896	0	0	0	0	0	0
Honduras	25,297	43,009	49,377	57,482	37,536	27,332	0	0	0	0	0	0
Jamaica	5	X	1	X	X	X	0	0	0	0	0	0
Mexico	20,983	25,734	42,104	49,993	74,172	85,501	0	0	0	0	0	0
Nicaragua	18,418	25,465	17,434	15,601	12,907	15,702	0	0	0	0	0	0
Panama	316	310	340	334	341	125	0	0	0	0	0	0
Trinidad and Tobago	8	3	3	X	X	X	0	0	0	0	0	0
United States	894	2,062	1,388	X	X	X	1	10	21	0	1	0

SOUTH AMERICA

Argentina	936	341	323	567	535	437	0	0	0	0	0	0
Bolivia	14,712	16,619	9,774	6,699	14,441	16,338	0	0	0	0	0	0
Brazil	147,630	176,237	205,544	221,939	297,667	378,257	0	0	0	0	0	0
Chile	X	X	X	X	X	X	0	0	0	0	0	0
Colombia	60,957	57,346	60,972	78,601	105,360	55,266	0	0	0	0	0	0
Ecuador	8,207	8,748	12,745	14,633	51,606	78,599	0	0	0	0	0	0
Guyana	2,294	3,202	2,065	1,700	2,102	3,017	0	0	0	0	0	0
Paraguay	116	140	73	66	49	544	0	0	0	0	0	0
Peru	17,127	14,982	14,812	14,613	28,563	36,621	0	0	0	0	0	0
Suriname	903	4,445	2,479	2,805	1,943	3,849	0	0	0	0	0	0
Uruguay	X	X	X	X	X	X	0	0	0	0	0	0
Venezuela	4,705	3,884	3,354	4,127	8,388	11,127	0	0	0	0	0	0

	Reported Malaria Cases						Reported Cholera Cases					
	1979	1980	1981	1982	1983	1984	1979	1980	1981	1982	1983	1984
ASIA												
Afghanistan	34,444	47,285	67,668	110,309	118,684	155,720	X	X	X	X	X	X
Bahrain	273	256	274	X	X	X	39	X	X	X	X	X
Bangladesh	49,776	67,727	45,902	38,204	40,303	31,787	2,154	X	X	X	X	X
Bhutan	5,375	X	X	X	5,213	18,356	X	X	X	X	X	X
Burma	14,515	16,469	42,019	42,021	36,647	60,488	874	1,018	54	X	989	X
China	2,384,543	3,300,349	3,059,653	2,041,359	1,377,647	903,802	85	88	X	X	X	X
Cyprus	1	2	6	X	X	X	X	X	X	X	X	X
India	3,064,697	2,844,815	2,622,639	2,160,447	1,911,149	2,023,462	5,073	9,522	5,237	4,656	8,542	2,519
Indonesia	165,911	175,239	149,576	220,129	147,887	92,527	28,738	5,541	18,354	8,183	12,964	7,921
Iran	22,175	32,635	29,655	42,808	45,916	30,835	1,856	1,599	6,034	427	270	531
Iraq	4,012	2,815	X	3,326	2,422	3,340	X	X	X	X	X	X
Israel	16	43	44	X	X	X	X	X	X	1	X	X
Japan	53	55	41	X	X	X	11	22	19	16	35	55
Jordan	320	202	274	X	X	X	141	X	908	X	X	X
Kampuchea, Dem	X	X	X	10,114	X	X	X	X	X	X	X	X
Korea, Dem People's Rep	X	X	X	X	X	X	X	170	X	X	X	X
Korea, Rep	X	X	X	X	X	X	X	145	X	X	X	X
Kuwait	98	98	142	X	X	X	3	X	9	X	X	X
Lao People's Dem Rep	X	12,603	X	X	5,564	7,210	X	X	X	X	X	X
Lebanon	9	4	9	X	X	X	X	X	X	X	X	X
Malaysia	44,912	44,552	59,422	43,915	22,218	32,094	502	106	479	516	2,195	67
Mongolia	X	X	X	X	X	X	X	X	X	X	X	X
Nepal	12,131	12,265	15,978	16,907	16,719	28,208	22	1	24	X	X	X
Oman	2,247	1,340	2,218	30,566	34,885	16,590	X	X	X	X	X	X
Pakistan	12,304	17,707	37,923	56,708	49,160	73,996	X	X	4	X	X	X
Philippines	87,668	105,750	97,557	97,531	90,319	107,301	933	836	864	345	X	X
Qatar	124	62	116	X	X	X	X	X	X	X	X	X
Saudi Arabia	3,192	6,496	5,543	15,167	17,956	11,091	23	2	13	X	X	X
Singapore	208	200	261	X	X	X	10	18	34	31	14	40
Sri Lanka	48,004	47,949	47,383	38,566	127,264	149,470	46	104	574	309	86	X
Syrian Arab Rep	2,550	1,481	1,828	2,183	1,260	840	689	X	X	X	X	X
Thailand	302,568	396,705	427,792	419,763	243,906	306,569	1,788	4,331	39	638	1,495	645
Turkey	29,323	34,154	55,551	X	66,681	55,382	X	X	X	X	X	X
United Arab Emirates	11,599	8,560	7,653	6,224	4,815	3,516	X	X	X	X	X	X
Viet Nam	40,782	31,763	42,714	50,920	63,649	58,806	365	978	374	50	390	22
Yemen	3,838	5,824	10,029	20,641	2,168	1,262	X	X	X	X	X	X
Yemen, Dem	4,083	2,153	4,079	7,609	9,294	3,615	1,953	720	X	X	X	X

	Reported Malaria Cases						Reported Cholera Cases					
	1979	1980	1981	1982	1983	1984	1979	1980	1981	1982	1983	1984
EUROPE												
Albania	X	X	X	X	X	X	X	X	X	X	X	X
Austria	35	44	54	X	X	X	X	X	2	X	X	X
Belgium	56	59	30	X	X	X	X	1	X	X	X	1
Bulgaria	102	128	420	X	X	X	X	X	X	X	X	X
Czechoslovakia	6	15	2	X	X	X	X	X	X	X	X	X
Denmark	110	70	104	X	X	X	X	X	X	X	X	X
Finland	13	13	14	X	X	X	X	X	1	X	X	X
France	99	111	77	X	X	X	X	3	20	18	3	1
German Dem Rep	22	16	35	X	X	X	X	X	X	X	X	X
Germany, Fed Rep	486	570	319	X	X	X	X	5	4	1	X	X
Greece	44	53	64	X	X	X	X	X	X	X	X	X
Hungary	13	6	34	X	X	X	X	X	X	X	X	X
Iceland	X	X	X	X	X	X	X	X	X	X	X	X
Ireland	32	22	25	X	X	X	X	X	X	X	X	X
Italy	164	176	143	X	X	X	8	X	X	X	X	X
Luxembourg	X	X	7	X	X	X	X	X	X	X	X	X
Malta	X	X	1	X	X	X	X	X	X	X	X	X
Netherlands	113	101	128	X	X	X	5	X	2	X	2	X
Norway	32	25	35	X	X	X	X	X	X	X	X	X
Poland	23	X	29	X	X	X	X	X	1	X	X	X
Portugal	45	26	27	X	X	X	X	X	X	X	X	X
Romania	19	14	22	X	X	X	X	X	X	X	X	X
Spain	52	90	129	X	X	X	267	4	2	1	2	4
Sweden	104	98	123	X	X	X	1	X	X	X	X	X
Switzerland	93	95	138	X	X	X	X	X	X	X	X	X
United Kingdom	2,053	1,670	1,576	X	X	X	X	6	12	1	5	5
Yugoslavia	55	83	58	X	X	X	X	X	2	X	X	X
USSR	**399**	**386**	**304**	**X**	**X**	**X**	**X**	**X**	**X**	**X**	**X**	**X**
OCEANIA												
Australia	473	629	497	X	X	X	1	2	2	1	4	1
Fiji	X	X	X	X	X	X	X	X	X	X	X	X
New Zealand	X	65	39	X	X	X	X	1	X	X	X	X
Papua New Guinea	117,670	118,390	122,743	109,306	126,930	150,328	X	X	X	X	X	X
Solomon Islands	26,357	35,028	61,108	69,829	84,526	72,108	X	X	X	X	X	X

whole world. Many deaths reported as diarrhea are believed to have been caused by cholera.

Despite these shortcomings, the figures, especially those for 1979, do give us an indication of the geographical distribution of the diseases, and the figures for some countries are continuous enough that it is possible to see trends over a six-year period. Probably one of the best ways of mapping the distribution of disease is by the use of dot distribution maps. Using this method, one dot represents a certain number of cases.

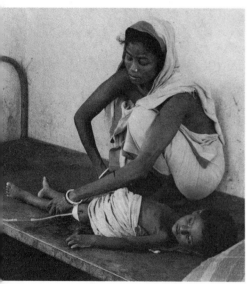

Cholera causes rapid dehydration, and is often fatal in young children. Fluids given intravenously are helping to keep this boy alive.

Question

17. (a) Using one dot to represent 1000 reported cases of malaria, and an outline political map of the world, produce a map to show the distribution of the disease in 1979.

(b) Using only your map as reference, describe the world distribution of the disease, relating your answers to continents, different climatic areas, and the different ''worlds'' as described in this chapter.

(c) Devise some other method of illustrating the incidence of reported cholera cases for a year of your choice.

(d) Explain the advantages and disadvantages of your method used in part (c) as opposed to the dot distribution method.

(e) Repeat part (b), this time for cholera.

(f) Using selected examples from five widely separated countries for which data is most complete, construct simple line graphs and write a commentary to describe trends in occurrences of the disease over the six-year period.

Ten million people are affected each year by the diseases listed in Table 2.3, and half of them die. These diseases are preventable by immunization, yet only one in five children has been protected, despite enormous efforts to increase this number. The need for cold storage of vaccines in remote regions limits the effectiveness of the campaigns. Health care is available in large centres but, for the ordinary citizen, the services and facilities do not compare with those normally available to each of us. Poor transportation facilities make local aid stations difficult to reach. Although such services are often free or subsidized, in some instances even the small fee charged may cripple a family's finances for years. Besides, lack of an adequate diet makes people more susceptible to disease. Polluted water supplies and crowded living conditions allow for the spread of parasites, bacteria, and viruses.

The Fight Against Disease in the Lesser Developed Nations

Attempts to improve the standard of health in poor nations must go beyond immunization. The program has to involve education, the supply of clean water, improved sanitation, the training and deployment of health care personnel, facilities, medicines, and equipment. In many cases, the achievement of independence from colonial control led to a deterioration of services for the people. These services now have to be restored in such a way as to be both effective and economical.

Because of the constraints of cost and the enormous task of supplying vast numbers of people with the help required, many nations use what is referred to as **grass-roots medicine** and **barefoot doctors**. Several representatives from each village are selected by the villagers themselves to be trained in medical centres, and they then return and teach the people what they have learned. They teach about covering supplies of water and avoiding the spread of diseases by using a dipper to dispense the water. They may also have been trained in midwifery or nutrition.

Examples of this practice can be seen in parts of India, where health care workers go on marches through local villages to convince women to eat papaya, which is rich in vitamin A. Vitamin A deficiency in pregnant and lactating women often causes blindness in young children. There was an old superstition that papaya caused sterility, but the healthy babies of the health care workers convinced the villagers that this was not true. As part of the program, women are given young papaya plants which will produce fruit in six months. Each woman has to raise ten seedlings and give them to other women in the village. Thus, the practice spreads throughout the area. The compliance of the women is checked by the local health care worker.

Health education where mothers are largely illiterate requires special approaches. Ballads are written and performed to explain how to prevent the spread of AIDS. Groups of health care workers in Nigeria put on plays in villages to explain the causes and treatment for diarrhea. Oral Rehydration Therapy, referred to earlier, in which a mixture of sugar, salt, and clean water is used to cure dehydration from diarrhea, is taught by demonstration and repetition. The use of local plants to produce nutritious weaning foods is shown through cooking demonstrations and sampling.

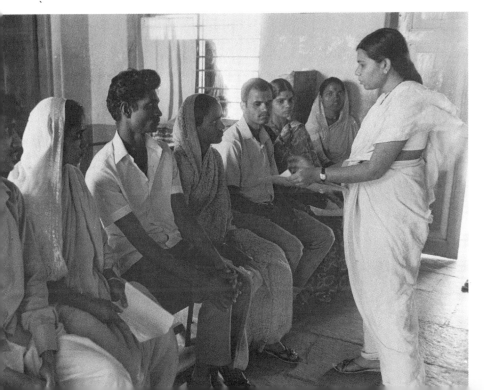

Family planning counselling is one aspect of health care in developing countries.

People must understand the connection between polluted water supplies and disease if they are to use a well rather than their traditional sources of water. Aid organizations such as UNICEF will often pay for a well to be drilled and finished, but the villagers must be shown how to use and maintain the pump for long-term benefits. In Togo, West Africa, **Canadian University Services Overseas (CUSO)** donates money to help equip villages with wells. As much money is spent on explaining the benefits of the clean water as on drilling the well. Certain local people are provided with motor bikes so that they can go from village to village to instruct.

Experience has shown that people will often return to polluted sources if they are not convinced of the benefits of clean water. A broken pump providing water from a clean source would not be fixed, but would be used for its scrap value. Hand pumps designed and built in Canada were not rugged enough for the non-stop use they received in the villages. Thus, CUSO brought in pumps designed in India, and made in Togo, and supplied training in the maintenance of these pumps. The villagers had to contribute toward the cost of the well, and thus they appreciated it more than if it had been a gift. The incidence of diarrhea and guinea worm is now decreasing, due to the improvement in the quality of water.

Question

18. The original Canadian approach in West Africa was to drill a well and leave. Explain why this method failed.

Minority Groups Within Societies

''I say to you today, my friends, that in spite of the difficulties and frustrations of the moment I still have a dream. It is a dream deeply rooted in the American dream. I have a dream that one day this nation will rise up and live out the true meaning of its creed: 'We hold these truths to be self evident, that all men are created equal.'

''I have a dream that one day on the red hills of Georgia, the sons of former slaves and the sons of former slave-owners will be able to sit down together at the table of brotherhood.

''I have a dream that one day even the state of Mississippi, a desert state sweltering with the heat of injustice and oppression, will be transformed into an oasis of freedom and justice.

''I have a dream my four little children will one day live in a nation where they will not be judged by the colour of their skin but by the content of their character.

''I have a dream today!''

Martin Luther King, August 28, 1963, at the Lincoln Memorial in Washington

Five years after uttering these words, Martin Luther King was assassinated. Even before his death, at the age of 39, Dr. King was becoming disheartened by the lack of progress toward real equality for blacks. Laws were in place to make all people equal, yet there was still a real difference between the economic condition of whites and blacks. With the passage of time since his death, there has been little improvement, as Figure 2.2 illustrates.

Figure 2.2
Some Indicators of the Quality of Life Among Blacks and Whites in the USA

RESPONSIBILITY
Households headed by women

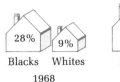 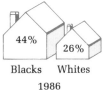

28%	9%	44%	26%
Blacks	Whites	Blacks	Whites
1968		1986	

OPPORTUNITY
High school graduates   Enrolled in college

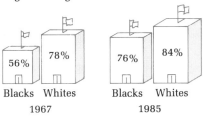 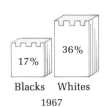 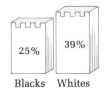

56%	78%	76%	84%	17%	36%	25%	39%
Blacks	Whites	Blacks	Whites	Blacks	Whites	Blacks	Whites
1967		1985		1967		1985	

AFFLUENCE
Median family income

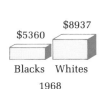 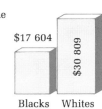

$5360	$8937	$17 604	$30 809
Blacks	Whites	Blacks	Whites
1968		1986	

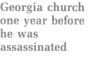

Martin Luther King preaching in his Atlanta, Georgia church one year before he was assassinated

Laws by themselves are not enough. Attitudes among both whites and blacks have to change before significant improvements will be achieved. Employment opportunities must increase, and living conditions must be improved. Education and training must be put within reach and used.

Even within the United States, where the constitution states that "all men are created equal," there are many groups which find themselves at a disadvantage because of racial discrimination. The same is true for most, if not all other countries, and Canada is not free of it either, although we think of ourselves as enlightened people.

UNESCO has defined **racism** as "the generalized, permanent exploitation of real or biological differences, to the advantage of the accuser and to the detriment of his victim, for the purpose of justifying aggression." **Prejudice** is an unfavourable opinion that is formed without any basis in fact.

Questions

19. Relate one or more instances of prejudice that have occurred in your school or local community. How was this incident dealt with by those concerned?

20. In your opinion, why do people have prejudices against those who are different from themselves?

21. Make three suggestions that could lead to the reduction of prejudice.

Cultural Diversity

The world is composed of people from many different backgrounds. This is **cultural diversity**, and consequently we live in a multicultural world. These tremendous variations lead to a rich mixture of art, music, medicine, religious beliefs, foods, and philosophies. Many cities have enclaves of people with different cultural traditions, and people of all backgrounds are able to experience the richness of such variety. Yet many cultures fear for their own future. The overwhelming pervasiveness of American popular culture threatens their existence. In recent history, government-sanctioned persecution of cultural groups has led to such catastrophes as the holocaust in which 6 million European Jews were exterminated, the exodus of many people of East Indian descent from newly independent nations of East Africa, and the apartheid policy of South Africa.

The Concerns of Native Groups

In North America, many native groups whose ancestral lands were taken from them without legal treaties are now seeking redress for past injustices. Native groups in many other parts of the world are also challenging the "status quo." When native groups claim land or monetary settlement for land with great economic potential, such as in the development of minerals, forests, or hydro-electric sites, agreements become more difficult to achieve. In such cases, pressure for just claims must be applied to the government from all parts of society, even from other countries.

Lubicon roadblock near Little Buffalo, Alberta, October 15, 1988

The Penen of Sarawak

One May day in 1987, surveyors arrived in a village on the upper reaches of the Baram River in Sarawak on the island of Borneo. This was the first that the Penen inhabitants had heard of a decision that would affect the lands they had farmed for generations. Permission had been granted to a firm to exploit timber in the area. A road put through to access the timber destroyed the rubber plantations and rice fields of 19 families, yet protests to the government brought no results. The native people blockaded the road and surrounded the logging camp, but police quickly arrived and arrested some of those involved. When the people appealed for help to their local politician, they found that he was part-owner of the logging company.

The government denies that native people have any legal claim to the forest. Timber is a most important part of the Sarawak economy, and certain people are given huge tracts of land in exchange for favours to the government. The forests are being cleared so fast that the whole state could be deforested in ten years.

The Penen people claim that not only have their lands been taken from them, but logging has caused silting and flooding in the river, with the resultant destruction of rice lands and fishing waters. Access to other products from the forests such as wood, fruits, roots, medicines, and meat has been denied them. They cannot harvest rattan from the forests, which they previously exchanged for salt. They also claim that the loggers have introduced cigarettes and alcohol to their communities and have harassed the women.

Situations such as this have led native groups to form action committees, demanding the return of their land and repair of the damage that has been done to it. Delegations are kept waiting for many days to see government officials, and it may take 12 years for any cases to be heard in court.

Logging in Sarawak, Borneo

Questions

22. The story of the Penen related above is paralleled in other parts of the world. Many of the nations involved are very poor and in need of import dollars.

    (a) Suggest strategies that you believe should be employed by the native groups and by the governments to improve the situation and yet avoid jeopardizing the economy of the country, both now and in the future.

    (b) In your opinion, can this be achieved without international co-operation? Justify your opinion and, if relevant, make suggestions about action which should be taken.

23. Large-scale developments that ignore the traditional lifestyle of native people also have little or no regard for environmental consequences.

    (a) Look at pages 237-243 and describe what environmental damage results from widespread forest clearance in tropical areas.

    (b) What are likely to be the long-term consequences of this damage for the countries in which it is occurring?

    (c) Will the destruction of the tropical forests have any impact on the lives of Canadians?

    (d) Does justice for native people's land claims cost a country too much in land and money? Explain your answer.

24. Explain the importance of politics in influencing the outcome of what is essentially a question of morality and justice.

25. Suggest strategies which should be adopted to protect the interests of native people in all parts of the world.

Women in Today's World

Women have made considerable progress socially during the past 50 years, yet, with a few exceptions, attitudes and traditions continue to favour men. A well-known statement made by the United Nations in 1980 says that, "On average, women work twice as many hours as men, but receive only one-tenth of the world's income and own only one-hundredth of the world's property." In many countries, laws are in place to ensure that males and females are paid the same for "work of equal value," yet the average wage of women workers is substantially less than that of men. In the UK, for example, female workers are paid 25 percent less, and in the USA, they receive 40 percent less than their male counterparts.

Mother and children waiting for food supplies in southwestern Ethiopia

There is still discrimination over what is considered a woman's job and, generally speaking, most women work at jobs with lower rates of pay. This could be attributed to the fact that many women have acquired a sense of inferiority which keeps them from taking advantage of all available opportunities.

Greater value needs to be attached to the traditional nurturing activities of women — cooking, cleaning, teaching, nursing, advising, gathering fuel, planting, weeding, etc. Often carried out in addition to paid work outside the home, this work is rarely given a monetary value, and tends to be taken for granted by the recipients.

In many parts of the lesser developed world, women have enormous obstacles to overcome if their lives are to improve. They do most of the agricultural work as well as their household tasks. They are often illiterate, and this makes it difficult to compete

Above, women in Nyasaland pounding maize. What is Nyasaland called today?; left, woman carrying firewood in Kenya

in a work force with men who are given access to any available education before women. Although most teachers in the world are women, the vast majority teach in pre-primary and primary schools rather than at universities.

Tradition often dictates that women eat last and consequently least. This often results in them not getting sufficient food to produce enough milk to breast-feed their infants or to nourish their developing babies when they are pregnant. Because malnutrition leads to poor health and anemia, it makes it more difficult for them to fulfill their demanding traditional roles.

When trouble strikes, women are responsible both for getting their children to safety and providing for their needs. Eighty percent of all refugees are women. In areas of high unemployment, men often leave their families to become migrant workers either in nearby cities or in

Above, women shopping in Bali, Indonesia; right, women in the developing world often spend hours each day collecting water for their families

other countries. This is especially the case in South and Southeast Asia and Central America. Some of these men abandon their families to the mothers' care.

Women usually do not have as great a say in the organization and activities of the group of which they are a part, even though they may have a better grasp of what is needed. In almost all nations, women have had the vote for a shorter period than men. In Kuwait and Bhutan, they still cannot vote. (There are some countries, notably Saudi Arabia, where nobody votes.) Where information is available from lesser developed nations, it is apparent that women have very little political power, often holding fewer than five percent of political posts.

The greater physical strength of men is sometimes used to intimidate women. Women generally are valued less than men. Seclusion, the practice of keeping women apart from the general public, and veiling, are very common in Muslim countries of the Middle East and North Africa. A woman is viewed as the ''property'' of her husband or father in many nations. In Bangladesh and Botswana, a woman's worth is judged primarily by the number of children she bears, particularly males.[2]

Question

26. The four preceding paragraphs almost exclusively address problems in lesser developed nations. As you were reading them, however, you may have thought that many of the statements made could be applied to nations such as Canada. Taking each point at a time, explain the similarities and/or differences as you see them existing in our society compared to those in lesser developed nations.

Only women work in the communal rice harvest of Central Java, Indonesia.

Housework

Wherever you are, food has to be cooked and served, clothes and houses must be cleaned, and the needs of children met. In 1973, Paul Giles, a young British criminal, was ordered to clean a senior citizens' home as punishment for a crime. Could housework, therefore, be considered as equivalent to a jail sentence? For many women, it has become just that. Recent studies indicate that labour-saving devices have increased the length of time per week that US women work on household chores. What has happened is that higher standards of cleanliness and a greater variety of food are expected, more clothes are cleaned, and other members of the household are not helping as much as before. In 1980, the annual value of domestic work in the United States was estimated at $14 500 per home.

Changes in the organization of society in lesser developed nations have also left their mark on women. Mati, who lives in a village in Zimbabwe, finds that she has more household chores to do than her mother did. This is because the children are busy at school, and so cannot help much around the house, and her husband is away, earning money to pay for the children's school fees.

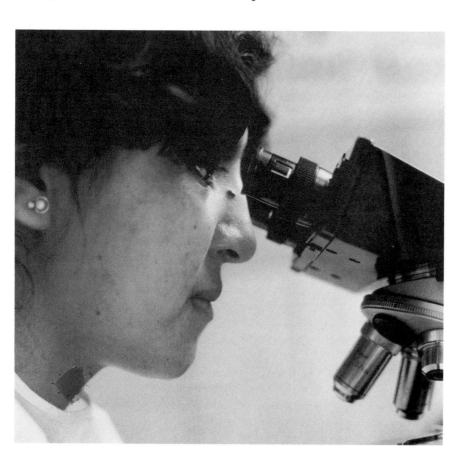

Left, a woman involved in medical research; above, this woman cares for her children and helps to run the family farm near Lennoxville, Quebec.

Living in the outskirts of Harare, in Zambezi, Elias found that acquiring additional material possessions meant more work in looking after them. She found she needed other activities, and so she is training to be a teacher. This career will give her the financial independence and status which she felt that she lacked, but she will need to employ someone to do the housework.

All over the world, maids, cleaning women, and nannies are employed so other women can work outside the home. They are often paid very low wages, may have very long hours with no days off, and few have any benefits. These jobs are almost exclusively the domain of women, as are jobs related to cleaning public buildings.

Trying to balance a career with a home and family is almost exclusively a bigger problem for women than for men. The responsibility carried by the woman for child care means that, more than men, they take part-time jobs. In the UK, 41 percent of women have part-time jobs compared to two percent of men. Many women are not free to train or put in overtime which might enhance their careers. It is estimated that lost overtime pay cost UK women $27 billion in 1987.

Women traditionally occupy poorer-paying jobs. In 1985, the average woman in the US earned less than two-thirds of the salary of her male counterpart. In the Philippines, men work an average of 41 h per week, while women work 61 h. In the USA, a man works an average of 1.6 h per day on household chores. A survey in Halifax revealed that among 60 married couples with both spouses working, women do 3.5 h of housework daily, while men do 1.5 h. Women also spend twice as much time with their children.[3]

Questions

27. (a) With the guidance of your teacher, design questions for a questionnaire on work to evaluate the relative situation of men and women in your area. You should consider the amount of money earned, type of employment, hours worked outside the house, rate of pay, hours worked inside the house, number and age of children, etc. You must attempt to word the questions so that you do not offend the person filling out your questionnaire, yet you must ensure that you are getting an accurate answer. Plan how you are going to explain what you are doing to the people you are interviewing. The answers must be in a form that is easy to evaluate collectively. Normally, a quantitative response, or a simple yes or no is the easiest to deal with. Asking for your subjects' comments at the end of the questionnaire will often make them feel more involved and will often produce interesting insights.

(b) Decide how you will attempt to achieve a representative sample.

(c) Allocate responsibilities within the class and decide on timelines.

(d) Analyze the results, using graphing techniques where appropriate.

28. Prepare a job description for a housewife. Use the headings listed below.
    Description
    Hours
    Payment
    Holidays
    Job Satisfaction
    Work Hazards
    Job Security
    Redundancy
    Payments
    Fringe Benefits

29. (a) Suggest three possible ways of correcting the problem of inequality that exists with respect to household responsibilities. Your answer should focus on solutions involving social agencies, political action, and personal activities.

(b) Describe how your solutions in part (a) might be achieved. Also, outline any foreseeable problems. Discuss your ideas with the class.

(c) Which three proposals or combination of proposals do you favour, and why?

30. (a) Why is equal access to education not a guarantee of equal access to economic opportunity?

(b) Why is the attitude of *both* sexes important in the improvement of the status of women in society? Give examples to back up your statements.

31. The education of women and girls in the lesser developed nations is considered vital for improving living conditions. Design a flow chart that shows the direct and indirect consequences that such education would have in a village of 500 people in either sub-Saharan Africa, Bangladesh, a native Indian village in the Brazilian forest, or in any other lesser developed nation with which you are familiar.

32. In order to gain entrance to the better public-funded high schools in Tokyo, a girl must have higher marks than a boy. What would be your reaction if this were the situation in Canada?

33. CIDA is encouraging the Canadian government to consider the impact of any aid programs on the women in the country or area involved. Among world organizations working towards bettering the position of women are Women's World Banking, which offers loans to Third World women, and the UN Voluntary Fund for Women, which raises money for development projects for women. Imagine yourself on a committee trying to advise one of these organizations. Briefly outline two or three recommendations that you would present to the Canadian government concerning funding for the building of a village school, the establishment of a village bank, and a plan to provide basic health care.

36. (a) Design a logo, such as might be used on buttons or posters, to symbolize a desire to improve the position of women. You could address the cause of women in the lesser developed world alone, or closer to home.

(b) Explain the symbolism that you have incorporated into your design for part (a).

Child Labour

Imagine yourself working for 12 h each day in oppressive heat and smoky conditions, being in constant danger of injury and yet earning less than $1 per day. Such is the life of a child worker in the glassworks of India. In the carpet factories of Morocco, children, some as young as four, work in cramped conditions hand-knotting carpets. Children as young as five or six in some Central American nations are in domestic service, doing back-breaking work from dawn to dusk. A month's wages for 13 h per day of such work might be $20. Similar scenes are repeated in many other poor nations. Laws are in place to prevent such activities, but bribery and corruption make law enforcers turn the other way. This situation also occurs in more developed nations from time to time.

The United Nations' International Labour Organization estimated that in 1986, 88 million children between the ages of 11 and 14 were working in virtual slavery. Such children usually do not have the opportunity to learn to read, and are thus at a disadvantage for the remainder of their lives. Often they are malnourished and suffer emotional problems from stress and deprivation.

There are approximately 1.1 billion children in the world between the ages of 5 and 14. Many parents, desperate for ways to support these children, allow them to work in appalling conditions. The factory owners prosper and, as the supply of cheap labour is so enormous, they can keep wages low. Companies and individuals who buy the products of child labour help to perpetuate the situation.

Above, young girls abandoned by poor families doing hand embroidery in Fez, Morocco; left, destitute street children in Thailand working to earn money for food

Table 2.5
A Profile of
World Youth

Criteria	World	More Developed	Less Developed	Canada	Bangladesh
Youth population (ages 15-24) 1985, millions	940	186	755	4.3	20.0
Youth population projected to 2020, millions	1261	172	1109	4.0	40.3
Total population 1985, millions	4845	1176	3671	25.4	101.5
Percentage of population below age 25, 1985	53	38	58	39	65
Percentage of children surviving to age 20	86	98	85	99	72
Average number of children per woman	3.6	2.0	4.2	1.7	6.4
Percentage of female teenagers aged 15-19 having a baby each year	5	3	6	3	13
Percentage enrolled in secondary school (male/female)	47/36	85/87	41/28	96/95	24/6

Above, this boy in an Asian city earns a living by hauling garbage; right, children in Nepal carrying heavy loads

Questions

35. What arguments can be made in favour of keeping the employment of children as it is, and against the current child labour situation?

36. Many people attribute the employment of children to a combination of improved health care and a lack of available schools.

    (a) Do you consider these arguments valid?

    (b) What are the other contributing factors?

Many young girls in Thailand work as street entertainers to support their families.

(c) Suggest strategies that might lead to a reduction in the abuse of children as a source of cheap labour.

37. (a) Use the statistics presented in Table 5.5 to illustrate the argument that youth in lesser developed nations face a grim future.

    (b) Suggest and briefly explain three necessary strategies for improving the future of world youth.

    (c) Some of the products of child labour are imported into Canada. Would you be in favour of, or would you object to, a ban on such imports? Explain your position. Some products produced by children are hand-knotted carpets from Morocco and India, glassware from India, and toys from Thailand.

This boy in Manila, Philippines works as a street vendor.

The International Debt Crisis

To be in debt is not in itself a problem; the crisis arises when we are unable to repay our debts. Such is the case for many poor nations who are currently US $1000 billion in debt and are unable to repay even the interest.

Impoverished nations struggling to meet their repayment commitments are forced to reduce basic services of health care, road building and repair, and industrial development. Thus, the economy of the countries concerned and the people's quality of life deteriorate and their governments may be obliged to borrow more money.

Nations are becoming more cautious about lending money to those who may not be able to repay the loan. If the major debtor nations fail to repay their debts, it will have very serious repercussions around the world.

So why did they borrow such huge sums of money? In 1945, many allied nations, including 15 developing nations, held the Bretton Woods Conference in New Hampshire, USA. The International Monetary Fund (IMF) and the World Bank were created at this conference to oversee and centralize major international monetary transactions. These two organizations wield massive power in such matters.

It was agreed that industrialized nations would sell manufactured goods to poorer nations which would, in turn, sell raw materials. However, prices for raw materials fluctuated wildly, and never rose as quickly as those of the manufactured goods that less developed nations were importing. Exporters of raw materials borrowed to pay for necessary imports.

As a result of increased oil prices in 1973, many banks in the richer nations found themselves in possession of enormous sums of money. They encouraged needy nations to borrow for development projects, expecting high rates of return. Oil-producing nations often invested their enormous profits in European banks, rather than use them to help those in need.

Some borrowed money was used to construct megaprojects such as the US $40-45 billion Itaipu hydroelectric project on the Brazil-Paraguay border and the Trans-Amazon Highway in Brazil. A few people benefitted, but the vast majority did

Table 2.6
The Major Third
World Debtor
Nations 1987

Country	Total External Debt ($Million)	Debt Service	
		% of GNP	% of Exports
Brazil	106 730	4.9	34.8
Mexico	97 429	8.5	48.2
Argentina	48 444	*not available	50.0 (1985)
South Korea	47 996	8.6	21.5
Indonesia	35 761	6.1	25.1
India	35 460	1.4	12.7
Venezuela	32 079	*not available	
Philippines	26 184	4.9	19.5
Turkey	26 124	7.1	32.1
Egypt	24 342	8.5	33.6

not, and are now suffering as the countries struggle to repay the debt. Some nations, such as Argentina, have used the money for military purposes. In 1981 and 1982, Argentina bought armaments worth US $13.9 billion from other nations. Some dictators, such as Sese Seko Mobuto of Zaire, Ferdinand Marcos of the Philippines, Anastasio Somoza of Nicaragua, and Jean-Claude Duvalier of Haiti, added some of the money they borrowed to their personal fortunes.

Further oil price increases, rising interest rates, the increase in the value of the US dollar compared to other currencies, and the world recession in 1983 are all part of the current crisis. Poorer nations were forced to borrow more as servicing or interest costs increased. For example, in 1975, Venezuela paid 42 cents of every dollar in interest on its loans. By 1981, that figure had risen to 66 cents.

The approximately 140 member nations of the IMF contribute money to the fund in amounts proportional to their gross national product. Because their voting power is also dictated by their contributions, the United States has a virtual veto on the activities of the IMF. Thus, the more developed nations are the ones making the decisions. The IMF determines which nations are credit worthy, and

imposes austerity measures on nations unable to repay debts. It has demanded, among other things:

· that the currencies of debtor nations should be devalued. (This makes imports for the debtor nation more expensive. Their exports also do not earn them as much on the international market);

· that subsidies be eliminated, resulting in increased costs for basic goods for a nation's citizens;

· that wages be frozen, so people have less money to spend; and

· that governments cut back basic services. (This is another penalty for local people.)

Such measures have not resulted in benefits either to the lenders or the debtors. Protectionist policies of developed nations (to prevent importation of cheaper products such as steel and clothing) make it impossible for debtor nations to improve their economies through trade. Changing from growing food for themselves to growing cash crops for export has meant a shortage of food in many countries.

Deteriorating infrastructure such as roads, hydro lines, and sewage disposal is one consequence of international debt.

What can be done to improve the situation? It seems very unlikely that the world's financial situation will change in a way that would enable the debtor nations to repay their loans. By dealing separately with individual countries, lenders have considerable influence in forcing austerity measures upon debtor nations, because they can threaten to withhold any future aid. Some debtor nations are offering ownership in industries in order to avoid incurring additional debts. Probably this will result in the creation of more "branch plants," with the attendant problem of profits going to the controlling nation. Others have agreed to set up conservation schemes aimed at preserving habitat and wildlife for the cancellation of some debts, or have offered their minerals in exchange.

Several nations have requested reduced rates of repayment, so that their economies are not so badly affected. In some cases, lending nations have "forgiven" or cancelled a debt, or delayed the repayment for a stated number of years. Canada has employed such measures with African nations. The creditor governments will have to repay the banks, and taxpayers will have to foot the bill. It is important that a solution to this problem be found and implemented quickly if people in the poorer nations are to improve their standard of living.

If a significant number of debtor nations were to agree to withhold repayment of their debts, they would be in a much stronger position in relation to their creditors. But if the richer nations would pay higher prices for commodities imported from debtor nations, the latter would be in a better position both to repay their debts and improve their economies.

Questions

38. Draw a flow chart based on the following information on the importing of shirts from Bangladesh to Canada. Continue your flow chart beyond the details given, to include details of the results of this situation in Bangladesh and in Canada.

In order to improve their economy and to provide employment for thousands of people, Bangladesh developed a shirt industry using locally grown cotton. In 1983, 16 000 of these shirts were imported into Canada. As exports grew, by 1985 20 000 Bangladesh workers were employed in the industry, and they in turn supported 100 000 more people. Canadian shirt makers protested to the Canadian government over these imports, however, and the number of shirts imported from Bangladesh was halved.

39. Canada and other richer nations have faced situations similar to that described in question 38. Examples have included shoes imported from India and cars imported from South Korea. In such cases, we have restricted imports or imposed tariffs on these cheaper manufactured goods.

(a) What arguments might be given to justify these actions? Give reasons for your answer.

(b) In what ways are we experiencing a moral dilemma?

40. (a) What would be the results in the more and the lesser developed nations, if there were more equitable prices for raw and manufactured goods?

(b) How could such a change come about?

Foreign Aid

A Canadian volunteer helping with a construction project in the Dominican Republic

Students in Honduras using learning materials supplied by UNICEF

Forms of Foreign Aid

Foreign aid takes many forms and can be channelled through a wide variety of agencies, both government-sponsored and privately operated. Its effectiveness will depend to some degree on the nature of the organization distributing it.

Bilateral aid is one of the most common forms of foreign aid. In this case, aid is sent directly from the donor country to the recipient country without going through an intermediate agency. Much bilateral aid is **tied aid**, given with certain conditions attached, for example, that the materials given must be purchased in the donor country. If a school in Kenya is being equipped through the Canadian foreign aid program, then the materials for that school would be largely supplied from Canada.

There are several disadvantages associated with tied aid. One is that some of the materials might be obtained less expensively from other countries. Also, equipment suitable for the donor country may be inappropriate for the recipient country. Tied aid can also be inefficient, since it requires a great deal of paperwork as well as the transportation of materials over a great distance. Tied aid can also bring pressure to get the recipient nation to conform to a particular policy or political viewpoint.

It should be noted, however, that tied aid has clearly benefitted recipient countries greatly and has resulted in the transference of a good deal of technology. Tying aid to certain conditions also may make giving aid more acceptable in the donor country. It can also be specifically tailored to the needs of the recipient.

Multilateral aid involves the transfer of aid from a number of donor countries through an international agency such as the Red Cross. Agencies involved in multilateral aid generally avoid making political statements and entering into conflict with the governments of the recipient countries, even where there is clear mismanagement of funds. The Food and Agricultural Organization (FAO) of the United Nations has had a major role in agricultural research and in the dissemination of the results of this research around the world. The **World Health Organization (WHO)** is another outstanding UN organization which has had a major role in monitoring health problems, coming up with solutions for them and disseminating the benefits. The WHO was primarily responsible, for example, for the campaign which eliminated smallpox from the earth.

One of the largest agencies administering multilateral aid is the World Bank. Founded in 1944, the World Bank is considered to be the world's single most powerful force for development. In 1986, it lent out over US $18 billion. It is located in Washington, D.C., but the money it lends reaches almost every corner of the developing world. The basic philosophy behind the operations of the World Bank is as follows. It receives funds from the wealthier industrialized countries such as France, Canada, the United States, and West Germany. With this capital, it lends to developing countries unable to borrow from regular commercial banks. Any profits which are accrued by the Bank are funnelled back into its various projects around the world.

Although the Bank has funded some small-scale projects, much of its money has been directed into extremely large developments, some more successful than others. One project which has received criticism is an $18 million cattle-grazing scheme in Botswana, Africa. Studies have indicated that this project has made the problem of overgrazing worse in that region of the country and has led to desertification. In addition, the cattle-grazing project threatens a nearby wildlife preserve.

Another World Bank project, called "Polonoroeste," involves the state of Rondonia in Northwest Brazil. A tropical rain forest was cleared to make room for a new highway through the region, leaving behind a rapidly deteriorating environment which cannot support even subsistence farming.

On the other hand, the World Bank has also been instrumental in developing some highly successful projects. Here is a sampling:

- financing for the construction of sewage tunnels under the city of Shanghai;
- rehabilitation of ten major port facilities in Madagascar;
- construction of two coal-fired electrical generating plants in East Java, Indonesia; and
- agricultural credit programs to supply loans to farmers in Ecuador.

One of the most important roles of the United Nations is not political but social, giving economic and social assistance to the countries in the developing world. Some of these UN agencies have become enormous, however, and consequently inefficient.

Questions

46. In what specific ways is the operation of the World Bank different from that of a regular commercial bank?

47. Judging from the sheer size of its operation, what problems does the World Bank face in administering its programs?

48. Explain why the World Bank is so little-known to the average North American.

A Bakery in Nairobi

In Nairobi, Kenya, a group of 40 poverty-stricken women decided that they would like to set up their own bakery. Although they had the ambition and drive to set up a business, they could not obtain a loan to purchase the necessary equipment.

The project might never have moved ahead if the Women's World Banking Organization had not stepped in and agreed to guarantee 50 percent of the loan of $3125. The Women's World Banking Organization was founded in 1978 by a woman named Michaela Walsh, who set up headquarters in the Netherlands. The organization's goal was to lend money to women setting up businesses in the developing world who would otherwise have no access to funding. The rest of the loan for the bakery was guaranteed by other sources and the money was made available to the women.

After an evaluation of the project, the women were given a one-month training program and then the bakery opened. At present, the bakery is operating successfully, and is paying back the loan at current rates.

Questions

41. Why are so many people in developing countries unable to obtain loans, while in industrialized countries most people have credit cards and some have more credit than they need?

42. What was the crucial element in the Nairobi project?

43. What lessons could be learned from this project by foreign aid organizations?

Foreign Aid: To Give or Not To Give

Although there is a great deal of news coverage on the need for foreign aid, many Canadians and others in the industrialized world have misgivings about the principle of foreign aid itself. Summarized below are arguments for and against foreign aid to the developing world.

In Favour of Foreign Aid

1) A feeling of moral responsibility for the welfare of all people leads us to help the less fortunate.

2) If underdeveloped countries can develop economically, they can be future markets for our goods.

3) We win friends who may be valuable allies in the future.

4) Money spent in Canada for materials to help LDCs creates employment in our country.

5) If we help to check disease in the developing world, this may prevent its spread to us.

Against Foreign Aid

1) We have enough problems in our own country without sending money to other countries.

2) We should not be spend-

ing our money on foreign aid when so much of it is wasted.

3) The people of the LDCs do not appreciate the aid we give them.

4) People in LDCs should learn to help themselves; foreign aid will only make them lazy.

5) When we provide foreign aid to people in the developing world, we inevitably impose values which may interfere with their way of life.

6) Many people in the LDCs are happy without the benefits of foreign aid and technology from the developed world.

7) Industries we set up in the developing world may eventually compete with our own.

8) By supplying aid to countries at war, we are indirectly fuelling that war.

Questions

44. Evaluate both sides of the argument on foreign aid. What is your point of view on this issue? Outline your reasoning carefully. If your own views conflict, explain how this is so.

45. If someone pointed out to you that there had been a large number of failures in the area of foreign aid, how might you justify continuing it?

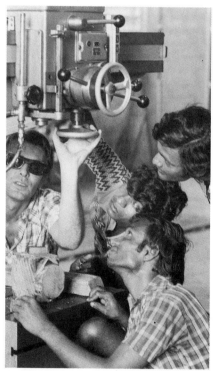

A Canadian volunteer teaching machining skills in Sri Lanka

Canadian International Development Agency (CIDA)

The **Canadian International Development Agency (CIDA)** is the largest government agency in Canada. It is responsible for administering the aid Canada sends to the developing world. With a budget of $2174 million per year, CIDA has a significant impact on many of the organizations which are involved in foreign aid. Table 2.7 illustrates CIDA's budget expenditures.

As can be seen from Table 2.7, CIDA distributes its money amongst a wide variety of aid programs. In general, this is a wise choice, since each form of aid has its own strengths.

CIDA tends to concentrate its aid in countries of the British Commonwealth or French-speaking countries. This reflects Canada's bilingual nature and its commitment to the Commonwealth. Table 2.8 on page 66 lists the various countries around the world which received Canadian foreign aid in 1987.

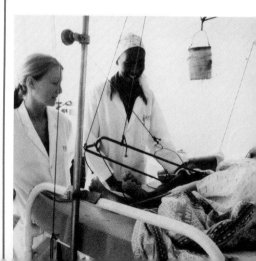

CIDA sponsored house construction in an African nation

A Canadian medical worker in Lesotho

Table 2.7 CIDA's Budget for 1986-1987

Nature of aid	Budget ($millions)	Percentage of CIDA budget	Number of projects	Number of countries
Bilateral food	211	8.4	35	45
Multilateral food	166	6.6	360	120
Bilateral non-food	756	30.0	1 000	105
Industrial co-operation	32	1.3	700 +	100
Development banks	588	2.3	1 000s	150 +
Multilateral non-food	182	7.2	10 000 +	all LDCs
Humanitarian	52	2.1	120	80
Private aid agencies	249	9.9	3 500	100 +
World Bank and other such organizations	157	6.2	10 000 +	150 +

**Table 2.8
Countries Receiving Canadian Government-to-Government Assistance in 1986-87.**

CIDA sponsored agricultural research in Peru

Central America	Africa		Europe
Mexico	Morocco	Zaire	Turkey
Guatemala	Algeria	Congo	**Asia**
Belize	Tunisia	Gabon	Jordan
El Salvadore	Egypt	Equatorial Guinea	Yemen
Honduras	Sudan	Cameroon	Democratic Yemen
Nicaragua	Ethiopia	Central African Republic	Pakistan
Costa Rica	Djibouti	Chad	India
Panama	Somalia	Niger	Nepal
Haiti	Kenya	Nigeria	Bhutan
Dominican Republic	Uganda	Benin	Bangladesh
South America	Rwanda	Togo	Burma
Colombia	Burundi	Ghana	Thailand
Venezuela	Tanzania	Burkina Faso	Malaysia
Guyana	Zambia	Ivory Coast	Indonesia
Brazil	Malawi	Liberia	Philippines
Ecuador	Mozambique	Sierra Leone	China
Peru	Madagascar	Guinea	
Bolivia	Lesotho	Mali	**Oceania**
Chile	Namibia	Guinea-Bisseau	Papua New Guinea
Paraguay	Botswana	Gambia	
Uruguay	Zimbabwe	Senegal	
Argentina	Angola	Mauritania	

Above, teaching surveying in St. Lucia; right, a Canadian teacher in Zimbabwe

Some projects funded by CIDA are described below.

- Honduras spent $1.3 million of its CIDA aid money to buy equipment from Canada for its El Cajon hydro-electric dam (1985-86).
- a $1.7 million project in Bangladesh employed 60 000 destitute women to improve and maintain rural roads (1985-86).
- $400 000 was spent in Niger and Burkina Faso on rural development projects such as schools, wells, seeds for farmers, and demonstration farms (1985-86).
- The International Committee of the Red Cross received $6.2 million in grain from CIDA for famine relief in Ethiopia (1985-86).

A significant portion of CIDA's budget is directed toward privately operated NGOs (non-governmental organizations) like the Red Cross, World Vision, UNICEF, Foster Parents Plan, various churches, and others. These organizations will be discussed in more detail later.

The very size of CIDA, with its enormous budget, means that there will be a certain amount of waste. Stricter controls might cost more than the projects themselves. In addition, as a government agency, CIDA has developed a large **bureaucracy** to administer aid. With so many people employed in its bureaucracy, decisions are made in Ottawa which may or may not be appropriate in the developing world.

Along with the success stories, there are also examples of CIDA projects which failed due to poor management. During the early 1980s, CIDA sponsored a development project in Haiti which was designed to aid farmers and the poverty-stricken in the countryside. The focal point of the development project was a road for shipping produce out and allowing modern technology in. However, this road was designed for vehicular traffic, of which there was almost none. Not only was the road of little value when it was finished, but also all the tools and equipment used to build it disappeared by the end of construction. Other mistakes involved installation of fire hydrants which were not connected to a source of water and which were placed in a region where no one was trained to fight fires. Elsewhere, a 60 t silo was constructed but never used.

There are other examples besides this one. Millions of dollars of aid money has been spent on the Tanzanian railway system which is scarcely operational and is on the verge of collapse. Canadian wheat sent to the Sahel in Africa in the late 1980s never reached those who needed it, but was sold on the black market. A shipload of potatoes sent to Haiti arrived saturated in salt water and unfit to eat.

These are disheartening incidents but, overall, CIDA carries out a very difficult task competently.

Question

49. (a) Construct a pie graph, using the percentage data from Table 2.7, to illustrate how CIDA's money is allocated to different kinds of projects.

(b) On an outline map of the world, colour and name the countries to which CIDA sends aid. Use Table 2.8.

(c) Referring to your graph, map, and other data in Table 2.7, write a 300-word summary of CIDA's involvement in and impact on the world.

Non-Governmental Organizations

Some of the most effective agencies for administering foreign aid are the **non-governmental organizations (NGOs)**. Although they may receive some government funding, their modest budgets rely on donations from private groups or individuals. NGOs concentrate on small-scale, practical programs.

There are several different types of aid provided by the NGOs. These are listed below.

- Aid for children includes such programs as child sponsorship, education for children, and child nutrition. Organizations such as UNICEF, Cansave, Foster Parents Plan, and World Vision give this type of aid.

- Human rights organizations such as Amnesty International and various anti-apartheid groups operate in an attempt to eliminate or reduce the abuses of human rights around the world.

- Canadian churches often send aid through churches in the developing world. This aid is efficiently spent because the recipient church keeps administrative costs to a minimum by using the money to fund small, local projects. Another example of the efficiency of church aid is demonstrated by a Markham, Ontario church. Money is collected from the congregation and sent to a project manager in Haiti who uses it to buy construction materials to make simple houses at a cost of $1500 each. Members of the Markham church who have experience in construction travel to Haiti (paying their own airfare) and work as volunteers for several weeks building houses with the assembled materials.

- Small, highly specialized, private aid agencies form an important component in foreign aid. Run largely by volunteers, they work with low budgets to operate an eye clinic in an African country, for example, or an orphanage in India. Examples of such organizations are Sleeping Children Around the World (SCAW) and the Evangelical Missionaries' Medical Aid Society.

- General aid organizations, like Oxfam-Canada, World Vision of Canada, or

CARE, are larger, although still privately operated, and provide money for a broad range of programs from rural development to nutrition and education. They also supply help to organizations which actually oversee the projects.

In general, the non-governmental organizations operate on a smaller scale than, say, the WHO or the World Bank. In some ways they can accomplish what larger organizations cannot. They do not, for example, impose the political restrictions of projects initiated by the Canadian or US governments. NGO programs make one-to-one contact with people in the developing world, and can therefore be more finely tuned to the needs of a local area. Small NGOs are sensitive to the care with which the money is spent, and realize that their very existence depends on continued public support.

Questions

50. What are some of the drawbacks of working through an NGO in attempting to solve the problems of the developing world?

51. For what reasons would a person give to an NGO even though larger international and governmental programs administer foreign aid?

52. In what ways would working for an NGO be an exciting and challenging job?

Agricultural machinery often becomes useless because people do not know how to make repairs. These Canadian volunteers in Central America are setting up repair shops so equipment can be maintained.

Canadian volunteers on a building project in Kenya

The Naam Movement

One of the most extraordinary and successful voluntary groups in Africa is the Naam Movement. This movement is involved in rural development at the grass-roots level, and is built on the imagination and work of thousands of ordinary people.

The origins of the Naam Movement go back to 1967 when a teacher in that country, Bernard Ledea Ouedraogo, determined to improve the lot of the average farmer. His philosophy was simple, stressing indigenous development and building on the best of the traditional ideas of an area. It was important, he believed, to start from where the peasant farmers were and work from there. The technologies were simple,

The name "Naam" came from the traditional village organization with which Ouedraogo was familiar. It was a grouping of young people formed co-operatively every rainy season to help with planting and harvesting.

Northern Burkina Faso is a difficult region in which to live and farm. It is on the southern edge of the Sahara Desert in the Sahel. There is supposed to be a rainy season every year, but it may be late or short or non-existent. The dry season is long and hot, and may extend for months or years. The soils are thin and often unproductive. Despite these formidable obstacles, the Naam Movement has prospered.

The Naam philosophy may not appear to be revolutionary, but it is. From its modest beginnings, the Naam Move-

ment expanded to over 1400 local groups by the time of its twentieth anniversary. In Somiaga, a village in northern Burkina Faso, the accomplishments are impressive: a pharmacy; a mill; a tree nursery; a woodlot; a cereal grain bank; a large dam to store water, prevent floods, irrigate, and provide fish; wells for drinking water; numerous farming improvements; a road to the outside world; introduction of new technology such as a fuel-efficient stove; and co-operation amongst farmers.

One of the simple improvements the Naam Movement has helped to bring about has been valuable in the semi-desert climate of the Sahel. Small piles of stones are laid in rows along the contours of the hills so that when rain does come it is trapped behind each of the

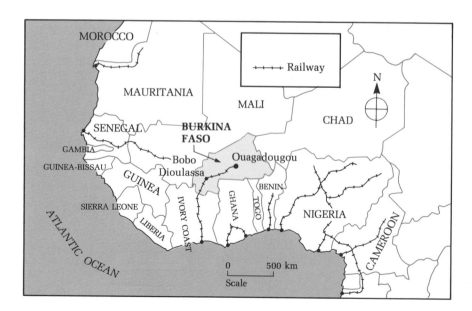

Figure 2.3
The Naam Movement began in Burkina Faso which is located in West Africa along the southern fringe of the Sahara in a region called the Sahel.

rows of stones and sinks into the ground. The productivity of the land has increased greatly because of this practice.

These developments are the result of the work but, more important, the ideas generated by the people themselves. When they needed help to drill wells, they called for outside help and the Lutheran World Relief Fund responded.

Similar self-help groups have developed in many places, and ideas for low-level technology have spread equally quickly.

Questions

53. Suggest reasons for the rapid spread of the Naam groups throughout Burkina Faso.

54. What aspect of the Naam approach would most appeal to the people who have become involved in it?

55. What important lessons can be learned from this movement that might be applied to the foreign aid programs administered by CIDA and other large government and United Nations agencies?

Conclusion

Living in an industrialized western nation, we are among the fortunate minority of world citizens who, generally speaking, have access to a high standard of living, good health, and a fairly high level of employment. The majority of people in other nations are struggling to survive in a world which offers them few of the advantages which we take for granted. As a nation which needs to trade to prosper, we are aware of global interdependence. Those nations and individuals who are in a position to improve the situation for those in need must take action for the benefit of all people.

Question

56. Stephen Lewis, formerly Canada's ambassador to the United Nations, has stated that the problems of the poorer nations cannot be solved without a three-pronged approach. This would involve more aid from wealthier nations, the adjustment or forgiveness of debts by wealthy nations, and the reduction of military spending by debtor nations. Comment on Mr. Lewis's observation.

Vocabulary

World Bank

North

South

urbanization

shanty towns, barrios, or favelas

geostationary orbit

water-related diseases

grass-roots medicine

barefoot doctors

Canadian University Services Overseas (CUSO)

racism

prejudice

cultural diversity

bilateral aid

multilateral aid

World Health Organization (WHO)

Canadian International Development Agency (CIDA)

bureaucracy

non-governmental organizations (NGOs)

Independent Study

1. "... there is no darkness but ignorance ....''
William Shakespeare, *Twelfth Night*, Act IV, scene ii

"Ignorance is the curse of God;
Knowledge the wing wherewith we fly to heaven.''
William Shakespeare, *Henry VI, Part 2*, Act IV, scene vii

"Knowledge itself is power.''
Francis Bacon, *Religious Meditation, Of Heresies*

"Ignorance is strength.''
George Orwell, *Nineteen eighty-four*

"They were a boy and girl. Yellow, meagre, ragged, scowling, wolfish; but prostrate, too, in their humility. 'They are Man's', said the Spirit, looking down upon them. 'And they cling to me, appealing from their fathers. This boy is Ignorance. This girl is Want. Beware of them both and all of their degree, but most of all beware this boy, for on his brow I see that written which is Doom, unless the writing be erased.' ''
Charles Dickens, *A Christmas Carol*

(a) Record the year in which each of the above quotations was first published.

(b) Explain the context of two of the quotations.

(c) Comment on the relevance of two of the quotations in today's world. Use different quotations from those used in part (b). Substantiate your arguments by using recent statistics. Where possible, compare these with earlier statistics.

2. Japan is a modern and progressive country, yet it is still considered more important for a woman to raise a family and support her husband than have a career outside the home.

(a) Research and report on the lives of women in Japan.

(b) In what ways do the lives of Japanese women differ from those of contemporary Canadian women?

(c) In 1980, Japan signed a United Nations pledge to end discrimination against women. In your opinion, how should they approach this task? Has Canada taken similar steps toward achieving equality for women, or are they still to be implemented here? Explain your answer.

3. Choose a minority group that has been affected by contact with "modern civilization.'' (Do not choose a group used as an example in this book.)

(a) Research and describe the history of the group and the traditional way of life of its members.

(b) Analyze how their way of life depended on free access to an unspoiled environment.

(c) Explain how and why their life was affected by outside influences.

(d) Relate what, if anything, has been done to redress any injustices that they have suffered.

(e) Suggest strategies that you would like to see implemented to improve their situation.

4. Choose a native group in Canada which is, or has been, involved in discussions concerning land claims and/or compensation at some time during the last 30 years.

(a) Describe the events which led to the claims being made.

(b) What solutions have been proposed, and which, if any, have been agreed upon?

(c) Compare the experiences of the group which you have researched to those of the Penen of Sarawak, described earlier in this chapter.

(d) In your opinion, how could this situation have been avoided in a way which was just for all parties concerned?

(e) Explain how your suggestions in answer to part (d) might be applied in the future.

5. Some people describe Canada as the "world's richest underdeveloped country."

(a) Research and report on five resource industries with largely foreign control and investment. Your report should give details of holdings in Canada and abroad.

(b) Comment on your findings and evaluate the consequences in terms of Canada's future.

(c) In your opinion, should we stop this trend?

(d) How could a reversal be achieved?

(e) What would be the short- and long-term consequences?

6. The disease referred to as AIDS (Acquired Immune Deficiency Syndrome) is spreading quickly throughout the world.

(a) Describe the mechanics of this condition. How does the AIDS virus attack the body, and what are the results?

(b) How is the virus transmitted, and which people are most vulnerable?

(c) Investigate and report on the history of this condition from its earliest discovery in Africa to its current distribution pattern. Include statistics concerning its occurrence around the world and present these in map and chart form.

(d) Bearing in mind the routes and means by which it is spread, use a map to project the distribution of future outbreaks of AIDS.

(e) Apart from a change in people's lifestyles, are there other methods that might be used to curb the geographical spread of AIDS throughout the world? (We suggest that you study the methods used to eradicate smallpox.) Upon what major breakthrough does such control depend?

7. Select two non-governmental organizations involved in sending foreign aid to the developing world, and for each one, obtain as much information as you can about:

- its budget and how it is spent, for as recent a year as you can find;

- its general philosophy and its goals for foreign aid;

- the regions of the world where it operates or sends its funds;

- two examples of the types of projects in which it is involved;

- its sources of funds (e.g., private donations, government funding, etc.); and

- an analysis of the organization as to its effectiveness.

Compare the two organizations for their strengths, weaknesses, general approach, and effectiveness.

8. List and describe ten examples of advertising or news items from the mass media dealing with foreign aid and the organizations which administer it. Include the date of the item, its source (with page number, if applicable) and author (if applicable).

(a) What general impression would a member of the public receive from the items you have listed?

(b) Do the news items and advertisements provide an accurate view of the foreign aid program? Explain your answer.

Kenneth Lumb

Grass-roots Dentistry in Canada's North

Dr. Kenneth Lumb graduated from dental school in 1969. He has worked in Toronto's Hospital for Sick Children and in private practice, and has also helped to provide dental care for those who live in isolated northern communities.

His first experiences of the North were at Sioux Lookout, in northern Ontario. As a fairly large community of approximately 2500 people, it could count on the services of a doctor and a dentist. Sioux Lookout also served as a base for nearby Indian reserves such as Big Trout Lake, Sandy Lake, and Lansdowne House. Each of these communities was 20 min to 1 h away by Cessna aircraft, and contained a nursing station to serve the local community of 300 to 800 people. At the nursing station, residents could receive immunization shots and basic health care, as well as emergency treatment when required. Each nursing station was in radio contact with three or four satellite clinics, each serving 25 to 175 people. At these clinics, community-trained lay dispensers administered first aid and occasionally dispensed drugs. Rounds of each satellite group were carried out every two or three weeks by nurses and physicians, and any patient requiring additional care would be flown to the nearest facility.

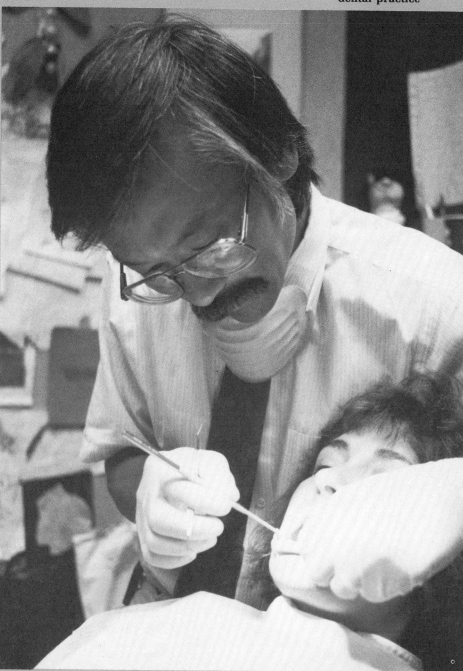

Dr. Lumb in his dental practice

Dental treatment was provided by means of portable equipment, transported by Cessna aircraft to the various communities.

Dr. Lumb trained people from isolated communities to become dental therapists. To do this, he was based at one of the facilities situated at an educational complex in Fort Smith, Northwest Territories, where many vocational skills were being taught. The aim of the program is to provide training for those interested without removing them from their northern homes, thus encouraging the graduate to stay in the North to work. Candidates for the course are required to have a grade 12 education, so some need to spend one or two years in Fort Smith upgrading their education before they qualify for entry. The course, funded by the federal government, takes two or more years to finish, after which the graduates work on children's teeth, doing extractions and fillings, X-rays, and cleaning. Those who graduated as dental therapists are also permitted to work on adults.

The School of Dental Therapy has now relocated to Prince Albert, Saskatchewan and, of the 18 to 20 students who enrol each year, usually seven or eight graduate. They return to northern communities to provide basic dental care, for which they are paid by the federal government.

Often, after many years of absence for educational training, the new graduates find adjustment to their remote new home a very difficult experience, and they may not stay there. They find that going back to their own community is even more difficult than working in a different one.

Providing medical and dental care to people in the North is frustrating, slow, and very expensive. Dr. Lumb cites the case of a man in Clyde River who was shot in an argument with another man. At the nursing station, he received basic treatment which stabilized him, but he was still in critical condition. An emergency flight to a hospital in Montreal was delayed two days by bad weather. He stayed in Iqaluit where attempts were made to regulate his vital functions before he was flown to Montreal on another chartered plane. Unfortunately, despite all these efforts, he died en route.

Questions:

1. Describe the ways in which medical care in remote areas of northern Canada is similar to grassroots medicine in many lesser developed nations.

2. What advantages do we have in caring for people in these remote areas that are not usually available in poorer nations?

3. Medical care in the north is far from ideal. Make a realistic suggestion for improving the service, bearing in mind the costs involved.

Part II

Geopolitical Issues of the World

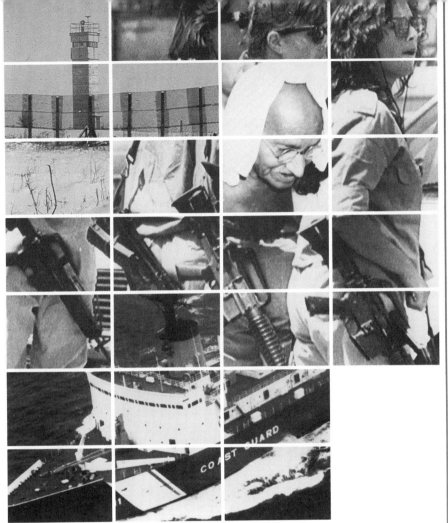

3

Geopolitics

By the end of this chapter, you should be able to:

- use examples to explain the significance of geography in determining the strategic importance of an area;

- analyze the causes of military conflicts and the reasons for the involvement of the superpowers;

- explain how arms are acquired by terrorist groups and less developed nations;

- evaluate the merits or drawbacks in spending money for military purposes in the place of social and economic development;

- analyze the possible causes and consequences of nuclear confrontation, and evaluate the efforts that have been made to reduce the risk of such a confrontation;

- describe the major military and other co-operative alliances and explain their aims; and

- explain how and why boundaries come into existence, and explain how boundaries and the status of nations have changed, especially since World War II.

Mozambique

Mozambique is a nation on the east coast of Africa, with the dubious distinction of being rated as the most miserable country in the world in which to live. The Human Suffering Index is a rating of the quality of life in each country based on income, water supply, energy use, freedom, adult literacy, population growth, job demand, inflation, and death rate. On this scale Switzerland has the least misery, and Canada is close to it, at number 9. In addition, in 1988, the World Bank ranked Mozambique as the world's sixth poorest country.

Mozambique's dismal situation provides us with an opportunity to assess the causes of impoverishment which plague this, and many other, lesser developed nations. Many people in Canada and other more developed nations do not realize that such poverty is due more

These homeless people in Mozambique were forced to leave their rural homes because of drought and guerilla activity.

to the results of geopolitics than to drought or large populations. **Geopolitics** involves the spatial (territorial) claims of nations and their orbit of influence beyond their political boundaries. This chapter will largely be concerned with demonstrating that political attitudes and activities, past and present, are the most important factor in determining the current world condition. These attitudes develop largely in response to geographical situation.

Apart from persistent drought, Mozambique's present situation can be attributed almost wholly to past colonial influences and present political activities.

Mozambique had been under Portuguese control since 1506. When the Portuguese relinquished power in 1975, following a ten-year war, they left behind a nation which was ill-prepared for self-government. Despite having had at their disposal a land rich in natural resources, Portuguese interests emphasized, first, trade with South Africa to obtain foreign currency and, second, a supply of agricultural goods for Portugal. Farming had not been developed in a way that would supply food for the Mozambican people. When the Portuguese left, the country was bankrupt, the people were unskilled, there was a 90 percent illiteracy rate, and there was virtually no internal organization of government and social agencies. Infrastructure such as railways, roads, and power lines were in desperate need of repair.

Add to this legacy the fighting that continues today. The Mozambique government supported the efforts of those who were trying to remove Prime Minister Ian Smith from power in Rhodesia, which had been a British colony until 1965. Mr. Smith's 15-year term ended in 1980, with the formation of a black regime which renamed the country Zimbabwe. The Rhodesian Intelligence tried to destabilize Mozambique. They established the Mozambican National Resistance (MNR) as a fifth column. **A fifth column** is a group of people who, although they live in their own country, act against it because they sympathize with an enemy.

When Zimbabwe gained independence, the MNR was recruited by the South African government, with mandate to "destabilize the Mozambican economy through acts of sabotage." (Report of the Delegation Visit to Canada of the Christian Council of Mozambique, 1988.) The

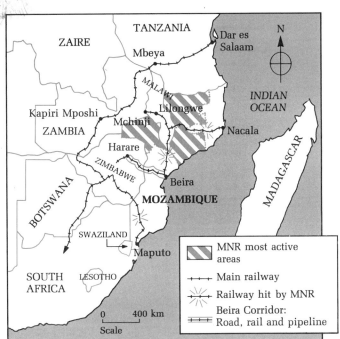

Figure 3.1
Mozambique and Its Surrounding Nations

MNR, also known as RENAMO, uses sabotage and murder to achieve its ends. South African government leaders feel much more secure when the black nations which flank its northern border are weak and dependent, for they present less of a challenge to their policy of apartheid. Because of their vulnerability to incursions from South Africa, these nations are referred to as the "front line" states. Canada is one of the nations attempting to strengthen them.

In 1987, a delegation of Canadians of varied backgrounds, and headed by the Honourable Walter McLean, M.P., spent one week in Mozambique specifically to gain a greater understanding of the country's problems. They travelled through much of Mozambique and talked unhindered to many people. In 1988, the Christian Council of Mozambique sent representatives to talk to Canadians. These meetings help to illustrate the genuine concern that Canada has for the welfare of the people of Mozambique.

Drought coupled with war has made food distribution to badly affected areas a special problem. Two hundred and fifty thousand people died in 1986 as a result of war-induced famine, and the United Nations estimated that four million others were in danger of starvation.

All of these factors have resulted in deteriorating conditions in Mozambique since 1982. The McLean Report of 1987 states that, "since 1982, Mozambique has actually regressed by almost every development criteria you could name . . . .[and its] well-being [is increasingly tied] to that of the apartheid state [of South Africa]." Over 5 million of the 14 million people in the country have been forced by the fighting to move; 250 000 people have fled, some to poor neighbouring countries, thus stretching already meagre resources. The GNP per capita income dropped from US $240 to

Summary September 1986

- Affected by food shortage .... 2.52 million
- Dislocated .... 1.03 million
- At short-term nutritional risk .... 0.41 million
TOTAL AFFECTED .... 3.96 million

TANZANIA
ZAMBIA
MALAWI
Lichinga
NAMPULA
ZAMBEZIA
Tete
Changara
Quelimane
Chindl
ZIMBABWE
MOZAMBIQUE
Mozambique Channel

0   200   400 km
Scale

SOUTH AFRICA
Panda
Maputo
SWAZILAND

Food scarcity caused by banditry
Drought-affected areas
Concentrations of dislocated people
Populations movements

$140 in the six years preceding 1987, and the mortality rate among children under five has risen to 325 per thousand, compared with ten per thousand in Canada.

Canada is committed to helping Mozambique. Aid supplied through government agencies between 1985 and 1989 has exceeded $50 million and, in addition, there are many non-governmental agencies involved. The Canadian delegation concluded that the problems of the nation are inextricably a combination of war, poor development, and dependency. There are many other nations willing to help, and it is important that their efforts be co-ordinated. Canada further suggests that it would be most beneficial to concentrate on the Beira Corridor, where there are vital communications links for Mozambique and other countries having a common border with South Africa.

To foster development and reduce dependency on other nations, Canadian investigators recommended focussing on improving agriculture, health, education and training, small enterprises, and infrastructure; that is, to restore Mozambique to a good state of management for the benefit of its citizens.

Questions

1. Make two short lists which identify the direct and the indirect causes of Mozambique's current crisis.

2. What was it in the past attitude of Portugal to Mozambique that still affects Mozambique today?

3. Why do other nations, including both the USA and USSR, have a special interest in the "front line" states?

4. What effects does fighting have on the economy and development of Mozambique?

5. Re-read the list of priorities that Canada has for helping Mozambique. Suggest one way in which Canadians could help, in each of the categories.

These refugees in Tete Province (see map on opposite page) have taken refuge at a railway station.

Introduction

Tales of conflict between nations and tribes have been recorded by scribes for thousands of years. The reasons for disputes have remained essentially the same. They include a need for land to provide resources for one's own people, and a powerful desire to expand one's own influence into other territories and to control strategic transportation routes. What has changed is the scale of hostilities and the potential devastation which does or could result.

The geographical perspective provides us with a valuable tool to help us analyze some of the causes of conflict. Theories put forward 80 to 100 years ago, concerning the expansion of a country's influence, have merit and are worthy of study in light of subsequent events. The accumulation and exploitation of empires have left many former colonies ill-prepared for independence. Many are impoverished by their military activities in which richer nations have a keen interest and overt or covert involvement for strategic reasons.

While there have been a few examples of nations splitting to become smaller units, the trend is toward economic and military alliances involving anything from two nations to over 100. The most significant modern changes in this regard are taking place within the European Economic Community where many independent nations have slowly become integrated into a union of approximately the same economic strength as the USA. Probably the greatest organization ever created, the United Nations includes almost all countries, and has contributed significantly to humanitarian and peacekeeping activities around the world.

It is very important to realize that a significant factor in world affairs and the well-being of the population is geographical location. Location affects the productivity of the land and its strategic importance. Thus, politics becomes interwined with geography, in the study of geopolitics.

The Nature of Geopolitics

Geopolitics is the study and analysis of the spatial (territorial) claims of nations and their orbit of influence beyond their political boundaries. It is most often concerned with the outer limits of the state, but can also encompass the push for sub-division within a state. A country may grow by acquiring territory, or split up into smaller units. Geopolitics attempts to analyze the factors which lead to the change of the geographical boundaries of various states. Some famous geopolitical ideas are outlined below.

Various theoretical attempts have been made to explain the principles of political influence. Friedrich Ratzel (1844-1904) was the first to propose that the state was like a developing organism, needing nourishment in the form of additional territories if it were to stay healthy. Some of Ratzel's students took his ideas and applied them as part of the Nazi expansionist ideas of the 1930s. One of these students, Karl Haushofer, was an associate of Adolf Hitler.

Other people had similar ideas. In 1904, Sir Halford Mackinder suggested that the land which he referred to as the **Pivot Area**, (Figure 3.2), had the potential to become a powerful state. He based this on the idea that it had natural protection, distance from the sea, and local resources. In particular, the absence of easily accessible waterways made it less vulnerable to invasion. The Pivot Area, then of little significance, has now developed into the Soviet Union.

Later, Mackinder included eastern Europe in his Pivot Area, and renamed the resulting combination the **Heartland.**

Mackinder formed the following hypothesis:

Who rules eastern Europe commands the Heartland.

Who rules the Heartland commands the World Island [Asia and Europe].

Who rules the World Island commands the World.

Even in today's missile age, the vast size of this Heartland gives the core some measure of protection through the number of minutes warning they would receive of an attack.

Japan's expansion, between 1870, when it became politically unified, and 1942, was carried out for reasons other than those suggested by Ratzel. The Japanese people had developed a very efficient "war machine," and were able to

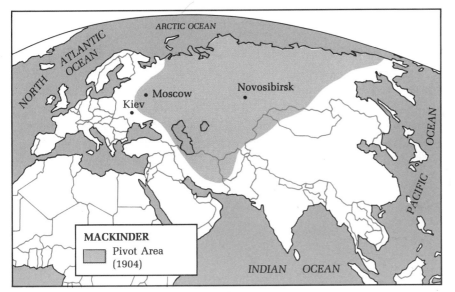

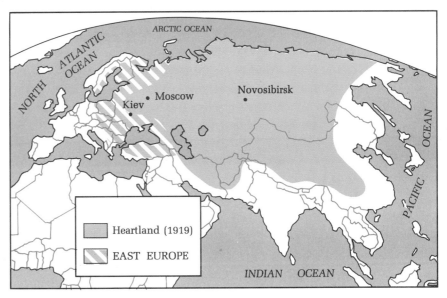

invade poorly defended islands and nearby parts of the mainland. This growth of influence was accompanied by increased Japanese economic activity based on imported raw materials and exported finished goods. Figure 3.3 illustrates this expansion.

At its height following World War II, the British Empire included such a variety of countries in all parts of the globe that it was said, "The sun never sets on the British Empire." It should also be remembered that Britain controlled the American colonies until the 1770s. The

Figure 3.3
The Japanese
Empire 1933-1942

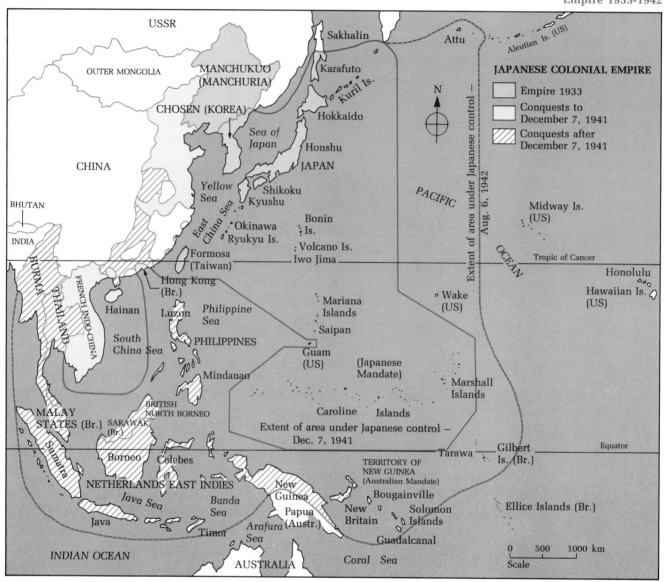

legacy of British influence remains widespread through culture, language, legal systems, and economic ties, even though most of the colonies are now independent.

Generally speaking, people's attitudes toward colonization have changed. It is believed to be wrong for one group of people to dominate another. Nevertheless, there still remain instances where powerful nations control less powerful ones through measures other than colonization.

Geopolitics also encompasses:

· the future division of land, such as in Antarctica, where many boundaries remain unresolved;

· the division of oceanic control; and

· the study of possible allocation of zones of control in space.

Questions

6. From your own knowledge of current events, list and briefly describe three examples of a powerful nation attempting to influence a less powerful one. Identify the countries concerned, state how the pressure is being applied, and try to explain why this is occurring.

7. (a) In what ways could a powerful nation benefit from territorial expansion or influence?

(b) In what ways could a weaker nation benefit from being invaded or influenced by another country?

(c) In what ways could a weaker nation suffer from the intervention of a foreign power?

Give examples, current or past, for each of the above questions, where you can.

8. In your opinion, under what circumstances, if any, would one nation be justified in invading another? Give reasons for your answer, using examples where appropriate.

9. (a) Study a map of Antarctica, showing its coastline and boundaries as they exist today.

(b) Why have disputes over territorial control in Antarctica remained insignificant? Identify another part of the world where similar arguments might apply.

(c) What changes are taking place that could make fixing these boundaries much more important?

10. Look at Figure 3.4, which shows world maritime claims, and read the note of explanation about "Exclusive Economic Zones" and the "World Lake Concept." Until recent years, most of the world's oceans have served as frontiers and routeways which we call the "high seas".

(a) Why did this attitude toward the seas exist until recently?

(b) Explain why this attitude is changing.

(c) Explain the UN decision to acknowledge the existence of Exclusive Economic Zones.

(d) What problems can you foresee developing from new situations?

(e) What measures can be taken to alleviate the problems you have outlined in part (d)?

11. Can you foresee a need to make some formal division of outer space? List arguments for and against the proposal.

12. Do you believe that the total area of oceans outside the EEZ should be divided between the nations? Or should they be left as the "high seas"? Justify your answer.

Figure 3.4
World Maritime
Claims

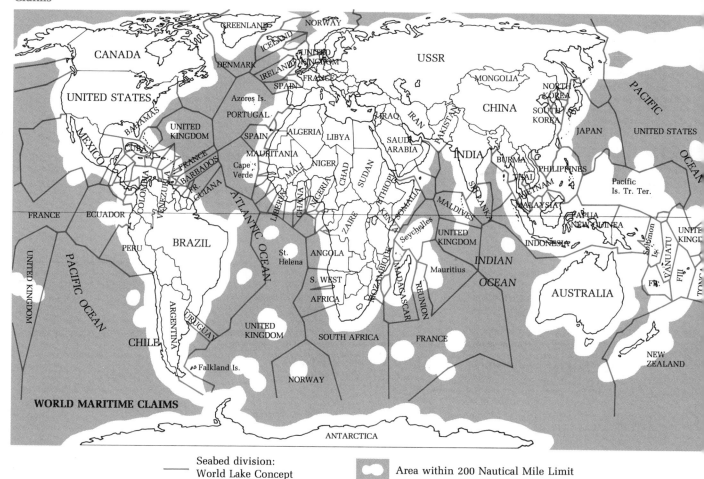

Seabed division:
World Lake Concept

Area within 200 Nautical Mile Limit

The United Nations has sanctioned the right of each maritime nation to claim an area of ocean, 370 km wide, out from its shores. Within that area, each nation has exclusive rights to control navigation, resource exploitation, and other factors of importance to the state. This zone is called the **Exclusive Economic Zone (EEZ)**.

The probable next step in dividing the oceans would be to divide them along median lines between two states. If this were adopted, it is obvious that the possession of islands in remote areas would be very beneficial to a few nations.

The Political Spectrum

Each country is governed according to a basic philosophy. This philosophy may vary, depending on who actually holds the reins of power, but such variation within a country is not normally as extreme as the differences between individual countries. Words such as *left, right, liberal, conservative, communist,* and *fascist* are used to describe political philosophies. Table 3.1 should help you to understand the meaning of the terms that are commonly used.

As in the case of the spectrum of light, where there is a gradual change from one part to the next, the political spectrum also forms a continuum.

Figure 3.5
The Political
Spectrum Viewed
as a Circle

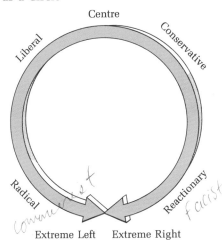

Some people consider that the two extremes of the spectrum are in fact very similar, and they illustrate this idea by arranging the political philosophies around an almost continuous circle, as shown in Figure 3.5.

Questions

13. In a recent provincial election, there were several "fringe" parties running.

(a) Draw a horizontal line across your page. On it write LEFT, CENTRE, and RIGHT, and show the position of the three major parties, using the bottom of Table 3.1 as a guide.

(b) Read each of the following policy statements from the fringe parties, and mark where you think they lie on the political spectrum. Refer to Table 3.1.

Libertarian Party: is for free enterprise, free trade, and freedom from overregulation by government. Wants to reduce taxes and clean up polluted beaches so that families will benefit.

Family Coalition Party: is against abortions and for traditional family life.

Green Party: is for preventing pollution (rather than just cleaning up the damage).

14. (a) Design a one-page policy statement for a political party that you would like to see in power.

(b) Explain how your ideas would be of benefit to people. Give at least five examples of their impact on, say, taxation and social benefits.

15. Communist countries such as the USSR and China are beginning to permit some measure of private enterprise and ownership. Why might they have considered that such a move would now be beneficial?

16. Many people believe that Canada leans toward the "left" because it has many social services. In what way do we benefit and/or suffer from the provision of these services?

17. Why do you think that many newly emerging nations, with initial ideals of democracy or communist philosophies, often end up as military dictatorships?

Table 3.1
The Political
Spectrum

Left		Centre			Right
Radical		**Liberal**	**Conservative**		**Reactionary**
Communist	**Social Democracy**	**Reform Liberalism**	**Classical Liberalism**	**Conservatism**	**Fascism**
Equality of condition	**Equality of opportunity**		**Equality of right**	**Aristocracy**	**Hierarchy**
Want quick and drastic change using illegal methods if necessary. Look ahead to 'Utopia'. Individual welfare is a priority, at the expense of individual free-doms. Everyone has an equal share and benefit. No private ownership (Karl Marx, Mao Tse Tung — Com-munism would come in by a dic-tatorship of the proletariat, then the government would disappear, and everyone would be free.) USSR, China have only accom-plished the former, so are more TOTALITARIAN, where the govern-ment strives for total control or domination over its citizens.	Want substantial change but by legal methods Support the ideal of freedom of the individual at the expense of too much state control Some private ownership		Change should be moderate and slow, using existing insti-tutions where possible Private ownership encouraged Government chosen by democratic elections		Strong opposition to change. Strength comes from the past. Use illegal methods to maintain status quo, if necessary. Some private ownership Authority centered in a leader (Mus-solini, Hitler, Franco). Dictator-ship where there is one-person rule

These descriptions are generalizations and variations exist which have not been included

Alliances and Blocs

There are about 160 nations in the world. Each has a combination of social and political characteristics which set it aside from all others. Despite these differences, alliances of many kinds have been forged between groups of nations for their mutual benefit. Such agreements are examples of

Figure 3.6
Members of the
United Nations

supranationalism, efforts at co-operation which, in effect, reduce or remove normal national barriers. They may be based on political beliefs, military concerns, or economic considerations, or a combination of these factors. There is one organization, the United Nations, that includes almost all countries of the world. For that reason, it is our greatest hope for the future, despite its continuing problems.

The United Nations

The initial concept of the United Nations came with the League of Nations in 1919. Established following World War I to prevent further aggression, it was hoped that all world nations would join. However, only half of the nations became members, and amongst the absentees was the United States. The League collapsed during World War II, but was replaced by the

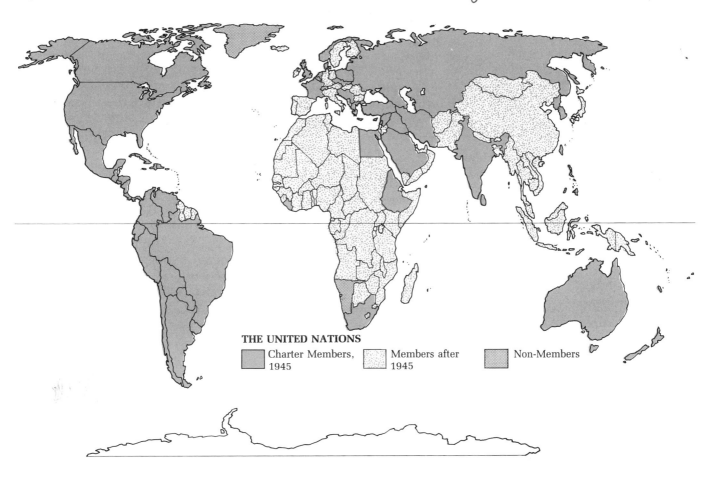

THE UNITED NATIONS

Charter Members, 1945   Members after 1945   Non-Members

United Nations in 1945. The United Nations has continued its very important function of providing a forum in which nations can address the General Assembly on matters of concern to them. Some other organizations which have developed as subsidiaries of the United Nations include the Food and Agricultural Organization (FAO), United Nations Educational, Social, and Cultural Organization (UNESCO), and the World Health Organization (WHO).

Another supranational organization, formed between the war years, was the Permanent Court of International Justice, now called the International Court of Justice. This court deals with international disputes such as fishing rights. For example, it ruled on a dispute between Canada and the USA over claims to exclusive fishing rights on a part of Georges Bank off the coast of Maine and New Brunswick.

Question

18. Explain what is at stake in the continued existence of organizations such as the UN and the International Court of Justice.

Major Military Alliances

The USSR and the USA are the two dominant nations in the world; for this reason, we refer to them as the **superpowers**. They have never fought a war against each other, but they have experienced a continuous conflict of ideologies since World War II. Each superpower attempts, and usually succeeds, to influence other countries' ideologies through economic or military pressure. In this way, it improves its own security. Differences in communist and capitalist ideology and a poor knowledge of life in the other's country, coupled with determined efforts by some individuals and organizations to promote distrust, have led to suspicion and fear of each other.

Following World War II, the USSR continued to occupy territory that it had held at the end of the war. The strength and expansion of this western boundary of the USSR worried the USA, together with many of the democratic nations of western Europe. If Mackinder's "Heartland" concept is correct, (see page 83), the Soviet Union was beginning the move to control the "World Island," which includes Eurasia and Africa. The next step would be world domination.

Whether or not this was the Soviet intention, the concern aroused in the minds of non-communist nations led to the formation of non-communist alliances called the **North Atlantic Treaty Organization (NATO**, formed in 1949 and still in operation), the **South East Asian Treaty Organization (SEATO**, 1954-1977), and the **Central Treaty Organization (CENTO**, 1959-1979). The countries involved in these treaty areas are shown in Figure 3.7.

The Soviets experienced horrific devastation as a result of two world wars and, before that, the Napoleonic War. This led them to conclude that their European border was their most vulnerable flank. To strengthen this border, they exerted economic and political control over the countries of eastern Europe, using military strength when necessary, to establish cooperation. Their defensive alliance, created in 1955, is called the **Warsaw Pact**. Member countries are also linked to the Soviet Union via the **Council for Mutual Economic Assistance (COMECON)**.

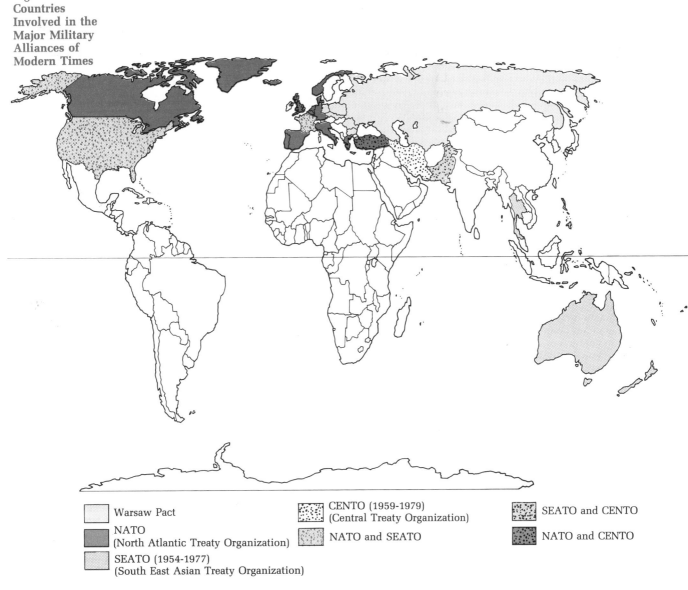

Figure 3.7
Countries
Involved in the
Major Military
Alliances of
Modern Times

Warsaw Pact

NATO
(North Atlantic Treaty Organization)

SEATO (1954-1977)
(South East Asian Treaty Organization)

CENTO (1959-1979)
(Central Treaty Organization)

NATO and SEATO

SEATO and CENTO

NATO and CENTO

Questions:

19. The military alliances of the non-communist world, illustrated in Figure 3.7, were designed as part of a "Containment Policy."

   (a) What was and is being contained?

   (b) How is this being achieved?

   (c) Do you consider that there was or is still a need for this containment?

20. Look at the two world hemisphere maps.

(a) Why does the USSR feel itself to be in a more vulnerable position, strategically, than the United States?

(b) Why did the US government react so swiftly and strongly when it found that the USSR was in the process of establishing missile bases in Cuba in 1962? (Details are given on pages 114-115).

(c) Compare the strategic locations of Cuba with respect to the USA, and Turkey with respect to the USSR.

(d) Name some places in Central America, and amongst the islands of the Caribbean, where the US government has a political interest. Why does this interest continue?

(e) In what countries of Europe or Asia might the Soviet Union have a political interest similar to that of the United States in Central America? Why does the Soviet Union have this concern, and how does it continue to show it?

Hemisphere centred on USSR

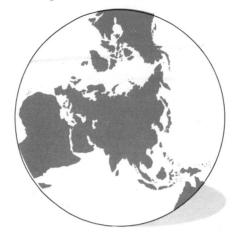

Hemisphere centred on USA

Table 3.2
A Strategic Comparison of Geographic Factors in the USA and USSR

USA	USSR
Fourth largest area in world (9 363 000 km²)	Largest area in the world (22 402 000 km²)
Isolated by oceans on the east and west, buffered by the Arctic Ocean	Oceans to the north and east, extensive land border
Major ports ice-free all year	Ports of north and east frozen in winter, access to Black Sea ports hindered by NATO countries
Agriculture usually produces surplus	Often has to import large quantities of grain
Limited oil and natural gas resources, large deposits of other energy and metallic resources	Large resource deposits of oil, natural gas, and other energy and metallic resources
Centres of population close to oceans	Centres of population far from oceans
Buffer zones of Canada to the north and Mexico to the south	Buffer zone of Warsaw Pact countries to the west
Fairly dense transportation network	Vast areas with poor transportation network

East German guard tower on the border between East an West Germany

21. From a Canadian perspective, do you consider that the United States should interfere in the affairs of its neighbouring countries? Justify your opinion in the light of potential arguments from people with a viewpoint opposed to your own.

22. (a) Take each of the points made in Table 3.2 in turn and explain its strategic significance.

(b) List and explain five other factors that you would research in order to determine which of the two countries has a strategic geographical advantage over the other.

23. Using a globe and an atlas, determine if there is any other country or area that could grow to achieve the importance of the USA or the USSR. Explain your answer with reference to three different countries or areas which you considered.

Canada's Role in Military Alliances

The Canadian government believes that we can best protect our way of life through collective security. That is, we work with other nations having similar ideologies.

The Canadian security policy has three main components:

· defence and collective security;

· arms control and disarmament; and

· the peaceful resolution of disputes.

Canadian Defence Policy

Canada's defensive policy is aimed at deterring potential aggressors against Canada and Canadian interests. We could not hope to protect Canada adequately by ourselves, so we have joined with the USA in North American Aerospace Defence (NORAD), and also help the United States in the surveillance of Soviet submarine forces. Together with our commitments to NATO, we are thus able to contribute to the survivability of the United States' strategic nuclear forces. These forces form a deterrent against Soviet attack.

Canada has strong cultural, historic, and economic ties with western Europe, committing itself in two world wars begun in Europe and fought around the globe. Canadian personnel form part of the NATO forces in Europe and help to maintain its uneasy peace.

We allow our allies to use Canadian territories and facilities in peacetime for operational training with unarmed aircraft. We have agreed that, during an international emergency, and given the necessary government approval, we would allow aircraft carrying nuclear weapons to fly over Canada. Tanker aircraft and interceptor planes would be permitted to use Canadian airfields.

Unarmed cruise missiles are tested over Canadian territory, and allied warships use our port facilities. Canadians are involved in combined exercises within Canadian territory.

Our geographical position, sandwiched between the Arctic Ocean and the USA, makes our involvement in any hostilities between the superpowers inevitable. The government contends, therefore, that it is better to work with the USA in creating a strong defence, than to dismantle our forces and depend on our allies in time of need. An adequate military force may also prove valuable if we find it necessary to affirm our sovereignty over remote areas of the Arctic.

Canada's success in peacekeeping has been widely recognized by other members of the United Nations. In the past, Canadian military personnel have been assigned to keep the peace in Egypt, Lebanon, the Congo, New Guinea, Yemen, the Dominican Republic, India, Pakistan, Cambodia, Laos, Vietnam, Nigeria. We currently help to keep the peace in India, Pakistan, Egypt, Israel, Jordan, Lebanon, Syria, Korea, Cyprus, and Afghanistan.

Another way in which Canada promotes peace is to formulate arms control proposals with its allies. We have also provided delegations in arms control talks at the United Nations, the Conference on Security and Cooperation in Europe, the Mutual and Balanced Force Reduction talks, and the Stockholm talks.

According to Canada's official defence policy, published in 1987, if we are to continue to play this important role in international affairs, we will need to upgrade our equipment, especially in air defence surveillance. Satellites may be designed and deployed for this purpose. The country remains committed to our involvement in NATO, NORAD, and the United Nations.

Figure 3.8
Defence
Expenditure in
NATO
(A) per capita
(B) as a % of GDP

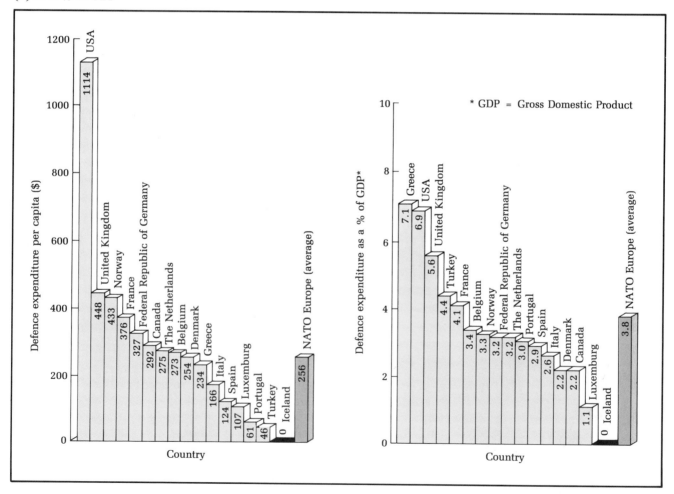

94   Part II   Geopolitical Issues

Questions

24. The phrase, ''The best offence is a good defence,'' is often used in connection with a discussion of war and prevention of war.
    (a) What does the phrase mean?
    (b) Do you agree? Justify your answer.

25. The greatest challenge that we have had to our Arctic sovereignty has come from the USA, which claims that the Northwest Passage is an international waterway. Comment on the significance of this development.

26. Give arguments for and against Canada's continuing involvement in international military organizations. Which side of the argument do you favour?

Major Economic Alliances

The arguments in favour of economic alliances are simple, on the face of it. By combining production and economic organization from transportation and marketing, economies of scale enable costs to be cut. Many people are reluctant to enter into such agreements, however, because this means giving up a degree of sovereignty.

There are four kinds of economic integration. At the lowest level there is **free trade**. Two or more countries agree to remove tariffs and other charges on all or certain goods traded between them. Each country still maintains the right to charge tariffs on goods from countries not involved in the agreement.

In a **customs union**, there is free trade but, in addition, all countries apply the same tariffs to goods from outside, and then pool and allocate the receipts. A **common market** is a customs union with the additional feature of capital and labour being free to move across international boundaries within the union without any penalty.

The greatest degree of integration comes in the **economic union** in which, in addition to the features mentioned above, there are common economic and monetary policies, common currency, banking and insurance systems, uniform taxes, and corporation laws. To achieve economic union would be virtually impossible without political union.

American ice breaker, The Polar Sea, sailing through the Northwest Passage in 1985

The European Economic Community

The **European Economic Community (EEC)** is approximately equivalent to the total economic strength of the United States. The initial move toward integration was made by Belgium and Luxemburg in 1922, with the Netherlands joining in 1944.

The European economy was devastated by World War II, so the United States funded a recovery program, the **Marshall Plan**, named after US Secretary of State George Marshall, that gave Europe about $12 billion between 1948 and 1952. Eighteen European countries had to work together to administer the use of these funds. This effort was known as the **Organization for European Economic Co-operation (OEEC)**. The success of this organization led eventually to the formation of the EEC, or **European Economic Community**, commonly called the Common Market.

The European Economic Community has progressed in some respects into the economic and political union envisaged by the French economist, Jean Monnet (1888-1979). There are over 100 countries with accredited diplomatic representatives to the EEC, and it functions as a unit in trade negotiations. The Treaty of Rome in 1957 marked the beginning of the European Common Market as we know it.

There are over 50 supranational organizations in the world aimed at improving some aspect of the economy or defence of the countries involved. None approaches the importance of the European Economic Community, although Latin America has made considerable progress towards economic co-operation. These Latin American organizations are summarized in Figure 3.10.

The United Nations Economic Commission for Latin America, with its headquarters in Santiago, is also pressing for the establishment of an area-wide common market. The **Latin America Economic System (SELA)** advocates co-operation involving the mutually beneficial organization of resource extraction, industrial organization, and trade. The countries also work together in the development of transportation, communications, tourism, and other economic and social matters.

Figure 3.9
Members of the European Economic Community

Figure 3.10
Organizations for
Economic
Integration in
Latin America

Andean Group
(also members of LAFTA)

Caricom
(Caribbean Community)

CACM
(Central American Common Market)

LAFTA
(Latin American Free Trade Association)

* Former member of the Andean Group

Questions

27. How differently would a co-operative economic effort be organized in a lesser developed nation as compared to a more developed nation?

28. Do you consider that the presence of United Nations organizations, such as the economic commissions described above, is justified and helpful for the economic development among lesser developed nations? Explain your conclusion.

29. Would the United Nations economic commissions be beneficial in developed nations? Explain your answer.

30. What advantages and disadvantages would there be in an expanded economic union of some kind between Canada and the United States?

Efforts have also been made in Africa to achieve economic co-operation. These are summarized in Figure 3.11

The United Nations has established ECA the **Economic Commission for Africa (ECA)**, with goals similar to those of its equivalent in Latin America. The most significant African organization is the **Economic Community of West African States (ECOWAS)**. It was founded in 1975 by 15 countries, and was joined two years later by Cape Verde.

**Figure 3.11
Organizations for
Economic
Integration in
Africa**

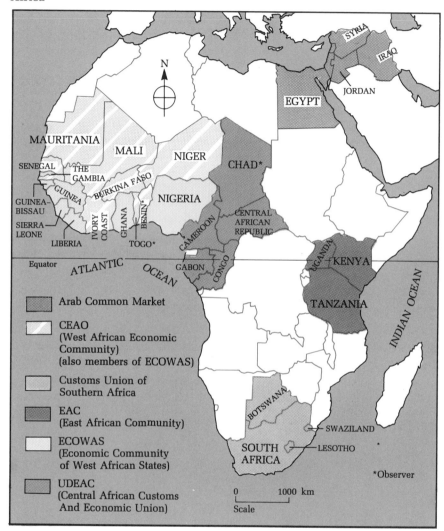

Arab Common Market

CEAO
(West African Economic
Community)
(also members of ECOWAS)

**Customs Union of
Southern Africa**

EAC
(East African Community)

ECOWAS
(Economic Community
of West African States)

UDEAC
(Central African Customs
And Economic Union)

*Observer

0   1000 km

Scale

Some attempts at economic co-operation have been made among the Arab, Asiatic, and Pacific countries, but there has been only limited progress. There remains much hostility between many nations; so far, the best results have been achieved with bilateral agreements.

Simulation

The leaders of three lesser developed nations have approached your organization for advice concerning possible future economic co-operation, possible mutual integration, and possible integration with other neighbouring states. The maps to the right summarize the characteristics of these states and their neighbours.

Using the information from the maps on page 99, produce a report which outlines your suggestions for development, and explain the advantages of your scheme. Your should divide your report into stages, with goals for each five or ten years.

Following your report, list three criticisms that might be made of your suggestions, and present arguments to support your viewpoint.

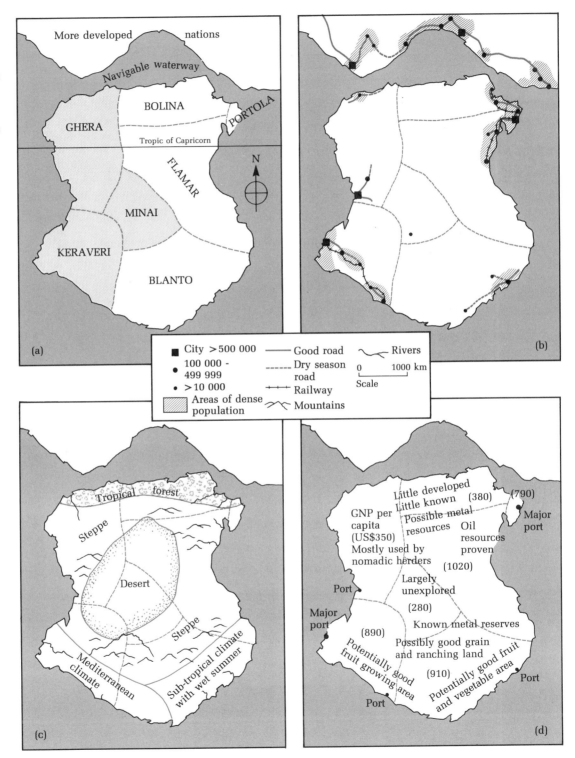

(a) Political
    Boundaries
(b) Population
    and
    Transportation
    Patterns
(c) Pertinent
    Physical
    Characteristics
(d) Economic
    Information

(a)

More developed   nations

Navigable waterway

BOLINA

PORTOLA

GHERA

Tropic of Capricorn

FLAMAR

N

MINAI

KERAVERI

BLANTO

(b)

City > 500 000
100 000 -
499 999
> 10 000
Areas of dense
population

Good road
Dry season
road
Railway
Mountains

Rivers

0   1000 km
Scale

(c)

Tropical   forest

Steppe

Desert

Steppe

Mediterranean
climate

Sub-tropical climate
with wet summer

(d)

Little developed
Little known   (380)   (790)

GNP per   Possible metal
capita   resources   Oil
(US$350)   resources
                               proven
Mostly used by
nomadic herders   (1020)

Largely
unexplored
(280)

Known metal reserves
Possibly good grain
and ranching land

Potentially good
fruit growing area

Potentially good fruit
and vegetable area

Major
port

Port

Major
port

(890)

(910)

Port

Port

The Evolution of Political Boundaries

Maps of the world made throughout human history reveal a constantly evolving pattern of political units. In the distant past, areas of dense population were separated from each other by natural barriers of mountains, seas, deserts, or distance. However, as population increased and the need and desire for more territory grew, the **frontiers** (zones of exploration and expansion) of adjacent countries overlapped. Boundaries had to be established between the political units. Even so, the boundary might turn out to be very disruptive to the development of the frontier area and to the lives of the inhabitants. There are no true political frontier areas remaining on land today, but **maritime states**, those which border the oceans, are expanding into the frontier of the adjacent oceans.

Within a country, there may be an area unknown and almost "mysterious" to the majority of citizens. Few people live there, and very few have visited it. It forms a frontier region within the boundaries of the country. Canada and the Soviet Union are both bounded by such areas. Their sparsely populated and inhospitable northern regions could supply valuable resources. Settlement is encouraged or sometimes even forced in these areas, for the sake of resource exploitation, or as a defensive measure to discourage encroachment or invasion by rival or even friendly nations.

A **boundary line** on a map represents the geographical limit of state sovereignty. In reality, the boundary is a vertical plane dividing the air, land, and water.

Figure 3.12
The Frontier and
the Boundary

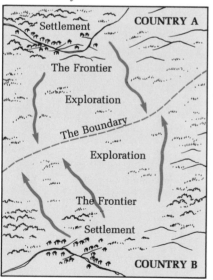

Figure 3.13
Cross Section of a
Boundary

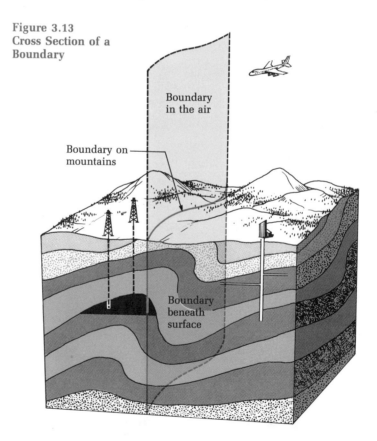

Ideally, the establishment of a boundary involves four stages:

· definition — describing the boundary:

· delimitation — marking it on a map;

· demarcation — marking it in reality; and

· administration — checking the boundary and applying laws.

Some nations of Africa have not finished the second stage of boundary making, and are finding the process difficult because the boundary was not defined in sufficient detail. Many nations have not completed demarcation, and often the boundary is just marked with poles or stones. Demarcation can be a very expensive process, so walls or fences are used only in very sensitive areas.

The characteristics that make the most effective boundary are difficult to identify. Some would advocate using the physical characteristics of the land, such as mountain divides and rivers. Others would prefer to divide on the basis of culture, language, or religion. All methods of division are, like other classifications, imperfect. A division based on the mountain crestline may hinder making transportation links. A division based on language or religion may generate hostility between the groups it separates.

Question

31. Using atlas maps, study the boundary between Canada and the United States.

(a) Looking at the boundary from west to east, list the criteria that were used to define this boundary.

(b) What advantages and disadvantages can you see in the criteria used, in light of subsequent economic developments?

(c) Consider any part of the Canada-US border where you think that a better decision could have been made. Map what would have made a better border. Explain why you made this choice, and anticipate the problems it would create for the governments of Canada and the USA.

Boundary Changes in the Last Few Decades

If you were to look at an old atlas, you would notice that there have been many changes in the boundaries, names, and status of various nations since it was published. In fact, since the conclusion of World War II, approximately 90 states have gained independence from the colonial powers. These changes were set in motion by the two world wars. Following World War I, Germany and Turkey were stripped of their empires. The countries thus liberated were put under the trusteeship of other nations under a system of mandates administered by the League of Nations. The intention was that the responsible nation would slowly lead its controlled territories to self-government.

During the inter-war period, nationalism grew in a quiet way. Following the war, violence erupted in many colonies such as Kenya, Malaysia, and Indo-China, in an attempt to speed independence. Mahatma Gandhi (1869-1948), is much admired for his efforts to reduce violence while at the same time working toward the independence of India. He developed the principle of ''non-violent civil disobedience'' and ''passive resistance,'' whereby his followers were instructed never to hurt others, and to subject themselves willingly to the law. This resulted in many of his followers being hurt, some being killed, and thousands being jailed. The method was very effective in that it caused great annoyance to the ruling authorities and speeded independence.

The Charter of the United Nations encourages colonial powers to lead their colonies toward self-government. In all but two trusteeship cases, the West Bank (claimed by both Israel and the Palestinians) and Namibia, these aims have been achieved.

Mahatma Ghandi on his seventy-eighth birthday

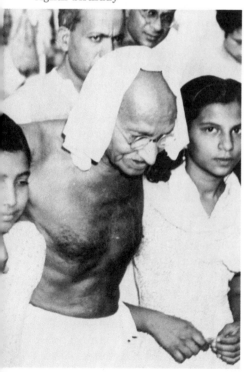

The Changing World Map

The changes we observe in the map of the world since World War II are primarily due to the independence achieved by former colonies. They are also due to the expansion of some nations to incorporate others into their own territory, or at least to get them under their control. Notable colonial powers were Great Britain, France, Spain, Portugal, Belgium, Denmark, Germany, Italy, and the Netherlands. Figure 3.14 shows the distribution of these empires. Japan, Australia, and New Zealand have also had a small measure of empire.

Although never referred to as "empire," the United States' interests in many other nations have changed the map of the world. These nations include Hawaii, Cuba, the Philippines, Puerto Rico, Guam, Wake Island, the Samoan Islands, Panama Canal Zone, Danish Virgin Islands, Ryukyu, the Volcono and Bonin Islands of Japan, and the Marshall, Caroline, and Mariana Islands. Russia and China have also expanded into surrounding territory, although this is not usually referred to as "empire," either. One nation can be influenced by another through means other than colonialism. Military threat is one very powerful method used by the

USSR to ensure the compliance of eastern European countries, and by the USA in its frequent military involvement in Central America. Another alternative is for one country to make another country dependent on it for economic support. Thus, the United States wields power in Latin America, Great Britain has considerable influence on the world's banking systems, and the nations of the Middle East have a major control over other countries through manipulation of energy supplies. Influence can also be exerted through culture and the spread of ideas, but this usually is followed by more concrete moves.

Question

32. (a) Using a blank world map, draw in the national divisions of the world as you believe they will be in about 50 years' time.

(b) Justify your predictions in part (a).

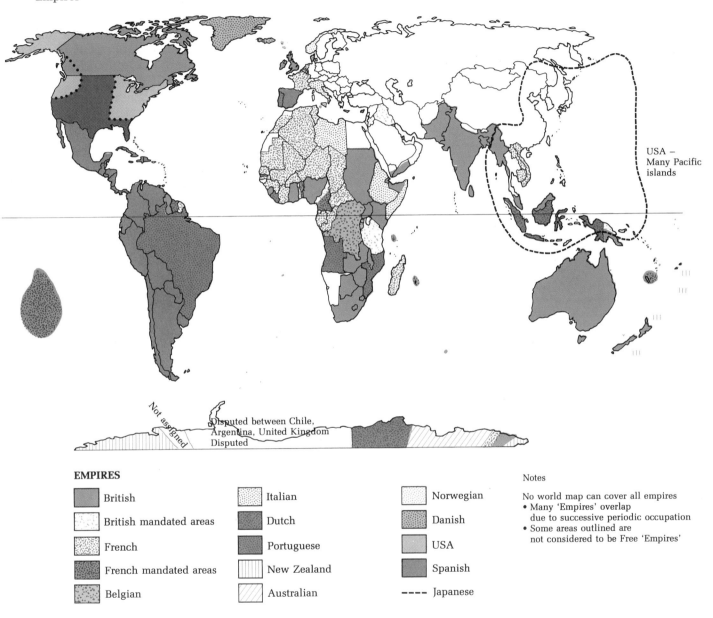

Figure 3.14
A Map of Modern Empires

USA –
Many Pacific
islands

Not assigned

Disputed between Chile,
Argentina, United Kingdom
Disputed

EMPIRES

British	Italian	Norwegian
British mandated areas	Dutch	Danish
French	Portuguese	USA
French mandated areas	New Zealand	Spanish
Belgian	Australian	---- Japanese

Notes

No world map can cover all empires
• Many 'Empires' overlap
  due to successive periodic occupation
• Some areas outlined are
  not considered to be Free 'Empires'

National Boundaries Within Africa

Africa is home to some of the most ancient humanoid remains, and yet it is also an area of many of the world's youngest nations. Most of the continent remains uneasy, with many incidents of guerilla warfare, military action, and considerable political upheaval. Until the European takeover of the continent in the nineteenth century, however, it had consisted of a succession of city states. A **city state** was an area of political influence that developed around a city important for its strategic location or trade.

Many of these states were stable, and had important centres of learning. When the slave trade that began along the west coast of Africa in the sixteenth century reached its height, it changed a pattern of development which had been in existence for about 2000 years. Although slavery was finally outlawed in the USA in 1865, it had already destroyed the fabric of society in many African coastal areas by that time. Most of the young men and many women were gone, children were orphaned, and communities were disrupted.

The great colonial powers had earlier nibbled at the edges of Africa, but in the 1870s there was a tremendous rush to claim the interior. Within ten years, 26 million

square kilometres, and 100 million people had been taken over! The rival European powers involved decided that, rather than resorting to military force, they would meet to divide Africa among them.

Fourteen nations attended this meeting (no African leaders were invited), and between November 1884 and February 1885, Africa was

divided up with no regard for geography, history, religion, culture, or any other reasonable grounds for division. Africa had been changed from hundreds of independent states into 40 colonies. Many of the current African problems can be traced to that division. (Following its defeat in World War I, Germany's colonies were confiscated and control of them was given to

**Figure 3.15
Early African
States**

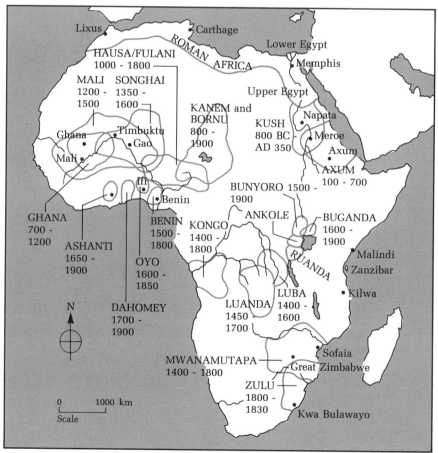

South Africa and the colonial powers of Europe.)

In the late 1940s and 1950s, when African nations were preparing for independence as a result of a United Nations recommendaton, there was an idealistic move to create a United States of Africa. Hopes for this were dashed because the potential leaders of each African nation were not willing to relinquish the power that they would be assuming from the departing colonial governments. Subsequently, each nation attempted to develop its own economy and infrastructure based on the legacy from the colonial empire. As these forms of organization were geared to servicing the needs of the former colonial power, they were not suitable for a newly independent nation. Many nations, starting with dreams of a prosperous and democratic future, have degenerated into poor, insecure dictatorships with enormous human and environmental problems.

Figure 3.16 Political Boundaries in Africa Established by European Powers in 1884-1885

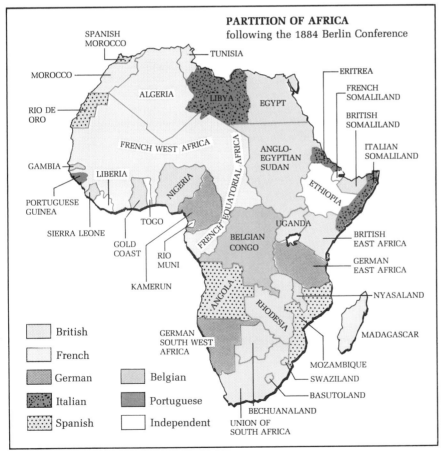

PARTITION OF AFRICA
following the 1884 Berlin Conference

SPANISH MOROCCO
TUNISIA
MOROCCO
ERITREA
ALGERIA
LIBYA
EGYPT
FRENCH SOMALILAND
RIO DE ORO
BRITISH SOMALILAND
FRENCH WEST AFRICA
ANGLO-EGYPTIAN SUDAN
ITALIAN SOMALILAND
GAMBIA
LIBERIA
NIGERIA
FRENCH EQUATORIAL AFRICA
ETHIOPIA
PORTUGUESE GUINEA
UGANDA
SIERRA LEONE
TOGO
BELGIAN CONGO
BRITISH EAST AFRICA
GOLD COAST
RIO MUNI
GERMAN EAST AFRICA
KAMERUN
ANGOLA
NYASALAND
RHODESIA
MADAGASCAR
GERMAN SOUTH WEST AFRICA
MOZAMBIQUE
SWAZILAND
BASUTOLAND
BECHUANALAND
UNION OF SOUTH AFRICA

British
French
German   Belgian
Italian   Portuguese
Spanish   Independent

Questions

33. What approach to administration and development would have been taken by a colonial power to a possession along the west coast of Africa and a possession farther inland? Where would the governing cities and the transportation links have been established? What other priorities would the colonial authorities have had? Would education and social services for the indigenous people have been a priority? Would they have trained sufficient numbers of local inhabitants to run and maintain the government and the infrastructure? Explain your answers fully, giving reasons for your opinions.

34. In what ways would the legacy of the colonial past have been a hindrance for the newly independent African nations described by you in question 33 above?

The Interest of The Superpowers in Africa Today

Besides the desire to benefit from trading relationships with the new African nations, the superpowers frequently try to influence political leanings, and the continent has become split between pro-western and pro-communist camps. Superpower interest results from:

· the strategic importance of Africa with respect to the world's oil supply;

· its large reserves of diamonds (70 percent of the world total), cobalt (90 percent), chromium (90 percent), gold (50 percent), platinum (40 percent), oil (8 percent), and uranium (one-third of the free world supply); and

· its large supply of cocoa (65 percent of the world total).

Sudan

Sudan is the largest country in Africa, and occupies a pivotal location between the Arab world and sub-Saharan Africa. It also flanks the Nile River and borders the vital international shipping lane through the Red Sea.

In 1985, a transitional military/civilian government took power in Sudan. In April 1986, as promised, there were free multi-party elections, but the new government had inherited formidable problems. The basic domestic aims of the democratic government are to end the civil war in the South, solve the country's enormous economic problems, and establish a constitution that will lead to a stable government. On the international scene, the government is aiming for amicable relationships with its neighbours and non-alignment with either superpower.

The particular problems faced by Sudan include heavy indebtedness to foreign governments and funding agencies, and an inability to take full advantage of its agricultural and mineral resources. This is due partly to poor government policies in the past and problems of climate and soil.

Within the country there are many different language, ethnic, and religious groups. The Islamic Arab North dominates. This sparked a separatist civil war from 1952-72 and then a rebellion that began in 1983, in which the Sudanese People's Liberation Movement demanded fair treatment for all Sudanese people, regardless of their religion. The

fighting in the South cannot be won by either side because government opponents are dominant in the rural areas, but cannot control urban environments. Fighting creates a drain of about 30 percent of total government expenses.

In a previous regime, Sudan had allied itself strongly with Egypt and had received much aid from the United States, whereas neighbouring Libya and Ethiopia had close ties with the USSR. The Ethiopians are supplying military aid to the Sudanese People's Liberation Army in the form of logistical support, sophisticated arms

**Figure 3.17
Sudan and Its
Neighbours**

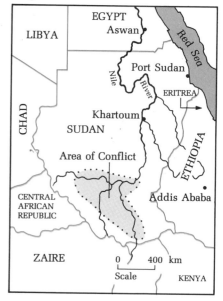

including SA-7 missiles, and training. They also provide a radio station and a political headquarters.

Sudan finds itself in a bleak economic situation. For a limited time after the government took office, western nations provided it with massive food aid, and Arab nations supplied free oil. Loans were rescheduled and spending cuts were imposed within the country. Despite these efforts, the International Monetary Fund declared Sudan in default in 1986. Inflation has increased to over 40 percent, and earnings from cotton exports have declined, because of crop damage and a poor world market. Sudan also has to import large quantities of oil. National expenditures are twice its revenues, and thus it remains dependent on loans and aid.

Because the Sudanese government has chosen a policy of non-alignment, the United States has reduced its aid considerably. Libya has attempted to influence the Sudanese government, but its efforts have been repelled. Relations between Egypt and Sudan have improved, however, and there has also been increased cooperation with Iran.

A sick refugee being carried by friends to a hospital in eastern Sudan

Questions

35. (a) Which of Sudan's problems can be directly related to the characteristics of the physical and cultural make-up of its territory? Use suitable maps to help illustrate your answers.

(b) In what ways is its international geopolitical situation an additional problem?

36. What do you believe should be three priorities for the Sudanese government? How would you attempt to achieve these objectives?

37. Suggest at least two ways that wealthy nations and international organizations could contribute to the improvement of the situation in countries such as Sudan. Show how these actions would help.

Armed Conflict and Its Causes

Since World War II, over 160 armed conflicts have broken out, mainly in lesser developed nations. There is a great deal of superpower involvement, supplying arms and advisors for local fighters. In some cases, the superpower may consider it necessary to send in its own troops, as happened in Vietnam and Afghanistan. The United States and the USSR each have about three-quarters of a million troops abroad. The US alone has 360 bases and outposts in many countries. Countries such as the UK, Cuba, France, Libya, Syria, South Africa, and Vietnam also have many troops stationed outside their borders.

There is growing unrest and resentment against the presence of United States bases in several countries, especially Spain, the Philippines, and Greece. In these countries, the United States supported the former right-wing dictatorships, which have now been replaced by democracies. Other countries no longer happy about US bases on their soil are Honduras, Portugal, and Turkey. Abandoning these bases would save the USA much money, but make it harder for Americans to respond to trouble. The USA also warns that a reduction in its conven-tional forces increases the comparative strength of Soviet conventional forces.

Question

38. (a) Refer to a political world map, and identify the six countries mentioned in the preceding paragraph.

(b) Carefully explain why each is of strategic importance to the United States.

(c) What do you foresee as the probable outcome of the removal of United States bases from those six countries?

When conflicts break out, civilians suffer death, injury, displacement, and deprivation. Often young adults are taken against their will to join in the fighting, while those who remain may be tortured or killed, accused of collaborating with the enemy. More than half of the 16 million people killed in these armed conflicts since 1945 were civilians!

There are many reasons why wars and other military conflicts break out. It has been claimed by political thinkers that the sole reason for the existence of a state is not to benefit its citizens, but to maintain its borders. If those borders are violated by another nation, war could result. The expansionist policies of Nazi Germany, which led to the violation of other nations' borders, were one of the root causes of World War II.

Some leaders appear to initiate hostilities for personal prestige or wealth, along with their more praiseworthy motives. One such leader from the past is Mao Zedong in China, with a current example being the Ayatollah Khomeini in Iran. Idi Amin of Uganda is an example of a person who desired personal aggrandizement and the accumulation of wealth, with little or no consideration for the rights of others.

Threats to national borders may cause a nation to take the offensive. In the six-day war of 1967, for example, Israel occupied additional territory when its security was threatened by surrounding countries.

Religious conflicts have frequently led to fighting or discord within a country. In Ireland, there was sufficient animosity between the people of the Protestant- and Roman Catholic-dominated areas to cause a division of that country in 1921. The situation is exacerbated by economic problems which result in a general lack of development and a high unemployment rate. Similarly, Pakistan was created in 1947 to give a home to Muslims away from the Hindu majority in India.

In 1971, Bangladesh was created after bitter fighting in East Pakistan. The reason for the formation of a new country here was different than in the case of Pakistan. The leaders of the rebellion justified it by stating that their part of the nation was not receiving as much economic

Figure 3.18
Military Strategy
and Fighting
Since World
War II

attention as the western part, where the capital city was located. They believed that, as an independent nation, their economy and consequently their living standards would improve. If a country such as Bangladesh does not possess, or have access to, sufficient resources, a war of desperation may result.

Any group of people who believe strongly enough that they are not being fairly treated by their own govern-

ment may resort to violence. If that violence is backed by outside support from other nations (who may have completely different motives), the oppressed may win their cause, but then find themselves indebted to the nation that assisted them. The strategic importance which could be achieved by support nations, such as the USA or USSR, is a major reason why both have become so involved in Third World conflicts.

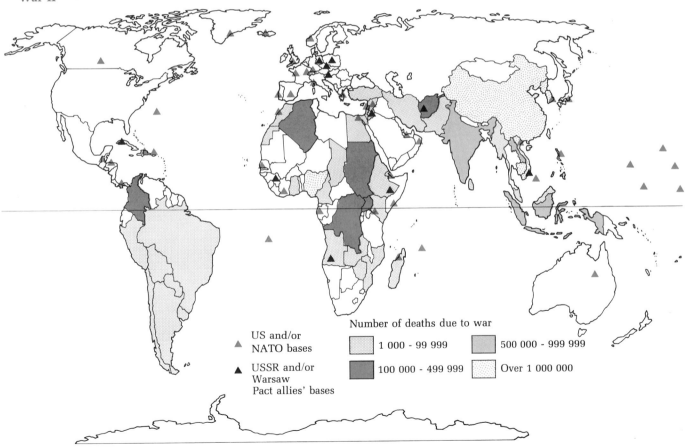

US and/or
NATO bases

USSR and/or
Warsaw
Pact allies' bases

Number of deaths due to war

1 000 - 99 999   500 000 - 999 999

100 000 - 499 999   Over 1 000 000

Israel and the Arabs

When the visiting archaeologist thought back over the events of that sunny winter's day in Rome, he remembered the way that the four men's eyes glittered. They walked unusually close together as they came from the automobile ramp into the terminal at Leonardo da Vinci Airport.

The men wore long coats, and their eyes were the only part of their faces visible through the scarves which were wrapped around their heads. It was strange that nobody else, not even the officials, seemed to notice them. Later, it was revealed that they were also high on drugs.

The American archaeology professor was on his way to Washington. He was standing at the Trans World Airways counter next to El Al Airlines of Israel. All of a sudden, the deafening sound of grenades and firing came from the four men, and he and his companions hit the floor.

He could see the airport security people returning fire, using long-barrelled revolvers that had been hidden beneath their coats. They were in plain clothes, and had hastily donned paper hats for identification. When the shooting ceased, there were shell casings all around, and the professor found that one of the terrorists lay only 3 m away from him.[1]

This event took place on the morning of December 25, 1985. There was a simultaneous attack at Vienna's Schwechat Airport. In all, 14 bystanders and four terrorists had been killed.

Subsequent investigations revealed that the terrorists were members of a breakaway faction of the PLO (Palestine Liberation Organization). There were also many international connections, implying co-operation by Libya, Iran, Syria, and Romania. Such incidents are staged to draw worldwide attention to the ongoing hostilities that exist between the Palestinians and the state of Israel.

The Dome of the Rock, Jerusalem. Israel contains a number of such sites valued by Moslems, Christians, and Jews.

The aftermath of the terrorist attack at Rome's Leonardo da Vinci airport.

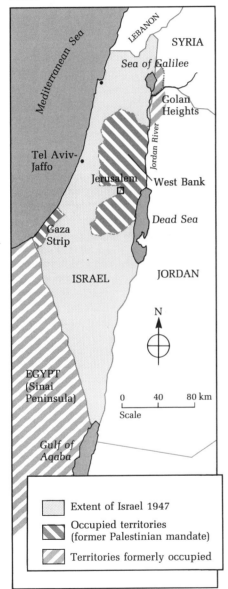

Figure 3.19
Israel, Its
Occupied
Territories, and
the Surrounding
Nations

Extent of Israel 1947

Occupied territories
(former Palestinian mandate)

Territories formerly occupied

Open warfare, guerilla activity, terrorism, and international political wrangling have plagued relations between Israel and other nations and groups since the country was officially created by the United Nations in 1947.

The history of the area, including present-day Israel, is long and fascinating. It was one of the **cradles of civilization**, with a measure of prosperity which permitted the existence of organized governments, armies, and religious practices. These existed for hundreds of years, before North America was discovered by Europeans.

There were periods of peace interspersed with inter-tribal wars and subjugation by such nations as Egypt, Greece, Rome, and Turkey. Its inhabitants included Arabs who followed the Islamic faith and Jewish people who were periodically subjected to persecution, attack, and exile.

Israel had been quite a powerful nation under Kings Saul, David, and Solomon, but wars and invasions led to its political extinction in 721 BC. The Jewish people generally existed as a persecuted group maintained by their religious belief in one God and their strict code of ethics. Another uniting factor was their desire to return to the land of Israel.

In 1896, Theodor Herzl (1860-1904), an Austro-Hungarian writer, founded the political Zionist movement which worked for the creation of an autonomous Jewish state in Palestine. He hoped to get help from the German emperor for this, but nothing came of his efforts. The British captured

Palestine from Turkey during World War I and, in 1917, Arthur Balfour, the British Secretary of State for Foreign Affairs, promised British support for a Jewish homeland. This was the **Balfour Declaration**, which included a proviso that "this should not affect the civil and religious rights of existing non-Jewish communities in Palestine." The United States President, Woodrow Wilson, endorsed the Balfour Declaration.

After much opposition, a British **mandate** (permission given by the League of Nations to administer a conquered nation) was implemented in Palestine, and it included the Balfour Declaration. The British presence, though, could not prevent fighting between the Arabs and Jews in the area. After 1933, when the Nazis came to power in Germany and began deporting and exterminating the Jews, many Jews fled to Palestine. Again, there was much Arab opposition, and the British decided that they were unable to carry out their responsibilities to both the Arabs and Jews. They recommended that, to keep the peace, a separate Jewish state should be established, involving the forced transfer of Arabs from the Jewish territory. This suggestion provoked armed conflict in which many Arabs, Jews, and British were killed.

During World War II, many more Jews arrived in Palestine. The Jewish people pressed for national status and a Jewish army. The Arabs threatened British and American interests and personnel in the Middle East if their own claims were disregarded. Britain withdrew from the situation and handed control over to the United Nations. The United Nations recommended dividing the country into two independent states — one Arab state and one Jewish state. The Arabs rejected this plan, and a vicious civil war broke out. In the midst of this controversy, an independent Israel was established on May 14, 1948. On that same day, Israel was attacked by five Arab nations. The Balfour Declaration did not stop Arab opposition, and fighting continued for months.

Israel was admitted to the United Nations in 1949. The nation, though, has continually had to fight for its existence. As a result of these wars, it has occupied territories outside the borders designated by the United Nations. In 1967, Israel captured most of the Sinai Peninsula in Egypt from which it has now withdrawn, and the Golan Heights in Syria which it has annexed. In the Yom Kippur war of 1973, Israel captured additonal territory after being attacked by both Syria and Egypt. Israel still occupies the West Bank and Gaza Strip (see Figure 3.19). However, it no longer controls most of this land.

At present, the Palestinians are a stateless people with no national territory under their control. About half of the original Palestinians and their descendants remain in the historic area of Palestine which includes Israel and the occupied territories, where their quality of life is not on a par with that of Jewish Israelis.

Thousands of Palestinians have chosen to leave the area of Israel and its occupied territories and move into neighbouring countries. Many of them live in poor conditions, such as in the refugee camps of Lebanon. As more and more refugees file into Lebanon, they find themselves less welcome in this country which is suffering from tremendous political turmoil.

In 1978, the United Nations recognized the PLO as the sole representative of the Palestinian people. For any kind of peace to be firmly established in this area of the Middle East, it would appear to be essential that other nations, in particular the USA and Israel, be willing to work with Palestinian leaders.

A Palestinian refugee camp

Young Israeli soldiers are considered by the government to be vital to national security.

Questions

39. For years, this part of the Middle East has been subjected to more conflict than most other parts of the world. Using an atlas, explain why geographic situation has had much to do with these conflicts. Contrast the Middle East with other areas as you make your observations.

40. In 1982, Israel invaded Lebanon to prevent further PLO attacks on its northern border. After extensive international and domestic criticism, Israel withdrew its troops in 1985. Discuss Israel's involvement in Lebanon. After establishing your viewpoint, find a newspaper or magazine article which takes a different view of the same situation. In a brief essay, compare the two points of view, giving possible reasons for the variation in outlook.

41. (a) Why do people commit acts of terrorism?

    (b) Why might some terrorist attacks by PLO factions be designed to discredit the PLO leaders?

42. Currently, the population of Israel is divided over the issue of surrendering ''land for peace.'' Taking into account Israel's demographic and geographic situation, develop a chart listing the pros and cons of this strategy.

43. (a) In what ways could the United Nations help to bring a lasting peace to this troubled area?

    (b) What would be the reaction of the Israelis and the Arabs to your suggestion in part (a)?

    (c) What important role can you see the superpowers playing in such conflicts?

The Underground Arms Trade

Some military and civilian personnel see the promotion of war as a means to easy wealth. This may or may not be carried out legally. Arms dealers in Brussels are ready to sell governments and terrorist groups anything from submachine guns to hand-held missile launchers, tanks, and helicopters. These pieces of equipment come from many sources. While they may actually pass through Brussels, more often just the paperwork is done there, possibly with the assistance of a bribed diplomat. In this way, governments and groups can buy or sell almost anything to anyone, without having to admit it officially. Brussels has thus become the centre for much illicit arms trading in the world.[2] The sale of narcotics often provides terrorist groups with the money to purchase weapons.

Questions

44. This section has outlined many reasons why hostilities may break out between nations and groups.

    (a) Choose any three reasons and account for the success or failure of the strategies adopted by a country or group initiating the offensive.

    (b) Choose any two of these reasons and explain how each could lead to a third world war. If you can think of another cause of war than those given, you are encouraged to use it as one of your examples.

45. (a) Do you believe that the underground trade in military equipment should be halted? Justify your answer.

    (b) What methods could be employed to reduce the illegal trade in arms?

The Threat of Nuclear War

The Cuban Missile Crisis

In October 1962, the world came very close to the outbreak of World War III. Photographs taken from a United States spy aircraft showed that Soviet missile bases were being set up in Cuba, within 150 km of the United States coastline. Air photo interpreters matched them to photographs taken from spy planes observing military bases in the USSR.

These bases posed a real threat to the USA, and President John F. Kennedy had troops moved into Florida on alert. Further photographic intelligence revealed that more Soviet military equipment was on ships approaching the Cuban shores, and President Kennedy stated publicly that a US **blockade** had been put in place to force them back.

Tension mounted. A United States U-2 spy plane was shot down over Cuba, an act that might have provoked the US to destroy the responsible missile base, as it had promised. Initial uncertainty over the cause of the crash of the spy plane led to a delay which gave Nikita Kruschev, the Soviet premier, time to announce the withdrawal of the missiles. Subsequent observation showed that the weapons were being dismantled and shipped out. Confrontation, possibly involving nuclear weapons, had been avoided, and anxious observers all over the world felt that they had been given a reprieve.

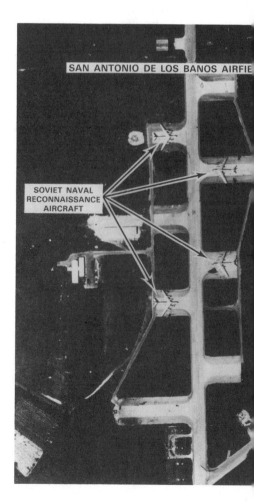

SAN ANTONIO DE LOS BANOS AIRFIE

SOVIET NAVAL RECONNAISSANCE AIRCRAFT

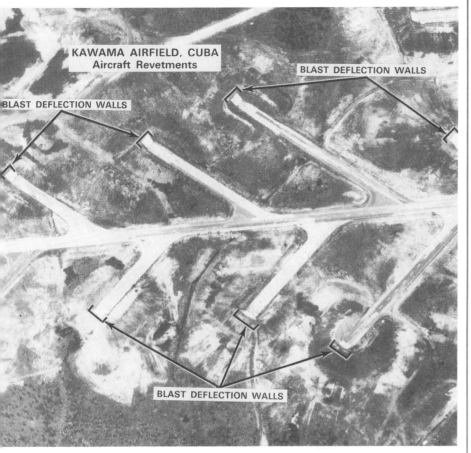

KAWAMA AIRFIELD, CUBA
Aircraft Revetments

BLAST DEFLECTION WALLS

BLAST DEFLECTION WALLS

BLAST DEFLECTION WALLS

SOVIET MIGs, WESTERN CUBA

MIG-23s

MIG-21s

Questions

46. Why is the word "reprieve" used at the end of the account, rather than an indication of the end to the problem?

47. In return for the recall of Soviet missiles from Cuba, the USA agreed to a Soviet demand that they dismantle their bases in Turkey. Using an atlas, comment on the reason for this demand.

48. "Spying, whether from satellites, planes, or in other ways is a most important instrument for peace."

   (a) Justify this statement, particularly with reference to bilateral arms agreements.

   (b) What might be the possible drawbacks to spying?

MICHAEL POWER HIGH SCHOOL
GEOGRAPHY DEPARTMENT

Table 3.3
The Vocabulary
of War

Here are some of the commonly used terms.

Antiballistic Missile (ABM) System   Interceptor missiles, radar, and other equipment used to intercept and destroy enemy ballistic missiles.

Assured Destruction   The ability to destroy enemy cities and military installations, even after having been attacked.

Ballistic Missile   A missile propelled by a rocket for the first part of its journey. It travels in an arc.

Conventional War   A war fought without the use of nuclear weapons.

Cruise Missile   A guided missile, the engine of which burns throughout flight. It is not usually detected by low-level radar, and is controlled by computer.

Deterrent   Weapons capable of retaliation that will make an enemy hesitate before attacking, or refrain from attacking altogether. (Deterrence is the policy which advocates this approach.)

Fall-out   Radioactive particles created by a nuclear explosion and returned to earth downwind, usually in precipitation.

First Strike (Pre-emptive Strike)   The first attack of a nuclear war.

Ground Zero   The point on the earth where a nuclear weapon is detonated (or the point directly below an airburst.)

Hard Target   A structure protected against the effects of nuclear attack, for example, a missile silo.

Hiroshima and Nagasaki   Two Japanese cities devastated in 1945 when atomic bombs were dropped on them.

ICBM   Intercontinental ballistic missile.

Kilotonne   The amount of energy that would be released by the simultaneous explosion of approximately 1000 t of TNT, a way of measuring the explosive power of a nuclear blast. The ''Little Boy'' bomb which destroyed Hiroshima was 13 kt, or 0.013 Mt.

Laser (Light Amplification by Stimulated Emission of Radiation)   A beam of light that could be used to destroy enemy installations from a satellite, for example.

Launch on Warning (Launch Under Attack)   A strategy of launching nuclear weapons when warning systems indicate that enemy missiles are going to attack.

Limited Nuclear War   A nuclear war in which a limited number of nuclear weapons (possibly 10 or 100) are used.

Megatonne   The amount of energy that would be released by the explosion of approximately 1 million tonnes of TNT, a way of measuring the explosive power of a nuclear blast. Eighty bombs like the one exploded at Hiroshima equals 1 Mt.

Multiple Independently Targetal Re-entry Vehicle (MIRV)   Multiple re-entry vehicles (many warheads) carried to enemy territory by a ballistic missile. Each of them has a mechanism to guide it to a separate target.

Mutually Assured Destruction (MAD)   A strategy to prevent nuclear war based on the assumption that each side is capable of destroying the other. Missiles involved are usually targeted at cities.

Nuclear club   Members are countries possessing one or more nuclear weapons. (USA 1945, USSR 1949, UK 1952, France 1960, China 1964, Israel late 1960s, India 1974; Pakistan is believed to have joined in 1987.)

Nuclear-Free Zone   An area in which nuclear weapons are not permitted, for any reason.

Nuclear Winter   The theory that multiple nuclear explosions will greatly alter the atmosphere and that temperatures in the succeeding year(s) will be so low that crops will not grow. Any people who survived the initial nuclear effects would likely freeze to death.

Pershing II   A US intermediate-range missile. It has a 1600 km range and, from bases in western Europe, could reach its target in 5 min with pinpoint accuracy.

Proliferation   The process which leads to more and more nations possessing nuclear weapons, or an increase in the number of nuclear weapons in one country.

Soft Target   A target not protected against the effects of nuclear attack, for example, a city.

SS20   The NATO way of describing a Soviet intermediate-range nuclear missile. From bases inside Warsaw Pact countries, this missile can reach its target in 10-15 min.

Strategic Defence Initiative — SDI (Star Wars)   In theory, an impenetrable shield over the United States which would keep out enemy missiles. It depends largely on satellites equipped with laser beams.

Triad   A combination of submarine-launched ballistic missiles, ICBMs and intercontinental bombers. Defence against simultaneous attack by all three would be difficult.

Verification   Determination of whether the potential combatants are complying with arms control agreements.

Yield   The amount of energy released in a nuclear explosion.

Zero-Option   A proposal for the scrapping of all intermediate-range Soviet and American nuclear missiles in Europe.

Question

49. With very few exceptions, the words listed in Table 3.3 have come into existence since 1945, and most of these are from the past 20 years. What is the significance of the addition of this group of words to the English language over such a short period?

NATO troops patrolling the border between East and West Germany

The Nuclear Threat — Is It Real?

The threat of nuclear war is very real. As the nuclear club grows, and the number of weapons increases, so does the danger that they present. There are many ways in which a nuclear war could start. There could be a conscious decision to attack, the attack could be an accident resulting from human or computer error, or nuclear weapons could be used by terrorists. One very real danger is the escalation of a conventional war into a nuclear war.

Superpower Confrontation

The border separating West and East Germany is considered to be one of the most likely flashpoints between the superpowers. A **flashpoint** is the place where fighting begins and then escalates rapidly. (Other areas which might lead to superpower confrontation are the Middle East and Southeast Asia.) Within a few hundred kilometres of the border between East and West Germany are housed over one-half of the world's total array of conventional forces. If reserves from NATO and Warsaw Pact members were included, the total number of

soldiers would equal 10 million! In addition, there are hundreds of nuclear missiles at hand, each capable of reaching enemy territory.

For many decades, concerned citizens from nations all over the world have protested, marched, held meetings, printed and distributed literature, and taken part in acts of civil disobedience. These activities are aimed at influencing other people, but in particular, politicians, to work toward a reduction, and eventual elimination, of nuclear weapons. Such pressure eventually produces results, one of which was the ban on mid-range nuclear weapons, signed by the superpowers on December 9, 1987. More details of this very significant treaty are included later in this chapter.

Peace activists demonstrating on Parliament Hill

The Consequences of Nuclear War

Nobody knows exactly what the resuts of widespread nuclear war would be. Experts make predictions, and often they disagree. However, it is important that we become aware of the potential damage to the environment, our food supply, health and livelihood. Below is a consensus of opinions.

If many cities were to be bombed, the resulting fires would release large quantities of soot into the air. Other radioactive particles from surface disturbance would also reach the upper atmosphere. Huge, dense clouds would reduce the amount of light and heat reaching the surface. Surface air temperatures even in summer would be reduced to below freezing, even in tropical areas. Upper air currents would spread the cloud around the world. Experts cannot agree on how long the smoke would take to clear, but they estimate that it would spread from the northern to the southern hemisphere in two weeks. This drastic cooling of the earth's surface is often referred to as "nuclear winter."

It is believed that nuclear fireballs in the upper atmosphere might reduce the concentration of ozone by as much as 20-30 percent, and locally by 70 percent. Ozone protects all living things on earth from excessive exposure to ultra-violet radiation from the sun. Without it, there would be increased incidence of cancer, genetic defects, and damage to vegetation. Chemical pollutants would be flung into the air, including those that could cause a significant increase in the acidity of rain. Pollutants might be trapped by inversions near large cities and industrial areas. These would further affect the health of any survivors. Fall-out, especially concentrated down-wind of surface attack, would increase the incidence of cancer and susceptibility to other ailments.

Nuclear explosions in the upper atmosphere could knock out communications and cause much confusion at a time when communications would be vital for organizing a war effort, treating civilian casualties, or, equally, for calling a halt to the combat.

Cooling and the reduction in light intensity would reduce the rate at which crops could grow. Normal supplies of seeds, fertilizers, fuels, means of transportation, and storage facilities would be drastically cut. Many crops would fail. Grain surpluses

To commemorate the dropping of nuclear bombs on Hiroshima and Nagasaki, protestors used washable paint to outline human figures on sidewalks. What do you think the outlines represent?

held in storage would not be sufficient to feed all of the survivors, and there would be much starvation. Radioactive fall-out might become concentrated in food sources, causing more health problems for those who managed to acquire food.

Questions

50. Imagine that you have survived a nuclear attack on a nearby city.
    (a) What would you do in the first day, week, and month to increase your chances of survival?
    (b) What facilities and services would have been destroyed? How would this affect your day-to-day existence?
    (c) Suggest three ways in which you as an individual, or in a group, could help those afflicted by such an attack.

51. Assume that a group of 85 survivors have reached a village, 150 km from the blast. Ten inhabitants still live there.
    (a) In what ways would social organization among a few survivors develop?
    (b) Why would social organization play a significant role in increasing the chances for survival?

Military Expenditure

Many people argue that military expenditure is good for the economy. It creates employment, triggers research, spins off new techniques and products for non-military use, and supports many businesses. The Canadian Ministry of National Defence estimated that in fiscal year 1985-86, $12 billion was spent on the military. This, in turn, generated $1.6 billion in taxes and 294 000 jobs, 178 000 of them in the private sector.

Table 3.4
Jobs in the
Private Sector
Which Resulted
from Military
Spending in
Canada 1985-86

Agriculture	2 000
Resource Industries	1 700
Aircraft Manufacturers	4 100
Shipbuilding	5 000
Construction	6 100
Transportation	11 000
Wholesale and Retail Trade	46 200
Communications	4 400
Financial Sector	14 700
Accommodation and Food	21 300
Education and Health	3 700
Other Personal Services	10 900
Other	46 900
Total	178 000

Questions

52. Try to list three kinds of employment within each category mentioned in Table 3.4 that could result from the needs of military personnel and operations.

53. Are such figures deceptive? To answer this, imagine what the effects on employment would be if there were no military organization.

There are many people who would prefer to see this money spent on other projects such as improving food supplies, health and education at home, and in lesser developed nations. Figure 3.20 illustrates some facts relevant to the controversy.

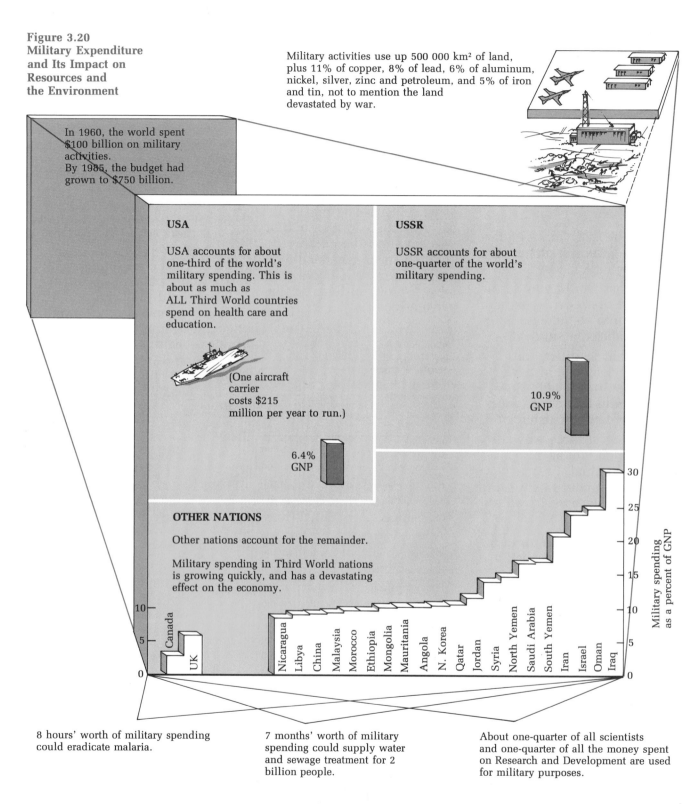

**Figure 3.20
Military Expenditure
and Its Impact on
Resources and
the Environment**

Military activities use up 500 000 km² of land,
plus 11% of copper, 8% of lead, 6% of aluminum,
nickel, silver, zinc and petroleum, and 5% of iron
and tin, not to mention the land
devastated by war.

In 1960, the world spent
$100 billion on military
activities.
By 1985, the budget had
grown to $750 billion.

USA

USA accounts for about
one-third of the world's
military spending. This is
about as much as
ALL Third World countries
spend on health care and
education.

(One aircraft
carrier
costs $215
million per year to run.)

6.4%
GNP

USSR

USSR accounts for about
one-quarter of the world's
military spending.

10.9%
GNP

OTHER NATIONS

Other nations account for the remainder.

Military spending in Third World nations
is growing quickly, and has a devastating
effect on the economy.

Military spending
as a percent of GNP

30
25
20
15
10
5
0

Canada
UK
Nicaragua
Libya
China
Malaysia
Morocco
Ethiopia
Mongolia
Mauritania
Angola
N. Korea
Qatar
Jordan
Syria
North Yemen
Saudi Arabia
South Yemen
Iran
Israel
Oman
Iraq

8 hours' worth of military spending
could eradicate malaria.

7 months' worth of military
spending could supply water
and sewage treatment for 2
billion people.

About one-quarter of all scientists
and one-quarter of all the money spent
on Research and Development are used
for military purposes.

As you can observe from Figure 3.20 lesser developed countries spend a great deal of money on military equipment and activities, and this is increasing each year. The figures illustrated in Figure 3.21 would indicate that among the more developed nations, the military burden reduces the value of productivity by a related value. Countries that spend a large part of their GNP on the military do not have as much growth in their manufacturing sectors.

Figure 3.21
Military Spending
Compared to
Productivity
1960-1983

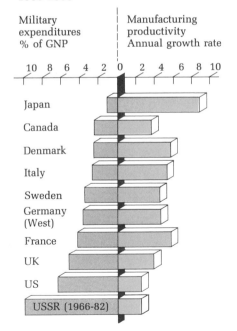

The Deterrent Power of Nuclear Weapons

There are many strategists and their followers who believe that it is important to have a nuclear arsenal, and there are others who feel that the existence of such weapons in itself creates a real threat of nuclear war.

Question

54. Read through Table 3.5. Choose any three arguments which you favour and, in each case, explain why.

Table 3.5
Two Sides to the Argument Concerning Whether or Not Nuclear Weapons Prevent War

In Support	In Opposition
Without nuclear defences, the West would be vulnerable to a Soviet takeover	The Soviets fear war
Unilateral disarmament makes a country vulnerable	Mutual agreement for removal in stages offers protection to both sides
Nuclear deterrence has kept the peace since 1945	There have been over 160 armed conflicts since 1945.
	There are about 100 false alarms in the USA per year
You must be stronger than your enemy before disarming	The arms race will never end in that case
Good civil defence will cope	No protection is sufficient
Peace workers are being used by the enemy	Peace workers are everywhere

Nuclear Proliferation

When the first nuclear bombs were tested and eventually used on Japan in 1945, the danger from short- or long-term radiation was not realized or understood. Following World War II, atmospheric testing continued in remote areas such as the Pacific islands. Radiation levels in the atmosphere increased and, in particular, Strontium 90 levels built up in milk. Strontium 90 is stored in bones, and can accumulate to create future health problems such as leukemia. Peace movements in many nations eventually persuaded governments to ban atmospheric testing, and levels of radioactivity have dropped as a result. Most nuclear testing is now done underground. From time to time, treaties by the superpowers have put a halt to it. Verification of compliance with such agreements comes largely from a network of seismographic stations, one of which is situated at Yellowknife, Northwest Territories.

Negotiations aimed at reducing the possibility of an outbreak of nuclear war between the superpowers have taken place intermittently for many years. They have largely centred on reducing the number of weapons produced and reducing the number of weapons deployed.

The great significance of the superpower treaty signed in December 1987 is that it will lead to the removal and destruction of nuclear weapons that have been deployed. As a result of this treaty, 364 US Cruise and Pershing 2 missiles deployed by NATO in western Europe and 553 Soviet SS-20 and SS-4 in east bloc countries will be destroyed over three years. Another 130 shorter-range Soviet missiles will be dismantled over 18 months.

Talks such as these are very difficult. Even though each country might be very sincere about its intention to reduce the risk of nuclear conflict, it does not wish to disarm in such a way as to allow its opponent a superior position should war break out. Thus, any such agreements are only arrived at following arduous and tedious discussion, requiring the involvement of many advisors and a great deal of highly complex language. The conditions of these agreements must be implemented in such a way that each party can observe whether or not the other is living up to the bargain before more progress can be made. The process of disarmament which will result from the 1987 treaty will be verified over a ten-year period by observers from each of the superpowers. For the individual who desperately wants peace, the process can seem unnecessarily drawn out. It is important that the people make clear their feelings regarding disarmament to their respective governments.

Question

55. Suggest strategies which could be used in the worldwide quest for peace. You should do this in groups and present your findings for class discussion.

A ground-launched cruise missile being tested

Conclusion

There are millions of people in the world living in real danger of death, injury, or deprivation resulting from military activities. Others, remote from warfare, still fear the possibility of nuclear annihilation and the aftermath for victor and vanquished. The world is certainly in a state of unrest, and we welcome anything that contributes to a reduction in world tension.

The reasons for fighting are many, involving politics, religion, separation from necessary resources, and ideology. The majority of conflicts are taking place in lesser developed nations, adding to the suffering of their citizens and using money which could be spent to improve basic living conditions. Often the superpowers or other developed nations may back these clashes, or become directly involved in them.

The history of human existence has been one of emerging nations, conflicts, and alliances. Geography, especially when concerned with resource distribution and strategic locations, continues to play an important role in the influence exerted by nations. Understanding these basic concepts might help us to improve our future prospects.

Vocabulary

geopolitics

fifth column

Pivot Area

Heartland

Exclusive Economic Zone (EEZ)

supranationalism

superpowers

North Atlantic Treaty Organization (NATO)

South East Asian Treaty Organization (SEATO)

Central Treaty Organization (CENTO)

Warsaw Pact

Council for Mutual Economic Assistance (COMECON)

free trade

customs union

common market

economic union

European Economic Community (EEC)

Marshall Plan

Organization for European Economic Co-operation (OEEC)

Latin American Economic System (SELA)

Economic Commission for Africa (ECA)

Economic Community of West African States (ECOWAS)

frontiers

maritime states

boundary line

city states

cradles of civilization

Balfour Declaration

mandate (League of Nations)

terrorism

blockade

Independent Study

1. Identify three strategic locations in the world. Mark them on a world map. In each case, explain why the area is strategically sensitive, analyze political and military interests in the area, and suggest and assess the possible and probable developments during the next decade. Present your conclusions in a report of approximately 1200 words.

2. (a) Using articles from recent newpapers and news magazines, prepare a report on terrorism. Your report should include an explanation of what is meant by the words "terrorist" and "terrorism," the characteristics and backgrounds of a number of terrorists, and a description of the aims and activities of three currently active terrorist groups. Two of these should be well-known, one less known, and if possible, one of these should have some connection with Canada.

   (b) Describe steps which have been taken to reduce terrorist activities. Evaluate their success or failure.

   (c) Suggest steps that could or should be taken to reduce terrorist activity in the future.

3. (a) Describe the sequence of events that some experts believe would follow an all-out nuclear war. These should include the physical, environmental, economic, and political consequences. Why does expert opinion vary? Which do you believe is probably the most accurate, description, and why?

   (b) Are the tactics used as the plot for several "post-nuclear war" movies an effective nuclear war deterrent, or do they engender a feeling of hopelessness and acceptance of the inevitable? Justify your answer.

   (c) Choose any peace movement that has a significant membership in Canada. Describe the beliefs of its members and how these members draw public attention to their cause. Evaluate their success or failure in promoting public pressure for peace. (If possible, interview a member of the group.)

4. Choose an area of the world where there is conflict at present. (Do not choose Israel, as this has been covered in this chapter.)

(a) Draw a map which clearly shows geographical information that is relevant to a study of the conflict.

(b) Collect articles from newspapers and magazines that describe and explain the conflict.

(c) Research the historical background that has led to the current situation.

(d) Describe the involvement, either direct or indirect, of world superpowers remote from the geographic area of the fighting. Attempt to explain the reasons for their interest.

(e) Predict the possible outcome of the current conflict. You may be able to see more than one possible outcome, in which case you should describe each and choose the most likely, giving reasons for your choice.

Combine your answers into a report of approximately 1000 words.

5. Investigate the policy of apartheid in South Africa.

(a) Research and summarize the history of the Afrikaners and the coloureds and blacks in South Africa.

(b) When was the policy of apartheid adopted, and what was the political process involved?

(c) What laws were established under the apartheid policy?

(d) Give reasons why the policy was implemented.

(e) In what ways have laws regarding apartheid been modified since the policy was originally established?

(f) Report on the contrasting lifestyles of blacks, coloureds, and whites which result from the apartheid policy in South Africa.

(g) Describe the outside forces which are directly or indirectly involved in the conflict between pro- and anti-apartheid factions.

(h) Suggest how the situation might be resolved with a minimum of bloodshed.

Part III

Human and Economic Issues of the World

By the end of this chapter, you should be able to:

- identify those regions of the world which are considered developed and those which are underdeveloped;

- explain some of the reasons why certain countries are highly industrialized and others are not;

- examine various important economic trends taking place in the world today, especially in industrial growth; and

- evaluate the positive and negative aspects of industrialization throughout the world.

4

Industrialization and Economic Development

South Korea

South Korea typifies many of the changes which are taking place in the developing world today. There are centres of rapid change and industrialization within the country which have brought about significant improvements in the standard of living for the average person. At the same time, some regions of the country exemplify older, more traditional ways of life. The government has sometimes been open to democratic changes, sometimes opposed. Its reluctance to deal with demands for political reform has led to social upheaval, including the riots of 1987 and 1988.

South Koreans have for centuries followed a rural way of life with a strong emphasis on the family and adherence to a strict moral code. Buddhism has been important as a religion and as the basis of a highly structured lifestyle. This began to change during the Japanese occupation of the country during World War II and in the Korean War which ended in 1954. Rebuilding from the devastation of the Korean War was accomplished by rapid industrialization and modernization. Education has been introduced to virtually all classes of society, while American capital has poured in to help finance new industry. The younger, better educated portion of the population has begun to demand

Top of this page, shanty town on the edge of Seoul; bottom, university students clash with riot police; top of facing page, new office construction in downtown Seoul; far right top, women working in a rice paddy; far right bottom, a temple in Seoul; right, workers in an electronics plant

higher wages and a say in government. Many South Korean leaders have been educated in the United States and understand the benefits of a more open and democratic political system.

It should be noted that the adjustments which South Korea is struggling with are being made throughout much of the developing world. The tension produced by rapid industrialization of a traditional society is one of the themes in this chapter.

Questions

1. Since the Korean War, South Korean workers have been willing to work long hours for low pay to make a living and benefit the country as a whole. Now the younger generation is resisting the country's strict economic and political policies. Suggest reasons for this change in attitude.

2. Why has the United States taken a special interest in South Korea? Refer to your atlas to help answer this question.

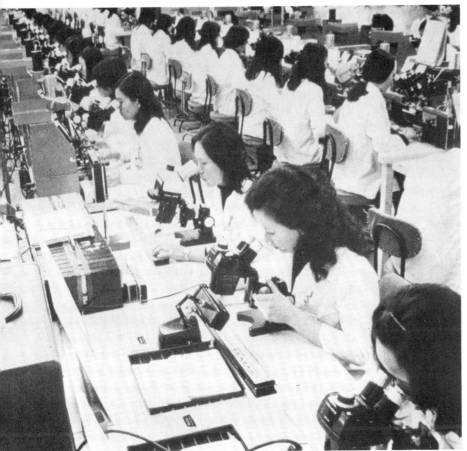

Introduction

Never in the history of the world have people achieved such widespread economic growth and prosperity as in the last 100 years. Standards of living for millions of people in the industrialized world have improved greatly. The affluence enjoyed today in countries such as Canada was undreamed of by previous generations. The benefits of this industrialization, however, have not reached every corner of the world, and the distribution of this wealth is very uneven. In this chapter, we will examine some of the forces which have brought about industrialization and the impact that this has had on the world.

Steel mill in a
developing nation

Industrialization

Economic development is a goal to which most countries in the world aspire. Differing philosophies, however, are proposed or used to reach that goal. Communism, for example, aims to attain economic development through people's unselfish devotion and hard work. Capitalism espouses a system where progress will come about as the result of individuals working hard and being allowed to keep the fruits of their labours. Democratic socialism covers the middle ground of mixed public and private initiative. Regardless of the route taken, it is now accepted almost universally that for a country to reach full economic development, industrialization must take place.

Industrialization is a process in which industry introduces modern, larger-scale technology to manufacture products. However, industrialization consists of more than technology, and brings about social, political, and economic changes that alter the nature and character of a country.

The United States has long been considered the prototype of the advanced industrialized nation. Through American television, movies, and other mass media, people in most parts of the world have been exposed to at least some aspect of American life. Even in countries such as Switzerland and Sweden, which have higher levels of affluence than the United States, the American way of life is perceived to be richer. Economic development, however, is a far more complex issue than attempting to replicate the American way of life.

The United States is a country where industrialization has taken place on a large scale. Almost all regions have gone through this process, and no aspect of life in the US has been unaffected by it. The migration of dispossessed agricultural workers to the industrial cities of the North, East, and Midwest, which began in the last century, is today mirrored in the social upheaval of developing nations of the Third World.

Industrialization has not occurred uniformly across the world, and in some regions it has barely gained a foothold. Without the same history or geography, the economic development in any two areas is bound to be different. A number of other factors must also be considered in accounting for this difference as we will see later on in this chapter.

Questions

3. Explain why the US model of industrialization might not be suitable for every country.

4. Examine the distribution of economic development around the world as shown in Figure 4.1.

(a) Comment on the location of those countries which are highly industrialized.

(b) Where, in general, are the countries which have experienced little economic development?

(c) Refer to the thematic maps of the world in your atlas to discover what other factors relate to either extensive or limited economic development.

Figure 4.1 Levels of Economic Development Around the World

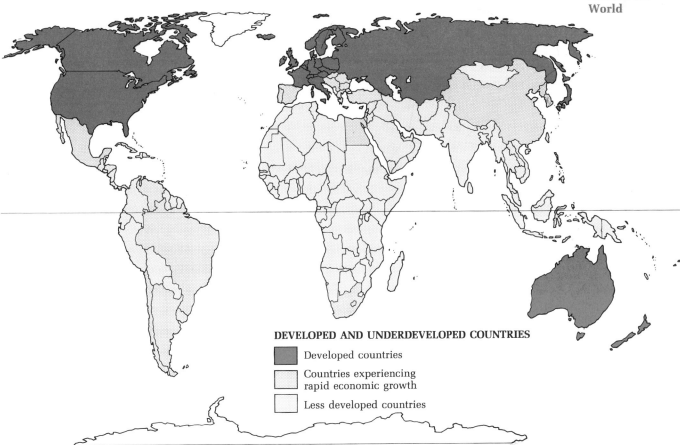

DEVELOPED AND UNDERDEVELOPED COUNTRIES

- Developed countries
- Countries experiencing rapid economic growth
- Less developed countries

The Desirability of Industrialization

As discussed earlier, most countries of the world have accepted the desirability of industrialization. There are drawbacks associated with this process, however. Problems such as rapid urbanization, the disruption of traditional values, and pollution are among the issues with which industrializing countries must wrestle.

Several factors influence the spread of modern industry. One is the introduction of universal education. As people learn to read, they become aware of the benefits of industrialization. The mass media and travellers from abroad expose large numbers of people to a more modern, affluent lifestyle. International trade has also been influential in encouraging lesser developed countries to industrialize. As modern manufactured products such as transistor radios, cameras, packaged and canned food, and television sets enter LDCs, the demand for them grows. In order to buy these products, people must have sufficient foreign currency to bring them into the country. This incentive is an important factor in introducing a country to the benefits of modern industry.

Modern industry does more than increase the level of affluence in a country, however. Not only does industrialization open up more jobs compared to traditional industry, but it also increases the variety of jobs available. It brings social change because it requires a work force which will accept standardized hours, is generally well-trained, and is prepared to agree to a wide range of restrictions imposed by the nature of the manufacturing process.

The building of modern factories entails considerable monetary cost and may lead to indebtedness that may, in the long run, override the benefits.

Industrialization also restructures a country's economy. A **money economy** is introduced, with a paper or coin currency and a central government bank which controls the currency. It takes the place of **bartering**, which is a system of trade where one object is exchanged for one or more others of equivalent

A paper mill in Sri Lanka

132

value. Some of the economies of LDCs are still based on bartering. In the Caribbean, for example, farm produce is exchanged openly and on a large scale through bartering. It is a practical way for farmers to obtain enough food without using scarce currency or having to enter the money economy to receive relatively low payments for their crops.

The money economy is important for LDCs, however, for it allows them to obtain needed goods on the international market. Farm equipment, cars, and consumer goods such as radios and television sets can be obtained through sales to other countries. LDCs therefore often have two economies in operation, each serving different needs.

In addition to the two economic systems discussed above, there is usually a black market as well. The role of the **black market** is to supply a country with currency or goods that are illegal or difficult to obtain any other way.

Industrialization also leads to the introduction of new technology. Large corporations bring in modern technology in order to manufacture goods in developing countries. Brazil, for example, currently produces aircraft, automobiles, and locomotives, using technology largely imported through large corporations. Yet because of restrictions such corporations often place on the use of the new technology, it sometimes has little application in LDCs beyond a single factory.

Appropriate technology has therefore been designed to meet the needs of the LDCs. Appropriate technology is well-suited to the recipient country and is **labour intensive**, taking a large number of people to perform the tasks required. The work is relatively unskilled, and the machines are ones an LDC could pay for, use, and repair. Also referred to as ''intermediate technology,'' appropriate technology will be discussed later in other contexts.

Questions

5. Describe some of the direct and indirect costs of introducing industrialization to a lesser developed country.

6. Quickly review the three types of market systems operating in many LDCs. How might statistics such as GNP per capita, which depend on currency figures, be misleading?

7. Name and explain the most attractive feature of industrialization in an LDC for each of the following people: a government administrator; a city dweller living in poverty; a manufacturer of electric wire; a farmer running a small farm; and a university student.

This urban improvement project in Peru is designed to provide housing for workers.

An Historical Perspective

In Europe 250 years ago, most manufacturing was carried out through **cottage industries**, which involved household manufacture of goods like cloth or pottery. Even today, cottage industries form an important part of the economy for many countries. Hand production of goods tends to be slow compared to industrialized manufacturing, although both methods of manufacture are laborious.

The economy of Europe in the 1700s is referred to now as a **pre-industrial economy**, since it was not based on large-scale industrial production but on small-scale production from cottage industry. Local exchange of goods was accomplished through barter.

It was into this setting that several new technologies were introduced and factories built to house them. Mechanized spinning and weaving, for example, allowed more work to be done quickly and cheaply. This was the beginning of **mass production**. The development and use of new machines and their effect on industry in Europe is referred to as the **Industrial Revolution**. Beginning first in Great Britain in the mid-1700s, its impact spread far beyond industry and affected all aspects of life in Europe.

The process of building factories and developing the machines to be used in them required a great deal of **capital**, or money. Banks were able to draw money from a number of different sources (e.g., from proprietors of giant trading companies), and fun-

nel it into industrial development. It should be noted that today a great deal of capital is still needed for industrialization. In fact, the process of industrialization in LDCs has been seriously hindered by a lack of such capital.

For Great Britain, as with other European countries such as France, its empire was important in the process of industrialization. Britain's empire was spread around the world, and supplied the mother country with a wide range of raw materials at low prices. In return, the colonies would purchase manufactured goods from Britain's new factories.

Although there was a proliferation of machines in British factories, there was also a great demand for labour to help run them. Labourers from the countryside flooded into the cities to work in these new industries. In many cases, these workers had been forced off the land by landlords and by changing conditions in the farming economy.

In the factories, the conditions were dismal, the pay was low, and the abuse of workers was widespread. The problems of the Industrial Revolution were not unlike those experienced in developing countries today.

Parallel to the introduction of new industrial technology in Great Britain were new developments in agriculture,

Figure 4.2
A Typical Cottage Industry in Great Britain in the Early 1700s

mining, and transportation. With this new technology, a smaller number of farmers was able to produce more food for the burgeoning cities. Improved roads and new railways got food to the markets and coal to the new factories. These developments did not take place without disruption or conflict, however. Competition arose between various European powers in the sale of industrial products and in the acquisition of new colonial territory.

By the 1800s, the Industrial Revolution spread throughout western Europe and reached the United States and Canada. In its wake came significant changes in social, political, and economic life. Large cities developed and, as a result, life for most Europeans changed dramatically.

Rural-based values gave way to urban values, and farm jobs were abandoned in favour of highly regimented factory-related jobs. Large-scale money economies flourished, along with international trade and the building of worldwide empires.

Today the drift to the cities is taking place on an unprecedented scale throughout the world. Many of those who arrive in these cities looking for work will not find it. Unemployment has become a way of life for tens of millions of people in giant urban centres. **Underemployment** is an equally serious problem. This occurs when a person in a given position has more qualifications than that position requires. Underemployment can also affect a whole region that has depended on a single industry. The closing-down of the Iron Ore Company of Canada at Shefferville, Quebec, in 1982 was such an event. The region remains rich in skilled workers, but the industry has disappeared. Further discussion of rural-urban migration and urban growth is found in Chapter 9.

Questions

8. Summarize the major developments which took place as a result of the Industrial Revolution in Europe.

9. What parallels can be drawn between the Industrial Revolution in Europe and current technological changes in the developing world?

Glasgow, an industrial city built during the Industrial Revolution in Great Britain, has changed little in appearance since that time.

The Legacy of Colonialism

During the eighteenth and nineteenth centuries, the major powers of Europe spread around the world to establish empires on every inhabited continent. The British, the French, the Portuguese, the Spanish, the Dutch, the Germans, and others scrambled to take over countries which they could occupy and which could serve their interests. Not only could the conquering powers dominate their **colonies** politically, but these acquired territories would also be useful economically. Colonies were of vital economic significance to the colonial power, since they would supply it with cheap raw materials and buy expensive manufactured goods in return.

It is precisely this unequal economic relationship that has led to some of the economic problems in the developing world today. Little manufacturing was established in the colonies because the imperial powers did not want competition for their own manufactured goods. As a result, colonial economies were developed around the production and export of cash crops. Rubber from Malaysia, cocoa from West Africa, sugar from the West Indies, and coffee from East Africa are examples of the cash crops which were introduced in colonial times and are still grown today.

West Africa provides an interesting example of the impact of colonialism on an area of the developing world. With a humid tropical climate, West Africa was an ideal location for the production of many of the crops which Europe desired. Coconuts, rubber, cocoa, sisal, and a number of minerals were

Figure 4.3 West Africa today. Note the location of the major cities and the orientation of the major transportation lines.

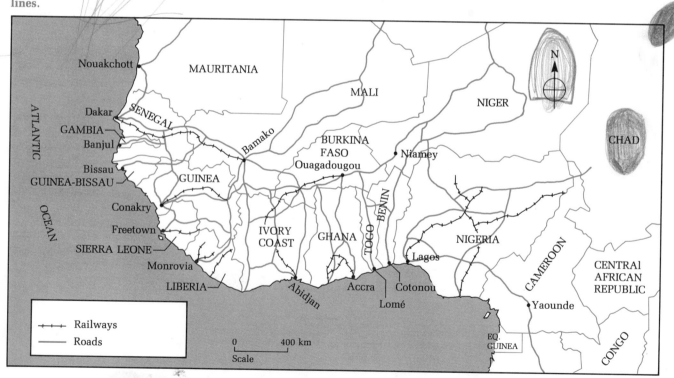

produced for export. Since labour was cheap, products could be exported inexpensively, often by large European producers who set up operations in that region. Traditional farming and domestic food production suffered as a result.

As can be seen in Figure 4.3, the major cities of West Africa are located along the Atlantic coast. The transportation routes generally run inland, perpendicular to the coastline. In many cases, the colonial powers of the last century established major cities along the coast to serve the economic needs of the empire. They built transportation routes for moving the raw materials from the sources of production to the coast for export.

This base has not served the interests of present-day development in West Africa. Wealth, education, and much of the modern development has been concentrated in the capital cities of West Africa, but the rest of each country has remained largely underdeveloped.

Colonialism has left other imprints around the world. When imperial powers took over a colony, the established political system was usually destroyed. A colonial government and imperial army sup-

planted it. When the colonies achieved independence, the imperial power left behind a foreign political system; often the only group which could take control of the country was the military. The result has been a dramatic increase in the amount of force used throughout former colonies as well as a large number of **insurrections**, the political overthrow of governments.

It should also be noted that the countries which were created by the imperial powers were often given artificial boundaries which cut across tribal or ethnic lines. Traditional enemies were lumped together in one nation, increasing the possibility of armed conflict.

Nigeria, Angola, the Central African Republic, and Uganda are examples of countries which have experienced political upheavals since achieving independence. Many citizens of these countries have been killed or

maimed during rebellions or civil wars.

Not all of the consequences of colonialism have been negative, however. Certain transportation and communication systems, like the East African railway system, are still in use today. Modern technology was absorbed to varying degrees by the colonies. Similarly, European languages were disseminated worldwide. The government of Singapore, for example, has credited some of its financial and manufacturing prowess to its use of English. India has used English to help unify an ethnically and linguistically diverse country. Schools, universities, governmental systems, religious institutions, and major business corporations were also set up within these colonies. Some of these legacies have had negative effects on the recipient countries, but it would be inaccurate to dismiss their value out of hand.

The University of Nairobi in Kenya

Questions

10. After independence, many former colonies actually experienced a decline in per capita wealth and economic output. Suggest reasons to explain this. Refer to Table 4.1.

11. When European powers withdrew from their empires in this century, there was an increase in violence, bloodshed, and armed conflict. Some people claim that this showed the former colonies were unable to manage their own affairs. Others claim that this showed the ultimate failure of colonialism. Which point of view do you support, and why?

Table 4.1
Changes in GNP
per Capita in
Africa 1965-1985

Country	Average annual growth rates (percent)
Benin	0.2
Botswana	8.3
Burkina Faso	1.3
Burundi	1.9
Cameroon	3.6
Central African Rep.	-0.2
Chad	-2.3
Congo, People's Rep.	3.8
Ethiopia	0.2
Ghana	-2.2
Guinea	0.8
Ivory Coast	0.9
Kenya	1.9
Lesotho	6.5
Liberia	-1.4
Madagascar	-1.9
Malawi	1.5
Mali	1.4
Mauritania	0.1
Mauritius	2.7
Mozambique	-
Niger	-2.1
Nigeria	2.2
Rwanda	1.8
Senegal	-0.6
Sierra Leone	1.1
Somalia	-0.7
South Africa	1.1
Sudan	0.0
Tanzania	0.0
Togo	0.3
Uganda	-2.6
Zaire	-2.1
Zambia	-1.6
Zimbabwe	1.6

Multinational Corporations

Some of the largest economic entities in the world are **multinational corporations**. This type of corporation is one which has its headquarters in one country but has branch plants elsewhere. Corporations such as General Motors or Exxon have branches in many countries and earn gross revenues which exceed the gross national product of a number of LDCs. There are no international laws to regulate them, and thus they are considered to be powers unto themselves to some extent.

Multinational corporations are not the only force which spurs contemporary industrialization, but they are often considered the most attractive or at least the most convenient. Figure 4.4 shows their advantages, but there is also a cost to the recipient country.

Multinational corporations (MNCs), sometimes referred to as "transnational corporations," will establish operations in a country if it appears to be profitable for them to do so. Perhaps a country has raw materials which an MNC wants, such as copper in Chile or timber resources in Borneo. A country may also offer cheap labour or freedom from labour-protection laws. Taiwan's economy has grown largely as a result of foreign investments taking advantage of its low wage rates and a hard-working labour force.

Countries sometimes offer corporations grants of money to come and locate within their borders. **Tax holidays** may also be used to attract companies. This means that a government exempts a corporation from taxes for a certain period after it establishes a plant in that country.

The size and prestige of many multinational corporations make their presence in a country a status symbol. In some cases, bidding wars for multinationals have emerged between countries. In the struggle, national govern-ments sometimes overlook small businesses which could provide more jobs but which do not have the high profile of larger operations.

One other potential danger associated with the operation of large multinational corpora-tions is that their prime con-cern is with profit and corporate survival. In some cases, these corporations carry out activities which are not in the national interests of the countries in which they oper-ate. In much of the develop-ing world, for example, growth hormones are sold freely even though in coun-tries like Canada such drugs are carefully administered through prescription only.[1] DDT, an insecticide long banned in Canada and the United States, is sold widely in many countries in the developing world.

When a corporation uses or exploits a country for its own interests in ways which are against that country's national interests, this process is called **neocolonialism**. In the Philippines, for example, the government has expropri-ated the land of poor farmers for conversion into plantations for a large multinational fruit company.[2] This type of activity resembles old-style

Figure 4.4
The operation of a multinational corporation involves the two-way movement of capital, personnel, technology, goods, and services.

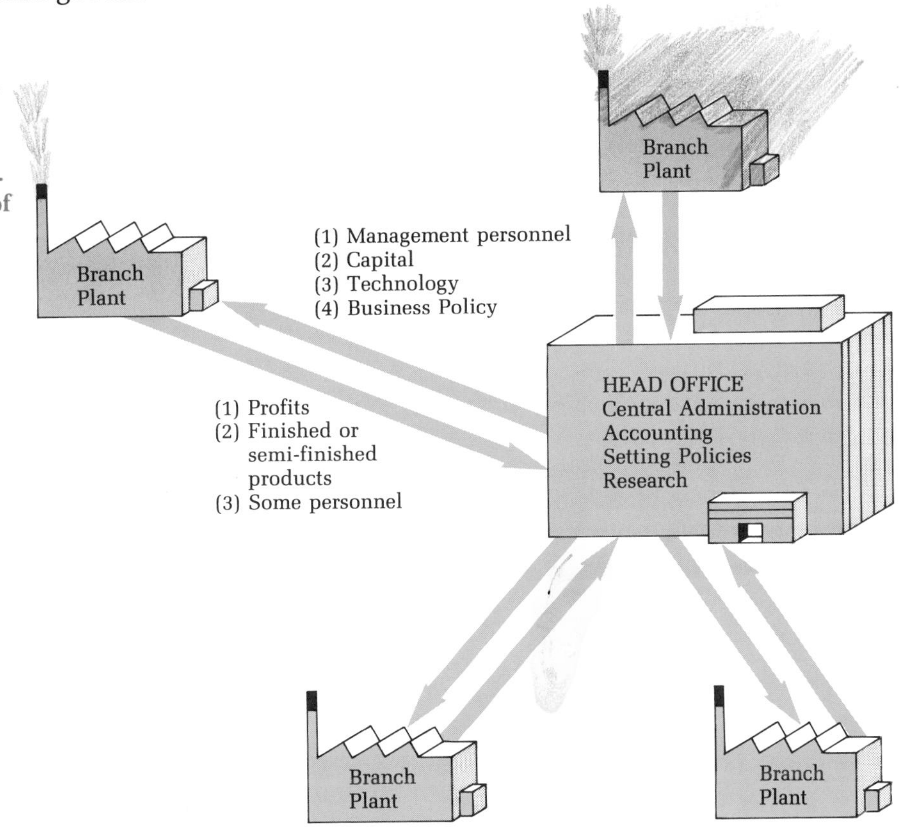

(1) Management personnel
(2) Capital
(3) Technology
(4) Business Policy

(1) Profits
(2) Finished or semi-finished products
(3) Some personnel

HEAD OFFICE
Central Administration
Accounting
Setting Policies
Research

Branch Plant

colonialism. The key difference is that the recipient country is not legally a colony.

Despite the drawbacks of multinational corporations, they have introduced significant technologies which have benefitted the entire world. Computers are products of multinational corporations, as are a variety of modern electronic equipment such as videotape recorders and television sets. Many valuable medications such as antibiotics have been developed by MNCs. Multinationals have the capability of raising large amounts of capital for research into and distribution of new products.

A McDonald's restaurant in Singapore

Company	Location of head office	Revenue/Sales, 1987 (millions US$)
1) General Motors Corp.	United States	101 782
2) Mitsubishi Corp.	Japan	96 606
3) C. Itoh & Co. Ltd.	Japan	92 356
4) Mitsui & Co. Ltd.	Japan	88 640
5) Marubeni Corp.	Japan	82 871
6) Sumitomo Corp.	Japan	81 709
7) Royal Dutch/Shell Group	Netherlands/UK	78 306
8) Exxon	United States	77 721
9) Nissho Iwai Corp.	Japan	75 441
10) Ford Motor Corp.	United States	71 643
11) Mobil Oil Corp.	United States	56 446
12) International Business Machines Ltd.	United States	54 217
13) American Telephone & Telegraph Ltd.	United States	51 209
14) Sears, Roebuck Ltd.	United States	48 440
15) British Petroleum Co. Plc	UK	45 198
16) Toyota Motor Corp.	Japan	43 637
17) IRI Group	Italy	41 287
18) Nippon Telegraph & Telephone Corp.	Japan	40 926
19) General Electric Corp.	United States	39 315
20) Nippon Life Insurance Co.	Japan	37 704

Table 4.2
The 20 Largest Multinational Corporations in the World by Sales, 1987

Questions

12. Examine the list of the 20 largest multinational corporations in the world in Table 4.2. Where are most of the corporations based? What does this indicate about the concentration of corporate power?

13. Why might countries enter into a bidding war to attract multinational corporations when there are other routes to economic development?

14. Are multinational corporations beneficial to most LDCs? Explain your answer carefully and include any limitations or conditions that might apply.

Economic Systems Around The World

Each economic system is closely tied to the political philosophy of a particular country; this makes it difficult to separate a nation's economic and political spheres. In some cases, the government takes a major role in controlling the economy, while in others, the initiative of individuals is vital.

One of the two most important economic philosophies in the world is **capitalism**. Capitalism refers to an economic system in which individuals can own and operate businesses and keep the profits generated. Capitalism is also referred to as the **free enterprise** system. Regardless of the name, this economic system is consumer- and profit-oriented. This means that the economy is geared to produce goods for individual consumption. Individual ownership provides a strong incentive for a person to work hard with the prospect of keeping the profits earned. Inherent in this system is economic competition. In theory, this competition encourages companies to produce goods more efficiently and more cost effectively than before.

Although capitalism is primarily an economic philosophy, it has political implications. In order for an individual to have the freedom to make economic decisions, there must be a certain degree of political freedom. As a result, in the last 200 years or so since Adam Smith described the theory of capitalism in *The Wealth of Nations*, capitalism and its variations have appeared most frequently in political democracies.

There are almost no nations today which have an unfettered capitalistic economy. Hong Kong, which will remain a British crown colony until 1997, may be closest to it. Great Britain during the early 1800s or the United States during the mid-1800s could be considered examples of true capitalist economies. Today, the United States, Great Britain, Canada, and many of the countries of western Europe have economies in which both private and public ownership of corporations occur.

True capitalism is not without its problems. For one, capitalism allows poverty to exist alongside great wealth. An individual has the right to work hard and become wealthy, but another person's inability to work means a life of poverty.

Capitalism also suffers from labour-management conflicts. Union leaders, because they represent the workers, frequently have different goals from owners and management, and the result of such conflicts may be a strike.

The free enterprise system is also affected by business cycles, where the economy experiences a boom or period of prosperity followed by a depression bringing business failures and increased poverty. Communism and socialism have been developed as a response to these weaknesses in the free enterprise system.

Communism, as practised in the world today, generally refers to an economic and political system in which the government controls or tightly regulates most aspects of life for the benefit of the average person. Economically, the government not only owns the means of production, the resources, and the marketing system, but also sets the

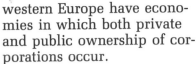

Figure 4.5 Adam Smith wrote *The Wealth of Nations* in which he described the philosophy of capitalism.

prices and keeps any profits which accrue. It should be noted that the communist system, as the German sociologist Karl Marx designed it in his famous treatise, *The Communist Manifesto*, was very different from the system that was established in Russia in 1917. According to Marx, the essential problem with capitalism was that the workers and the peasants remained poor while the ruling class became wealthy. The only solution, according to Marx, was revolution that would remove the **bourgeoisie**, or middle class, and replace it with a communist system operated by the people. All people were considered to be equal and were to give to the state according to their ability and to receive according to their need. This aspect of communist thought is directly opposed to Adam Smith's capitalism.

Figure 4.6
Karl Marx's writings helped change the course of human history in the twentieth century.

The governments in communist countries own most or all of the natural resources as well as the means of production. Most prices are controlled by the state, and profit is frowned upon. The rationale for these policies of economic control is simple; the state operates the economy for the benefit of all people in society rather than a small elite. No one is to get rich at the expense of others. So far as available statistics can show, the modern communist states have managed to establish a fairly equitable distribution of income within their societies. Yet, since prices are kept artificially low and profits are not condoned, supplies of food and essential goods are often in short supply. In the USSR, Poland, East Germany, and Romania, line-ups are common and stores find it hard to stock their shelves. Moreover, the kind of central control which dominates the political and economic life of the country curtails citizens' civil liberties.

Many countries have now developed economies which, although still profit- and consumer-oriented, have safety legislation for consumers and workers, limited price controls, transportation regulations, and extensive corporate tax laws. In some situations, the government actually owns companies and operates them in the national or public interest. Such an economy is referred to as a **mixed economy** or a **socialist economy**, since it embodies both public and private ownership as well as government regulation.

Questions

15. Contrast the role of the individual in the economies of the communist and the capitalist state. Use a chart or table as part of your comparison. What does this show about the priorities of the two systems?

16. Why would the communist system have such widespread appeal for the poor in the developing world?

17. What flaws are there in the communist and the capitalist systems?

18. What impact does the nature of an economic system have on the life of the average person in a society?

Hungary

Hungary is a country located in eastern Europe, bordering on the USSR. The Soviet Union dominates Hungary militarily as part of the so-called buffer zone between the Soviet Union and western Europe. Since Hungary is dominated by the Soviet Union, it has adopted a communist political and economic system. Although officially communist, the Hungarian economy operates very differently from that of the USSR and most other communist states.

The government in Hungary is firmly in control of the direction of economy, but there is considerable freedom for individuals to receive some of the profits of their labour. There is, for example, freedom to own and manage one's own business and keep some of the profits from its operation. Farmers are able to sell a significant portion of their produce on the private market. There are also bonuses for workers who produce particularly well in their factory or on the construction site, as is true in the USSR.

While other communist states suffer from food shortages and falling factory production levels, Hungary has generated a relatively high standard of living for its citizens while publicly adhering to a strict communist philosophy.

In 1956, Soviet troops crushed a popular uprising against the USSR's dominance of Hungary. The Hungarians learned that if they wanted to improve their lives, they must learn to accommodate the wishes of the Soviet Union.

The Hungarian government now sets the prices for less than 50 percent of all retail goods, but dictates the prices for most important goods. Close to one-third of the national budget is spent on subsidies for food and other necessities.

Figure 4.7 Hungary is located at what has for centuries been considered the crossroads of Europe.

Questions

19. In your own words, explain why the Hungarian economy has prospered while that of the other communist nations has not.

20. Examine Figure 4.7 and maps of Europe in your atlas.
    (a) In what ways is Hungary at a crossroads in Europe?
    (b) How is Hungary's location beneficial economically?

21. What lessons can other nations, communist or non-communist, learn from Hungary?

22. (a) Compare the growth of the GNP of Hungary with that of the other countries listed in Table 4.3.
    (b) Construct graphs to compare the selected countries. How do they compare?

Table 4.3
The Economic Growth and Changes in Standards of Living in Hungary, Japan, Canada, and Haiti

Country	Real growth rate of GNP per capita 1973-1986	Life expectancy 1970	Life expectancy 1985	School enrolment* 1970	School enrolment* 1984	Average annual growth rate (%) Agriculture 1965-80	Average annual growth rate (%) Agriculture 80-86	Average annual growth rate (%) Industry 1965-80	Average annual growth rate (%) Industry 80-86
Hungary	3.6	70	71	84	92	2.7	2.8	6.4	1.3
Japan	3.4	72	77	91	97	0.8	1.0	8.5	5.0
Canada	1.2	73	76	100+	98	0.7	2.8	3.4	2.9
Haiti	0.4	49	54	n.a.	48	1.0	-1.3	7.1	-2.4

How Countries Industrialize

Rostow's Theory of Economic Growth

Earlier in this chapter, we examined the Industrial Revolution in Europe and noted the impact it had on European society and the world generally. An American professor of economics by the name of W.W. Rostow developed a theory of economic growth to explain how a country actually industrializes. He based his work primarily upon research in Europe.

Rostow's theory centres on five stages through which an economy progresses. The stages are like building blocks because, if one is missing, the economy cannot progress further.

In Stage 1 of his theory, Rostow describes the Traditional Society, characterized by a small but dominant upper class, a tiny middle class, and a very large lower class of peasants and urban workers. Such a society is referred to as a **hierarchy** because it is highly structured with few at the top and a great many at the bottom. Great Britain before the Industrial Revolution or Russia before the Russian Revolution are two historical examples of countries in Stage 1. Today, there are many countries of the developing world, like Bangladesh or Ethiopia, which would fit into this category.

In Stage 1, there is little population growth, for the birth rates and the death rates are both high. Manufacturing is done in cottage industries and the standard of living is low.

Stage 2 is called the Pre-Conditions for Take-Off, a transition from the traditional society to the more economically developed and complex stages to come. Though sometimes welcomed, this stage may also be forced upon a country by war or colonization. India, for example, was forced into this stage when it was absorbed into the British Empire, and experienced the rapid growth of cities and imposition of a foreign educational and political system.

Stage 2 is characterized by a number of key developments. One of these is the accumulation of savings or capital which is then invested in promising areas of the economy. This process is aided by well-managed banks and an effective central government which helps direct economic development. Transportation and communications flourish, as does modernized farming needed to provide for a rapidly growing population.

For Stage 3, or Economic Take-off, to take place, there have to be major social changes. Education is essential, for literacy provides one of the building blocks for new industries. Death rates begin to decline rapidly and birth rates show a downward trend because of improved health care. Rapid urbanization is also a characteristic of this stage of economic development, as displaced rural workers move to new jobs in industry.

Economic take-off is usually triggered by a major event such as a war or a revolution. Although it was tragic in terms of the enormous loss of human life, the American Civil War was also the catalyst for the economic take-off in the United States. The post-war boom was aided by the joint growth of railways and the steel industry. In the case of Great Britain, the stimulus was provided by the textile industry.

Stage 4, called the Drive to Maturity, is actually an extension of Stage 3. The benefits of the rapid industrialization of Stage 3 gradually percolate throughout the entire society. Traditional ways of life are superseded and levels of affluence increase, allowing more people to travel, enjoy recreation, and pursue their own personal goals. Cities continue to grow, but at a reduced rate, and social services are available to more people.

Stage 5 of Rostow's theory is The Age of High Mass Consumption. According to Rostow, virtually everyone enjoys a high level of affluence in this ultimate stage of industrialization, and service industries multiply. As the amount of leisure time increases, people are able to pursue a wide variety of interests and are free to concern themselves with such public issues as pollution of the environment.

Questions

23. (a) If Rostow is correct in his theory, what sacrifices must a country make if it wants to achieve substantial economic progress?

(b) Why would the decisions that you identified in your answer to part (a) be difficult ones for many of the lesser developed countries to make today?

24. What flaws can you detect in Rostow's assumptions?

25. Does a theory like Rostow's have value, whether it "fits" or not? Explain your view.

26. What is the likely economic future of a country which has reached Stage 5 and then continues to develop, such as the United States, Great Britain, or Canada? Suggest reasons for your answer.

Why Are Some Countries Underdeveloped?

Geographic Problems

The greatest concentrations of industry in the world are to be found almost exclusively where the terrain and climate offer many natural advantages in terms of resources and agriculture. Some countries of the world, however, have serious physical problems to overcome in developing economically. Mountainous terrain like Nepal's, for example, can seriously handicap economic improvements. Deserts, extreme cold, or perhaps tropical rain forests each present a range of difficulties to be overcome. Farming and economic development have been severely hampered in the countries of the Sahel, which is a semi-desert and drought-ridden region lying along the southern edge of the Sahara Desert.

It should not be assumed, however, that economic development or the lack of it is determined wholly by the physical environment. Human effort pitted against considerable obstacles has brought about major improvements in standards of living. Extensive rice farming in the mountainous regions of Taiwan and the development of irrigated farming in Israel are two examples of determined efforts to farm or industrialize despite physical obstacles. Compared to Israel, the Kalahari Desert of southwestern Africa has a low level of technology, exemplifying the principle that the higher the level of technology applied to a difficult environment, the greater the opportunity for successful and profitable development. This principle is also evident if you compare the Soviet Union's city-building in the sub-Arctic with the static economic development of the semi-desert region of the Sahel in Africa.

The physical geography of Nepal makes farming and other human activity very difficult.

27. What other factors must also be present, besides a high level of technology, in order for a difficult environment to be profitably developed?

28. Using your atlas as a guide, select six different environments which present difficulties for human development. Explain the nature of the difficulties and suggest possible steps to overcome them.

Top, locally organized co-operatives dig wells and irrigate farmland in Burkina Faso; bottom, camels are considered appropriate transportation for much of the hot desert area of the world.

Infrastructure

Industry does not develop in isolation, but in response to and in relationship with various factors in its environment. One of the most important factors is **infrastructure**, which refers to the economic skeleton of an economy, such as roads, communications networks, schools, banks, and markets.

When an industry is established, it draws upon the infrastructure in order to operate. Imagine, for example, a small factory which produces leather sandals for local consumption as well as export. The following diagram, Figure 4.8, illustrates the various inputs and outputs which such a simple factory would require in order to be successful.

A street market in an Asian city

Figure 4.8
The Importance of the Infrastructure to a Small Sandal Factory

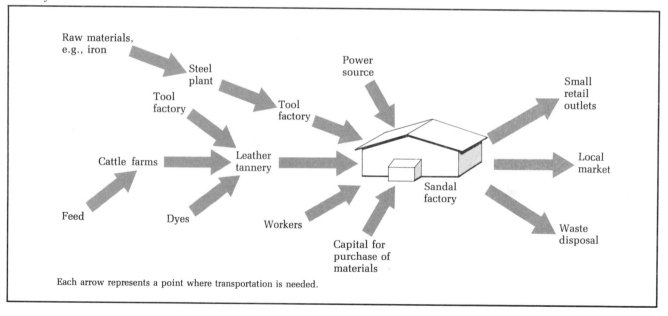

Raw materials, e.g., iron

Steel plant

Tool factory

Tool factory

Power source

Cattle farms

Leather tannery

Sandal factory

Small retail outlets

Local market

Waste disposal

Feed

Dyes

Workers

Capital for purchase of materials

Each arrow represents a point where transportation is needed.

If any of the required inputs for this factory are not available, or are only partially functioning, then the results can be devastating, both for the factory and for the economic growth of the region where it is located.

Because they allow the exchange of goods and services, markets are a particularly important part of the economic system of any country of the world. The functioning of the New York Stock Exchange, for example, has an impact all over the world. Billions of dollars' worth of stocks and bonds are traded on the exchange every day.

On a much smaller scale, rural markets in the developing world have a very important role in those economies. Efficient market systems help to increase the consumption of goods in a country and to generate new wealth.

Just as the markets serve an important role in the various economies of the world, so each part of the infrastructure has a key role to play as well.

Questions

29. Examine the photograph below. The region illustrated produced a wide range of tropical fruits and vegetables, as well as simple handicrafts. It is largely self-sufficient in food, but is very poor, and there is little contact with the outside word. What impact do you think there would be in this region if markets were established at the three main towns, and all-weather roads were built to link the towns and connect them with the outside world? Outline your reasoning.

30. Select three examples of markets with which you are familiar. How do they operate, and what importance do they have in the economy of your local area?

31. What difficulties can you see arising during construction of the infrastructure in a developing country?

32. What changes might follow in a country where a university, an electrical power system, and a banking system were constructed for the first time?

An isolated portion of central Africa, with little infrastructure to support industrial development

Automation

When machinery is introduced to perform tasks which otherwise would have had to be carried out by human labour, it is referred to as **automation**. Automation is not always appropriate for industry in the LDCs of the world. In a country such as Ecuador, for example, where there is a great deal of unemployment and average wages are low, factory automation has limited validity. Although the governments of LDCs compete with one another to attract multinational corporations to locate in their countries, the real benefits of a highly automated factory may be limited.

The development of automation requires a large input of capital to be successful. Automation is therefore referred to as **capital-intensive**. LDCs frequently lack capital, and therefore attempting to establish a factory or industry which is capital-intensive is inappropriate, if not harmful.

Small-scale industries can provide a variety of benefits in the developing world. They can be initiated by local needs. The machinery used is tailored to the requirements of the local business person. In

A highly automated factory in Brazil

addition, the capital investment will not exceed the ability of the individual to pay.

Questions

33. Modern, highly automated factories are desired as a symbol of success in LDCs. Explain why such a factory is actually a mixed blessing to a country in the developing world.

34. What problems might a small business operator face in the developing world?

35. Explain why a mix of businesses best suits a developing country.

A small business operating in Malaysia

Other Obstacles to Economic Growth

A wide variety of other factors comes into play to retard a country's economic development. Where the economy is dependent on one or two major export commodities and the world demand for those commodities collapses, or the price declines, the impact is serious. In Argentina, for example, world prices for wheat and beef went into a long decline during the late 1960s. This had a serious effect on the whole Argentinian economy and led to unemployment and other economic problems. The fall of world tin prices in the 1970s hurt the Bolivian economy; so was Zambia hurt by the fall in copper prices.

Government mismanagement has seriously jeopardized the development of numerous LDCs. The government of Libya has spent billions of dollars on military expenses and various military campaigns during the 1980s, while it has neglected basic economic and industrial development. Other countries, such as Haiti and the Philippines, have had political leaders who have stolen millions of dollars of public money for private use.

Ecological mismanagement is another factor which has contributed to the economic woes of a number of countries. The highlands of Kenya and Ethiopia have been severely denuded of trees in some regions. The resultant erosion, as well as the financial loss from the destruction of firewood, has retarded and even prevented any major economic development.

Natural disasters, wars, and other external factors have also hampered economic development. It is obviously subject to a complex set of forces.

Question

36. Outline the relationships among the economic problems which have been discussed in this section of the text.

Problems Associated with Industrialization

As industrialization comes into developing countries, it provides tangible benefits, as we have already seen, but there are also considerable costs. These costs refer not only to capital investment but also to the human, environmental, and social impact on a society. If industrialization comes quickly to a country unprepared for it, the impact can be especially drastic.

As mentioned earlier in the chapter, industrialization involves the centralization of major activities in an economy. In Thailand, for example, industrialization has brought about the concentration of transportation, communications, factories, labour, and governmental functions in Bangkok, the capital. In order to fill the demand for labour, the process of **urbanization** accelerates. This movement of people from rural to urban areas is accompanied by a degree of social breakdown and the loss of traditional values. Strong rural family units can break apart under the pressures of the urban environment. As values change, crime and social unrest may increase.

Industrialization also opens up opportunities for some entrepreneurs to make a great deal of money. **Entrepreneurs** are business people who invest money in the hope of making a profit. Some of them make spectacular profits, yet in the same cities are people who are very poor. Industrialization tends to increase the economic disparity between the rich and the poor. A rapidly industrializing LDC lacks the support systems families need to help them cope with unemployment, feelings of isolation, and other problems of the big city.

The pressures of industrialization create a great demand for cheap labour, a demand which, in some countries, is filled by children. Child labour is well-documented in the Philippines and Thailand, for example. Children working for low wages to support themselves or their families are robbed of the opportunity to attend school. They are forced prematurely into an adult world. In Lima, Peru, there are an estimated 10 000 abandoned children who live as street kids and are part of the child labour force.[3]

Environmental damage is another factor which must be evaluated when assessing the impact of industrialization on a country. Cairo is facing difficulties with air pollution from industrial plants to the north and south of the city.

Table 4.4
Factors That Contribute to the Process of Urbanization

Push Factors	Pull Factors
farm mechanization and resultant loss of jobs	hope for jobs
inadequate education and health care facilities, and other basic social services	desire for better health and social services
small plots of land or sharecropping conditions make it hard to grow enough food to eat	superior education facilities, etc.
	friends, family may already be in city to aid migrants
boredom with rural life	enjoyment of city attractions
natural disasters, crop failures, etc.	children can earn money to help the family

Bogota, Colombia, has a beautiful setting in a mountain valley, but that very setting traps pollution, causing the quality of the air to deteriorate to unacceptable levels. In Indonesia, industry's demand for wood has contributed to the loss of valuable tropical forests and extensive erosion. New York City produces mountains of garbage, but has no acceptable method of disposing of it.

Industrial accidents also present problems wherever there is modern industry. Factories are often old and dangerous, and in much of the developing world there are few government inspectors to monitor workplace safety. Larger-scale industrial accidents can affect thousands of people, as evidenced by the disaster at the Union Carbide plant in Bhopal, India, in December 1984. Originally the plant was built well beyond the outer limits of Bhopal but, as people migrated to the city in search of jobs, shanty towns appeared on the land around it. This accident will be discussed in greater detail in Chapter 7.

A large factory in Indonesia

Problems often
associated with
industrialization
include over-
crowding (top)
and sewage
disposal (bottom).

Questions

37. When considering the
process of industrializa-
tion, many developing
countries do not take into
account all of the costs
entailed, whether direct or
indirect. Suggest reasons
to explain this.

38. Select four problems
associated with industrialization. Suggest ways in
which the government of a
developing country could
act to reduce the impact of
each of these problems. Be
sure not to impose such
severe restrictions that the
industry will not develop
at all.

39. What factors in city life
can tend to undermine the
family?

Simulation

Imagine that you are called in to make recommendations to a multinational corporation which produces a wide range of personal consumer products such as soaps, deodorants, and skin creams. Your instructions are to recommend the most suitable country in which to locate a new factory to manufacture these products. In addition to the manufacture of consumer goods, your company will have to advertise heavily in the country of location and set up a sales network.

The region you are examining is southern Asia, and you are faced with a difficult choice, because five countries have petitioned you to locate within their boundaries. The best long-term interests of the company must be considered, and its need to produce significant profits. Examine the statistics given in Table 4.2 and then make your decision.

Question

40. Make your decision based on the information given in Table 4.5, and write up a full rationale for your selection. What facts could help you make your decision?

Table 4.5
Statistics for
Countries Under
Consideration

	Country A	Country B	Country C	Country D	Country E
GNP per capita ($)	250	475	550	300	700
Population (millions)	36	10	11	45	5
Rating of infra-structure	poor	poor	moderate	poor	well-developed
Number of cities over 500,000	6	2	4	10	1
Access to ocean	yes	no, landlocked	no, landlocked	yes	yes, an island
T.V.s per 1000 population	15	45	110	35	260
Illiteracy rate (%)	16	29	71	60	91
Number of other large MNCs in the country	2	6	27	8	17
Government incentives	free land, 5-year tax holiday	free land, 2-year tax holiday	cheap land, 2-year tax holiday	free land, 1-year tax holiday	market priced land

Future Trends in the World Economy

The Industrial Revolution signalled the change in Europe's economy ~~from cottage industry to a large-scale factory-centered system.~~ the world is entering what has been referred to as a second Industrial Revolution. Now, the emphasis is not on the production of industrial goods such as iron and steel, but on the management, storage, and retrieval of "information." We have entered the Information Age, characterized by the information explosion. The **information explosion** is the rapid increase in the amount of knowledge and the communication of this knowledge throughout the world. Corporations like IBM, Bell Canada Enterprises, and American Telephone and Telegraph have emerged which specialize in the collection, storage, and dissemination of information.

Several centres of high tech have arisen, especially in the United States, in response to this new emphasis on information. **High tech** refers to those sophisticated forms of technology, such as computers, that are able to perform many functions with great speed and ease. Silicon Valley near San Jose, California, the Research Triangle near Raleigh, North Carolina, and the centre close to M.I.T.

(Massachussetts Institute of Technology, Boston) are three of the major centres of high tech in the United States. Canada has a similar but smaller centre near Kanata, outside Ottawa, Ontario.

The rise of these information-oriented companies has occurred simultaneously with the decline of traditional heavy industries in the developed world. The United States, Great Britain, France, West Germany, and Belgium, once industrial giants, have experienced factory closings and heavy losses in iron and steel, textiles, shipbuilding, and even automobile manufacturing.

At the same time, some LDCs have built up a sizeable heavy industrial base. With their lower wage rates, fewer government regulations, and tax advantages, corporations find such LDCs as Taiwan, South Korea, Malaysia, and Singapore attractive as locations for heavy industries.

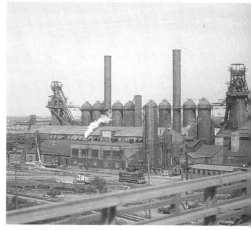

A US steel plant which has been closed, and a large shipbuilding facility in South Korea

This shift of so-called traditional industries has implications for both ends of the process. In the industrialized world, for example, jobs and taxes are lost when factories close and communities search for new industries to replace them.

Other trends are developing in industry and the world economy as well. A new trend in the world economy is the amassing of large concentrations of capital by a few banks and financial organizations. Some of this money can be moved around the world quickly to be invested for the best rate of return. This influences the rise and fall of the value of world currencies such as the American dollar and the British pound.

In October 1987, the stock markets of the world experienced the greatest fall in stock values in the twentieth century. What began as nervousness on the stock market in Tokyo spread around the world within hours. Billions of dollars were slashed off the values of stocks, and the world financial markets were severely shaken. The interdependency of national economies was made visible, as well as the importance of the movement of funds around the world.

There is also a great deal of centralization in other areas. National governments have become enormous entities, sometimes the largest employer in a country. As outlined in the discussion on multinational corporations, when decisions are made at the head office, the impact is felt around the world.

At the same time, there is a trend toward decentralization in other areas of the economy. Many small businesses have developed, even in the industrialized world, and decision making is decentralized. Protests from separatist groups show the trend toward the creation of smaller political units which are more meaningful to the people who support them. Separatists active in Sri Lanka, northern Spain, Northern Ireland, and the Philippines are examples of the people's desire to develop more autonomous political entities. Clearly, they meet opposition from the governments in power.

Questions

41. In our society, why is information becoming so important to our lifestyles and our industries?

42. As the emphasis in the industrialized world begins to shift from the traditional manufacturing industries to informational industries, what changes will likely occur in the types of skills that are required?

43. What benefit is there for the industrialized world in the loss of traditional industries to other countries?

44. As more countries become involved in the production of manufactured goods, what trends begin to develop in the world economy as a whole?

45. What positive and negative results are to be expected from the increasing centralization of great amounts of capital in large corporations?

Conclusion

The world is changing very quickly at present from an economic standpoint. Important trends include the development of global money markets, the introduction of new computer-related technology, the improvement of communications, and the rapid growth of a wide range of service and information-related industries. At the same time, some countries have not participated in the economic growth and prosperity enjoyed by the industrialized world. Such countries are experiencing problems because of unwise leadership, lack of infrastructure and education, and an inability to sell their products to countries that want them. These two opposite trends characterize the world economic scene today and foreshadow the patterns for the future.

Vocabulary

industrialization

money economy

bartering

black market

appropriate technology

labour-intensive

cottage industries

pre-industrial economy

Industrial Revolution

mass production

capital

underemployment

colonies

insurrections

multinational corporations

tax holiday

neocolonialism

capitalism

free enterprise

communism

bourgeoisie

mixed economy

socialist economy

hierarchy

infrastructure

automation

capital-intensive

urbanization

entrepreneurs

information explosion

high tech

Independent Study

1. (a) On a map of the world, mark the major empires of the world around the year 1900.

   (b) List these empires in order of size, from largest to smallest.

   (c) Using your atlas, list the various raw materials which each imperial power would receive from its respective colonies.

   (d) What difficulties can you discover, from a geographic point of view, in maintaining empires of the size you have noted?

   (e) After the collapse of the empires, what economic or trading patterns were likely to be maintained? Suggest reasons for your answers.

2. (a) Select a large multinational corporation and name the location of its head office. Describe the range of goods or services it produces, the extent of its operations beyond its country of origin, and its basic financial data such as sales, profits, growth, etc.

   (b) What role does this company play in the transfer of technology to the developing world?

   (c) What events or long-term developments might threaten the economic future of this company?

   (d) What aspects of the company's activities might an LDC government find attractive?

   (e) Based on the information you have gathered, evaluate this company's role in the world economy.

3. Select a developing nation and analyze its past and present economic conditions and the future prospects for its economic development. Use the following as guidelines for your research:

   - its geographic location, including climate, physical features, agricultural base, etc.;

   - its historical background, including any colonial legacy;

   - the current level of development, including GNP per capita and other indicators of the standard of living in that country; and

   - obstacles that the country faces in its economic development, such as those which you have already researched in the preceding sections.

4. (a) Using financial newspapers and magazines, list the major industrial trends taking place in the world which could have a major impact in the next 20 years. Be specific, and give examples of where these trends are beginning to be felt today.

   (b) Compare the impact of these trends on the developed world as opposed to the developing world.

5. (a) Identify three or four major issues that affect the international economic scene today. Briefly describe each one.

   (b) What factors can you identify which influence the value of the American dollar and the Japanese yen?

   (c) What evidence can you find that the international flow of large quantities of money is important to the world economy?

   (d) How do the emotions attached to buying and selling stocks and currencies affect the international economic scene?

By the end of this chapter, you should be able to:

- identify those regions of the world where hunger, malnutrition, and related diseases are most common;
- understand some of the reasons why hunger and its related problems are so prevalent in some countries;
- examine the various possible solutions to hunger; and
- evaluate the changes which need to be implemented in underdeveloped countries to reduce the incidence of hunger.

5

Hunger

Ethiopia

Ethiopia has become a symbol to people in the developed world of the devastating effect that hunger can have on a country. Repeated droughts and famines have ravaged Ethiopia and claimed millions of lives; unfortunately, the future appears somewhat bleak for that country.

As early as 253 BC, there were reports of serious droughts and starvation in Ethiopia. Since that time, the country has experienced numerous droughts interspersed with years of relatively plentiful rainfall. In 1888, close to one-third of the population died from starvation and related diseases.

Although the outside world had been to some extent aware of the effects of Ethiopia's drought and starvation in earlier years, it was during the 1980s that the plight of this nation came to the world's attention. Mass media coverage alerted millions to the threat of starvation. In 1984-85, the country experienced a serious drought; 2 million people eventually died from hunger and related problems. In northern Ethiopia, the areas worst hit by drought, close to 80 percent of the crops failed. The government has been blamed for serious mismanagement in its efforts to deal with this situation; only after hundreds of thousands of people died from hunger-related causes did it admit to having a serious problem.

In 1987-88, another drought hit, with many of the same results as in the earlier drought. The port facilities for importing food into Ethiopia are inadequate, while roads are poor or non-existent. The government has been involved in civil war, fighting 23 rebel groups and factions in all parts of the country. Unfortunately, the region of the country which is held by the largest rebel group is also worst hit by drought and hunger. Both the government and the rebels have withheld or disrupted food shipments to the hungry for political purposes. The result has been that people have starved to death while food was available not far away.

The Ethiopian government has also launched agricultural schemes which have led to increased hunger. One such program is the establishment of Soviet-style collective farms which have produced little food. There has also been a resettlement scheme which has attempted to move more than 1.5 million farmers from the northern portion of the country to the more fertile South. Tens of thousands have died in this forced movement.

Coincident with this, the entire country has experienced serious environmental deterioration. Soil erosion has led to the loss of much rich soil and the continued deforestation has robbed the country of needed fuel as well as protection for the soil. Farming methods remain backward, food production is meagre, and living standards are among the lowest in the world.

As Ethiopia struggles for survival, observers in the developed world wonder whether those people who have donated food in the past will tire of giving and simply stop. Will there be any escape for Ethiopia from the cycles of drought and hunger?

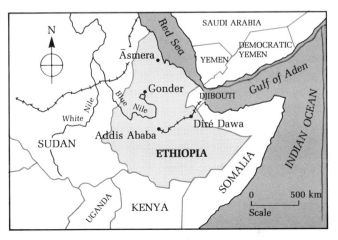

Figure 5.1
Ethiopia is located on the horn of Africa. There are some rich agricultural areas as well as regions of desert and semi-desert where the rainfall is highly erratic and the soil is poor.

Introduction

Hunger is one of the most important issues in the world today, yet its exact nature is seldom understood. What is real hunger? Who suffers from hunger? Why do we have hunger in a world of seeming plenty? These are all questions which are essential to an understanding of the issue and which will be discussed in this chapter.

Hundreds of people gather at a relief camp in northeastern Ethiopia, where food is distributed to the hungry.

What is Hunger?

In Canada, people will often make the comment "I'm hungry" when it's time for a meal or a snack. This temporary sensation is very different from the hunger experienced in many areas of the developing world. In the case of the LDCs, **hunger** can be defined as the painful sensation or state of weakness caused by the need for food. Hunger for many people is a lifelong experience. It has been estimated that approximately 600 million people around the world suffer from serious inadequacies of food intake, and the number has been growing over the last few decades.

Although hunger exists on a world scale, the starving child is not found everywhere in the developing world. This fact, however, should not affect how seriously we examine this problem.

Clearly, a great deal of suffering accompanies hunger. An adequate and balanced diet is essential for the maintenance of good health. When an individual experiences hunger over a long period of time, or has major inadequacies in the quality of his or her diet, this results in a state of **malnutrition**.

Question

1. Without reading any further in the chapter, write down your thoughts on the following topics. These will be useful later on, for you to come back to and re-examine.

   (a) Where do you think hunger is a serious problem in the world? Be specific and name regions and countries where this problem exists.

   (b) Who will suffer the most from the effects of hunger? Explain your answer.

   (c) Why do you think people are starving in the world today, despite the fact that there appears to be plenty of food?

   (d) Is significant progress being made in the fight against hunger? Explain your answer.

When someone has a diet deficient in quantity of food intake, that person is said to suffer from **undernutrition**. In simple terms, such a person does not have enough food to eat.

The states of malnutrition and undernutrition pose a major threat to human health in the developing world. When the body is weakened by lack of adequate food intake, it is open to a wide variety of diseases.

In general, there are two types of disease from which a malnourished person can suffer. The first category of illness is caused by a dietary deficiency and includes diseases such as kwashiorkor, scurvy, and marasmus. The second category is made up of infectious diseases which may lead to serious physical damage or death. Although measles or dysentery, for example, are generally not considered to be a serious health problem in the industrialized world, in the developing world they are major killers.

Children are most often the victims of both deficiency and infectious diseases. UNICEF estimates that up to 14 million children die every year from diseases associated with malnutrition. Close to 5 million children die every year from dysentery alone.

Questions

2. Why are children so often the ones to suffer from hunger and malnutrition?

3. (a) What patterns can you detect from the map in Figure 5.2?

   (b) Obtain an atlas and examine some of the thematic maps of the world. What physical geographic problems are located in those areas which currently experience the highest levels of malnutrition?

   (c) Judging from other thematic maps in your atlas, what major economic activities are carried out or are lacking in those areas of the world that are severely affected by malnutrition?

The plight of children in the developing world is frequently tragic. Their small body size as well as their lack of resistance to illness leaves them open to attacks of disease. In addition, children often suffer from a poorly balanced diet and lack of proper medical care. In the event of the loss of a parent, the children are caught without outside assistance to help in their survival.

**Figure 5.2
The Distribution of Serious Malnutrition Around the World**

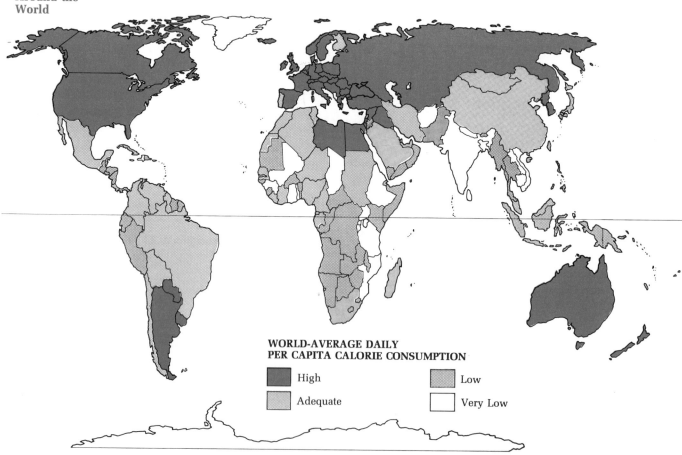

**WORLD-AVERAGE DAILY
PER CAPITA CALORIE CONSUMPTION**

High

Adequate

Low

Very Low

Early deficiencies in a child's diet can cause permanent damage. For example, 90 percent of the growth of the human brain is completed before the age of five. Inadequate diet can seriously impair brain development and scar a child for life. One estimate indicates that each year in Africa alone, 5 million children die and 5 million are crippled permanently as a result of hunger and malnutrition. In order to protect our human "capital," steps must be taken to protect today's children.

Question

4. (a) In which ways are the children of the world human "capital?"

   (b) What impact will there be on a continent such as Africa 20 years in the future as a result of the impact of malnutrition on its children today?

   (c) Why do you think that female children suffer from malnutrition and its associated problems more often than male children?

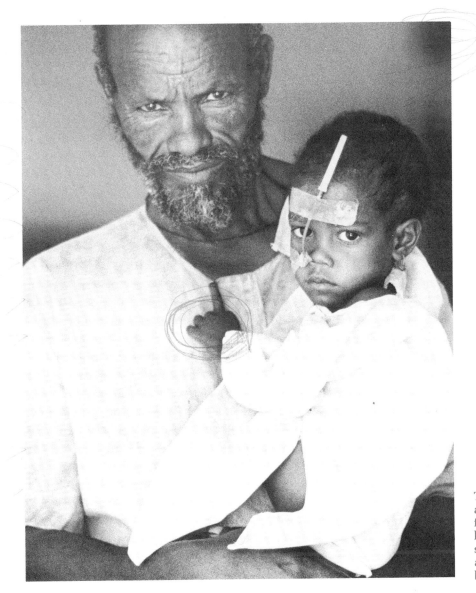

This child, in the arms of his father, no longer has enough strength to eat, and must be fed by perfusion.

Following is a summary chart of some of the major diet deficiency diseases affecting people living in the developing world particularly.

Table 5.1
Diet Deficiency
Disease

Disease	Cause	Symptoms	Cure
Kwashiorkor	severe protein deficiency	- loss of skin colour and hair colour - diarrhea, anemia - depression - weak, thin muscles - water-logged tissue cells - can lead to death	- well-balanced diet
Marasmus	diet deficient in both protein and calories (common with bottle-fed babies in LDCs, sometimes referred to as the disease of starvation)	- progressive wasting of body tissue - low temperature - wasted limbs - sunken eyes - appearance of old age - loose skin in folds - can cause death	- restoration of a diet high in protein and calories (children over six months of age survive better)
Beriberi	a severe vitamin B1 deficiency caused by diets overly dependent on cereals for energy (common among people who eat a great deal of rice that has been excessively milled)	- emaciation or swelling of body - personality changes - damage of nerves and heart - paralysis of body - listlessness	- balanced diet
Pellagra	deficiency of niacin and tryptophan (occurs among populations which are overly dependent on maize)	- skin ulcers - digestive and mental problems - cracking of skin - inflammation of mouth, tongue - diarrhea, vomiting, loss of weight - can lead to death	- high-calorie diet with rest
Scurvy	severe vitamin C deficiency	- extreme weakness, low fever, weight loss - loss of appetite - spongy gums - bleeding gums, lips - bleeding under skin - can cause death if not caught in time	- diet high in vitamin C
Rickets	severe vitamin D deficiency and a lack of calcium and phosphorus	- defective bone growth - pot belly, bent bones - bowed legs	- balanced diet with enough vitamin D, calcium, phosphorus

As mentioned before, children who are weakened by malnutrition or undernutrition are highly susceptible to infectious diseases. Measles, mumps, tetanus, and whooping cough, for example, are all diseases which take a high human toll every day in the developing world. It should be noted that, with only a very small investment of ten cents or less per child, inoculations can be administered to children. Such inoculations are highly cost effective, since they immunize a child against a variety of diseases for years.

Possible Solutions

UNICEF has been involved in helping children from its inception following World War II. In the years since, UNICEF has been active in advocacy for children, protecting them from hunger, abuse, and neglect. From its years of work, UNICEF has identified five strategies for saving the lives of children in the developing world as well as for improving standards of living.

1. **Oral Rehydration Therapy (ORT)** involves mixing salt, sugar, and clean water, and feeding it to children with diarrhea. ORT stops the diarrhea and the resultant dehydration. The cost is approximately ten cents for one packet of ORT to treat one child.

2. Growth charts for infants and young children are used to monitor their physical progress. Those children whose growth lags behind the norm require special attention before the damage to their bodies is permanent.

3. The use of vaccines to protect children from common infectious diseases is a major weapon in achieving better health. An immunization "gun" can be used to vaccinate hundreds of children in a short period of time.

4. Promotion of breastfeeding is important, since it is not only cheap but also more nutritious, more sanitary, and safer for infants than bottle-feeding.

5. Food supplements for infants are supplied when necessary. Vitamin A or iodine are good examples of possible supplements.

Questions

5. (a) Where in North America would you expect to see deficiency diseases? Give reasons for your answer.

   (b) Why are these diseases said to be a "silent crisis?"

6. (a) What role can education play in providing adequate diets for the children?

   (b) What form should dietary education take? Be specific in your answer and mention the groups you would target, as well as the type of individual you would select to do the teaching. Keep in mind that most people in the developing world still live in villages and that education must not be considered by itself but in conjunction with other programs or changes.

7. (a) What major differences do you notice between the diseases that have been listed in Table 5.1 and the types of diseases that are common in industrialized countries such as Canada?

   (b) What do you think accounts for these differences?

   (c) Why are the most deadly diseases of the developed world more difficult to cure or eliminate than the major diseases of the developing world?

8. Which of the five programs would be the most difficult to implement fully? Explain your reasoning.

Primary Health Care

Many countries such as China, North Yemen, and Pakistan have begun to introduce **primary health care** to help reduce the ravages of disease and malnutrition. The concept is to train large numbers of local health care workers to work in their own villages. After only a few weeks' training, these health care workers are equipped to diagnose simple health problems, prescribe basic medicines, and educate the local people in the area of health care. More serious problems are referred to larger clinics or hospitals, where they are available.

Questions

9. Why are these local health care workers sometimes referred to as "barefoot doctors?"

10. Suggest several reasons why the training of local health care workers is an appropriate undertaking for much of the developing world.

Right, mothers with their children wait at a small clinic in Ghana to see a local health care worker; below, a young boy is examined by a local health care worker in a rural district in Ghana.

Profiles of Hunger

Hunger is widespread throughout the world, and its effects are devastating. However, for each person or family experiencing it, it is an individual catastrophe. This is true wherever it occurs. The following profiles have been chosen from widely different areas around the world to illustrate some of the forces that have acted to bring about hunger, poverty, and malnutrition.

Profile #1

Jose lives in the countryside of the Dominican Republic. He and his wife have eight children, all of them under the age of 14. Jose and his wife had four other children who died from infectious diseases before they reached the age of three.

With only 2 ha of land to farm, one mule, and virtually no modern farming technology, Jose has struggled hard to wrest a living from the land. Over the last few years, he has had poor harvests and has not been able to feed his family well. As a result, he has borrowed heavily at high interest rates to buy grain to plant and to buy food for his family. This year, unfortunately, Jose was unable to pay the interest due on his loans and the large landholder who lent him the money repossessed his land. Now, to farm it, Jose must rent back the land that was once his. This means that he has less money than before, and cannot afford to produce as much food.

Jose wonders what kind of future there will be for his family. Despite their industriousness, Jose and his family have major problems to overcome.

Profile #2

Gita is a 20-year-old mother who lives on the streets of Calcutta, India. She was born in a small village north of Calcutta in the state of West Bengal. With only one year of formal schooling, Gita left the village and her 14 brothers and sisters to come to Calcutta. At the time, she was only 13 years of age.

Since her arrival in Calcutta, she has worked as a maid for two middle-class familes who help her out with clothing for her and her daughter from time to time. Until two years ago, she lived in a **bustee**, a registered community of the very poor. When the cost of living became too great, Gita moved out and began to live on the streets. "Life is better here than in my village," she says. On average, she earns 90 cents a day for a 60 h work week.

Gita's husband no longer lives with her and her three-year-old daughter, but Gita feels pleased just to be able to survive. Her diet is far from adequate, but she tries to provide food for her daughter every day. Gita does not try to look too far into the future, although she does hope for a better day to come.

Profile #3

Abdul is 42 years old and lives in northern Nigeria with his wife and six children. Two older children have married and moved away from home. Three other children died in early childhood. The family is able to cope well with adversity, however, and works long hours on the farm.

Abdul's farm is 5 ha in size and is located on the southern edge of the semi-desert region called the Sahel. The rainfall is erratic at best, and the desert blows sand in from the north. This year, the village well has gone dry and the villagers have not been able to dig it out again. Crops have been poor over the last few years and the prospects do not appear to be improving. Many nights, Abdul and his family go hungry.

Abdul's wife does most of the work on the farm itself, as most women in rural Nigeria do, and she spends much of the day travelling to obtain water and carry it back home. She has never seen the crops as poor as they are this year.

Abdul spends his days in discussion of village matters with the other men of the local area. He does some of the work on the land and some general work such as repairs to the family house.

Two of their children have received some education, and Abdul is optimistic that his children will achieve a higher standard of living than he and his wife share.

Profile #4

Zhang lives on a large collective farm south of Beijing, China. She is 23 years old and is not married. Zhang grew up knowing hunger first-hand. One of 12 children, she lived on a very poor collective where crops were often insufficient to feed the people who worked the farm. Zhang did attend school for six years, and left home to work on a larger collective at the age of 17.

Under the new regulations governing the operation of collective farms, those who work hard are able to keep increased profits. Zhang is one of those who have benefitted from this new scheme. Although her diet is far from that of a woman in the developed world, she is now able to have one substantial meal per day. Her diet lacks protein, but she has access to clean water and even some fruit. At night, though, she often feels that hungry sensation.

Zhang has plans to marry two years from now and looks forward to having the one child that parents are permitted to have in China under the population control policies. The future holds promise for Zhang and she eagerly anticipates what will come. The long 16 h days that she works seem to have paid off for her.

Questions

11. (a) After examining the four personal profiles presented above, what similarities can you note among the situations of all the people discussed?

    (b) What do you think is meant by the term "putting a face on poverty and hunger?"

12. (a) Suggest some of the causes of the hunger and malnutrition depicted in each one of the profiles.

    (b) In the light of these profiles, evaluate the following statement: "People are poor and hungry because they are lazy and refuse to work hard."

    (c) To what extent are these four people and their families victims of forces beyond their control?

    (d) How might agricultural education have improved the lives of the people in the profiles? What would have been necessary to include in this education?

13. How have these people reacted to poverty and hunger in each case?

14. (a) For each of the four people here, suggest options which might help them escape from their current state of hunger and poverty.

    (b) What obstacles could prevent the implementation of the plans which you suggested in part (a)?

Government Policy

This issue of hunger in the developing world is extremely complex, and involves many interrelated factors. Considering any one of the factors which contribute to hunger without dealing with other ones leads to an incomplete understanding of the issue. When the role of pests is considered in the context of hunger, for example, it is important to evaluate government policy toward pest management as well as attempts by local farmers to control such pests.

Governments of developing countries can be seen to be part of the hunger problem rather than part of its solution. Some government policies can actually discourage the production of food. In a typical situation, the government is concerned about unrest in the cities and is anxious to keep food prices low. Officials believe this will prevent riots or disorder, so they buy food cheaply on world markets. The prices they pay to their own farmers for crops fall, therefore, and many farmers are forced into bankruptcy. The farmers leave the farms and head for the cities where they may obtain a low-paying job, if they are fortunate. Later on, the government may run short of cash and be unable to purchase cheap food any longer. The result is that hunger spreads among both the urban and rural poor.

The problems associated with importing cheap food into countries of the developing world are made more serious by the shipment of free grain from countries such as Canada. Free grain is often sent to developing countries as part of the effort to fight hunger. When it arrives at its destination, it has much the same effect on the local farm economy as the cheap food which is bought on the international market. Farmers suffer as the local market prices are depressed, and there is little incentive for the government to increase local food production.

One side effect of the flood of food imported into the developing world is the change in local eating habits. People begin to switch from traditional to westernized foods. In some cases, the traditional foods are nutritionally better, but lose out in the competition against fast foods and western food tastes.

Questions

15. How might the governments of the developing countries, suffering from low food production on their farms, satisfy both the farmers and the urban dwellers?

16. Canada and the United States have benefitted from exporting food to the developing world. In the short run, these exports may appear to be beneficial to all concerned. What problems might appear in the future? Explain your answer fully.

Other General Factors Which Contribute to Hunger

So far in this chapter, a number of different reasons have been examined for the hunger and poverty which so much of the world is experiencing. There are, however, additional factors which influence the production, distribution, and consumption of food. Because of the great variety of geographical and political conditions found within the developing world, each of the factors will be more or less important according to the country or region being discussed.

Pests

Rats, locusts, beetles, and other pests destroy large quantities of food throughout the world. As much as 40-50 percent of crops in the developing world is damaged by these pests to some extent. Of the various pests in the world, the rat is generally considered to be the single most destructive. Rats are extremely hardy and are able to survive and thrive under adverse conditions. The rat is omnivorous and is ingenious at obtaining food.

Rats can also reproduce very quickly. If all the offspring from a single pair of rats were to survive, there would be 20 million rats at the end of three years. Rapid reproduction makes the rat a more serious threat than it would be otherwise. Whatever food a rat does not consume, it can contaminate through droppings or through bacteria it can carry. In India, it has been estimated that 10-25 percent of the total grain output is destroyed by rats. In north central India, however, rats are honoured and are fed rather than fought.

In recent years, some rats have developed an immunity to certain poisons used against them. These rats have been dubbed "super-rats."

Questions

17. (a) What conditions in the industrialized world encourage the presence of rats?

    (b) What could be done to reduce the rat populations of the world?

18. Alberta is one province which is considered to be rat-free. What type of program do you think would be effective in Alberta to keep it this way?

19. If it is technically possible to eliminate rats from at least certain areas of Canada, why do you think it has not been done? Explain your answer fully.

20. (a) Why is the rat considered to be such an imposing enemy in the developing world?

    (b) What could happen if rat control programs were allowed to deteriorate in the tropical developing world? Explain your answer.

Other pests can do considerable damage to crops and stored food as well. Beetles, for example, can infest grain which is stored improperly. Various beetles live, eat, and lay eggs in stored grain. Locusts also pose serious threats to crops. When they move in swarms of several hundred million, locusts can devour thousands of tonnes of grain within a few weeks. Some locust swarms have been known to darken the skies as they fly overhead. In recent years, Africa has been particularly hard hit by locusts. Spraying breeding areas early in the locust life cycle has helped to eliminate some of the dangers of the locust swarms.

Figure 5.3
A Norway rat

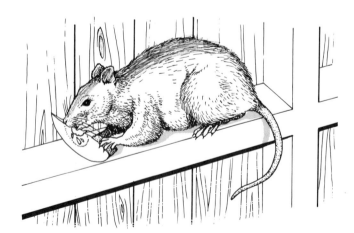

Figure 5.4
Loss of Food
During Crop
Production and
Distribution

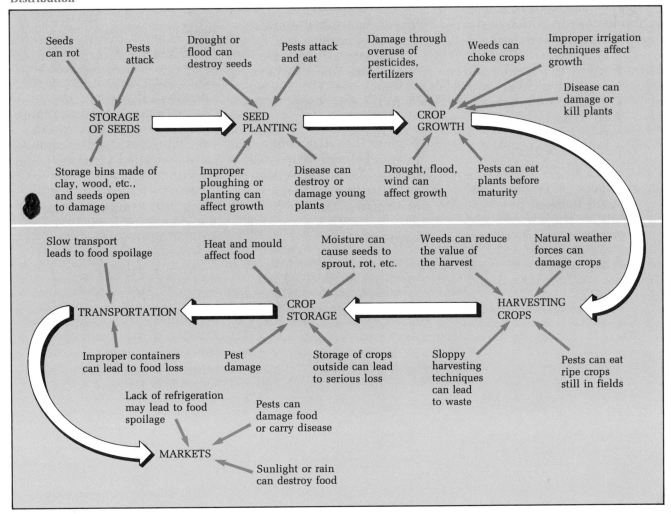

STORAGE OF SEEDS

Seeds can rot
Pests attack
Storage bins made of clay, wood, etc., and seeds open to damage

SEED PLANTING

Drought or flood can destroy seeds
Pests attack and eat
Improper ploughing or planting can affect growth
Disease can destroy or damage young plants

CROP GROWTH

Damage through overuse of pesticides, fertilizers
Weeds can choke crops
Improper irrigation techniques affect growth
Disease can damage or kill plants
Drought, flood, wind can affect growth
Pests can eat plants before maturity

TRANSPORTATION

Slow transport leads to food spoilage
Improper containers can lead to food loss

CROP STORAGE

Heat and mould affect food
Moisture can cause seeds to sprout, rot, etc.
Pest damage
Storage of crops outside can lead to serious loss

HARVESTING CROPS

Weeds can reduce the value of the harvest
Natural weather forces can damage crops
Sloppy harvesting techniques can lead to waste
Pests can eat ripe crops still in fields

MARKETS

Lack of refrigeration may lead to food spoilage
Pests can damage food or carry disease
Sunlight or rain can destroy food

Questions

21. How do pests contribute to food losses? Refer to the specific stages of food production in which pests are particularly active.

22. (a) Suggest five simple and inexpensive changes you think might reduce food losses and help ease the hunger problems of the developing world.

    (b) What specific obstacles could there be to introducing the changes you have suggested?

    (c) What general approach could ensure that the suggestions you made in part (a) would be implemented?

    (d) At what income level would farmers be helped most by the changes that you have suggested? Give reasons to back up your answer.

23. Discuss this statement fully: "Human mismanagement of food production and distribution is the key to an understanding of food losses in the developing world."

A locust in Uganda

Pest Control

Efforts to control or eliminate pests have achieved varying degrees of success around the world. Pests like locusts have been brought under control in much of southern Africa, for example. Yet, in other situations, such as in a few of the islands of Indonesia, the rat population is almost out of control. Success in pest control, therefore, holds promise only if applied vigorously and consistently.

Pesticides are a potent weapon in controlling the destruction of food. When applied wisely, pesticides can destroy up to 97 percent of the insects in a rice field, for example. When used indiscriminately, however, pesticides can poison people, their food, their animals, or their water supply. In addition, insect pests have begun to develop resistance to certain pesticides, allowing them to thrive despite the use of potent chemicals. In some cases, stronger and stronger pesticides have been developed to battle the pests. Unfortunately, these more potent chemicals pose a great threat to human life.

Natural pest control systems are being developed, and the future of these systems looks promising. The concept here is not to try to wipe out all pests, but to keep insects at tolerable levels. This means applying natural restraints like planting mixed crops in the same fields, cleaning up insect breeding grounds like mosquito swamps, and introducing natural predators.

Mixed cropping is a particularly interesting option for pest control. When mixed crops are planted in the same field and crops are rotated, the soil is able to maintain its fertility. It also reduces pest invasions and provides a green cover on the soil under tall crops such as maize. Mixed cropping also prevents excessive moisture loss and reduces soil erosion.

A wide range of other alternatives has been suggested for controlling pests. Irradiation of food kills bacteria and insects and prolongs the storage life of foods. In this case, X-rays, gamma rays, or high energy electrons are used to preserve food. Some objections have been raised to this practice, because of the possible effects radiation would have on people's health. Food can also be frozen to slow bacterial or enzyme action which leads to food spoilage. Even refrigeration of foods reduces food spoilage.

Questions

24. What disadvantages would intercropping or mixed cropping present to many farmers?

25. What other techniques can be used to prevent food spoilage?

Intercropping is a common practice in much of the developing world. In this photo, you can see bean plants growing around the stalks of maize plants. Beans return to the soil some of the nutrients which maize uses, thereby increasing the food productivity per hectare.

Bangladesh

Bangladesh is one of the poorest countries in the world. It faces all the basic problems which confront nations of the developing world, yet it faces other serious obstacles, too. The statistics in Table 5.2 illustrate some of these obstacles.

**Table 5.2
Basic Statistics
for Bangladesh**

Population: 102 000 000 (8th largest in the world)

Population Density: 714 people /km²

Age Distribution: 0-14: 43%; 15-59: 52%; 60 + : 4% (figures are rounded)

Population Growth Rate: 2.8% per year

Life Expectancy: 47 years

Illiteracy rate: 25%

Religion: 83% Moslem; 16% Hindu; 1% Christian, Buddhist, other

Infant Mortality Rate: 153 per 1000 live births

Climate: Hot and humid; average temperature 29°C, with one of the highest rainfall totals in the world

Land Quality: 66% is arable

Doctors: 6.9 per 10 000 population

Disease risks: Malaria, yellow fever and cholera are still common

GNP per capita: $120

Labour Profile: 77% of the work force is employed in agriculture, forestry, and fishing

10% of the work force is employed by government

5% of the work force is in manufacturing

4% of the work force is in trade

4% of the work force is in construction, services, etc.

Roads: 4000 km of paved roads

Television: 3 per 1000 population

**Figure 5.5
Bangladesh and
Its Location
Relative to Other
Countries of
Southern Asia**

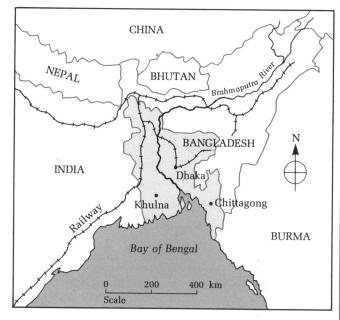

Questions

26. (a) Examine Table 5.2. Compare these statistics for Bangladesh to those of Canada available in the Appendix to this book. What major differences can you note? Explain their significance.

    (b) What specific major problems does Bangladesh face?

    (c) Which statistics would appear to indicate that Bangladesh has a serious hunger problem? Explain your reasoning.

Historical Background of Bangladesh

Over 1600 years ago, Bangladesh was the part of the Gupta Empire which stretched across northern India. The Gupta culture flourished for over 160 years. From that time to this, many outside forces have moved across Bangladesh, the most recent of these being the prolonged rule of the British over India, of which Bangladesh was a part. Bangladesh was incorporated as part of the British Empire, but after World War II, Britain withdrew from southern Asia. When it withdrew, it left behind conflicts which were to erupt into violence within a generation.

The British divided up the Indian sub-continent into basically two countries — India, which was largely Hindu, and Pakistan, which was essentially Moslem. Unfortunately, Pakistan was split geographically into East and West, on either side of India. This geographic split presented fundamental problems of transportation and economics, as well as the political near-impossibility of governing a country in two halves, 1600 km apart. The people of East Pakistan (later Bangladesh) resented the power that West Pakistan had over them as well as political decisions which paid little attention to their particular needs.

These frustrations reached a head in the late 1960s and, in 1971, Bangladesh proclaimed independence from Pakistan. This action precipitated a civil war which lasted until 1972, when Bangladesh won the war and achieved full independence. The geographic separation of Pakistan from Bangladesh, as well as India's support of Bangladesh, contributed to the outcome of the war.

Clearly, Bangladesh's birth as an independent nation was a violent one. Since 1972, a number of coups and political crises have shaken Bangladesh. Other incidents, such as rioting over government-imposed food policies, have demonstrated the pressures people live under.

No less serious than the political problems have been the physical disasters which have assaulted the country. In July of 1985, for example, a monsoon devastated portions of northern Bangladesh, killing thousands and leaving 400 000 stranded and homeless. Other storms of massive proportions have flooded large areas of the country since it declared independence in 1972.

Since much of the country is flat and only a few metres above sea level, it is particularly vulnerable to serious flooding. The worst flooding in the country's history occurred in September 1988, when three-quarters of the country was submerged, leaving 25 million people homeless.

Although the soil is rich throughout much of Bangladesh, farms are small and farmers poor. Farming techniques tend to be backward, and few farmers are able to afford fertilizers or pesticides for their crops.

Bangladesh is one country of Asia where the pressure on the land is great. The population growth rate being high, new land for the growing rural population is in short supply. The delta of the Ganges River is one region where new land is being created. With the abundance of soil that is washed down from the mountains, hills, and plains of India and Bangladesh, the new islands that are formed in the Bay of Bengal are both fertile and flat. The rural poor of Bangladesh have moved onto these newly created islands in search of land to farm. Unfortunately, this land is also prone to flooding from the tropical storms which move onshore from the Indian Ocean. The results can be devastating; since 1972, tens of thousands have lost their lives on or near these islands.

Bangladesh has received a great deal of foreign aid, from outright gifts of food to technical agricultural aid. The impact on the country has not been significant, however, and some critics maintain that Bangladesh is actually suffering as a result of inappropriate aid. Free grain distributed to the hungry has led to hardship among farmers (as outlined earlier in this chapter, for example).

As can be seen in the statistics given for the country, Bangladesh has a very limited industrial base and little international trade. Its imports include large quantities of grains, fuels, and manufactured goods. Bangladesh exports far less than it imports, in dollar terms. The infrastructure in Bangladesh is limited, and few farmers have access to resources which could help improve crop output or improve life expectancy for themselves or their families.

Questions

27. Although average citizens of Bangladesh may not have been actually involved in a civil war or political upheavals, what repercussions might they have felt from the political problems of the country?

28. Besides the political factors which have affected Bangladesh, what others have contributed to its widespread hunger and malnutrition?

This family in Bangladesh faces a life with little food and the threat of natural disaster.

29. (a) Examine Table 5.2 once again, with particular emphasis on the labour profile. How does the percentage of the work force employed by the government compare to other sectors of the economy? What significance does the size of the government payroll have for a very poor country such as Bangladesh?

(b) What statistics listed in Table 5.2 indicate that the introduction of new ideas and technology in the country could be a slow process?

30. Bangladesh is considered to be caught in a "cycle of poverty." Using the information which has been provided, create a diagram to illustrate what is meant by the term "cycle of poverty." For your diagram, use a full sheet of paper and arrows to connect the various headings. Include as many details as you can, and show their relationship to each other.

Statistical Analysis #1

Statistics provide useful insight into the nature of hunger in the developing world. Africa is a continent which, south of the Sahara Desert, suffers from hunger and its related problems as much as other regions, and sometimes more. It should be noted that Africa also contains large quantities of natural resources such as oil in the north, gold in South Africa, and numerous minerals in the central portion of the continent. The statistics on pages 180 and 181 will help to identify some of the problems which Africa faces as well as some of their causes and effects.

Questions

To answer questions 31 to 35, examine Table 5.3.

31. What could explain the absence of statistics for so many countries in Africa?

32. (a) Which statistics reveal a major difference in quality of life between the urban and rural dwellers of Africa?

(b) What importance do the statistics you cited in part (a) have on the movement of people within African countries?

(c) What reasons can you suggest for such a difference between rural and urban standards of living?

33. (a) Explain the meaning of the last column in Table 5.3 on household income share.

(b) Although statistics on household income are missing for many African countries, what pattern would you expect to see? Explain your reasoning.

(c) What importance would these statistics on household income have for Africa?

(d) How might the pattern of household income be changed to benefit Africans with the lowest income? What might be the effect on other categories illustrated in Table 5.3?

34. What signs of hope or progress can you identify in Africa?

35. Is there a relationship between different columns of statistics in Table 5.3? If so, what are these relationships? Explain your answer fully.

**Table 5.3
Statistical
Analysis of
Africa**

	% access to clean water (1987)		Population Per Physician (000's) (1987)*	Population annual growth rate (1987)*		% in absolute poverty		Household income share	
	urban	rural		total	urban	urban	rural	top 20%	bottom 40%
East Africa*									
Burundi	90	20	45.4	2.2	2.3	55	85	-	-
Comoros	53	20	16.0	2.6	13.2	-	-	-	-
Djibouti	50	20	2.2	6.0	7.9	-	-	-	-
Ethiopia	93	4	88.1	2.7	8.0	60	65	-	-
Kenya	61	21	10.1	4.0	7.5	10	55	60	9
Madagascar	73	9	10.0	2.9	5.6	50	50	-	-
Mauritius	100	98	1.9	1.4	3.4	12	12	55	14
Rwanda	55	60	29.1	3.3	6.6	30	90	-	-
Seychelles	86	80	2.2	1.1	4.4	-	-	-	-
Somalia	60	20	15.6	2.8	5.4	40	70	-	-
Sudan	-	-	9.1	2.9	7.3	-	85	50	14
Uganda	45	12	21.3	2.8	0.5	-	-	47	17
Southern Africa									
Angola	85	10	-	2.5	5.8	-	-	-	-
Botswana	98	72	7.4	-	-	40	55	60	8
Lesotho	37	14	18.7	2.6	18.9	50	55	-	-
Malawi	82	54	47.6	3.3	8.2	25	85	51	22
Mozambique	82	2	39.2	2.6	6.4	-	-	-	-
Swaziland	80	30	7.2	3.4	10.9	45	50	-	-
Tanzania	85	47	24.3	3.4	8.5	10	60	50	16
Zambia	70	32	7.1	3.3	6.1	25	-	63	10
Zimbabwe	100	10	6.1	3.2	5.8	-	-	69	8
Central Africa									
Cameroon	35	22	13.7	3.2	8.1	15	40	-	-
Cen. Af. Rep.	40	5	22.4	2.3	4.6	-	91	-	-

Country									
Chad	–	–	56	30	6.5	2.2	47.9	30	30
Congo	–	–	–	–	5.4	3.1	5.3	46	8
Equat. Guinea	–	–	–	–	5.9	1.7	62.0	47	–
Gabon	9	68	–	–	5.9	3.0	11.6	75	34
Zaire	–	–	80	–	7.9	3.0	13.5	43	5
West Africa									
Benin	–	–	65	–	5.0	2.8	17.5	26	15
Burkina Faso	–	–	–	–	4.8	1.8	55.9	27	31
Cape Verde	–	–	–	–	3.8	1.6	6.4	100	21
Gambia	–	40	–	–	6.7	3.5	11.6	100	33
Ghana	–	–	–	–	4.8	2.7	6.7	72	39
Guinea	–	–	–	–	5.8	2.2	8.1	91	2
Guinea-Bissau	–	–	–	–	6.5	3.7	7.5	21	37
Ivory Coast	20	50	26	30	8.3	4.5	–	51	75
Liberia	11	73	–	23	5.5	3.4	12.4	50	24
Mali	–	–	48	27	10.7	2.5	25.4	58	20
Mauritania	14	55	12	12	7.0	2.1	14.1	80	16
Niger	–	–	35	–	7.0	3.0	37.2	48	34
Nigeria	–	–	–	–	4.7	2.8	10.5	60	30
Sao Tome	–	–	–	–	5.5	2.2	2.5	98	79
Senegal	–	–	82	–	3.9	2.8	13.1	63	27
Sierra Leone	15	53	65	–	3.8	1.9	17.3	58	8
Togo	–	–	–	42	6.5	2.8	18.5	68	26

Possible Solutions to Problems of Hunger in the Developing World

At times, our mass media portray hunger as an insoluble problem which steadily worsens. Indeed, hunger is a complex and sometimes baffling issue. It is unfair to assume that nothing can be done about it, however, or that those people who are caught in the midst of it are incapable of doing much to escape it. There have been many successes in the battle to rid the world of hunger, though not as spectacular as one would hope. Slowly, however, signs of progress are beginning to emerge. A few of these signs of hope will be discussed in the next few pages.

Breast-feeding

Breast-feeding has become a key health issue in the developing world, and one which is essential to the elimination or reduction of hunger. Simple and cost effective, breast-feeding provides a solution to infant nutritional problems which can dramatically alter infant death rates and ultimately the future of all nations in the developing world.

Bottle-feeding Versus Breast-feeding

Until a generation or so ago, breast-feeding was standard practice. Perfectly suited for the nutritional needs of the infant, mothers' milk is high in quality and purity. If breast-feeding were accepted universally in the developing world, the incidence of infant deaths, malnutrition, and disease would be significantly decreased. Despite its advantages, breast-feeding is losing out in popularity to bottle-feeding. Especially in the developing world, bottle-feeding is becoming the preferred method of infant nutrition.

There are a number of negative aspects to the adoption of bottle-feeding. One of these is cost. Although few Canadian parents consider the cost of formula to be burdensome, some families in the developing world can spend as much as one-third of their annual income on infant formula. The problems associated with the use of formula in the developing countries, however, extend beyond the cost. Proper hygiene is essential in its preparation, a difficult condition to meet in much of the developing world. Clean water, for example, is rare in places.

Table 5.4
Advantages and Disadvantages of Breast-feeding and Bottle-feeding

Breast-Feeding Advantages	Bottle Feeding Advantages
1) Breast milk supplies all the nutrients a baby needs; it is perfectly suited for an infant.	1) Someone besides the mother can feed the baby, when necessary.
2) Colostrum, a fluid produced before the breast milk comes in, contains antibodies which protect the infant from disease.	2) In rare cases, a mother cannot breast-feed, and bottle-feeding is a viable option.
3) There is little or no cost, apart from ensuring an adequate diet for the mother.	3) Bottle-feeding gives the mother freedom to work where her infant cannot be taken.
4) Breast milk is sanitary.	4) Bottle-feeding may prevent deterioration of health of a malnourished mother.
5) Breast-feeding is convenient for mothers working in fields, etc.	5) Formula can be sterile if used properly.
6) Feeding on demand can act as a method of birth control.	6) Baby can be kept alive if mother is seriously ill or dies.
7) Breast-feeding develops a close mother-child relationship.	
8) Breast-feeding can help the mother to lose weight gained in pregnancy.	
9) Breast-feeding can reduce the possibility of later allergies to food.	
10) Breast-fed babies experience fewer skin disorders and only rare constipation.	
11) Breast milk is always at the proper temperature.	

Disadvantages	Disadvantages
1) The mother is not free to leave the baby for long between feedings.	1) Formula is expensive.
2) Some malnourished mothers produce milk that is lower in quality than desired.	2) Formula must be mixed exactly according to instructions. This is difficult for illiterate mothers.
3) Nursing can be tiring for the mother.	3) Bottles and nipples must be sterilized before use. This requires precious fuel, and is difficult.
4) Nursing may be painful or difficult for the mother.	4) Water must be boiled to use in formula.
5) A mother with a breast infection may not be able to feed her child.	5) Formula should be kept in refrigerator after mixing.
	6) Formula contains large amounts of sugar.
	7) Some infants can develop an allergy to formula.

An infant who is fed formula which is improperly prepared, as with impure water, will often experience **gastroenteritis**, a serious upset of the digestive system. Gastroenteritis can bring on severe diarrhea, dehydration, and even death. UNICEF has estimated that close to 1 million children die each year from problems associated with bottle-feeding.

Under the impact of aggressive, western-style radio and television advertising, bottle-feeding is gaining widespread acceptance. Some corporations, like Nestlé's of Switzerland, have been accused of using unacceptable sales techniques, such as distribution of free samples of infant formula to mothers after childbirth. Although Nestlé's has agreed to discontinue unethical advertising in the developing countries, there is still widespread concern that infant formula advertising by international corporations puts unfair pressure on families in the poorer countries.

Questions

36. Bottle-feeding has been criticized as being illogical and impractical for developing countries. Do you agree or disagree with this statement? Give reasons for your answer.

37. Which advantages of breast-feeding would apply to rural areas of the tropical developing world? Explain your answer.

38. What costs, both direct and indirect, would a country of the developing world encounter if a majority of its population switched from breast-feeding to bottle-feeding? Evaluate specifically all aspects of life that would be affected.

39. Imagine that you are a consultant to the health minister for an underdeveloped country. What regulations or restrictions, if any, would you recommend be applied to multinational food corporations which marketed infant formula in your country? Refer to advertising and marketing strategies as well as to other aspects of the companies' operations.

40. (a) What advantages would prompt a Canadian mother to breast-feed her baby rather than bottle-feed?

    (b) What aspects of present-day Canadian lifestyle work against a mother breast-feeding her baby?

    (c) Considering your answer to part (a), how might employers or health officials encourage breast-feeding of infants?

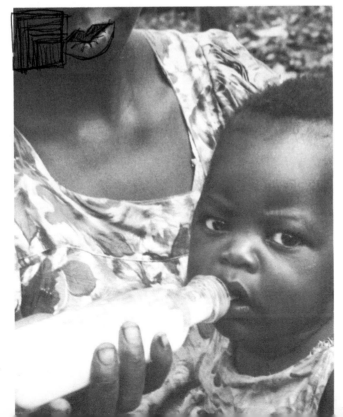

Bottle-feeding of infants has become an increasingly popular option for many families in the developing world.

Land Ownership

Farmers work on the land, and their very life depends on the land itself; this has meant that farmers since earliest times have identified very closely with the land and land ownership. If a farmer is to pour thousands of hours into producing crops from a parcel of land, it is important to be able to keep the produce. In much of the world, however, farmers do not have ownership of the land which they work, and they do not control how the land is managed or how the produce is handled. The result is that they do not have that bond with the land which is so important to successful farming. In fact, land ownership patterns in Asia and Latin America indicate that many farmers are landless and many others do not own enough land to support a family.

Much of the land in the developing world is owned by large landowners. In Latin America particularly, large farms predominate; small farmers are confined to poorer agricultural areas or to renting land from large landowners.

This inequitable distribution of land produces several problems as a consequence. First, the large landowners use only a small proportion of the land for farming. In extreme cases, as little as 10-15 percent of the land is actually used for crop produc-tion. On small farms, often over 70 percent is farmed. The small farmer must practise intensive farming in order to survive and have enough food to sell to local markets.

The rent to large land-owners is usually paid as a share of the crop, and can be as much as 60 percent, or more of a given harvest. This system of land rental and pay-ment is referred to as **sharecropping**.

Questions

41. What makes sharecropping an inequitable system of land tenure? Refer particu-larly to the owner-tenant relationship.

42. Would a sharecropper be anxious to adopt new tech-nology to improve crop yields? Explain your answer.

Large landholdings play an important role in the economy of many countries in the developing world. They are often plantations which produce cash crops for export to industrialized countries. **Cash crops** are agricultural products that are grown primarily for export to bring foreign currency into the country. Coffee, sugar, cotton, bananas, pineapples, and peanuts are among the cash crops that are widely grown

A large European-owned farm in East Africa

in the developing world. The proceeds from the sale of cash crops return to the large land-holders in the form of foreign currency which allows the country to buy manufactured products from the industrialized world such as cars, electronic goods, and consumer products. The land used for growing cash crops, however, is not available for food production within the home country.

Although not widely known or understood in the industrialized world, land tenure and land reform are major issues in many countries of the developing world whose distribution of land is inequitable. El Salvador, Brazil, Peru, Kenya, and the Philippines are among those countries.

Land reform has strong proponents and strong opponents. In simple terms, it reflects the conflict between the rich and the poor over the control of a very important resource. Land reform legislation exists for most countries of the developing world where there is a concentration of land ownership in the hands of a few wealthy people. Yet this legislation is rarely implemented in full, and as a result, it has been assumed that land reform is a failure.

Figure 5.6
How Land
Reform Changes
a Large
Landholding

This farmer works his small plot of land in northeastern Brazil.

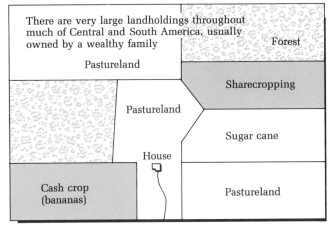

Before land reform

There are very large landholdings throughout much of Central and South America, usually owned by a wealthy family

Forest

Pastureland

Pastureland

Sharecropping

House

Sugar cane

Cash crop (bananas)

Pastureland

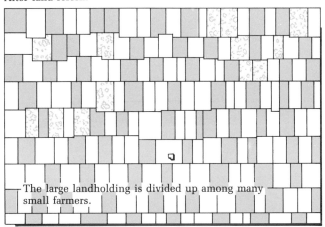

After land reform

The large landholding is divided up among many small farmers.

Table 5.5
Arguments For
and Against Land
Reform

Arguments In Favour of Land Reform	Arguments Against Land Reform
1) Land reform is socially just and equitable.	1) Land reform robs the rich of their land.
2) A higher percentage of land is actually used for food production.	2) There is a loss of export earnings and taxes from the drop of cash crops.
3) Land reform may reduce the pressure for revolutionary activity.	3) It can alienate the wealthy who often control industry, government, etc.
4) There is less hunger and malnutrition since the poor can grow their own food.	4) Deterioration in the quality of farming practices may follow, leading to soil erosion, loss of forests, etc.
5) Migration to cities slows down.	5) Extensive government programs would be needed to train farmers, provide seeds, fertilizers, etc.
6) Numerous small markets develop to sell produce and therefore there is more "grass-roots" economic activity.	6) Multinational food corporations would be angry at the loss of a source of cash crops.
7) Wealth is spread more evenly throughout the population.	7) Some jobs would be lost in the production and processing of cash crops.
8) More jobs are created as people are able to farm their own land.	

Questions

43. (a) In many countries of Central America, the land ownership pattern is marked by the presence of a few large landowners and many sharecroppers and small farmers. Why are such countries ripe for rural revolution and attempts to overthrow the government? Explain what the thinking of the average farmer in the country might be.

(b) What steps might the government take to try to defuse the situation which you have described in part (a)?

(c) What possible reactions to the government action outlined in part (b) might there be amongst the rich or the poor?

(d) In what ways does the land ownership issue appear to be a "no-win" situation in Central America?

44. What do you think are the most serious problems that face any government trying to implement land reform? Give reasons for your answer.

45. Assume that you had the role of an organizer of poor landless farmers who desperately wanted land to farm in Central America. What steps would you take, and would you have the farmers take, in order to achieve their goals?

46. Why do you think the issue of land reform is so little understood in the developed world?

47. The redistribution of land to poor farmers is insufficient by itself to bring about major improvements in the world hunger situation. What else must be done at the same time to ensure that land reform will have the greatest positive effect?

The Green Revolution

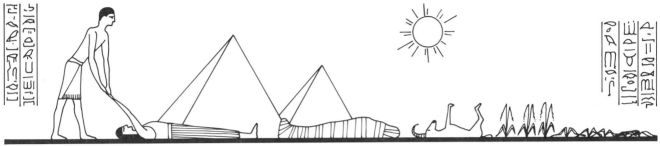

Figure 5.7
A Hieroglyphic
Depiction of
Famine in
Ancient Egypt

For centuries, starvation has been occurring on a large scale in the world. Even in biblical times, there were accounts of widespread famine in Egypt. It has always been believed that, to eliminate hunger, more food must be produced. It was upon this premise that the Green Revolution was founded.

The **Green Revolution**, which received international acclaim in the 1950s and 1960s, refers to the effort to stimulate agriculture in the developing nations through the use of **High-Yielding Varieties (HYV)**, especially of wheat and rice. These new hybrid grains tended to have short, stiff stalks, a quick response to fertilizer, and a strong resistance to common pests and diseases. They were highly productive under ''ideal'' growing conditions. These conditions included the use of insecticides, pesticides, irrigation, and the application of fertilizers, as well as other farming practices widely used in the developed world.

The earliest successes of hybrid grain production came in Mexico, where research into hybrid wheat plants took place. Within 15 years of the introduction of the hybrids, Mexico went from being a large-scale wheat importer to a net wheat exporter. The yield of wheat per hectare went up as much as five times. **Yield** refers to the amount of a crop produced per year from a given area. In India, yields increased from 1 t/ha to as much as 5 t/ha after the introduction of hybrid wheat varieties.

Similar gains in crop yields were produced with hybrid rice. The International Rice Research Institute in the Philippines spearheaded research into HYVs. The

Figure 5.8
An Older Variety
of Wheat
Contrasted with a
Newer High-
Yielding Variety

results of planting these HYVs on individual farms have been spectacular. Yields went up from just over 1 t/ha to as much as 7 t/ha in Asian countries such as India and the Philippines.

The Green Revolution would appear to have unlocked the secret of producing enough food for the world's population. Many people thought it would break the cycle of hunger and malnutrition and free people forever from lack of food. As valuable as the Green Revolution has been, however, hunger and malnutrition still exist on a vast scale. To understand this seemingly contradictory situation, it is necessary to examine the true impact of the new HYVs.

There are some facts the statistics do not reveal about these hybrids. It is important to know that the HYVs were most widely adopted by wealthy and middle-class farmers in the LDCs. They were the ones with the capital and the know-how to purchase the necessary fertilizers and pesticides. The poorer farmers were effectively excluded from this process. In addition, subsistence farmers are often reluctant to experiment with new and untried seeds. If the seeds fail, the farmer's family is left with no food. Also, the skills and expertise needed to use the new hybrid seeds are difficult for a small farmer to obtain.

There are other economic factors that keep the poor farmers from profiting from the use of the HYVs. As total grain production increases through the widespread adoption of the new seeds, prices for the grain crops decline. Therefore, without government price supports, the poor farmers become poorer. Some of the small farmers may actually be pushed to bankruptcy. This situation allows the richer farmers to purchase farmland from them at depressed prices. The poorer farmers often drift to the cities where they rarely obtain the food they need.

Ultimately, more and more land is controlled by a smaller and smaller number of people. This may allow for more efficient farming, but it does very little to ease the hunger situation. The poor who were suffering from a lack of food before the Green Revolution are no better off after it has swept the countryside. In fact, as a result of the Green Revolution, there are more poor than before.

Questions

48. (a) Construct bar graphs to illustrate the information shown in Tables 5.6 and 5.7.

(b) What accounts for the rapid adoption of the HYVs in so many countries of the world where the farmers have been thought of as very conservative and resistant to change?

49. (a) These statistics give information about the adoption of HYVs, but what do they show us about the impact of the Green Revolution on the problem of hunger?

(b) Considering the answers that you gave in part (a), in what ways could the statistics be misleading for people concerned about the problem of hunger?

50. Some critics have claimed that the Green Revolution has little value in and of itself. Do you agree? Explain your answer.

51. What do you think could be done to allow the Green Revolution to be of benefit to the poor farmers of the world? Outline your proposals in detail.

52. Considering the impact of the Green Revolution, explain how it could happen that an LDC could export food while its people suffered from a lack of food.

53. Discuss the validity of this statement: "Modern technology alone provides little hope in solving the hunger problems of the world."

Table 5.6
The Increase in
Cropland Given
to HYVs in South
Asia 1965-1982

Year	Millions of hectares
1965	0
1966	1
1967	4
1968	8
1969	9
1970	10
1971	12
1972	14
1973	15
1974	15
1975	17
1976	19
1977	20
1978	22
1979	22
1980	23
1981	24
1982	25

Note: Figures are rounded.

Table 5.7
Total Increase in
World Grain
Production Between
1970-1974 and
1980-1984

Region	Total Increase (Million of tonnes)
Asia	200.3
North America	86.0
W. Europe	31.3
Latin America	23.9
Eastern Europe and U.S.S.R.	8.8
Oceania	8.4
Africa	8.2

Note: Only a portion of the total increase in grain production can be directly attributed to the introduction of HYVs, but such increases are unprecedented and most grain production is of HYV grain.

Figure 5.9
Cross-Breeding
Plants to Produce
a Superior Strain

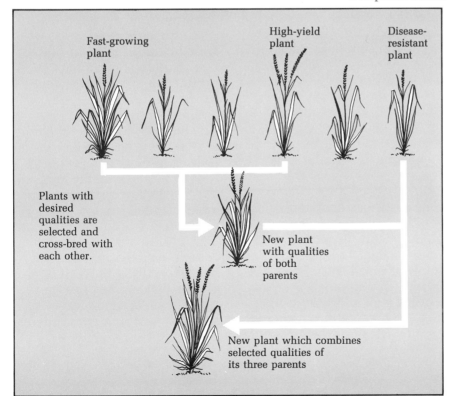

Fast-growing plant

High-yield plant

Disease-resistant plant

Plants with desired qualities are selected and cross-bred with each other.

New plant with qualities of both parents

New plant which combines selected qualities of its three parents

A New Green Revolution

Another Green Revolution is under way at the present time. It differs from the first one in that it is developing plants that grow quickly but under such conditions as poor soils, irregular rainfall, and changeable weather. Promising results have appeared, and research is continuing.

In order to develop new crops, it is necessary to **cross-breed** plants with other plants having different but desirable characteristics. The result of this cross-breeding will be the production of a new and superior plant. Figure 5.9 illustrates the process.

Successful cross-breeding depends upon several factors. First, the researchers must have a wide variety of wild or domestic plants from which to choose. Second, much time is required to allow for the cross-breeding process to take place. Since each new seed that is developed must be planted and grown to see if it has the desired characteristics, this process of cross-breeding takes many years. Lastly, it is important that once a new strain of a crop is developed, it is made available to those farmers who need it, wherever they may be around the world.

Questions

54. What problems can you foresee in the whole process of cross-breeding?

55. When new strains of crops are developed, what should be done to ensure that they are used to help farmers in the developing world who are poor and who need them? Refer to the section on the Green Revolution to help in your answer.

Genetic Engineering

Imagine a wheat plant which grows quickly, even in poor soils, and produces four times the grain that traditional wheat does. This wheat plant is also resistant to insect damage and produces a natural herbicide which kills weeds growing around it. What a boon this plant would be to farmers all over the world! Is this type of plant simply a product of science fiction, or is there some hint of reality to it?

Until recently, the very thought of a "super-plant" such as the one described above would have been dismissed as wishful thinking. New advances in the area of genetic engineering, however, have begun to change the way in which plants are developed.

The principle of genetic engineering is simple. Every living cell of every living plant or animal contains genes. Genes contain the information regarding the characteristics of each living organism, for example, its size or its resistance to drought. Each gene, therefore, contains those characteristics which make a plant or animal unique. With genetic engineering, the desirable genes of one plant can be spliced into another to create a brand new plant with its own characteristics. Although the process of genetic engineering may appear to be simple in theory, it is a very complex procedure in practice.

One of the prerequisites for the effective development of genetically engineered plants is the availability of a wide variety of plants from which to select genetic material. This includes the wild varieties of modern domesticated crops. Unfortunately, as the techniques of modern agriculture have spread, fewer and fewer varieties of crops are grown. The wild cousins of modern crops are slowly disappearing from their areas of origin. Crop specialists have begun to realize, therefore, that there is an urgent need to preserve a wide variety of wild plants from which to draw genetic material.

Some recent examples of genetic engineering in practice include experiments to produce an orange tree capable of surviving sub-freezing temperatures for a few days. This development alone could save farmers in Florida millions of dollars per year. Research is also being carried out to develop a wheat plant which is able to grow in soil which has a high salt content.

Up to this point, most genetic engineering research has taken place in well-established universities and colleges or in laboratories of companies which are funded by large corporations.

Although much of the research is theoretical and risky, solid progress has been made.

Synthetic Foods

Significant progress has been made in developing synthetic foods. One example is tofu, which is a soybean curd product. It contains no cholesterol, is high in protein, and is relatively inexpensive. Tofu is a practical food because it acquires the taste of the foods it is mixed with. Synthetic foods have also been developed from spirulina algae, which grows in ponds of fresh water. Spirulina is high in protein and is easy to grow and to process.

Modern food research has resulted in the creation of artificial flavours as well as artificial foods. Artificial milk, hamburgers, jam, and vegetable soup, for example, are very high in protein and vitamins and actually resemble real foods.

Questions

56. Compare the appeal of plants which are genetically engineered to those which were a product of the Green Revolution. Outline the advantages and the disadvantages of each.

57. (a) What impact would genetically engineered crops have on farming in the developing world?
    (b) What should be done in order to ensure that ordinary farmers of the developing world benefit as much as possible from these new crops?

58. (a) Considering the importance of the preservation of a wide variety of plants to be used in plant breeding or genetic engineering, what steps should be taken toward this end? Be practical and specific in your suggestions.
    (b) Many of the plants which are necessary for plant breeding are native to countries of the developing world. What attitude do you think LDCs would have to the use of their plants for research and development of new plants?

59. (a) What advantages would genetic engineering have over traditional plant breeding?
    (b) What problems might there be in setting up genetic engineering laboratories?

60. What appeal would synthetic foods have for both the public and the manufacturer?

61. (a) Do you think synthetic foods offer a solution to the hunger problem of the world? Explain your answer.
    (b) Under which specific circumstances might synthetic foods be useful in the developing world?

62. Why might synthetic foods be rejected by consumers?

63. Have you ever eaten foods that are largely or partially artificial? How did you react to them? Would you eat them again?

Forgotten Crops

Of the roughly 30 000 edible crops in the world, only 150 are intensively cultivated and only 30 provide the basis for people's diets. Clearly, there is a great potential for developing some of the other available edible crops. Many of these little-known crops are tasty and highly nutritious and will grow under adverse conditions. In fact, some of them were once important crops in some part of the world, but have since been abandoned. These forgotten crops are still grown in parts of the developing world, but are not accepted by much of the affluent world. Why are these crops so little-known beyond small geographic areas? In this section, we will attempt to answer that question.

The tepary bean is one of the most drought- and heat-resistant food crops known. The seeds contain more protein than most commercial beans, and the tepary bean requires only one downpour to begin growth and the production of seeds. It will grow easily in a hot, sunny, dry climate.

In the southwestern desert of North America, Indians have cultivated the amaranth. It grows roughly 1 m high and requires little care. Each plant can produce a seed head weighing perhaps 3-4 kg. The seeds can be used in cereals or popped like popcorn. In addition, the leaves are edible and high in vitamins and minerals. The amaranth is well-adapted to growth in the tropics.

The groundnut is another little-known food crop that grows wild in eastern North America. Often mistaken for a weed, the groundnut produces

Figure 5.10
The tepary bean, the groundnut, and the amaranth are all highly nutritious "forgotten crops" which are well-suited for growing under poor conditions of thin soil and irregular supplies of moisture.

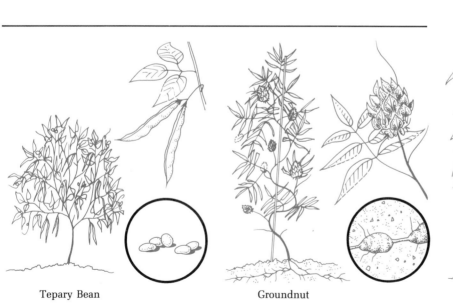
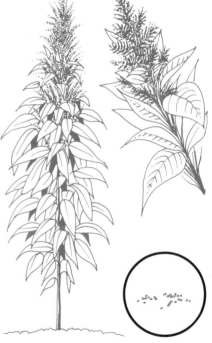

Tepary Bean   Groundnut   Amaranth

dozens of underground tubers. Each tuber is high in protein and has a taste not unlike the potato. Groundnuts also enrich the soil by fixing nitrogen in the soil.

Questions

64. With all the advantages of these forgotten crops, why have they not been accepted as the major crops of the world have been? Be specific in your answer.

65. What do you think would be necessary to make these crops widely accepted?

66. What precise advantages would any of these three crops have for drought-stricken regions of the developing world?

Statistical Analysis #2

Questions

For the following questions, refer to Table 5.8.

67. (a) Overall, in Africa, what has been the trend in the growth rate of GNP per capita?

(b) Considering the information contained in both Table 5.8 and Table 5.3, what implications does your answer to part (a) have for the future of Africa?

68. (a) Describe the trend for life expectancy and adult literacy in Africa over the period indicated.

(b) Suggest reasons for the differences between male and female literacy rates. Considering the important role of women in African society and in the African economy, what significance does your answer have for the continent?

(c) Suggest reasons for the dramatic changes in life expectancy for Africa over the period shown.

69. (a) Considering Table 5.8 and Table 5.3, would rural or urban dwellers have a greater life expectancy?

(b) Most African governments put urban needs first. Do you think this is wise in view of the statistics you have examined? Explain your answer.

(c) Suggest why the governments of so many LDCs emphasize urban programs.

70. (a) Which regions of Africa appear to suffer from the greatest degree of serious poverty?

(b) Which regions within Africa have benefitted from the production of one or two natural resources such as oil or a mineral? Refer to the thematic maps in your atlas as well as Table 5.8.

71. (a) Does there appear to be a relationship between the growth of the GNP per capita and improvements in life expectancy and adult literacy? Explain your answer, using graphs where possible.

(b) How does Africa compare to other regions of the developing world economically? Be specific in your answer.

Table 5.8 Selected Statistics for Sub-Saharan Africa

	GNP per capita (US$)	GNP per capita real growth rate %	Life expectancy		Adult literacy (%)				literacy rate
					male/female		male/female		
	1986	1973-86	1960	1985	1970		1981		1984
East Africa									
Burundi	240	1.1	38	48	29	10	35	13	34
Comoros	280	0.4	43	50	-	-	64	39	-
Djibouti	-	-	-	48	-	-	-	-	-
Ethiopia	120	0.6	36	45	9	4	11	5	15
Kenya	300	0.2	42	54	44	19	61	38	59
Madagascar	230	3.2	41	52	56	43	68	55	68
Mauritius	1200	2.0	59	66	77	59	68	-	83
Rwanda	290	2.0	42	48	43	21	51	27	57
Seychelles	1726	-	-	69	56	60	-	-	-
Somalia	280	-0.3	36	46	5	1	11	3	12
Sudan	320	-0.8	39	48	28	6	38	14	31
Uganda	425	-	43	49	52	30	65	41	57
Southern Africa									
Angola	940	-	33	44	16	7	36	19	39
Botswana	840	6.4	45	57	41	43	61	61	71
Lesotho	410	4.0	40	54	49	74	58	81	74
Malawi	160	-0.5	36	45	42	18	37	16	41
Mozambique	210	-	40	47	29	14	44	12	38
Swaziland	600	0.7	39	53	51	45	57	54	68
Tanzania	240	-1.7	41	52	48	18	62	31	85
Zambia	300	-2.6	42	52	66	37	79	58	76
Zimbabwe	620	-0.1	45	57	63	47	77	61	74
Central Africa									
Cameroon	910	6.1	39	55	47	19	55	25	56
Cen. Af. Rep.	290	-2.0	35	49	26	6	48	19	40
Chad	136	-	35	45	20	2	35	8	25
Congo	1040	4.0	38	58	50	19	70	44	63
Equat. Guinea	425	-	36	43	-	-	-	-	40
Gabon	3020	-3.6	41	50	43	22	63	44	62
Zaire	160	-3.6	40	51	61	22	74	37	61
West Africa									
Benin	270	-0.1	35	49	23	8	25	10	28
Burkina Faso	150	1.1	33	45	13	3	15	3	13
Cape Verde	360	4.7	47	62					

Country									
Gambia	230	-1.5	31	41	16	6	29	12	25
Ghana	390	-3.2	43	53	45	20	59	37	53
Guinea	320	-0.2	33	40	21	7	35	14	28
Guinea-Bissau	170	-1.4	36	39	13	6	33	9	–
Ivory Coast	740	-0.5	38	53	26	10	50	28	43
Liberia	450	-4.0	40	50	27	8	42	18	35
Mali	170	0.4	35	45	11	4	14	6	17
Mauritania	440	-0.3	36	47	–	–	–	–	17
Niger	260	-0.8	35	44	6	2	14	6	14
Nigeria	640	-2.6	40	50	35	14	66	38	42
Sao Tome	340	0.4	52	64	–	–	73	42	–
Senegal	420	-0.7	37	47	18	5	31	14	28
Sierra Leone	310	0.4	30	40	18	8	31	17	29
Togo	250	-1.4	39	51	30	8	46	20	41

Conclusion

Although hunger is an age-old problem, it has only risen to international prominence in the last quarter of the twentieth century. The mass media have helped to focus attention on the hunger issue, thereby creating opportunities for people in more developed countries to help alleviate the problem.

The gains in the fight against hunger are impressive, as can be seen from some of the evidence discussed in this chapter. From longer life expectancies to improved standards of living, health, and food distribution, much has been done to reduce the incidence of hunger and the related human suffering. There is, however, a great deal to be done yet; those in the developed world can take a key role in reducing hunger. The technology is now available to eliminate hunger; what is needed is the human will, both in the developed and the underdeveloped world, to use that technology.

Vocabulary

hunger

malnutrition

undernutrition

Oral Rehydration Therapy (ORT)

primary health care

bustee

gastroenteritis

sharecropping

cash crops

Green Revolution

High-Yielding Varieties (HYVs)

yield

cross-breed

Independent Study

1. Obtain at least eight issues of a major daily newspaper that covers international affairs. Obtain them over a period of at least three or four weeks to get an adequate sampling of news items. Examine the newspapers to answer the following questions.

   (a) Make a list of all the news coverage of the developing world, as defined in Chapter 1. Name the country mentioned in each case, as well as the nature of the news event covered.

   (b) What is the general impression of the developing world which you obtain from the news items? How might the nature of the articles you have found influence readers' opinions?

   (c) List the various wire services which have supplied the news articles. (Their names appear at the top of the article just after the headline.) Does the paper have a writer of its own reporting from anywhere in the developing world? In total, how many different sources have been used by this newspaper? What is your estimation of the depth of coverage assigned to the developing world?

   (d) Which specific articles deal with the issue of hunger or other related topics? What point of view is taken in the articles about these topics?

   (e) In your survey of the newspapers, have you detected any bias in the reporting of events in the developing world, especially those events related to the issue of hunger? If so, what is that bias?

   (f) It has been suggested that it is not what is said about a subject that matters, but what is not said. Evaluate this statement in light of your examination of the newspaper coverage of the developing world.

2. Select two of the following countries to use as a basis of research: Brazil, Peru, Ethiopia, Thailand, India, Zaire, Burkina Faso, or Costa Rica. For each of the two countries, carry out the following research.

   (a) Record the basic geographic data for the countries you have selected, such as population, population density, GNP per capita, and infant mortality rate, as well as any figures that relate to the hunger issue.

   (b) Develop a brief historical sketch of the two countries. Concentrate primarily on political or other developments within the last 20 years that may have influenced the development of the countries as a whole.

   (c) Identify any current events covered in the Canadian mass media which have given these countries greater visibility here.

   (d) Identify five problems which you feel are significant in each country today. Explain fully your reasons for your selection.

   (e) Compare the two countries which you have selected and outline the similarities and differences in the nature of the problems which they face and the approaches taken to try to solve them. Resources which you could use to research this assignment include mass circulation newspapers, periodicals such as weekly news magazines (both Canadian and foreign), encyclopedias, world almanacs, vertical files in the library, and textbooks.

3. (a) Prepare a questionnaire for the students in your school or neighbourhood to discover their knowledge of and attitudes toward issues relating to hunger. Draw up a list of ten questions which are to form the basis of your questionnaire. Be certain that the questions are clearly written and do not suggest an answer to the interviewees. Avoid questions such as, ''You think hunger is a serious problem in South America, don't you?'' since it suggests a desired answer. Instead, phrase the question to read, ''Do you think that hunger is a serious problem in South America?''

(b) Make 20 copies of your questionnaire and then interview the appropriate number of students. Attempt to interview a cross-section of age groups, since that will produce a more varied set of answers.

(c) Once you have received all the completed questionnaires, summarize the answers, expressing the answers to each question as percentages, wherever possible.

(d) Draw conclusions from your collected data, and compare the results with what you had anticipated.

(e) Evaluate your survey. Were any questions inappropriately worded? How would you change the questionnaire if you were to distribute it again?

4. Research the following topics related to futuristic methods of food production:
   • hydroponics (growing plants without soil, but with a growing medium and water containing high levels of nutrients);
   • growth of new foods from bacteria or from food wastes;
   • food production in unusual locations such as abandoned mines, old factories, or reclaimed open-pit mines;
   • plant growth in a space station; and
   • high-tech raising of crops in sterile greenhouses.
   Once you have completed the basic research, evaluate the future of the techniques. Which ones, if any, could be valuable in combatting hunger?

5. Using the information that has been provided in this text as a starting point, evaluate each one of the following statements as to its relevance and truth.
   (a) ''Hunger results from too little food production in the world.''
   (b) ''The issue of hunger really pits the rich world against the poor. To solve the problem of hunger, this basic conflict must be resolved.''
   (c) ''Hunger is such a complex problem that we can never hope to solve it.''
   (d) ''The major causes of hunger in the developing world are natural disasters such as floods and droughts. These disasters are essentially beyond our control.''

Peter Cameron
Picking Coffee Beans in Nicaragua

Peter Cameron, 34, was among a group of 23 Canadians who, in 1986, spent one month over Christmas picking coffee beans in Las Rosas, a Nicaraguan village. They were members of the Alliance for Non-violent Action, and included among their number a retired doctor, a priest, artists, students, a steelworker, and a mother on welfare. To cover their fare, food, and transportation costs, each member had to contribute about $1500. They conducted fundraising events to raise some of the money. The welfare mother received much financial help from others who were her neighbours in the same housing project.

The group members flew to Costa Rica, and then travelled the rest of the way by truck on deteriorating roads. On the way, they observed damaged buildings, tanks, much abandoned mechanical equipment, and a dearth of young men. Many young Nicaraguan men had been conscripted into the army, and many others had been killed. This meant that there were not enough people to pick the coffee beans, so the Canadian group came to help the villagers with the harvest.

They eventually arrived in the village, which consisted of white shacks on the slope near a river. Each small shack was home to a family of about eight people. Nobody starved in the vi'lage, though they were certainly poor. There was free medical care and a school, but the village was dominated by the coffee mill. When the Somoza family, who had ruled Nicaragua for 44 years, had been ousted by an uprising in 1979, the wealthy local land-owners, who owned about 100 km² of land, escaped to Florida, and the farmland became run-down. When the new government started land reform, a small plot of land was given to each family so that they could grow vegetables or raise chickens for themselves. The rest of the land was taken over as a state farm on which some people worked for wages on a full-time, part-time, or seasonal basis.

Peter and his companions unrolled their sleeping bags on the floor in the attic above the coffee mill. It was quite chilly at night, about 5°C, with myriads of stars in a jet-black sky. The village had posted guards to warn the people of any Contra attack.

The group members rose at about 4:30 a.m., had a breakfast of beans, rice, and tortillas, and walked to the slopes where they would start picking the coffee beans by 6:00 a.m. At first, they were so slow that even a child would pick three times as much in one day. By the end of their stay, however, they were about as fast as the children, though that was still much slower than the men or women. The coffee beans were like firm cherries which had to be picked very carefully so that the bushes were not damaged, as this would reduce next year's crop.

Once picked, the beans were taken by donkey to the coffee mill. The water-powered grinder removed the hulls, and the beans were then washed down a sluice. The hulls could be used as fer-tilizer or combined with soy-beans or grain for animal feed. The pale green coffee beans were dried in the sun, and were sold in the raw form, mainly for export.

Lunch of beans, rice, and tor-tillas would be brought out to workers in the fields, and at the end of the day, they would have a supper of — you've guessed it — bean, rice, and tortillas. Occa-sionally with supper, there might be a little meat or a little salad. For their Christmas meal, the vil-lagers roasted a pig. There were fresh grapefruit, oranges, and bananas available and, as the gardens improve, the variety in the villagers' diet should increase.

When they left, Peter's group were paid for the amount of coffee beans that they had picked, but they returned the money to the villagers so that they could buy supplies. They also left behind many of their personal belongings, such as sleeping bags, clothing, flash-lights, toothbrushes, and toothpaste.

If there is one impression that sticks out in Peter's mind, it is the extreme hardship that the Nicaraguan peasants face daily. ''Most Canadians take their lifestyle for granted — three good meals a day, adequate clothing and housing for a start.

''One day, I watched an old Nicaraguan coffee picker walk up the hill, and realized that the man had no shoes. By the look of his toughened, callous soles, I could see that he had never worn them . . . . Suddenly, my bag of coffee beans became much lighter, and I was able to pick much more quickly, as I realized my good fortune.''

Questions

1. List and briefly describe three ways in which your life would be different had you been born into a family in Las Rosas.

2. (a) In what ways did the Nicaraguans benefit from the Canadians' visit?

   (b) What, in your opinion, were the benefits for the Canadians involved?

3. What would you like and/or dislike about taking part in such a project? Suggest ideas for improve-ments if you have any.

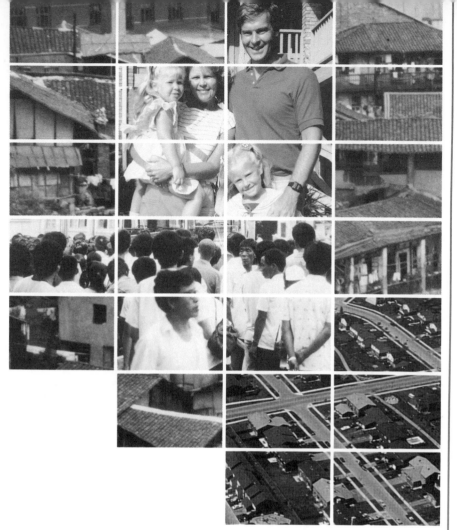

By the end of this chapter,
you should be able to:

- identify reasons for concern about population
  growth in various parts of
  the world;

- demonstrate a knowledge
  of the basic elements of
  demography and their significance; and

- show an understanding of
  the trends toward a declining population in the
  industrialized world.

6

Population

Sao Paulo, A City in Crisis

Brazil is an extraordinary country, with some of the most sophisticated and advanced industries in the world. The city of Sao Paulo has been called the engine which propels the Brazilian vehicle. With its sprawling factories, seemingly endless suburbs, and a population of over 6 million people, Sao Paulo is one of the world's largest and fastest growing cities. However, it also faces problems which threaten to consume it.

Sao Paulo has been referred to as a city with a split personality. On the one side, it has an enormous and progressive industrial base. Its factories produce items as varied as aircraft, automobiles, toys, processed food, and gasoline. Billions of dollars are generated by these industries, and some of the richest families in the world make their homes in the city.

But the city has a darker side. As its rapid industrial expansion took place, hundreds of thousands of Brazilians flooded into the city in search of jobs. Unfortunately, there were not enough for all of these new

Sao Paulo is a city of the rich and the poor living side by side.

arrivals, and they have settled into a life which excludes them from the prosperity at Sao Paulo's heart. Many live in abject poverty, occupying favelas or shanty towns encircling the city. People live in cardboard shacks with no running water, electricity, or proper sewage disposal. Medical treatment is an unknown for many people, and a complete education is just a dream for millions. Sao Paulo is bursting at the seams with people, and unable to accommodate the new arrivals.

An oil refinery, part of Sao Paulo's huge industrial complex

The city has a high crime rate, and many people are afraid to walk the streets for fear of being robbed or assaulted. During the 1980s, several major riots, including food riots, took place. Some residents have accused the police and city officials of being corrupt and allowing the city to enter a serious state of decline.

Many in the middle class point to Sao Paulo as an example of a world rapidly becoming overcrowded — a city that is out of control. They claim that Sao Paulo is an example of overpopulation at its worst; the only solution is a drastic reduction in the number of people allowed to migrate there. Yet the crushing poverty of the Brazilian countryside has forced hundreds of thousands of people to leave their farms and move to the cities in search of a more amenable way of life. Sao Paulo, however, has received more migrants than it can reasonably handle. In this view, if the city had fewer people, it would have fewer problems.

Introduction

Population problems are some of the most pressing issues facing the world today. Clearly, some of the world's urban centres, such as Sao Paulo, are desperately overcrowded. With close to four babies born every second in the world, population growth appears to be spiralling upward at a dangerously high rate. Major cities, especially those in the developing world, are growing more quickly than any other settled areas. Are we facing a world where there will be standing room only? What solutions are there to this perceived problem?

The basis of this chapter is an examination of the extent to which overpopulation, or "the population issue," is a major crisis. To help focus your thinking in this area, see if you can answer the following questions. Write your answers on a separate sheet of paper.

(a) What is the approximate population of the world today?

   i) 5 billion

   ii) 4 billion

   iii) 3.5 billion

   iv) 3 billion

(b) The most populous country in the world is:

   i) India.

   ii) Indonesia.

   iii) USSR.

   iv) China.

(c) A population growth rate of 2.8 percent is considered:

   i) low.

   ii) average.

   iii) high.

(d) The population of the world has never grown at a faster rate than it has in the last ten years.

   True   False

(e) The length of time required to double the population of the world is:

   i) 35 years.

   ii) 48 years.

   iii) 55 years.

   iv) 120 years.

(f) Canada's population growth rate is declining.

   True   False

(g) The most crowded country (not city state) in the world from the point of view of population density is:

   i) India.

   ii) Vietnam.

   iii) Egypt.

   iv) the Netherlands.

(h) In the year AD 1, the approximate population of the world was:

   i) 1 billion

   ii) 2 billion

   iii) 750 million

   iv) 250 million

(i) The most populous city in the world is probably:

   i) Shanghai.

   ii) New York City.

   iii) Tokyo.

   iv) Mexico City.

(j) Approximately what percentage of the world's population lives in rural areas or villages?

   i) 85 percent

   ii) 70 percent

   iii) 50 percent

   iv) 30 percent

Answers

a) i b) iv c) iii d) False e) i f) True g) iv h) i i) i j) iii

An Historical Perspective

Throughout human history, population growth has been viewed as positive and even necessary. Most great empires, such as the British, French, and Spanish empires of the seventeenth, eighteenth, and nineteenth centuries, have encouraged large families as an essential element to ensure continuance of political and military power. The Romans, two thousand years earlier, needed a large population from which to draw personnel for their army, since the Roman Empire extended the full length of the Mediterranean Sea and demanded a significant military presence.

Other empires, such as the enormous Mongol Empire of Genghis Khan, encouraged population growth as well. This empire stretched from China to the Middle East. Clearly, a sizeable population was desirable to settle this vast amount of land.

Traditionally, Jewish, Christian, and Moslem philosophies have been **populationist** as well, teaching that population growth was beneficial to a country. A populationist viewpoint has been common in much of the world for centuries. In the Book of Genesis, God instructs Noah and his sons to be "fruitful and increase in number; multiply on the earth and increase upon it." This injunction to Noah has echoed down through the centuries in Jewish, Christian, and Islamic thought, and is still followed in many places today.

Part of this attitude was, no doubt, a realistic response to conditions of life. Before the twentieth century, health conditions throughout the world were poor, and many children died in infancy. Death of a mother in childbirth was not uncommon; life expectancy was limited, and infectious disease posed a very real threat to life. Within such a context, it is not surprising to see the various organized religions encourage couples to have large families. If parents had a large number of children, perhaps a few would survive. In addition,

for many centuries the world had only a fraction of its current population. At the time of Christ, for example, it is estimated that there were 250 million people in the entire world, which is roughly the current population of the United States.

Today, the attitude toward population growth has changed significantly, and in the industrialized world the trend is for parents to have small families with one or two children. In the majority of countries of the developing world, the population growth rate is slowing and large families are becoming less common. Table 6.1 illustrates the historic growth of world population. Although these figures are estimates, the trend is clear.

Questions

1. What general factors can you cite to explain the change in attitude to population growth in the latter part of the twentieth century as opposed to earlier times? Refer specifically to the attitudes in the industrialized world, as you have been able to observe them.

2. (a) Using the statistics from Table 6.1, construct a line graph to illustrate world population growth.

   (b) What general conclusions can you draw from the graphs you have constructed? Consider factors such as varying rates of population growth, as well as the importance of certain historical events or developments which can be drawn from your general knowledge.

**Table 6.1
Historic Growth
of World
Population**

Date	Population
8000 BC	5 000 000
4000 BC	87 000 000
AD 1	250 000 000
1650	500 000 000
1850	1 100 000 000
1930	2 000 000 000
1950	2 500 000 000
1970	3 600 000 000
1988	5 100 000 000

An Overview of World Population Distribution

Population density refers to the average number of people per square kilometre of a certain area. Figure 6.1 on page 206 illustrates some of the significant variations of population density around the world.

Questions

3. (a) Examine Figure 6.1. Which regions of the world have little or no permanent human population? Suggest reasons for this pattern.

   (b) Which regions of the world appear to have the greatest population densities? Refer to the thematic maps in your atlas and suggest reasons for the patterns you have noted.

   (c) What is the general standard of living of these regions? Refer to the statistics in the Appendix of this book to help with this question.

   (d) Which continents appear to have the greatest population densities?

   (e) If all the regions of the world which have high population densities but low standards of living were able to boost their affluence to a level comparable to that of the industrialized world, how would it affect other aspects of life in those countries?

   (f) Which specific countries have a high population density and yet a high standard of living? By examining thematic maps in your atlas, suggest reasons why these countries are in such a positive situation.

4. (a) What general problems would you expect to find in the regions of the world having high population densities?

   (b) What is the relationship between those areas of the world with high population densities and:
   i) most major cities of the world?
   ii) the world's most productive farmland?

   Discuss the implications of your answers.

Figure 6.1
The Distribution
of Population
Around the
World

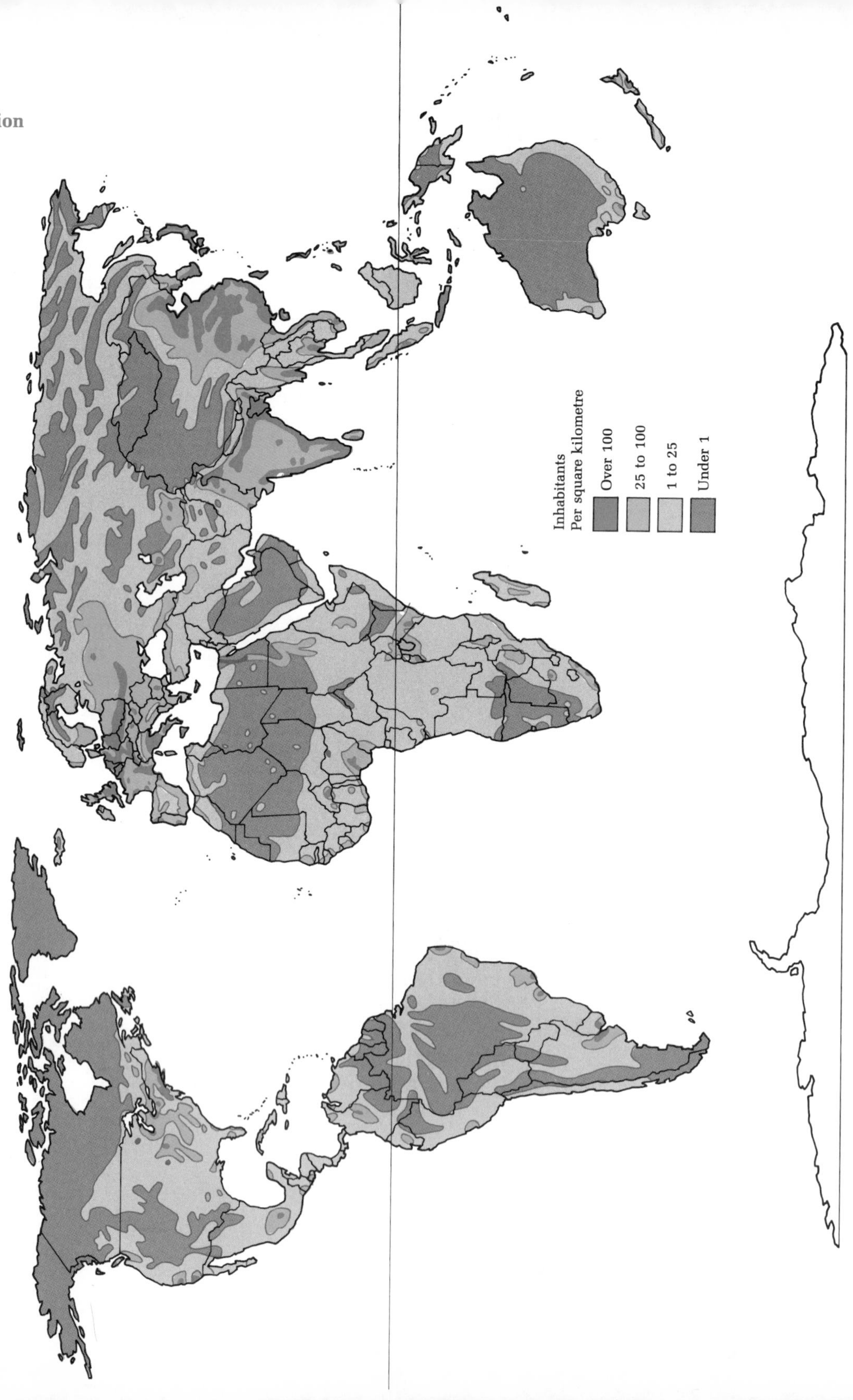

Inhabitants
Per square kilometre

Over 100
25 to 100
1 to 25
Under 1

Measuring Population Growth

Demography is the study of population and its changes and patterns. The chief concerns of demography are the number of births and deaths in a certain population, the number of years people live, and the trends that can be seen in these figure over time. The basic terms of demography discussed here help us to understand more clearly how human populations change. These terms will also help us to identify crucial questions concerning global population.

One important term in the study of population is **population growth rate**. Usually expressed as a percentage, population growth rate refers to the speed at which a population grows per year. For example, if the population growth rate of a country is 2.8 percent, that population is growing at a very rapid rate, close to the upper limit at which a human population can grow. Table 6.2 illustrates the impact of different population growth rates over a number of years.

Questions

5. Examine the growth of the two populations over the five years given. How do the two countries compare in overall growth?

6. Compare the total population growth of Country B in five years with that of Country A in one year. What conclusions can you draw?

The population growth rate of a country is influenced by a number of factors. One of these is the birth rate of its population. **Birth rate** refers to the number of live births in a country per 1000 population per year. The **death rate** of a country is also important, referring as it does to the number of deaths per 1000 population per year. If the birth rate is higher than the death rate, then the difference between the two is referred to as a **natural increase**. A **natural decrease**, on the other hands, occurs when the death rate is higher than the birth rate. Most countries of the world are presently experiencing a natural increase in their populations. Mexico, Brazil, South Korea, Kenya, and Zaire have among the highest natural increases in the world. (It should be noted that natural increase does not include immigration into a country. Immigration is included in a country's population growth rate.) A small

Table 6.2
The Importance of Population Growth Rates for Countries

Country A (population growth rate 2.8%)	Country B (population growth rate 0.2%)
Year 1: 20 000 000	Year 1: 20 000 000
Year 2: 20 560 000	Year 2: 20 040 000
Year 3: 21 135 680	Year 3: 20 080 080
Year 4: 21 727 479	Year 4: 20 120 240
Year 5: 22 335 848	Year 5: 20 160 481

number of countries are currently experiencing a natural decrease, for example, West Germany, Ireland, and Poland. If a country experiences a natural decrease, its total population will be decreasing in size, assuming that there is no large-scale immigration.

The **infant mortality rate (IMR)** is another important measure of the nature of a population and its health. The IMR is the number of infant deaths per 1000 live births in a population. In countries where the standard of living is poor, there tends to be a high IMR, whereas in developed countries such as Canada, the IMR is low.

Questions

7. In general, which types of countries tend to have the highest natural increases? Suggest reasons for this pattern.

8. Construct a chart similar to the one on page 209 and complete it by filling in the birth rates, death rates, or natural increases or decreases.

9. Refer to the Appendix at the back of the book. What appears to be the relationship between IMR and the birth rate of a country? Give reasons for the relationship you have found.

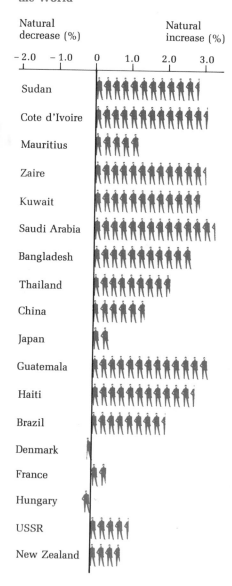

Table 6.3
Natural Increase and Natural Decrease Statistics from Selected Countries Around the World

Source: Population Reference Bureau 1988 Population Data Sheet

Rule of 72

One method of evaluating the rate of growth of a population is the use of the **rule of 72**. This rule provides a simple method for calculating the number of years required for a population to double in size, as in the following equation.

$$\text{The number of years required for a population to double} = \frac{72}{\text{Annual percentage rate of population increase}}$$

The number of years required for a population to double in size is referred to as the **doubling time**.

Country	Birth Rate (per 1000 population/yr)	Death Rate (per 1000 population/yr)	Natural Increase	Natural Decrease
Country A	50.5	26.8		
Country B	12.6	11.8		
Country C	44.2		20.6	
Country D		10.6		1.2
Country E		16.9	7.7	
Country F	10.4	11.6		

Question

10. (a) Using the statistics *p9 346* from the Appendix in this text, discover the doubling time for each of these countries, using the rule of 72.
   i) Canada
   ii) USA
   iii) USSR
   iv) Kenya
   v) Mexico
   vi) Thailand
   vii) India
   viii) the Philippines

   (b) Group these countries into three categories, according to their doubling times.

(c) Judging by other statistics in the Appendix, what factors do all or most of the countries with short doubling times have? What influence might these factors have upon these countries that would account for their short doubling times?

(d) What implications are there for the future of those countries with short and medium doubling times?

Rapid population growth causes hardship for families such as this one in northeastern Brazil.

Population Pyramids

Population pyramids are one of the most important tools that can be employed in demography. A **population pyramid** is composed of two bar graphs back-to-back and constructed vertically. The value of the population pyramid is that one can see the age distribution of a population at a glance. For example, the broader the base of the pyramid, the younger the population is. Examine Figure 6.2 to see examples of pyramids from different countries around the world.

✳ The **dependency load** of a population refers to the percentage of that population which is over 65, and the percentage under 15, combined. These portions of a population are considered to be out of the general work force and therefore must be supported by the rest of the population. In many LDCs, the dependency load includes large numbers of children under the age of 15, for example.

Table 6.2
The Importance of Population Growth Rates for Countries

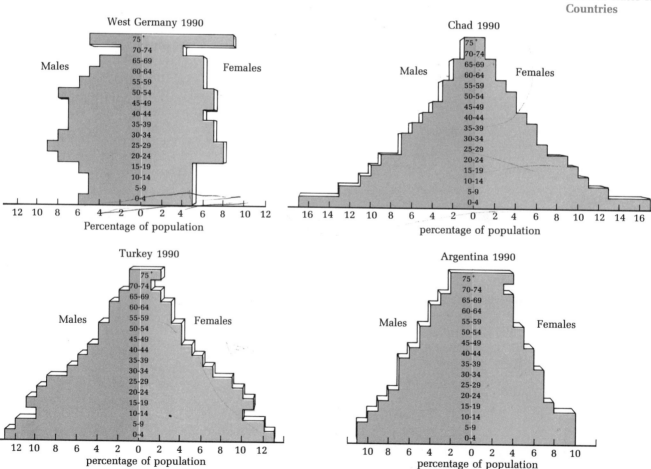

Part III   Human/Economic Issues

Questions

11. (a) Which of the countries illustrated in Figure 6.2 appears to have the youngest population?

    (b) How would you describe the overall shape of the population pyramid for the country you selected in part (a)?

    (c) What specific problems would your selected country have in providing services for its population, considering its age structure? Refer to the provision of the basic necessities for human survival as well as the income-earning capacity of the population.

    (d) What would happen to the appearance and the shape of the pyramid if the population growth rate suddenly dropped? Sketch a pyramid of the country as it would appear 25 years after the beginning of a rapid decline in the population growth rate.

12. (a) Which country appears to have the oldest population? Give reasons for your answer.

    (b) What specific problems might this country have in providing for its population?

Preschool children exercise outside their daycare centre in Puno Province, Peru.

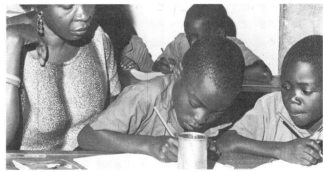

These children in Uganda are learning to read and write through a UNICEF/UNESCO program.

(c) Compare the nature of the country you selected as the "oldest" with the one you selected as the "youngest." Refer to such factors as the relative growth rates of the population and the major concerns of the country (as illustrated by the pyramids). What is the outlook for these countries?

13. How can accurate population pyramids help government planners in making decisions about government expenditures? Explain your answer fully.

14. How might a major war, a massive drought and resultant starvation, and a sudden rapid increase in wealth at all levels of society affect the population pyramid of a country? Explain your reasoning for each answer.

15. (a) Examine all of the pyramids of Figure 6.2.

**Table 6.4
Population by
Age Groups for
Canada 1955**

Male Age groups	Percentage of Male Population	Female Age groups	Percentage of Female Population
0- 4	12	0- 4	12
5- 9	10	5- 9	11
10-14	8	10-14	9
15-19	6	15-19	7
20-24	6	20-24	7
25-29	7	25-29	8
30-34	7	30-34	8
35-39	6	35-39	7
40-44	6	40-44	6
45-49	5	45-49	5
50-54	4	50-54	4
55-59	4	55-59	4
60-64	3	60-64	3
65-69	3	65-69	3
70-74	2	70-74	2
75 +	2	75 +	3

**Table 6.5
Population by
Age Groups for
Canada 1975**

Age groups	Male Percentage of Male Population	Female Age groups	Percentage of Female Population
0- 4	8	0- 4	7
5- 9	9	5- 9	8
10-14	11	10-14	10
15-19	10	15-19	10
20-24	9	20-24	9
25-29	9	25-29	8
30-34	7	30-34	7
35-39	6	35-39	6
40-44	6	40-44	5
45-49	6	45-49	5
50-54	5	50-54	5
55-59	4	55-59	4
60-64	4	60-64	4
65-69	3	65-69	3
70-74	2	70-74	3
75 +	3	75 +	4

**Table 6.6
Population by
Age Groups for
Canada**

Males Age groups	Percentage of Male Population	Females Age groups	Percentage of Female Population
0- 4	8	0- 4	7
5- 9	8	5- 9	7
10-14	7	10-14	7
15-19	7	15-19	6
20-24	8	20-24	7
25-29	9	25-29	9
30-34	9	30-34	9
35-39	8	35-39	8
40-44	8	40-44	7
45-49	6	45-49	6
50-54	5	50-54	5
55-59	4	55-59	4
60-64	4	60-64	4
65-69	3	65-69	4
70-74	2	70-74	3
75 +	3	75 +	5

Table 6.7
Population by Age Groups for Tanzania

Males Age groups	Percentage of Male Population	Females Age groups	Percentage of Female Population
0- 4	20	0- 4	19
5- 9	15	5- 9	15
10-14	12	10-14	12
15-19	11	15-19	11
20-24	9	20-24	9
25-29	7	25-29	7
30-34	6	30-34	6
35-39	5	35-39	5
40-44	4	40-44	4
45-49	3	45-49	3
50-54	3	50-54	3
55-59	2	55-59	2
60-64	2	60-64	2
65-69	1	65-69	1
70-74	1	70-74	1
75 +	1	75 +	1

Note: Figures may add to more than 100% due to rounding

Table 6.8
Population by Age Groups for Peru

Males Age groups	Percentage of Male Population	Females Age groups	Percentage of Female Population
0- 4	14	0- 4	14
5- 9	12	5- 9	12
10-14	12	10-14	11
15-19	12	15-19	11
20-24	10	20-24	10
25-29	8	25-29	8
30-34	7	30-34	7
35-39	5	35-39	6
40-44	4	40-44	4
45-49	4	45-49	4
50-54	3	50-54	3
55-59	3	55-59	3
60-64	2	60-64	2
65-69	1	65-69	2
70-74	1	70-74	1
75 +	1	75 +	1

Is there evidence that any of the countries experienced a population "boom" within the last 30 years or so? If so, which countries were they?

(b) What happened to the population growth rate after that boom?

16. (a) Using the data from Tables 6.4, 6.5, and 6.6, construct a series of three population pyramids for Canada.

(b) Describe the changes that have taken place over the given time period for Canada.

(c) When did Canada experience a baby boom?

(d) How old are the baby boomers today?

(e) What happened to the population in the wake of the baby boom?

(f) In what ways have the baby boomers influenced our priorities in Canada?

17. (a) Construct population pyramids for Tanzania and Peru.

(b) Describe the characteristics of each population. Refer to the relative age of each one.

(c) Compare the population figures for both of these countries with the figures for Canada.

Current Population Concerns

Malthusianism

Thomas Robert Malthus was an Englishman who lived in the late 1700s and the early 1800s. As a political economist, he recorded some of the concerns he had about population growth and food supply in the world. Europe in his day was entering a period of rapid industrialization.

At the same time, it was experiencing very rapid population growth and widespread political and economic upheaval. All of these conditions concerned Malthus, for he saw the quality of life deteriorating and widespread revolution and bloodshed becoming a real possibility.

At the heart of the changes occurring in Europe in the early nineteenth century, Malthus saw a dilemma: the population appeared to be increasing more quickly than the food supply. The consequences of this situation, as Malthus saw it, would be disasters such as famine or plague, riots, warfare, and the toppling of governments. In effect, there would be a breakdown of the established order.

To put it another way, overpopulation would inevitably be followed by events that would interfere with population growth. These events, now referred to as **Malthusian checks**, prevent a population from increasing too far beyond the food supply available to it.

Table 6.9
The Malthusian Theory of Population Growth and the Food Supply

Time Period	I	II	III	IV	V	VI
Population which increases at a geometric rate	1	2	4	8	16	32
Food Supply which increases at an arithmetic rate	1	2	3	4	5	6

Top, a crowded street in Beijing, China; bottom, a famine-stricken region of Ethiopia

As can be seen in Table 6.9, the population increases very quickly, with the same pattern or rate that Malthus had observed in Europe. By Stage III, the food supply proves to be inadequate to provide for the growing population. Factors such as inadequate agricultural technology and insufficient transportation and marketing systems contribute to the food shortage. It is during Stage III that the Malthusian checks begin to come into play.

By Stage IV, these checks have gone so far as to precipitate a disaster which in turn would reduce the population. Once the checks had run their course, the population would return to Stage II and the process would begin again.

The raw data to support Malthus's claims were abundant during that time in history. In India, for example, there had been a number of very serious famines. During the great Indian famine of 1770, close to one-third of the entire population of the country was annihilated. In the state of Bengal alone, for example, it has been estimated that close to 10 million people died.

Malthus also used the French Revolution to support his claim that the world was reaching a crisis point in terms of population growth, but he could not prove that the French were starving.

It should be noted, however, that even during his lifetime Malthus had many critics, including Karl Marx. Both men saw the great poverty of the cities of Europe, but Marx believed that it was due more to the effects of the capitalist economic system than to population growth.

Other social theorists believed that additional factors would come into play to reduce human population growth rates without such serious repercussions.

Malthus's dire predictions for the future of Europe did not come to pass and today seem remote indeed. In the latter quarter of the twentieth century, western Europe is struggling to deal with a massive food surplus and a population which is barely growing at all.

Contemporary demographers have applied Malthusian theory, not to Europe, but to areas of the developing world where famine and the threat of famine are very real. These modern theories are referred to as **neo-Malthusianism**, since they adapt Malthus's theory to current events and conditions.

Questions

18. (a) Select three specific examples that you are familiar with from television news or the newspapers or magazines you have read which would support a neo-Malthusian point of view.

(b) Suggest general reasons to explain why neo-Malthusian thought has considerable support today.

(c) On what grounds could neo-Malthusian theories be criticized?

19. Re-read the case study on Sao Paulo. Do the problems in Sao Paulo support or go against a neo-Malthusian point of view? Explain your answer.

Urban Growth

Problems associated with cities are among the most pressing which have ever been faced by humanity. In the large cities of the developing world, not only are the conditions of life for many people marginal at best, but the rate of urban growth is very high. Cities which had an inadequate site to begin with (e.g., swampland, mountainsides) now have millions of people crowding each other out. The populations of these cities have grown to the point where they equal or exceed the populations of whole countries.

Questions

20. (a) Examine Table 6.10 and indicate which continents contain the most cities in the top ten. What does this reveal about those continents?

(b) How many of the ten largest cities in the year 2000 will be located in the industrialized world?

(c) What does your answer to part (b) reveal about the differences between the industrialized and developing countries?

Table 6.10
The Ten Largest Cities in the World, as Estimated for the Year 2000

City	Population (millions)
Mexico City	27.6
Shanghai	25.9
Tokyo/Yokohama	23.8
Peking	22.8
Sao Paulo	21.5
New York/Northeastern New Jersey	19.5
Greater Bombay	16.3
Calcutta	15.9
Jakarta	14.3
Rio de Janeiro	14.2

21. (a) Using the information from Table 6.11, construct four graphs, with your choice of design, to illustrate the data.

(b) What changes in technology have allowed the trends you have graphed to take place?

Rapid growth is a characteristic of many North American cities.

Table 6.11
World Urbanization

Year	Percentage of population that is rural	Percentage population in cities under one million	Percentage of population in cities over one million
1900	86.4	12	1.6
1950	71.1	21.4	7.5
1985	56.7	27.5	15.8
2020 (est.)	37.5	35.4	27.1

The Aging of The Population of The Developed World

The population of the industrialized countries of the world is undergoing rapid changes. Couples are having smaller families of one or two children. At the same time, the median age of this population is increasing. Over the last 40 years or so, these changes have intensified in developed countries.

There was a decline in family size in industrialized countries during the Great Depression of the thirties. Then family size grew again after World War II. The capitalist and communist worlds both have experienced unparalleled economic prosperity in the years since World War II. People have decided to have smaller families in an effort to improve their standard of living. Families with four or five children were fairly common in this country until a generation ago, but few Canadian couples are having that many children now.

Women's roles have begun to change, and have contributed to the changes in family size. More women who have attained higher levels of education, for example, have decided to postpone having children in order to pursue a career. Many women are having their first children after the age of 30. This fact alone reduces the number of children a woman can have during her reproductive years.

Some couples see children as a hindrance to their lifestyle, and prefer to pursue their own activities without interference from children. Once considered almost an automatic part of marriage, children and their role in a family are being re-evaluated.

It should also be recognized that the **nuclear family**, with a father, mother, and children, is only one of a number of family styles seen today in the industrialized world. Many families are headed by a single parent, most commonly the mother. Divorce is common, as is remarriage. Birth rates and population growth rates are affected by these changes in the structure of the Canadian family.

Many Canadian couples are having smaller families.

Questions

22. (a) Examine Tables 6.12, 6.13, and 6.14. Graph the information found in the tables, using a multiple line graph, to show the changes of birth and death rates over the years for those three countries.

    (b) What similarities can you observe between all three countries' rates? Explain why you think they followed similar patterns.

    (c) What impact does the recent change in Canada's birth rate have on our society in general? Refer to the effect on schools, job prospects for the young and the old, immigration, the housing industry, hospital services, and pension plans as well as other areas of life.

    (d) What you have described in your answer to part (c) has been referred to as the "revenge of the empty cradle." What do you think is meant by this term?

23. (a) List as many family styles as you are familiar with, along with the characteristics of each.

    (b) How has each of the family styles you listed influenced the birth rates in Canada?

24. What is your attitude toward having children yourself? How does your attitude reflect or differ from the current Canadian attitude toward having children?

Table 6.12
Historic Birth and
Death Rates for
Canada

Period	Birth rate	Death rate
1851-61	45.2	21.6
1861-71	39.6	20.8
1871-81	36.9	18.8
1881-91	33.6	18.0
1891-1901	30.3	16.2
1901-11	30.7	12.9
1911-21	29.2	12.4
1921-31	25.2	11.0
1931-41	21.0	9.8
1941-51	25.3	9.7
1951-61	27.8	8.2
1961-71	21.1	7.4

Table 6.13
Historic Birth and
Death Rates for
the United States

Period	Birth rate	Death rate
1840	51.8	-
1860	44.3	18.7*
1880	39.8	18.8*
1900	32.3	17.2
1910	30.1	14.7
1920	27.7	13.0
1930	21.3	11.3
1940	19.4	10.8
1950	24.1	9.6
1960	23.7	9.5
1970	18.4	9.5

Table 6.14
Historic Birth and
Death Rates for
England and
Wales

Period	Birth rate	Death rate
1851-55	34.0	23.5
1871-75	35.5	23.3
1900-05	28.2	16.0
1931-35	15.0	12.0
1951-55	15.3	11.7
1971-75	14.0	11.9

Population Control

The Theory of Demographic Transition

A study of the past can help predict the future, so a study of the changes within countries already industrialized is valuable for predicting population change in the developing world. As can be seen with the historic patterns and changes in birth rates in Tables 6.12, 6.13, and 6.14, countries in the industrialized world once had very high birth rates which have fallen drastically. Many developing countries are now experiencing falling birth rates as well. Although there are clearly exceptions, taking the countries of western Europe as a basis, there appears to be a pattern to the rise and fall of birth rates, death rates, and the resultant natural increases.

The pattern has been as follows. When sanitation was primitive and life expectancy was short, there were high birth and death rates. The result was a relatively stable population size. As modern medicine was introduced and the standard of living improved, the death rates declined but the birth rates remained high. The product of these conditions was a rapidly increasing population. With a high standard of living, people began to refrain from having large numbers of children. They no longer needed their children's labour, and it made sense to have fewer children if more babies were able to survive to adulthood. These changes are summarized in Figure 6.3.

Questions

25. In both Phase I and IV of the theory of demographic transition, there is a low population growth rate. In your own words, describe the key differences between these two phases.

26. What evidence would you look for to help you decide if a country was in Phase II or not? Be specific, and refer to evidence that would be found upon visiting the country and gathering information first-hand.

27. What assumption would have to be made if this theory were to be applied to countries of the developing world today?

Figure 6.3
The Theory of Demographic Transition

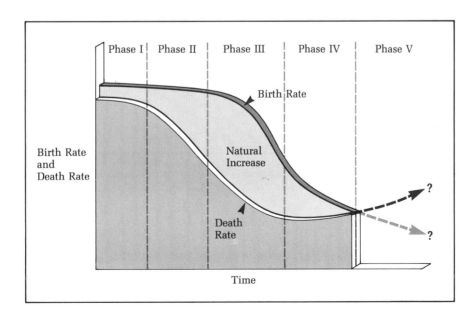

Family Size

One of the most important considerations in dealing with the issue of population growth is the decision-making process which goes on before a child is conceived. Deciding to have or not to have children is usually a deliberate process, and parents generally have a clear idea as to what role the children will fill in their lives as well as why they want them. Sometimes it is incorrectly assumed that parents do not consider carefully their reasons for having children. The statistics in Table 6.15 illustrate the fact that, around the world, the decision to have children is well thought out in most cases. It should also be noted that parents in the industrialized world have children for very different reasons than parents in developing countries.

Table 6.15
Reasons for
Having Children

Country	Mexico	Singapore	USA
Nature of birth rate	high	medium	low
Reasons for having children (% of parents)			
a) Economic support	72	19	4
b) Companionship	-	44	47
c) To strengthen the marriage	-	7	15
d) Psychological benefits to parents	16	21	26
e) Miscellaneous	12	9	8
GNP per capita (U.S.$)	$1 850	$7 410	$17 500

Questions

28. (a) Explain why 72 percent of Mexican parents have children primarily for economic reasons, compared to only four percent of American parents.

    (b) In general, what appears to be the relationship between economic factors and parents' decision to have children?

29. In which country in Table 6.15 do the reasons for having children appear to be the most complex? Suggest reasons for your conclusion.

30. In a country such as the United States, birth control devices are widely available. What role do you think birth control plays in affecting the birth rate? Explain your answer fully.

31. What relationship is there between Table 6.15 on the reasons why parents have children and the upcoming Table 6.16 (page 224) on the demographic and economic factors which affect population growth?

China

With over 1 billion people, China has a population dilemma unmatched in the world. A 2.5 percent growth rate in that country means that in one year, the population will grow by a figure that represents the entire population of Canada! The enormity of China's population sets up a unique population-management situation.

In China, the world's most populous country, much of the countryside has high population density, and many of its large cities are overcrowded. These two photos reflect China's population crisis.

In order to try to control the rate of population growth, China instituted a one-child policy. The thrust of this policy is that couples were offered a salary bonus if they would limit their family to one child. In a few cases, couples were allowed to have a second child under this agreement if their first child was handicapped in some way, or was a girl. Clearly, this policy has had some impact on reducing the rate of population growth in the world's most populous country. It has been estimated that the government of China spends close to $1 billion per year on population-control measures. This push to limit population growth has resulted in Chinese couples now practising some form of birth control.

Not all the couples in China, however, are willing to sign the one-child pledge. The State Planning Commission reports that only one-quarter of the couples in their child-bearing years have signed it. Despite the pressure from government programs, most couples continue to make their own decisions on family size.

Why do so many couples insist on having more than one child when the government so strongly opposes them? One common reason is that many couples in China will continue to have children until they have a son. The

desire to have a son is a deeply rooted cultural value which came from the days when sons were able to help on the farm and girls were considered an economic burden. Parents had to give their girls a dowry upon marriage into another family, which could amount to a great deal of money, while sons remained with the family to help on the farm. China's traditionally high infant mortality rates also meant that parents would have to have a large number of children to ensure the survival of a smaller number.

In China, there is still a strong belief that the larger one's family, the better off one is. In addition, despite the cash incentives to have only one child, there are other ways for couples to earn extra money than through the one-child government bonus.

At the present time, China's natural increase is 1.4 percent, but the prospects for reducing it significantly in the near future are not bright.

Top, a village in Central China; left, a residential area in Changqing; above, the main railway station in Beijing

Questions

32. (a) What direct and indirect costs will there be for the Chinese government if the population growth rate is not reduced soon?

(b) How do the interests of individual Chinese couples differ from the interests of their government regarding population growth and birth rates?

33. (a) How much force or compulsion should a government use to bring down the rate of population growth?

(b) Which of the following methods of reducing the growth rate would be viable options?
   (i) Apply tax penalties to those who have more than one child.
   (ii) Introduce forced sterilizations on couples with more than two children.
   (iii) Expand voluntary birth control programs.
   (iv) Expand instruction about birth control in schools.

Be sure to consider both the positive and negative aspects of each option.

Demographic-Economic Analysis

In the analysis that you have just completed of the population changes in the industrialized world and the Theory of Demographic Transition, you have seen that increasing affluence has brought about a decline in the birth rate. Using the statistics in Table 6.16, you will discover whether this is true for some developing countries today.

Questions

34. (a) Which countries have experienced the most rapid fall in birth rates since 1960?

(b) What do each of the countries you have selected in part (a) have in common with each other? Explain the significance of these common factors.

35. (a) Considering your answer to question 1, what should countries with rapidly growing populations do if they want to slow down that rate of growth?

(b) What obstacles might stand in the way of a government carrying out the changes you have suggested?

Table 6.16
Demographic-
Economic
Analysis

	The Philippines	Taiwan	Mexico	Brazil	South Korea
Births per 1000 1960:	45	39	44	41	42
1970:	44	26	41	38	30
1988:	35	16	30	28	19
Death rate per 1000	7	5	6	8	6
Natural increase	2.8%	1.1%	2.4%	2.0%	1.3%
Infant mortality per 1000 live births	51	6.9	50	63	30
Life expectancy (years)	66	73	66	65	68
Population density	142	213	31	13	345
Per capita income 1960:	$169	$ 176	$ 441	$ 268	$ 138
1969:	$208	$ 334	$ 606	$ 348	$ 242
1982:	$510	$1 400	$1 290	$1 570	$1 160
1986:	$570	$3 099	$1 850	$1 810	$2 370
Unemployment and gross underemployment	15%	4%	13%	12%	7.5%
Ratio of income of top 20% to bottom 20%	16:1	5:1	16:1	25:1	5:1
Income improvement of poorest 20% over past 20 years	negligible	200%	negligible	negligible	>100%
Investment cost of increasing GNP by $1	$3.50	$2.10	$3.10	$2.80	$1.70
Literacy rate	85%	85%	80%	70%	91%
Population with safe drinking water	50%	78%	62%	55%	66%
Agricultural working population per 100 hectares	71	195	35	43	197
Farmers belonging to co-operatives	17%	virtually 100%	5%	28%	virtually 100%
Yield per hectare for food grains	458	1 428	490	512	1 140
Food energy in kJ per capita	9 019	12 110	11 166	10 555	11 224
Daily protein output per person	52 g	80 g	66 g	61 g	73 g
Effective land reform	no	yes	no	no	yes

36. Examine the statistics in Table 6.16 once again. Choose a country with a high natural population increase and one with a low natural increase. Select a group of statistics which reflect some of the key differences between these two countries in terms of birth rates and factors which influence birth rates. Construct a multiple line graph to illustrate the differences.

Population Growth

Many different aspects of the world's changing demography have been examined in this chapter. The question remains, however: does our current population growth spell disaster or progress? The answer to that question will be important in helping to mould our view of the world. Table 6.17 summarizes two different points of view.

Table 6.17
Conflicting Views of Population Growth

Viewpoint One Growth means progress.	Viewpoint Two Continued massive growth brings disastrous problems of hunger and homelessness.
1) A growing population means a larger market for goods and thus more prosperity and industrial growth.	1) What point is there in having a growing population if it cannot be fed, clothed, or educated?
2) A large population gives a country greater political and military power.	2) More people simply strain the economy if they cannot find jobs or if the economy is in decline.
3) When a country has a large population, there is a greater pool of human resources to draw from and thus more progress is possible in all fields.	3) We are running out of easily accessible natural resources, and future exploitation of resources will be more difficult and costly.
4) We are not running out of resources, since we learn to use them more efficiently and discover new sources for them, including recycling them.	4) In an age of nuclear weapons, large populations do not automatically translate into political or military power.
5) Some of the richest countries in the world have high population densities and yet are not considered to be overpopulated (e.g., Great Britain, Holland, etc.).	5) The smaller a country's population is, the more manageable it is, regardless of its level of wealth.
6) Not all crowded cities have urban problems such as crime. Poor economic management and corrupt governments are among the reasons for urban problems, as opposed to simply overpopulation.	6) Many of the social problems in the world such as pollution, rising crime rates, and other social problems are the result, directly or indirectly, of overcrowding in cities and towns (e.g., Sao Paulo in Brazil, Lagos in Nigeria).

Questions

37. Examine both points of view outlined in Table 6.17. From the reading that you have done in this chapter on population, which side do you feel has the stronger argument? Write a full analysis to substantiate your answer.

38. What implications are there for a government or an international planning agency in supporting either of these two points of view? Think of both long- and short-term implications.

Conclusion

In this chapter, we have seen that many factors influence why people have children. Complex cultural and economic forces in a society come into play to mould parents' attitudes toward family size. But while population growth is a product of societal forces, it also produces conditions which affect the society. There is a general downward trend in rates of population growth worldwide and conditions will continue to change in all likelihood in the future. Population growth may be seen not so much as a problem but as a reflection of various forces operating within a country, and an opportunity to harness human potential for the future.

Vocabulary

populationist
population density
demography
population growth rate
birth rate
death rate
natural increase
natural decrease
infant mortality rate (IMR)
rule of 72
doubling time
population pyramid
dependency load
Malthusian checks
neo-Malthusianism
nuclear family

Education is a key to developing human potential. This Colombian boy is learning to read and write through a government sponsored program.

Independent Study

1. (a) Select three very large cities which have not been studied in this book, and for each one, research the following: the city's size, rate of growth, location, and history; its major industries and its economic role in the country; its major problems; and its outlook for the future.

   (b) What similarities and differences exist among these cities? Are they of a major or minor type?

   (c) What conclusions can you draw about the nature of very large cities and their management?

2. Collect a variety of newspapers and magazines that deal with issues in Canada and the United States.

   (a) Read through the articles and develop a list of the issues or topics which deal with the aging of North America's population. In particular, look for references to the growing number of senior citizens and the increasing importance of meeting their needs. Refer also to the advertisements which you see in these publications.

   (b) What major trends can you observe in the age structure of the North American population?

   (c) If current trends continue, what are the prospects for life in Canada in 25 years? Explain your answer fully.

3. Choose a major region of the world, such as South America or Southeast Asia, for which you will complete a demographic analysis.

   (a) What are the average birth rates, death rates, natural increases, and infant mortality rates for the countries of this region?

   (b) How have these rates changed in the region over the last 25 years or so?

   (c) What other changes have been taking place in this region over this time period? Refer to economic statistics such as GNP per capita and food supply per person, as well as other events such as political upheavals, wars, or natural disasters.

   (d) How might the events mentioned in question 3(c) have influenced the demographic trends of the region?

   (e) Are there significant variations between countries of this region? If so, are those variations demographic or economic, and what reasons can you suggest for them?

   (f) From your study so far, what conclusions can you draw about some of the factors which affect demographics?

4. (a) As the retirement age for people in the developed world decreases, the number of years of active retirement increases. What specific activities are available for retirees?

   (b) What lifestyle changes do people experience once they retire? Give specific examples .

   (c) How does the disposable income of many retired people compare with those in other age groups?

   (d) What changes are coming about in consumer products and advertising to appeal to retired people?

Part IV

Major Environmental and Resource Issues

By the end of this chapter, you should be able to:

- outline the interdependency of all environmental systems;
- describe and explain the causes, effects, and possible future implications of the following issues:
  - the loss of forests, especially in tropical environments;
  - soil erosion and degradation;
  - desertification;
  - atmospheric, water, and land pollution;
  - water shortages;
  - habitat and wildlife destruction, and
  - damage to permafrost environments;
- suggest what might help alleviate these problems.

7

Environmental Issues

The Destruction of the Ozone Layer

In the frigid conditions of Canada's northernmost manned meteorological station, at Alert on Ellesmere Island, scientists ready a helium balloon and the box of instruments it will carry aloft.

The instruments will be carried to a height of about 32 km where they will relay information about the ozone layer, which filters out much of the ultraviolet radiation emitted by the sun. During the past 20 years, the amount of ozone has been decreasing, bringing about increased exposure to ultraviolet radiation. This, in turn, has caused a noticeable increase in the incidence of skin cancer. In addition, excessive exposure to ultraviolet rays increases the incidence of cataracts and harms the immune system by slowing the production of white blood cells. It also affects crops and aquatic life. Shrimp and crab larvae are known to die when exposed to high doses of ultraviolet light, and many believe that major food crops like wheat and rice would be affected as a consequence of leaf damage.

Ozone depletion may eventually affect weather patterns and enhance the greenhouse effect caused by the current buildup of carbon dioxide in

A helium balloon being prepared for launch into the upper atmosphere

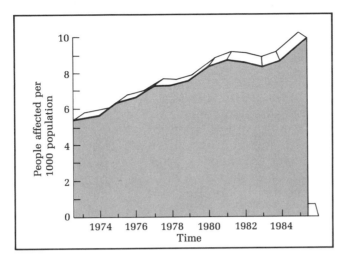

Figure 7.1
Increases in the Incidence of Skin Cancer in the USA

the atmosphere. This development, along with the increased risk to the health of the population, has sparked international concern about further deterioration of the ozone layer.

Ozone is created naturally when lightning or ultraviolet light passes through oxygen; in fact, ozone is just a special form of oxygen with three atoms in each molecule instead of two. Early in the history of the earth there was

Figure 7.2
The Results of Ozone Depletion in the Upper Atmosphere

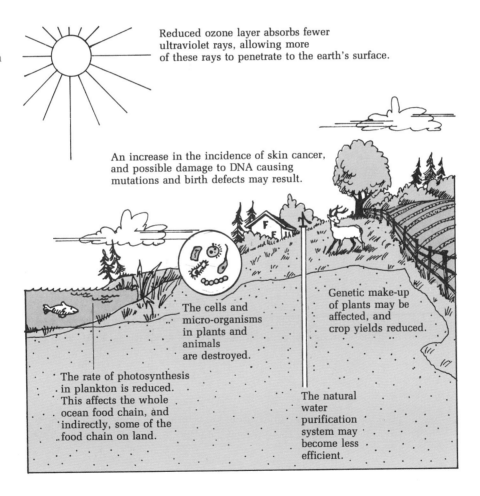

Reduced ozone layer absorbs fewer ultraviolet rays, allowing more of these rays to penetrate to the earth's surface.

An increase in the incidence of skin cancer, and possible damage to DNA causing mutations and birth defects may result.

The cells and micro-organisms in plants and animals are destroyed.

Genetic make-up of plants may be affected, and crop yields reduced.

The rate of photosynthesis in plankton is reduced. This affects the whole ocean food chain, and indirectly, some of the food chain on land.

The natural water purification system may become less efficient.

little oxygen, therefore little oxygen, and animals lived in the protected environment of the oceans.

Ozone is being destroyed by chlorofluorocarbons (CFCs). CFCs are used extensively in many of our modern systems and products and escape to the atmosphere. Figure 7.3 gives you some idea of the widespread use of CFCs. They slowly work their way to the upper atmosphere, where the sun breaks them apart to release the chlorine atoms. It is the chlorine atoms which react with the ozone. Some scientists believe that nitric oxides can also have a destructive effect on ozone. Nitrogen oxides are released directly into the stratosphere by supersonic jets, in addition to diffusing up from the surface of the earth from such sources as automobiles.

Twenty nations, including Canada, signed a pact in 1987 to protect the planet's ozone shield. In September 1987, 24 nations met in Montreal and agreed to freeze the use of CFCs at 1986 levels within two years, then make a further 20 percent reduction by 1993, and another 30 percent decrease by 1998. CFCs are no longer used as a propellant in spray cans in many countries, but there are numerous other products which still use them. In 1988, the Canadian government declared its intention of

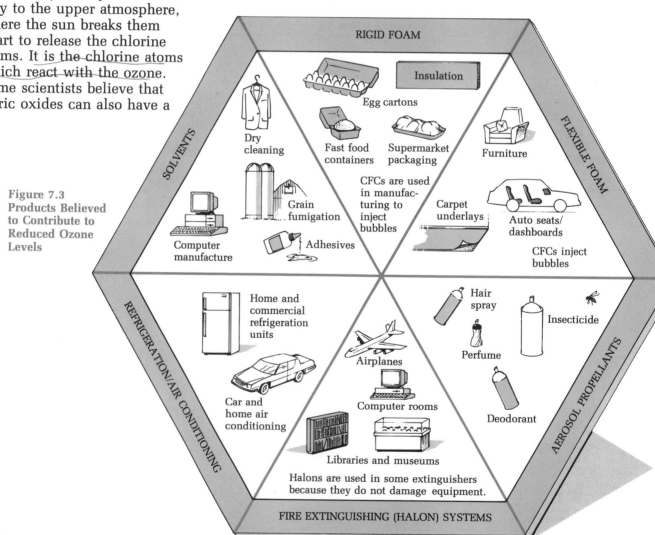

Figure 7.3
Products Believed to Contribute to Reduced Ozone Levels

banning the use of CFCs, except where the product is essential and where no substitute exists.

It was estimated in 1987 that the world produced 854 million kilograms of CFCs each year, about four times the amount produced 20 years before. In 1984, world concern was generated by the report of thinning of the ozone layer over Antarctica. Commonly referred to as a "hole," it was the size of continental USA. This hole has subsequently reappeared each spring and then closed up again. Canadian scientists have found a smaller hole over the Canadian Arctic and northern Europe. Since the mid-1970s, ozone concentrations have decreased worldwide. In the Toronto area, the reduction has been three to four percent; over Antarctica, the reduction has been 50 percent! It is estimated that for each one percent decrease in ozone, there will be a corresponding four percent increase in the incidence of skin cancer.

Alex Chisholm, of the Canadian Atmospheric Environmental Service, estimated in 1986 that we could start to see the detrimental effects of the loss of ozone concentrations in 10 to 15 years. By then, he says, it would be too late to do anything which would have an immediate effect, and it would take 100 years for the ozone layer to recover its original thickness. In fact, we are beginning to observe the effects already. Any controls we impose on ozone-destroying substances will have more benefit for our children and grandchildren than for us.

Questions

1. Look at Figure 7.3 which shows where CFCs are found.

   (a) Suggest three products whose use could be discontinued or replaced to reduce the production of CFCs.

   (b) In what ways would each of the changes you propose affect people and the environment?

2. It is estimated that CFCs started to damage the atmosphere about 25 years ago. They triggered widespread scientific interest about ten years later, and reports began to alert the general public about ten years after that.

   (a) In what ways have we benefitted from the production and use of CFCs?

   (b) How might we have known, in advance, the long-term effects of their use?

   (c) Produce arguments to support opposing sides in a discussion on the merits of more extensive testing of industrial chemicals. Which side do you support?

   (d) What do you believe would have happened if further testing, decades ago, had revealed the destructive potential of CFCs? Explain your answer carefully.

3. Pollution control has become an international problem.

   (a) Why is this?

   (b) How does this make the problem much more difficult than if each nation could deal with its pollution problems independently? Give some specific examples to illustrate your answer.

Introduction

The earth is essentially a closed system. Very little is added, and very little leaves it. There are a few exceptions, such as those space probes which will not return, the exchange of a few molecules from the upper atmosphere, and the arrival of small pieces of debris from space. These may be of local consequence, but have little worldwide impact.

One very important entity which does enter our atmosphere and has a very great influence is radiant heat from the sun. Until very recently, it was believed that all life forms depended directly or indirectly on the sun for their survival. Recently discovered exceptions include some creatures living in the deepest parts of the oceans. They sustain life by ingesting minerals which issue from vents in the ocean bottom, and are warmed by the exuding magma. The vast majority of life, however, still depends on the sun for survival.

The sun permits photosynthesis to take place, and it keeps the temperature of the surface of the earth in a range in which life can survive and water is available to us. To balance this, however, the earth also radiates energy to space. If it did not do this, the earth would be a fiery furnace on which life could not exist. When the gain and loss of radiant energy at the earth's surface are balanced, the overall temperature of the earth remains constant.

Within the earth's closed system are a myriad of interconnecting systems which result from, and contribute to, the dynamism of the earth. It would be impossible at present, even for the most sophisticated of our computers, to fully analyze all of the interconnections. The study of meteorology and weather forecasting, for exam-

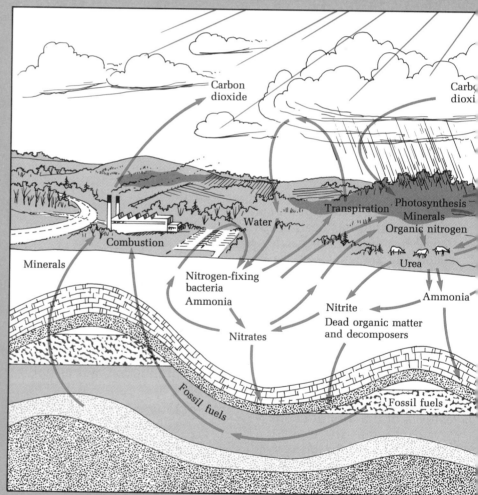

ple, is far from an exact science, even though it deals with only a fraction of those interconnecting systems. Figure 7.4 attempts to show the major cycles of the biosphere. The **biosphere** refers to the part of the earth's surface where living organisms can maintain themselves.

This diagram should help you to understand some of the interactions which are vital for the continuation of life within the finite realm of the earth.

This chapter concentrates on the impact that people are having on these interconnecting systems. Of great concern to many is the destruction of vast areas of tropical forest resulting in soil erosion and climatic change. In addition, the pollutants that we pump into the air are believed to be causing a general warming trend in the earth's atmosphere, referred to as the greenhouse effect. Pollutants in our air, water, and food are affecting our health and that of the plants and animals which form an integral part of our ecosystem. The demand for more water is putting a tremendous strain on existing supplies. The extinction of many wild species, largely as a result of the destruction of their habitat, is reducing the genetic variety which we could use in the future in developing new food sources and medical cures.

A growing awareness of these issues in the general population is evident, but the solutions are difficult and expensive to achieve. Ignoring the problems will not make them go away, however. The situation will continue to deteriorate until we take appropriate action.

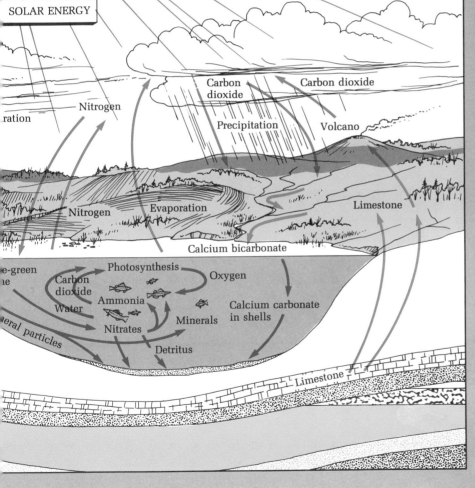

SOLAR ENERGY

Carbon dioxide

Carbon dioxide

Nitrogen

Precipitation

Volcano

ration

Nitrogen

Evaporation

Limestone

Calcium bicarbonate

e-green
e

Photosynthesis

Oxygen

Carbon dioxide

Water

Ammonia

Nitrates

Minerals

Calcium carbonate in shells

eral particles

Detritus

Limestone

**Figure 7.4
Major Cycles of
the Biosphere**

Deforestation, Soil Erosion and Degradation, and The Problem of Desertification

As the number of people inhabiting the earth increases, there is a corresponding increase in demand for those things necessary to sustain their lives. In areas where there is a rising standard of living, the demands grow more quickly than the increase in population would suggest. Growing industrialization and changing technology result in ever-increasing use of resources from all over the world. It has also led to the creation of wastes which are threatening the air, water, and land. Some of these problems of pollution, and the misuse and overuse of resources will be discussed in this chapter, followed by a subsequent chapter which outlines the impact that resource extraction has had on the world. Because the cycles which order the earth are intricately interconnected, any violation of one part of the system will have an impact on other parts. Thus, it is hard to divide this area of study satisfactorily.

**Figure 7.5
Distribution of
the World's
Forests**

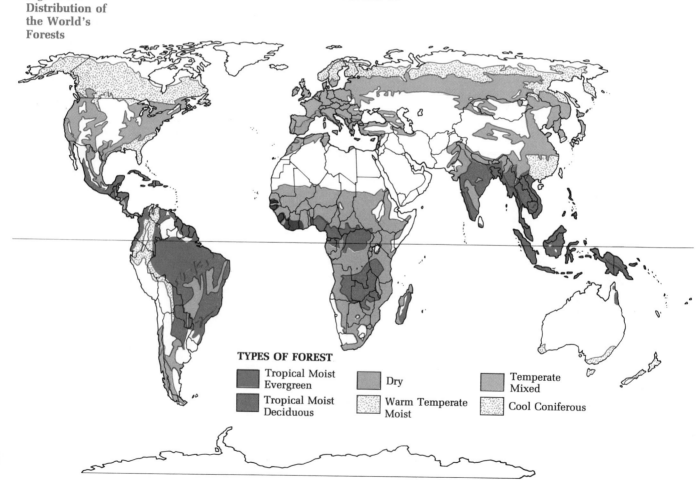

TYPES OF FOREST

- Tropical Moist Evergreen
- Tropical Moist Deciduous
- Dry
- Warm Temperate Moist
- Temperate Mixed
- Cool Coniferous

Deforestation

Forests cover approximately one-third of the land area of the world. Forest products are essential resources and provide employment for millions of people. They supply fuelwood, which is the greatest source of household energy for those who live in lesser developed countries. International trade in wood products exceeds $100 billion each year.

In addition to the vast range of products they provide, forests also form the habitat for plants and animals, reduce the rate of soil loss, convert carbon dioxide into oxygen, and provide us with an aesthetically pleasing environment.

A giant tree in the rain forest in northern Thailand

Tropical Forests

From a height of 800 km above the earth's surface, satellites have observed fires consuming the forests of southeast Asia. These forests are being deliberately burned to supply more agricultural land and animal grazing land for the increasing population. Tropical forests in Central and South America and in equatorial Africa are also being cleared at an alarming rate.

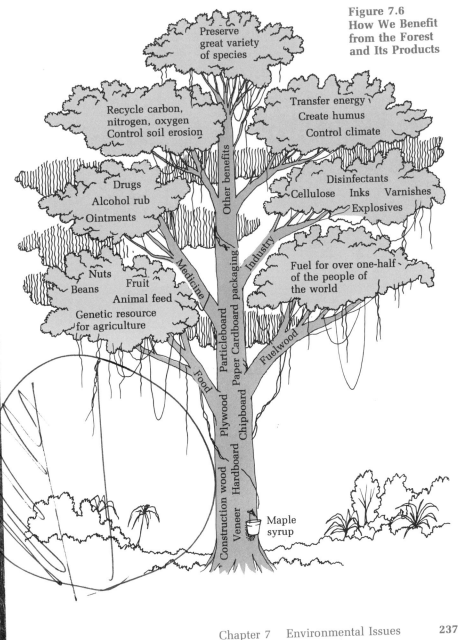

Figure 7.6 How We Benefit from the Forest and Its Products

Preserve great variety of species

Recycle carbon, nitrogen, oxygen Control soil erosion

Transfer energy
Create humus
Control climate

Drugs
Alcohol rub
Ointments

Disinfectants
Cellulose   Inks   Varnishes
Explosives

Other benefits

Nuts
Beans
Fruit
Animal feed
Genetic resource for agriculture

Medicine

Industry

Fuel for over one-half of the people of the world

Food

Particleboard
Plywood   Paper   Cardboard packaging

Fuelwood

Construction wood
Veneer   Hardboard   Chipboard

Maple syrup

Forests are being cleared all over the world, but it is in the tropical areas that most losses are occurring and about which there is the greatest current concern.

Forty percent of the tropical forests have already been cleared or degraded, and in many countries it is feared that the forests will have disappeared completely in 20 to 30 years. Each year, an estimated 11 million hectares of prime woodland is cleared. That is approximately the size of Nova Scotia and New Brunswick combined! Norman Myers, who has studied the world's forests in great detail, has estimated that the only large areas of tropical forests which will survive into the early part of the next century will be found in the western Amazon and Zaire Basins. Of the timber which is removed from the forests, 20 percent is used for local building materials and 47 percent for fuelwood. Timber sales abroad are the lesser developed world's fifth biggest export. In addition, vast areas are being cleared for agriculture and animal pasture land, using the "slash-and-burn" clearing method. Only one-tenth of this area grows back into forest.

Figure 7.7
The Shrinking
Forests

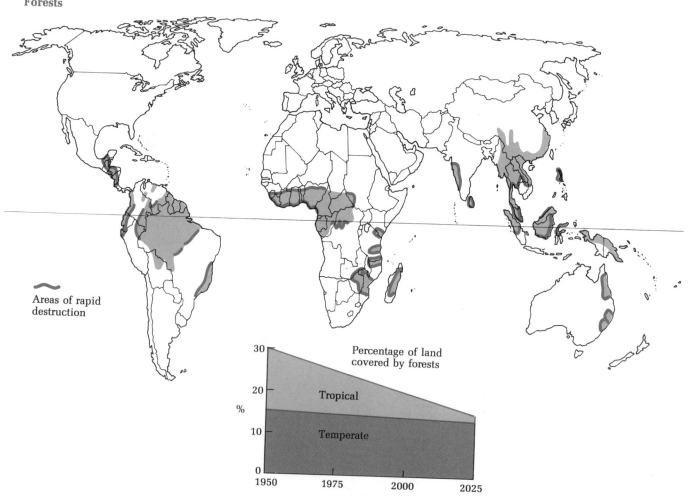

Areas of rapid destruction

Percentage of land covered by forests

30

20

%

10

0

Tropical

Temperate

1950   1975   2000   2025

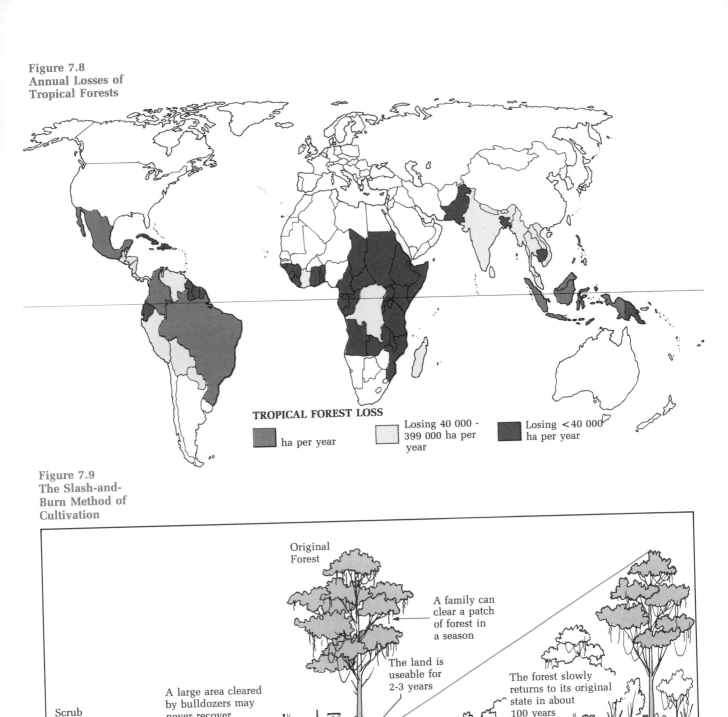

**Figure 7.8
Annual Losses of
Tropical Forests**

TROPICAL FOREST LOSS

Losing 40 000 - 399 000 ha per year

Losing <40 000 ha per year

**Figure 7.9
The Slash-and-
Burn Method of
Cultivation**

Original Forest

A family can clear a patch of forest in a season

The land is useable for 2-3 years

A large area cleared by bulldozers may never recover

The forest slowly returns to its original state in about 100 years

Scrub

100

← Years

0 4

Years →

100

Questions

4. (a) Why are the tropical forests being cleared?

   (b) What would be the results if no more tropical forests were to be cleared? Categorize those results as benefits to lesser developed nations, problems for lesser developed nations, benefits to more developed nations, or problems for more developed nations.

5. (a) Suggest approaches which might be adopted by a tropical country to slow the clearing of the tropical forests without destroying the benefits that come from their exploitation.

   (b) What measures would have to be taken to implement your suggestions?

The soils of the tropical forests are not fertile, since the vital nutrients are held above the soil itself. When leaves fall or a tree topples to the ground, soil bacteria decompose them within a few weeks, so that the plant materials become available to aid the growth of other plants. (In the temperate forests, this process may take years.) Thus, the supply of nutrients in the soils of the tropical forest is depleted extremely quickly, once the forest cover is removed.

The rural population of the developing nations depends upon growing its own food for survival. These people are often forced into marginal upland areas where the clearing of the forest results in devastating soil erosion. Downstream, the rivers become laden with silt and, with increased rates of surface run-off, they frequently flood, causing damage to crops, settlements, and communications. Reservoirs get choked and irrigation schemes become less efficient or even useless. In India, for example, it is estimated that slash-and-burn practices have caused about $1 billion in damage to lowland areas each year since 1978. In such circumstances, the livelihood of ten lowland dwellers is endangered by the activities of one upland farmer.

There are other consequences, too. An estimated 2 billion of the world's people still rely on fuelwood for cooking and heating. At present, some of these people can spend 7 h each day collecting it. As the supply further dwindles, gathering the wood will take more time away from other, more productive activities such as tending crops, and malnutrition will increase. Where animal dung is used instead of wood for fuel, there is less natural fertilizer to be recycled into the already overworked soils. Such a reduction in fertilizer is estimated to have lowered the developing world's grain harvest by more than 14 million tonnes a year. This is about double the food aid sent by the USA, Canada, and Australia. One simple development, the bio-gas unit, has been introduced to cope with dwindling sources of fuelwood.

Questions

6. Use Figure 7.10 to explain the principle and operation of the bio-gas unit.

7. Why are bio-gas units so suitable for use in rural areas of many developing nations?

8. Suggest other simple techniques which could be used under similar circumstances to reduce the need for fuelwood. Why do you think these have not been implemented in many areas?

Figure 7.10
A bio-gas unit

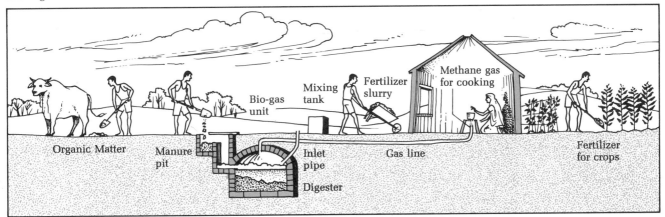

Organic Matter · Manure pit · Bio-gas unit · Mixing tank · Fertilizer slurry · Methane gas for cooking · Inlet pipe · Digester · Gas line · Fertilizer for crops

Land being cleared in Sri Lanka

The dollar value of timber exported by lesser developed countries is expected to fall from $7 billion to $2 billion by the end of the century, providing only 10 percent of their income instead of the current 30 percent. In fact, 14 lesser developed countries which have the right environment to produce forest products are now importing nearly $4 billion worth of lumber each year. Low cutting fees demanded by governments for timber lands have encouraged speedy removal of the trees. Those who lease or own the lands usually employ clear-cutting techniques which are efficient, but so destructive that the forest is unable to regenerate. In Brazil, in 1973, land in the Amazon area was sold for $5/ha. The owners are still making a fortune logging the vast tracts they bought from the government then, and little or no effort is made to replant the forest.

Questions

9. Imagine you were in a position of political influence and wished to instate a policy of conservation and proper management of the tropical forests in your country.
   (a) What opposition would you face?
   (b) What benefits and problems could result from your actions?

10. Suggest actions which importers of wood from tropical countries could take to encourage the exporting nations to use their forest resources more carefully.

Another consequence of clearing the tropical forests is the destruction of the specialized forms of life that inhabit them. Although the tropical rain forests cover only seven percent of the world's land surface, they are believed to contain 50-80 percent of its life forms, many of which have not yet been identified and studied. For example, a researcher identified 41 000 species of insect life alone in 1 ha section of the Peruvian rain forest. It is estimated that 1000 to 10 000 forms of life are destroyed in the forests each year. This destruction has been likened to burning whole libraries before they are read. Moreover, the forests probably have much to offer in the form of foods and medicines of which we are not yet aware.

The destruction of the tropical forests is believed to be contributing to the buildup of carbon dioxide in the atmosphere. (See the section on the "greenhouse effect.") Nature would normally be able to compensate for this increase over a long period of time, as plants would grow more vigorously in an environment rich in carbon dioxide, but present circumstances make this corrective action impossible.

The tropical forests also release prodigious amounts of water vapour into the air. Experiments carried out in Brazil in 1982 revealed that the Amazon creates 50 percent of its own rain and creates weather patterns that influence climate throughout

Latin America. But in areas of the Amazon Basin which have been cleared, local rainfall has dropped from 2000 mm to 800 mm per year.

In many countries where the forests have been cleared, water levels fluctuate greatly from one season to another. Waterways become unnavigable, and water supplies undependable. Even the Panama Canal is threatened. This canal depends on water from a natural and an artificial lake. Today, only one-quarter of the hills surrounding these lakes are still covered by trees, and further destruction is continuing.

Figure 7.11
Foods and Medicines Which Have Come From the Tropical Forests

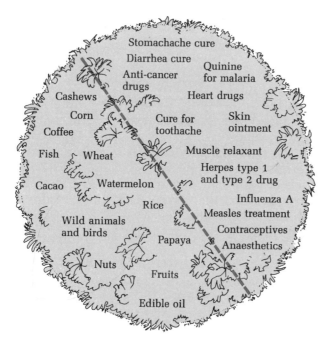

Stomachache cure
Diarrhea cure
Anti-cancer drugs
Quinine for malaria
Cashews
Heart drugs
Corn
Cure for toothache
Skin ointment
Coffee
Fish
Wheat
Muscle relaxant
Cacao
Watermelon
Herpes type 1 and type 2 drug
Rice
Influenza A
Wild animals and birds
Measles treatment
Papaya
Contraceptives
Anaesthetics
Nuts
Fruits
Edible oil

Water levels in the canal are dropping, and silt is building up on the floor. If the Panama Canal could no longer function, the economy of Panama would be devastated, and other nations currently using the canal would have to find new, more expensive, dangerous, and time-consuming routes, such as those around the southern tips of South America and South Africa.

Questions

11. What alternative actions could be taken by the government of Panama to ensure the future viability of the Panama Canal?

12. Some ships are too large to be able to use the Panama Canal.

   (a) What arguments could be made for or against building a new canal through the Central American isthmus?

   (b) Briefly explain the problems that would be encountered in such an undertaking.

   (c) Suggest safeguards that should be implemented to ensure that this new canal does not suffer the same fate as the Panama Canal.

Above, clearing forest for agricultural use in Thailand. Such action often results in soil erosion; left, burning tropical rain forest to provide land for cattle ranching in Brazil

Some Suggested Solutions

The solutions are not easy to accomplish, but they must be attempted if this trend toward self-destruction is to be slowed and reversed. It has been suggested that an international cartel, the Organization of Timber Exporting Countries, be developed to force world timber prices up. Increased prices would reduce consumption and make the return to the timber-cutter valuable enough so that reforestation would be undertaken, in particular, the growing of plantations of more efficient trees.

Another course of action is to ensure that industrialized countries import only wood grown on tree farms, none cut from the rain forest, and buy only meat from animals raised on established ranches, not from recently cleared land which has been created by burning forests.

Better cooking technology could be introduced in places where fuelwood is now used. This would include fuel-efficient stoves which are being used successfully in some areas, and the use of methane, produced from plant and animal wastes when they decompose in an anaerobic environment. This is the bio-gas technique described previously.

One other suggestion is that, in tropical areas, food

should be grown on the most productive soils. In many cases, this would require a new system of land ownership.

Some Success Stories

In some lesser developed nations, the people themselves are having an impact. For example, peasant women in northern India blocked the passage of giant bulldozers which are going to clear the nearby forest. This led to a conservation movement in the area which has resulted in the replanting of more than one million cypress, walnut, oak, and poplar trees, and significant progress in the conservation of the remaining forest. Such local movements are occurring in other parts of the world also.

Large sums of money are being used for research into the problem. For example, the Canadian International Development Agency (CIDA) spends about $80 million per year, and the US government's Aid for International Development contributes $140 million annually.

Scientists have developed new strains of plants to replace the depleted tropical forests. These grow to maturity in six years and, because they are legumes, they also help to fertilize the soil.

In China and South Korea, there has been much success with rigidly enforced village tree-replanting quotas. In Algeria, a strip of trees one kilometre wide and several hundred kilometres long has been planted in an attempt to stop the advance of the Sahara Desert.

Question

13. In many lesser developed nations, conservation is frequently regarded as a luxury, and advice from foreign scientists is often not welcomed. Why is this?

Many experts believe that once 10-20 percent of the tropical forest trees are removed, the forests will no longer be capable of regeneration. The experts consider that the best course of action is to show the nations' leaders the success stories, and let them take the ideas back to their own countries.

The problem is certainly one which the industrialized nations cannot ignore, and help will be needed from around the world. The World Resources Institute, based in Washington, is recommending that $8 billion should be invested over a period of five years to encourage and finance conservation, training, research, and tree planting. The money would come from both developed countries and from those receiving the assistance.

The Temperate Forests

There is an outcry from many concerned groups in North America that the temperate forests are not being replanted at a rate which will ensure renewal. Although you can observe from Figure 7.8 that the rate of clearance is much slower than in the tropics, nevertheless, it is a problem which North Americans should address. In Sweden, for example, the problem of disappearing forests was recognized a century ago. For about 90 years, the country's forests have been carefully replanted, fertilized, trimmed, and sprayed. The Swedish people invest five to six times more money per hectare in their forests than do Canadians!

In addition to being threatened by the lack of a large-scale replanting program, temperate forests are also being assailed by pollution, in particular, acid precipitation. The effects of pollution are covered later in this chapter.

Soil Erosion and Degradation

A resource which we have tended to take for granted until recent years has been the earth's fragile cover of soil. Soil may take hundreds or thousands of years to develop from the underlying parent material and from organic materials, but it can be destroyed within the course of a few years by forest clearance, poor agricultural practices, pollution, or urban encroachment.

The loss of soil is a worldwide phenomenon. It is occurring in more developed and lesser developed nations alike, and takes the form of erosion and degradation.

In areas of tropical forests, where large tracts of land are being cleared for agriculture, for fuelwood for the rural population, or for lumber, the unprotected soil loses its fertility very quickly. The heavy rains wash unprotected soils on slopes away, leaving useless areas of gullied land and causing mud slides and floods on the lowland areas below.

**Figure 7.12
Major Areas of
Soil Erosion
Around the
World**

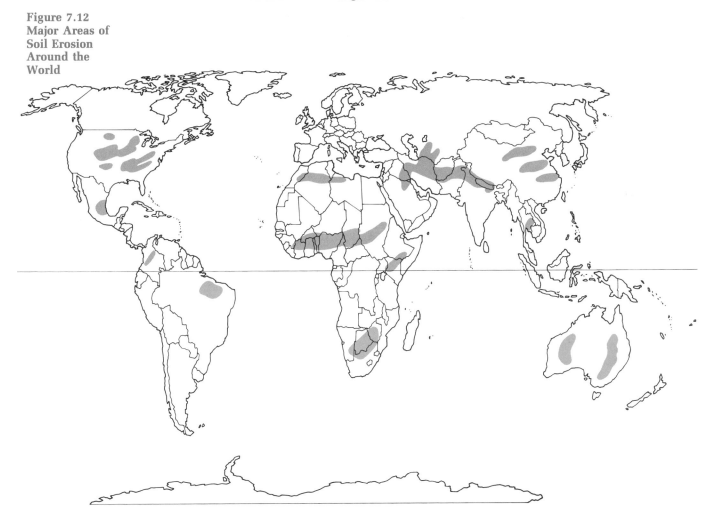

A typical example of "slumping" due to erosion after the removal of rain forest in Madagascar

In the vast areas of land in countries such as Canada, the United States, and the Soviet Union, where the natural cover of forests and grassland has been removed, surface soils are washing and blowing away and are being poisoned by the accumulation of pesticides, herbicides, and fertilizers. Yields of cereal grains decline where good topsoil has been removed, and the sediment which ends up in streams and lakes is a pollutant which not only chokes these waterways, but also tends to spoil them as a healthy environment for marine organisms, particularly fish.

In Canada, millions of hectares of good soil have already been destroyed or degraded.

Our land will have only a fraction of its potential productivity of 50 years ago if this trend is not halted. Our Prairie soils have lost up to 60 percent of the organic material from the top 15 cm of topsoil, due to the agricultural methods employed in growing crops such as wheat. Drought is also a problem, because it leads to increased wind erosion on exposed soils.

In Quebec, 30-60 percent of the organic content has been lost where the soil has been continuously used for growing row crops like potatoes, corn, or beans. The cropping practices employed expose the soil to wind and water erosion much more than if it had been left under a cover of grain or grasses. In southern Ontario, the cost of soil erosion is estimated to be $68 million annually.

Who is to blame for the situation? We all are, because consumers constantly demand low prices for food, farmers use farming techniques which are economically efficient but hard on the land, and the governments are slow to recognize the problem and even slower to act.

The results of this lack of concern for the environment will be higher food prices, declining food quality, and less food to supply a hungry world in the future. The four major problems and possible solutions are listed in Table 7.1.

Contour furrowing for tree planting in southern Ontario

Table 7.1
Soil Erosion in Canada

Problem	Area, description, cause	Suggested solutions
Wind erosion	Especially Prairies. Cut shelterbelts, reduced cattle and feed crops. Summer fallow causes loss of moisture in topsoil.	Build shelterbelts. Reduce summer fallow. Introduce other crops which cover the surface more closely. Use zero or minimal tillage.
Water erosion	Parts of B.C., the Prairies, and Ontario. Reduction of vegetative cover.	Plow in organic residues, use mulching, and contour cultivation. Use grass waterways, design better drainage systems. Use zero tillage.
Salination (calcification)	Drier Prairies. Humus removal permits water to soak down through soil, then be drawn to the surface with high salt concentrations during dry spells.	Plough organic material and residues into soil. Retain grass cover.
Acidity	Prairies and southern Ontario. Acids come from fertilizers, some natural-gas processing plants, smelters, and coal-fired thermal electric plants. (Fertilizers contribute nearly three times as much acid to the soil as does acid rain.)	Reduce sources of acid rain. Rotate crops with legumes which fix nitrates. Breed cereal crops that can fix nitrates into the soil.

An example of soil erosion near Guelph, Ontario

The Francis Family of Waterford, Ontario

Richard and Gail Francis bought their 20 ha farm in 1960. At that time, 100 ha were used to grow forage crops for their cattle and sheep, and there were no visible signs of any soil problems. Along with many of their neighbours, they changed their farm operation to one of growing more profitable cash crops, and soon began to notice soil problems developing. Small gullies were appearing and waterways began filling with topsoil which had washed down from higher land. In one sloping area, 30 cm of topsoil had washed from higher land over the course of 11 years, and was deposited in the lower fields. Yields from these higher areas started to decline by as much as 25 percent when compared to areas of deposition. Soil tests showed that the major cause of yield reductions was the removal of humus from the soil.

The Francises' concern led Richard to nearby Michigan, where much progress had been made in combatting such problems. As a result of this trip, the Francises introduced many new practices onto their farm. These included:

- arranging the fields and ploughing across slopes wherever possible (**contour ploughing**);
- grassing waterways;
- creating terraces with sub-surface drains where necessary;
- creating windbreaks at the edges of terraces and fields, using shrubs and trees;
- reforesting the rough land;
- introducing a four-year rotation consisting of two years of corn, one of soybeans, and one of cereal grains;
- using zero-till cropping practices on sloping land; and
- reducing tillage to a minimum on the remaining land.

Modified contour ploughing

Right, zero-tillage; below, a windbreak at the edge of a cornfield reduces wind erosion.

The new techniques took time to learn and considerable money for new equipment, but the results are promising. Using zero tillage, yields of barley and corn are higher than with conventional tillage. Results have varied, depending on soil type, and different practices have been adopted on various soils.

The Francises have found that the new practices have reduced their labour costs and the wear and tear on their equipment. They need to hire fewer helpers during the planting season, and because they don't need to use heavy machinery while the soil is still wet, it doesn't get compacted. The Francis family is confident that their new farming methods will be beneficial for themselves, but more importantly, for those who work the farm after them.

Certain problems remain, however. Agricultural companies need to find a herbicide to control perennial weeds. Also, more research is needed in the development of equipment better suited to zero tillage.

Left, a form of crop rotation; below, planting a new crop

Questions

14. List the problems which developed on the Francises' farm and carefully explain their causes.

15. In what ways did research, education, and openness of mind play key roles in the improvement of their farm?

16. What disadvantages, if any, do you see in adopting conservation farming techniques?

17. If you were appointed to try to persuade other farmers to adopt some or all of the soil conservation techniques practised on the Francises' farm, how would you go about it?

Desertification

Intimately linked with the disappearance of much of the forests and the erosion and degradation of our soils is the problem of desertification. **Desertification** is the destruction of the biological activity of the land that eventually leads to desert-like conditions. No doubt climatic change is responsible for some of the encroachment of the deserts (this spread, when due to natural change alone, is called **desertization**), but the effects have been accelerated by human activities.

The areas which are most at risk are the drylands, where rainfall is low and variable. Figure 7.13 illustrates the sequence of events which leads to desertification.

Desertification ranges from moderate damage, where productivity is reduced up to 25 percent, to very severe damage, where productivity is reduced by more than 50 percent. The table below shows estimates of the areas which are experiencing some degree of desertification.

Table 7.2
Desertification in
the Early 1980s

Location	Area of Drylands (million ha)	Percentage Desertified
Sudano-Sahelian Africa	473	88
Southern Africa	304	80
Mediterranean Africa	101	83
Western Asia	142	82
Southern Asia	359	70
USSR in Asia	298	55
China and Mongolia	315	69
Australia	491	23
Mediterranean Europe	76	39
South America and Mexico	293	71
North America	405	40
Total	**3257**	**61**

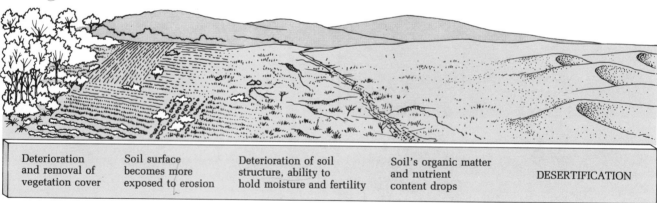

Deterioration and removal of vegetation cover	Soil surface becomes more exposed to erosion	Deterioration of soil structure, ability to hold moisture and fertility	Soil's organic matter and nutrient content drops	DESERTIFICATION

Figure 7.13
The Sequence of
Events Leading to
Desertification

Question

18. Using a world map and the statistics for desertification in Table 7.2, devise a method to show the extent of the desertification problem around the world. You might choose to superimpose bar graphs, proportionate circles, squares, or other symbols on relevant parts of a world map.

As you will observe from Table 7.2, several more developed nations are experiencing desertification. The basic cause of this process in all parts of the world is similar; that is, these marginal lands are being worked too hard. In wealthy nations, it is possible to allow some of this land to go out of production without much effect on the general economy. The country is sufficiently resilient to absorb the losses and to help those who are personally affected. The story is very different where, as this land goes out of production, there is little or nothing to take its place and few social services to help the people who are directly affected. Furthermore, if these countries are the ones undergoing large population growth, there is increased pressure on the land for food production.

Effects of the Spreading Desert in Mali

Mali, a country in West Africa, is experiencing severe desertification in its northern areas. Since the early 1970s, rainfall totals have been low, and the desert is taking over forests and cities. The River Niger is a very important inland waterway, and, 17 years ago, Timbuktu was a bustling port where grain was unloaded. Now, grain has to be unloaded 5 km away because the river has disappeared. The river in Timbuktu used to be an important fishing area, but now it is a sandy desert. Where there used to be forests, now there are only a few trees, and even these depend on hand watering for their survival.

There was once a busy market in the town, where piles of vegetables and fish were sold. Now the market is very small; there are still some spices and fruits, but few green vegetables. A few years ago, there was beef and then mutton; now there is

**Figure 7.14
The Location of
Mali and Some
Key Places
Within the
Country**

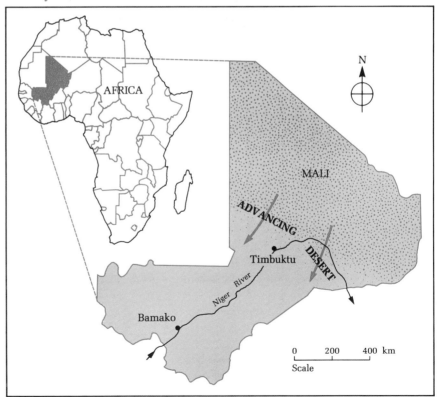

little meat for sale. Wells were dug to obtain water for the livestock, but by that time the cattle had died. The old river bed has now been dug out by hand to a depth of 20 m to reach water. Water is hauled in buckets to the small fields of corn, rice, and vegetables.

In the nearby villages, children used to help by looking after the herds of animals. Each morning, now, they come to the village centre where they are provided with their one meal per day. They are suffering from the effects of poor nutrition over the course of the last few years. Half of the children die before they reach the age of five.

The women and girls spend most of their day wandering through the desert to collect sticks to use as fuel. In the past, the boys used to strip the few remaining trees and bushes to feed to their animals, when no forage was available on the ground. Only a few goats now live where there used to be cattle.

As the trees and shrubs disappear, so also does the last defence against the desert. Very little help is being given to these northern areas, on the grounds that it is better to help the South where there is more hope for recovery. Thousands of refugees are moving south to try and keep ahead of the desert. Their villages are left empty, and the desert covers them over. As they move south, their cattle destroy the fragile vegetation cover.

Some villagers have opted to stay in the North. CIDA has helped these villagers by digging wells to a depth of 40 m when the villagers' own 18 m wells failed to reach water. With this water, tree nurseries have been started, and limited agriculture has resumed. CIDA has been working on several small projects in the area over the past 12 years, but during that time the desert has advanced 200-300 km. It is necessary to stop the spread of the desert in such countries as Mali, if their civilizations are to survive into the future.

Questions

19. List and briefly explain all of the factors which have led to the spread of the desert in Mali.

20. It has been suggested that it would be better to concentrate on the southern part of the country than to "waste" money in helping the North. Do you agree? Justify your answer.

21. (a) In what ways does Mali illustrate that it is important to act quickly when the first signs of desertification appear?

    (b) What action should be taken in response to the early evidence of the spread of the deserts? Clearly explain how local people, national governments, and international agencies would be involved.

Women pounding grain in a village in Mali

The State of The Atmosphere

The atmosphere is an integral part of the environment, vital to all forms of life and affected by every process which occurs. The composition of the air and the directions in which it moves have local, national, and international implications, because the atmospheric circulatory patterns carry noxious emissions far from their sources. Some of the pollutants come from natural sources, but human activities are responsible for the concentration of a great variety of additional pollutants in urban areas. Also, the construction of artificial environments in houses, office blocks, and other buildings has caused a dangerous concentration of certain toxic substances within them.

An example of desertification in Mauritania

When the quantities of pollutants produced were small and the chemicals involved were biodegradable, natural processes could quickly render them harmless. But now, with its escalating numbers and increased industrial activity, the world's population is creating a situation with which these natural processes cannot cope. The global effects of the accumulation of pollutants are most clearly seen in atmospheric processes, because the movements involved are faster than those of water. However, sampling of the oceans has revealed that pollutants are being spread by circulating currents, even into the remotest parts of the Antarctic, Arctic, and Pacific Oceans.

Table 7.3
Some Air
Pollutants and
Their Effects on
Health

Urban Pollution

Emphysema, which is a condition affecting the air sacs of the lungs and which limits the lungs' ability to absorb oxygen, is the fastest growing cause of death in urban areas. More than 50 000 United States citizens die annually as a result of the disease. Bronchitis and lung cancer occur twice as often in air-polluted cities as in rural areas. There is half the incidence of lung cancer in Norway, for example, where air pollution concentrations are low compared to the USA.

There are many air pollutants contributing to poor health. Some of these, and their effects, are listed in Table 7.3.

Carbon monoxide	Combines readily with oxygen in the blood, making it unavailable for cell metabolism. High concentrations are dangerous for persons with heart disease, asthma, and anemia.
Sulphur oxides and dioxides	Irritate the eyes, nose, and throat, and damage the lungs. They also kill plants, rust metals, and reduce visibility.
Nitrogen oxides and dioxides	Cause a stinking brown haze which irritates the nose and also blocks sunlight.
Hydrocarbons	Result from combustion, and react with atmospheric components to create smog, which has been shown to cause cancer in animals.
Particulates	Tiny particles of solids and liquids may themselves be poisonous or may carry other pollutants deep into the lungs, where they are trapped.
Photochemical smog	A mixture of gases and particles oxidized by the sun irritates the eyes, nose, and throat. It makes breathing difficult.

There are many hundreds of other air pollutants, some of which are known to affect human health, and others which are suspected of causing health problems.

Pollution in cities of industrialized nations is often brought to our attention. It is monitored, and laws have been put in place to reduce the amount of pollutants released into the atmosphere. In many developing nations, however, air pollution problems are much greater, but have hardly been addressed at all. Ted Munn, a respected Canadian meteorologist, reports that pollution problems in New Delhi, India, are so bad that it is often difficult to see for more than two blocks. He blames the burning of dung as a fuel and the lack of emission controls on cars for creating this situation. Particulate matter is a major problem where wood and charcoal fires are still used for heating, cooking, and fuelling cottage industries. There are similar problems in the following cities: Bagdad, Iraq; Tehran, Iran; Bombay and Calcutta, India; Jakarta, Indonesia; Lahore, Pakistan; and Kuala Lumpur, Malaysia.

Mexico City

Air pollution from a factory complex in China

Air quality in Mexico City changes drastically according to weather conditions.

Imagine a city where people joke about it being better to exhale than inhale, where jogging can be hazardous to your health, where just breathing is equivalent to smoking two packs of cigarettes a day, and where US Embassy staff are given extra pay or extra credit toward retirement for working in such a polluted environment! This is Mexico City, which is situated on an intermontane plateau where inversions frequently develop, trapping pollutants close to the surface, as seen in Figure 7.15. It is estimated that 40 percent of the population suffers from chronic bronchitis, and thousands die each year from pollution-related diseases.

The pollution levels in Mexico City are so high that you can actually contract hepatitis simply by breathing. A large number of people are treated each year for mental disorders which local experts attribute directly to pollutants in the air. The pollution problems are constant, but are usually greatest in January when the inversions are strongest and most persistent. At this time, many pregnant women and women with small children leave the city for a while.

With a population estimated to grow to between 30 and 36 million by the end of the century, Mexico will doubtless experience increasing problems with air pollution. The country has enormous economic difficulties and, although it has some of the toughest anti-pollution laws in the world, they go virtually ignored because of the economic consequences that would result if they were to be strictly enforced. There are more than 130 000 industries in Mexico City, in addition to 2.8 million motor vehicles with virtually no emission controls. Ninety percent of the gasoline sold to fuel these vehicles contains lead. Mexico City's pollution problems show what could result in cities of the developing world in the future.

A joint United Nations-World Health Organization (WHO) report says that air pollution in most world cities is down from previous levels, but over one-half of the industrial areas of 63 major world cities have air pollution levels exceeding WHO standards.

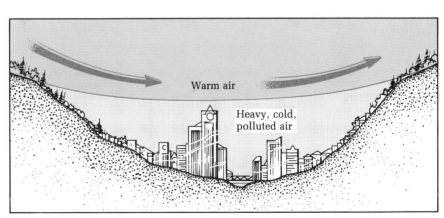

Warm air

Heavy, cold, polluted air

Figure 7.15
How An
Inversion Traps
Pollution

Questions

22. Re-read the description of Mexico City's pollution problems.

    (a) List the problems and their causes.

    (b) Citing specific examples, explain how and why this pollution differs from that of the large cities of the industrialized world.

23. Bearing in mind the other enormous problems experienced by Mexico City, suggest strategies which might be undertaken to improve the situation. Your suggestions should include efforts to be made by the government of Mexico, private corporations, and other countries.

24. (a) Use line graphs to plot the figures given in Table 7.4. Plot all of the lines on one graph. (You will need a second scale on the right-hand side of the graph to plot lead emissions.)

    (b) Describe and explain the observations which you can make from your graph.

Coal burning thermal power plants, such as this one in Canada, are a major source of air pollution.

Figure 7.16 Suspended Particulate Matter in Selected Cities

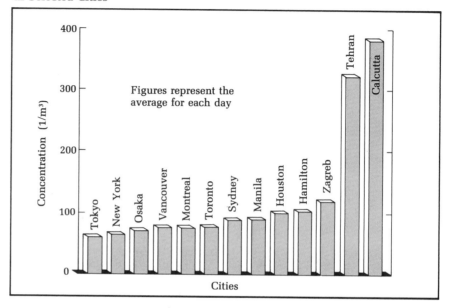

Figures represent the average for each day

Table 7.4
National Emission
Estimates in the
United States
1940-1984

Year	Particulates (PM)[a]	Sulfur Oxides (SO$_x$)[a]	Nitrogen Oxides (NO$_x$)[a]	Volatile Organics (VOC)[a]	Carbon Monoxide (CO)[a]	Lead (Pb)[b]
1940	22.4	18.0	6.7	17.7	79.4	X
1950	24.2	20.3	9.3	20.3	84.8	X
1960	20.9	20.0	12.8	23.3	87.5	X
1970	18.0	28.2	18.1	27.0	98.3	20.0
1971	16.7	26.8	18.5	26.3	96.3	22.0
1972	15.0	27.4	19.7	26.3	93.8	23.0
1973	13.9	28.7	20.2	25.7	89.5	202.7
1974	12.2	27.0	19.6	24.1	84.6	162.1
1975	10.3	25.6	19.1	22.7	80.5	147.0
1976	9.6	26.2	20.3	23.8	85.3	153.1
1977	9.0	26.3	20.9	23.6	81.1	141.2
1978	8.9	24.5	21.0	24.2	80.6	127.9
1979	8.8	24.5	21.1	23.5	77.4	108.7
1980	8.3	23.2	20.3	22.3	75.0	70.6
1981	7.7	22.3	20.5	21.0	72.3	55.9
1982	6.8	21.3	19.6	19.4	66.1	54.4
1983	6.9	20.8	19.4	19.9	67.6	46.9
Percent						
Change 1940-1983	-69	+ 16	+ 190	+ 12	-15	X
Change 1970-1983	-62	-26	+ 7	-26	-31	-77
Change 1975-1983	-33	-19	+ 2	-12	-16	-68

X = not available
Notes:
a. Unit of measurements is teragrams/year (10^6 metric tons per year).
b. Unit of measurement is gigagrams/year (10^3 metric tons per year).

The accidental release of toxic air pollutants occurs from time to time in all parts of the world. Occasionally, the release is so significant that it becomes headline news around the world. Such an accident occurred in Bhopal, India, on December 3, 1984. On that date, a white cloud of poison billowed out of a US-owned Union Carbide factory and drifted across the city. The toxic cloud killed more than 2000 people and seriously affected over 200 000 others, many of whom will be permanently handicapped. Poorly equipped and overcrowded hospitals were unable to deal adequately with the situation. In the court case which followed, accusations were levelled against Union Carbide for having poor equipment and careless procedures. Undoubtedly, litigation will continue for many years, but as an interim measure, a court in India ruled that

Union Carbide should pay $280 million in compensation. Union Carbide appealed the decision on the grounds that it amounted to conviction without trial. The appeal judge reduced the amount of compensation to $192 million. The corporation will appeal this further, for the same reason.

Residents waiting to leave Bhopal, India after the Union Carbide accident

Question

25. Many lesser developed nations are anxious to acquire branch plants of multinational corporations which will generate employment and thus improve living standards. The multinationals are attracted to these places because of lower labour costs and less stringent labour laws and environmental standards. Whose responsibility should it be to ensure the health of the worker and the cleanliness of the surrounding environment? Discuss the issues and summarize your conclusions.

The Spread of Air Pollution Beyond the City

The pollutants which are generated by urban activities spread outside the cities and affect remote and rural areas. In addition, some of the activities in rural areas also create pollution. Of particular concern are the chemicals used by farmers to control weeds and pests. When they are applied by aerial spraying, only 15 percent may reach the intended target, while the rest settles onto other land or water areas.

Acid and Toxic Precipitation

Much has been said and written about acid rain, more correctly referred to as "acid precipitation." Recently, concern has also been voiced about the other toxins in the air which fall as dry deposits or are absorbed by moisture first. These substances threaten our drinking water, accumulate in the food chain, and damage forests and agricultural crops.

Pollutants which cause acid precipitation come from two chief sources, industry and transportation, and their sources are easily traceable. Many industries emit sulphur dioxide, and transportation vehicles are largely responsible for nitrogen oxides. These combine with the air and moisture to create acids which damage living tissues and corrode building materials.

The results of acid precipitation pollution first became evident in Europe, where industrial activity is concentrated and where it has been carried out over a longer period than anywhere else in the world. In Germany, one-third of the forests are dead or dying; 25 percent of the fir trees and ten percent of the spruce trees in Switzerland are dead. The problem has spread into other countries such as Poland, Czechoslovakia, Austria, Sweden, the USSR, the Netherlands, and Romania. Areas of the lesser developed world where industrialization is in progress, such as in Latin America, are beginning to suffer the results of acid precipitation.

Similar observations are being made in North America. In 1983, there was little damage to forests of the United States. By 1984, it was estimated that eight percent of the forests had been affected, and by 1986, 34 percent had been damaged. In Canada, much concern has been voiced over the damage being done to maple trees, especially in Quebec where making maple syrup is an important industry. There are also possible repercussions for tourism in areas that are badly affected.

**Figure 7.17
The pH Scale of Acidity**

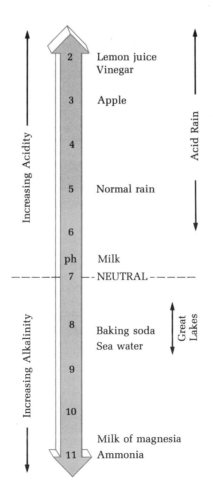

Sulphur Dioxide Emissions

The high incidence of colon cancer and breast cancer in northeastern North America has, for many years, been attributed to a diet rich in fat. However, Dr. Frank Garland, a California researcher, considers that this conclusion is not justified. His studies of data supplied by the National Cancer Institute of the United States revealed lower incidences of these cancers among people who live in the southern United States, yet whose diets include a greater proportion of animal fats than those of people living in the Northeast.

Dr. Garland and his brother Cedric, an epidemiologist (one who studies factors associated

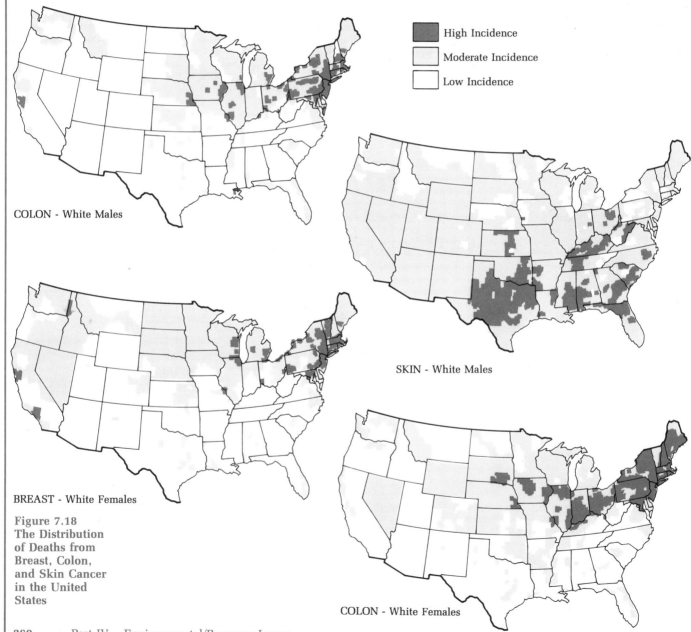

**Figure 7.18
The Distribution of Deaths from Breast, Colon, and Skin Cancer in the United States**

with diseases), studied maps showing the incidence of colon, breast, and skin cancer in the United States. They noted that colon and breast cancer deaths were much more prevalent in proportion to the population in the Northeast, and that the pattern of skin cancer was the opposite; that is, skin cancer occurred almost exclusively outside the Northeast. Dr. Garland and his brother began to wonder if the incidence of colon and breast cancer is related to lowered vitamin D levels caused by decreased exposure to the ultraviolet rays of the sun. Sulphur dioxide, one of the gases that create acid precipitation, also blocks ultraviolet rays. Similar correlations were found on maps of Canada and northern Europe. In Montreal, the incidence of colon cancer is 23.8 per 100 000 inhabitants, compared to 15.1 in Toronto. Comparable figures for breast cancer are 30.8 and 25.5 respectively. The doctors attributed differences in the incidence of these cancers to wind patterns which caused more pollutants to become concentrated in the Montreal area.

These two cancers are very rare in Japan, and the researchers suggest that the reason lies in the fact that the Japanese consume large quantities of fish which is rich in vitamin D. As a result of their findings, the researchers conclude that a diet with large amounts of vitamin D and calcium (the absorption of the latter is made possible by sufficient quantities of vitamin D) would help to reduce the incidence of colon and breast cancer in areas subjected to high levels of sulphur dioxide pollution. Both of these nutrients are found in milk.

Solving the Problem

The problem of acid precipitation is an international one, with pollutants being spread by the circulating currents of the atmosphere. For example, Sweden and Norway now receive 75-90 percent of their sulphur pollutants from outside sources, while Denmark exports approximately 75 percent of its sulphur dioxide emissions and receives about

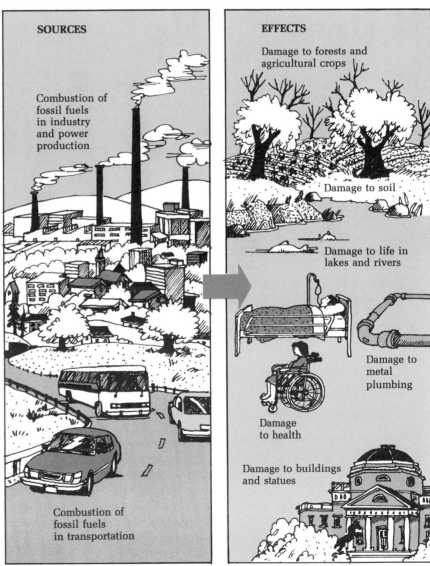

**Figure 7.19
The Sources and Effects of Acid Precipitation**

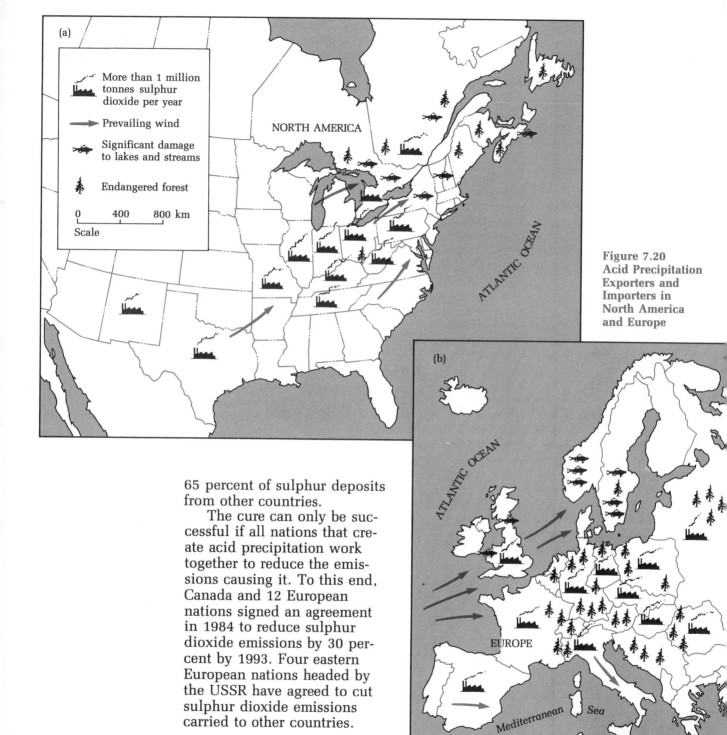

**Figure 7.20
Acid Precipitation
Exporters and
Importers in
North America
and Europe**

65 percent of sulphur deposits from other countries.

The cure can only be successful if all nations that create acid precipitation work together to reduce the emissions causing it. To this end, Canada and 12 European nations signed an agreement in 1984 to reduce sulphur dioxide emissions by 30 percent by 1993. Four eastern European nations headed by the USSR have agreed to cut sulphur dioxide emissions carried to other countries.

Canada continues to put pressure on the USA to make a similar move. It is estimated that, in Canada, half of the **acid deposition** which includes acid precipitation and dry acidic deposits, comes from the United States, while only ten percent of the fall-out in the United States comes from Canada. The USA has signed a treaty with Mexico to control acid precipitation.

Question

26. Why do you think the USA is readier to sign an acid precipitation treaty with Mexico than with Canada?

Figure 7.21 shows the distribution of acid precipitation in the world. It can be observed that the problem is almost exclusively in the northern hemisphere, but no doubt as the southern hemisphere becomes more industralized, similar problems will emerge.

It is also widely acknowledged that the acidification of the water is causing much damage to aquatic environments. This is occurring especially where the local bedrock is unable to buffer or neutralize this acid. The granitic shield areas, such as the Canadian Shield and the Baltic Shield of Scandinavia, together with the shield areas of South America, Africa, Australia, India, and the USSR, are particularly susceptible to the damaging effects of acid precipitation. In Canada

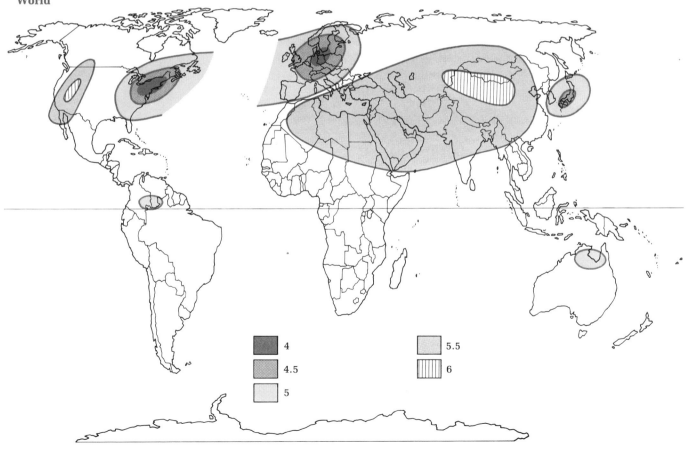

alone, it is estimated that 14 000 lakes are dead and 40 000 are seriously threatened by high acid levels. Not only does the acid cause the death of the organisms in the lake, it also may make the water hazardous to drink. The acids dissolve metals such as aluminum in the rocks and in lead and copper plumbing, and this may cause health problems.

The Special Problem Associated With Snowmelt

Acid snow and acid fall-out may accumulate on the land surface throughout the winter months. When temperatures rise, the melting snow and trapped pollutants are flushed into lakes and streams. The sudden increase in acidity in the water often proves fatal for marine organisms.

Toxic Precipitation

This term encompasses many more kinds of pollutants than acid precipitation. The mechanics of toxic pollution are similar, in that the pollution is usually brought to the ground by precipitation, but it comes from many more sources and is much more difficult to trace. Chemical reactions often take place, changing the composition of the precipitation as it travels. It crosses international boundaries and moves from air to land and water. Laws designed to control it would be difficult to draw up, let alone enforce.

Toxic deposition comes in the form of rain or snow or dry fall-out. It is believed to cause about $200 million in crop damage per year in Ontario alone, in addition to the damage it does to forests. People living near the Great Lakes have more toxic contamination in their food than anyone else in North America, including dioxins, PCBs (polychlorinated biphenols), and pesticides. PCBs and the insecticide DDT (dichloro-diphenyl trichloroethane) have been found in mother's milk and are passed on to nursing babies. These chemicals are believed to increase the risk of mutations and neurological, respiratory, and behavioural problems. Toxic precipitation is considered to be responsible for 2000 cancer deaths in the USA each year.

Radioactive Pollution

Pollution can result from nuclear accidents and the subsequent release of radioactive material into the air or water. Radioactive pollution can also be caused by the solid radioactive residues associated with mining or the disposal of used radioactive materials. Nuclear weapons and their potential effect on the environment continue to cause great concern, worldwide.

Case Study

The Chernobyl Nuclear Reactor Fire

In the early hours of April 26, 1986, after 24 h of experimentation, Unit 4 of the nuclear reactor at Chernobyl in the Ukraine went out of control.

A fire severely damaged the building which housed the unit, and a deadly radioactive plume escaped into the sky. Thirty-one people died soon after the incident from the effects of radiation exposure, and hundreds still suffer from serious radiation sickness. It is expected that thou-sands will have early deaths due to cancer.

Within nine months, the reactor was encased in cement, the remainder of the plant had resumed operations, and thousands of residents who had been evacuated returned home. Many people around the world are concerned that the evacuees' exposure to high levels of radiation will damage their health. Genetic problems and blood disorders may be a consequence. Doctors who have been working with the people exposed to high levels of radiation report better rates of improvement than expected, but the long-term results will obviously not be known for many years.

The effects on the local inhabitants were devastating, and repercussions were felt in many parts of the world, as radioactive rain fell on crops and pasturelands. Canada turned back shipments of green produce from as far away from Chernobyl as Italy because they contained high levels of radiation, and there was much concern in Europe over the contamination of food and water supplies.

In the months of investigation that followed the accident, it was determined that the explosion had resulted from an unauthorized experiment during which safety regulations were ignored. (There will be further investigations to determine if any design flaws contributed to the explosion.) In July 1987, judgement was passed on those individuals responsible for the disaster. The three officials in charge at the time were each sentenced to ten years' hard labour, with other workers receiving shorter sentences. This is the maximum sentence allowable in the USSR

Figure 7.22
The Spread of Radioactivity Following the Explosion at Chernobyl

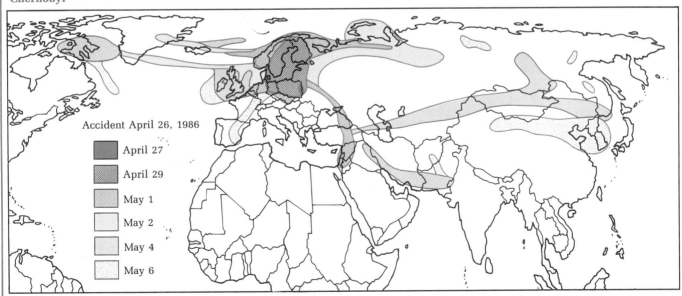

Accident April 26, 1986

- April 27
- April 29
- May 1
- May 2
- May 4
- May 6

for failure to ensure that safety precautions are observed when explosions can occur.

In addition to his ten-year sentence, the director was given a five-year concurrent sentence for abusing his power. Specifically, this involved failure to implement emergency plans once the blast and fire had occurred. As a result, people were exposed to more radioactivity than would have been the case if emergency plans had gone into effect.

The Chernobyl accident released only four percent of the total inventory of radioisotopes contained in just one of the nuclear reactors there. A major wartime attack on such a reactor would release more than 100 times that amount, and that is nothing compared to the potential of a nuclear war!

Questions

27. Following the Chernobyl accident, it was discovered that the level of radioactivity in the meat of reindeer was high.

   (a) What tests should have been done to determine whether or not the Chernobyl explosion was the cause?

   (b) If the explosion was not to blame, what other factors might have been?

28. What would be your reaction if, to avoid the economic consequences of higher radiation levels in food, the Canadian government was to suggest that allowable radioactivity levels should be raised, so that the food is deemed fit for human consumption? Explain your answer carefully.

29. The convictions of the officials in charge of the Chernobyl nuclear reactor are believed to be the first of their kind in the world.

   (a) What effect do you think the convictions would have on nuclear reactor employees in the USSR and in other nations?

   (b) Comment on the severity of the sentences.

30. In what other circumstances do you consider that failure to act responsibly should bring severe penalties? Justify your answer.

The damaged reactor at the Chernobyl nuclear power station is seen below the chimney at the centre of this photo.

The Greenhouse Effect

Apart from the pollution problems which have already been mentioned, there is growing awareness and concern that human activities, in particular industrialization, are having a subtle yet profound effect on the atmosphere. The "greenhouse effect" is caused largely by the increased concentration of carbon dioxide in the atmosphere.

When fossil fuels and other organic materials are burned, the carbon they contain is changed into carbon dioxide, which is released into the atmosphere. In the past, the normal balance of carbon dioxide in the air has been kept fairly even by its use in photosynthesis, a process which releases oxygen. Carbon dioxide is also absorbed by the oceans. However, as the major forests of the world are cut and burned, the concentration of carbon dioxide in the air increases. It has increased by about 25 percent in the last 100 years, from 275 parts per million in the late nineteenth century to 343 parts per million in 1984.

Carbon dioxide is a colourless, odourless gas which allows short-wave radiation (which includes the light rays from the sun) to penetrate the atmosphere. However, much of that incoming radiation is absorbed by the surface of the earth and, because the earth's surface is much cooler than the sun's, it is re-radiated in the form of long waves. Carbon dioxide absorbs this long-wave radiation, and this process heats up the atmosphere. The warming that results is called the **greenhouse effect**. This name is used because the air inside a greenhouse is heated when long-wave radiation is trapped by the enclosing glass. The greater the concentration of carbon dioxide, the greater the heating effect.

The record of global temperatures over the past centuries shows cycles of warming and cooling. Figure 7.24 shows quite clearly that the overall trend in this century is one of warming. The anticipated warming of the earth's

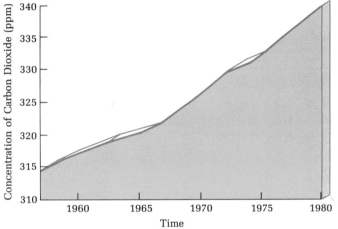

Figure 7.23
Mean Monthly Concentrations of Atmospheric Carbon Dioxide at Mauna Loa 1958-1980

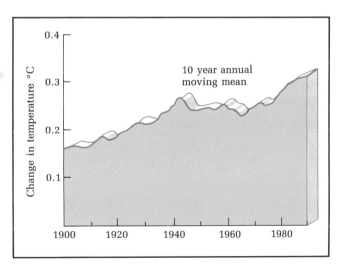

Figure 7.24
Global Mean Annual Surface Temperature 1900-1985

Figure 7.25
Some of the
Results of the
Greenhouse Effect

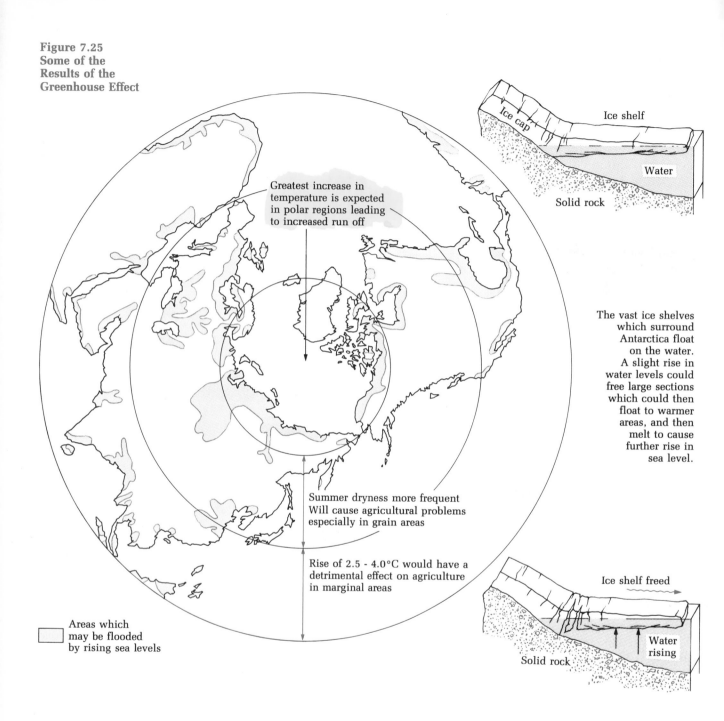

Greatest increase in
temperature is expected
in polar regions leading
to increased run off

Summer dryness more frequent
Will cause agricultural problems
especially in grain areas

Rise of 2.5 - 4.0°C would have a
detrimental effect on agriculture
in marginal areas

Areas which
may be flooded
by rising sea levels

Ice cap

Ice shelf

Water

Solid rock

The vast ice shelves
which surround
Antarctica float
on the water.
A slight rise in
water levels could
free large sections
which could then
float to warmer
areas, and then
melt to cause
further rise in
sea level.

Ice shelf freed

Water
rising

Solid rock

surface is not expected to be evenly distributed. The effects will probably not be as pronounced in the equatorial areas as they will be in the polar areas, yet the repercussions for the entire world will be great. There will be a shift in the climatic regions of the world. Slight changes in temperature and precipitation will have significant effects on agricultural production. Temperature increases will also cause a rise in sea level, although estimates of the change in sea level vary greatly.

Questions

31. Construct a flow chart which summarizes the causes and results of the greenhouse effect.

32. What changes would have to take place around the world in economic activities and lifestyles to reduce the threat which results from rising earth temperatures?

33. In what ways should we be preparing for the impending rise in temperature?

34. What advantageous results could follow a global increase in temperature? Would this offset its negative effects? Explain your answers.

Water Supplies and Water Pollution

Water is vital to all forms of life. Approximately 71 percent of the earth's surface is covered by the oceans which form the habitat of millions of marine creatures. Estimates of actual volumes vary, but most indicate that, of the total of 1.4 billion cubic kilometres, 97 percent is in the oceans and three percent is fresh. Of this fresh water, 77.2 percent is frozen in ice caps and glaciers, 22.4 percent consists of **groundwater** in the rocks and soil, 0.35 percent is in lakes and swamps, and 0.05 percent is in rivers and streams.

Question

35. Use the water statistics given above to produce a diagram or graph showing how small a proportion of fresh water is available for use when compared to the total volume. For best results, you will need to calculate percentages of the *total* volume for all values.

The volume of water in its various forms is finite. It is circulated through the hydrologic cycle, which is illustrated in Figure 7.26.

Figure 7.26
The Global Circulation of Water

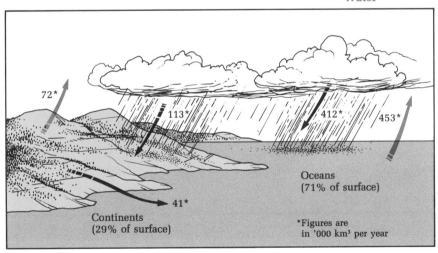

72* 113* 412* 453*

Oceans
(71% of surface)

41*

Continents
(29% of surface)

*Figures are
in '000 km³ per year

When averaged, there is plenty of water in the world for all personal, agricultural, and industrial use, but the circulation of water through the hydrologic cycle does not spread it evenly on the earth's surface nor to where it is most needed. The land surface can be divided into areas of water surplus and water deficiency, as seen in Figure 7.27.

Figure 7.27
Global Water Surplus and Deficiency

Water surplus occurs when precipitation is plentiful enough to supply the vegetation with its requirements for optimum growth. **Water deficiency** occurs when the water supply cannot meet the potential demand. Water supply problems are complicated by seasonal supply, the reliability of run-off, the density of population, the uses to which the water is put, and whether or not the source is polluted.

Water Supply Problems and Possible Solutions

Water is consumed domestically, in industry, and in agriculture. An individual could survive on a bare minimum of 2 L per day, but a reasonable quality of life depends on having about 80 L per day. (This figure does not include the water used in food and other manufacturing industries.) In Canada, our

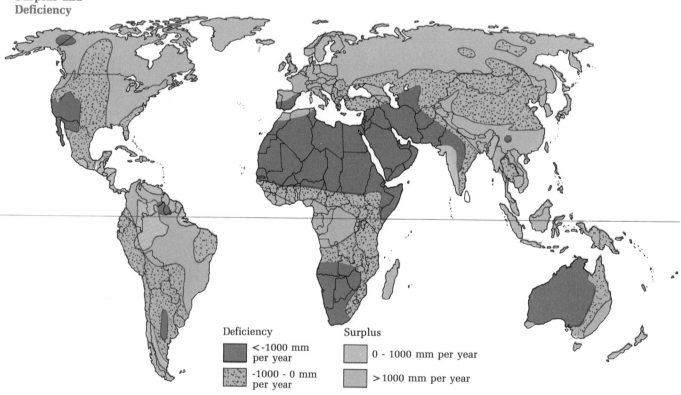

Deficiency

■ <-1000 mm per year

▦ -1000 - 0 mm per year

Surplus

▨ 0 - 1000 mm per year

▧ >1000 mm per year

'Surplus' and 'Deficiency' are defined as the difference between annual precipitation and evapotranspiration. Evapotranspiration is the water demand made by a crop when there is no shortage of water.

use is much greater than this. We each use an average of 285 L per day, varying from 90 to 320 L. If you were to add on the water used in preparing manufactured goods, the total would be a colossal 4100 L per person, second only to the USA at 6300 L per person, per day! Some of the domestic, industrial, and agricultural uses are illustrated in Figure 7.28.

In other parts of the world, the story is very different. As you can observe from Figure 7.29, most of the world's water is used in agriculture. About 12 percent of the cultivated land is irrigated, bringing immense returns in increased food production. In some areas, double or triple cropping is made possible. The large drawback to this use of water is that about 73 percent of the water does not return directly into surface sources. Instead, it re-enters the hydrologic cycle via the processes of evaporation and transpiration. Industry uses about 22 percent and households five percent, but up to 90 percent of this returns to sources which can be used again very quickly.

Figure 7.28
Use of Water in Canada

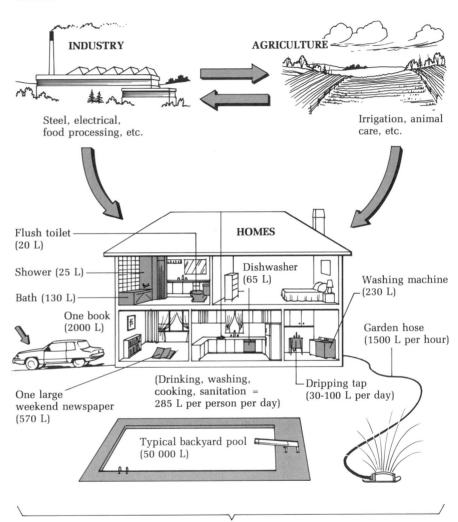

INDUSTRY

Steel, electrical, food processing, etc.

AGRICULTURE

Irrigation, animal care, etc.

HOMES

Flush toilet (20 L)

Shower (25 L)

Bath (130 L)

One book (2000 L)

One large weekend newspaper (570 L)

Dishwasher (65 L)

Washing machine (230 L)

Garden hose (1500 L per hour)

(Drinking, washing, cooking, sanitation = 285 L per person per day)

Dripping tap (30-100 L per day)

Typical backyard pool (50 000 L)

Total average use of water in industry, agriculture, and for domestic purposes is approximately 4 100 L per person per day!

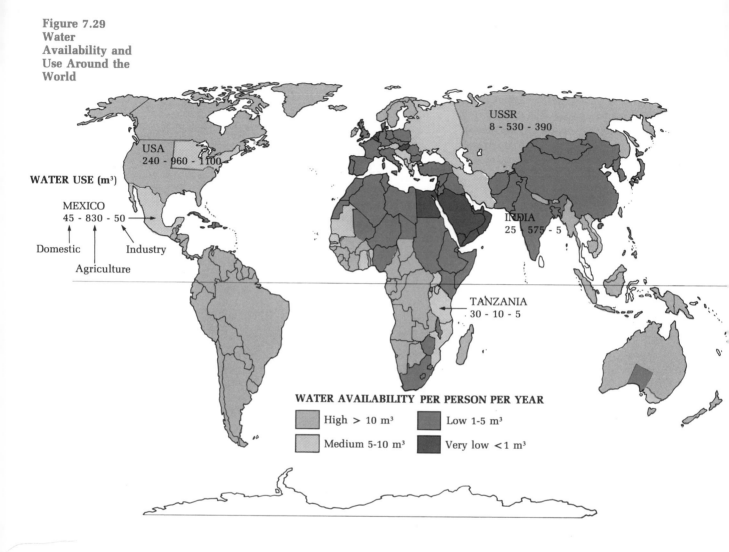

Figure 7.29
Water
Availability and
Use Around the
World

USSR
8 - 530 - 390

USA
240 - 960 - 1100

WATER USE (m³)

MEXICO
45 - 830 - 50

Domestic   Industry

Agriculture

INDIA
25 - 575 - 5

TANZANIA
30 - 10 - 5

WATER AVAILABILITY PER PERSON PER YEAR

High > 10 m³   Low 1-5 m³

Medium 5-10 m³   Very low <1 m³

Question

36. List and briefly explain the factors which contribute to the differences in water consumption in each of the following countries. Figures are based on consumption levels in 1980.

Country	Total (millions of m³)	Per Capita (m³)	Public %	Irrigation %	Industry %
Canada	36 153	1 509.0	12.6	7.8	48.4
USA	525 053	2 306.3	8.9	39.5	50.1
Germany	42 204	685.5	11.8	0.4	67.2
Greece	6 945	720.2	10.8	82.7	2.1

You may want to refer to thematic maps and other sources of information to find out about each country's climate, its standard of living, and the extent of its industry and agriculture.

Improving World Water Supplies

Any improvement in people's living standards depends directly and indirectly on an adequate and safe water supply. This can be achieved, but it has to be done carefully, with deliberate planning which involves overall health care strategies, political co-operation, the education and involvement of local inhabitants, and the wise use of money.

In the past, enormous irrigation and water supply schemes were considered to be the answer. Some megaprojects are still in the construction, planning, or proposal stages, but many people now view these with scepticism. Some general problems which have developed are summarized in Figure 7.30.

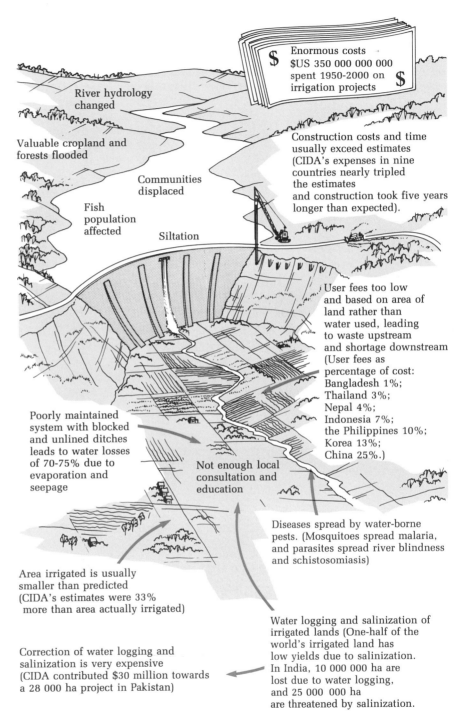

Enormous costs
$US 350 000 000 000
spent 1950-2000 on
irrigation projects

River hydrology changed

Valuable cropland and forests flooded

Communities displaced

Fish population affected

Siltation

Construction costs and time usually exceed estimates (CIDA's expenses in nine countries nearly tripled the estimates and construction took five years longer than expected).

User fees too low and based on area of land rather than water used, leading to waste upstream and shortage downstream (User fees as percentage of cost: Bangladesh 1%; Thailand 3%; Nepal 4%; Indonesia 7%; the Philippines 10%; Korea 13%; China 25%.)

Poorly maintained system with blocked and unlined ditches leads to water losses of 70-75% due to evaporation and seepage

Not enough local consultation and education

Diseases spread by water-borne pests. (Mosquitoes spread malaria, and parasites spread river blindness and schistosomiasis)

Area irrigated is usually smaller than predicted (CIDA's estimates were 33% more than area actually irrigated)

Correction of water logging and salinization is very expensive (CIDA contributed $30 million towards a 28 000 ha project in Pakistan)

Water logging and salinization of irrigated lands (One-half of the world's irrigated land has low yields due to salinization. In India, 10 000 000 ha are lost due to water logging, and 25 000 000 ha are threatened by salinization.

Figure 7.30 Problems Associated with Many Huge Water Projects

Through CIDA, Canada is now investing hundreds of thousands of dollars in draining and rehabilitating irrigated land made useless by imperfect irrigation technology. For example, Canada is adding $30 million to money supplied by the World Bank and the Pakistani government to drain and flush salts from 28 000 ha of water-logged cropland in the northwestern part of Pakistan. Yet we continue to invest in new irrigation schemes, and some people worry that the technology is still not sufficiently exact for long-term success. Maybe the alternatives are to consider small-scale projects or carry out further experimentation.

More and more, people are realizing that better solutions involve smaller projects in which investment from outside sources is coupled with local commitment.

Bandong, Thailand

The village of Bandong is in the northeastern part of Thailand where rainfall is concentrated in the summer months. This area exhibits some of the problems of the developing world — a dense population, a shortage of clean water, and eroded and exhausted soil which makes it difficult to grow food. The village people have committed themselves to working with agencies such as UNICEF and the government of Thailand to improve their living conditions.

The seven months of dry weather creates serious water shortages, so people use the brackish and polluted surface water for washing and cleaning. Children, usually girls, take about 5 h each day collecting water from a swamp on the outskirts of the village.

In the rainy season, water is collected in huge jars from the run-off from the roof. With long periods of storage, however, this water becomes contaminated. Larger, safer units made of bamboo-reinforced concrete are used by some of the people, but such units are expensive.

One of the important aims of

the villagers has been to prevent such diseases as dysentery by ensuring a pure drinking water supply. The World Health Organization estimates that 80 percent of sickness in poor communities can be traced to water-borne bacteria.

The people are tackling this problem in two ways.

The first approach includes the education of the people about sanitation. Latrines are built, and the villagers are helped to understand how flies spread disease from exposed human wastes. People are taught to cover stored water to prevent contamination, and to add chlorine to their home cisterns. As a result of these simple improvements, the incidence of dysentery has dropped markedly.

The second approach, a much larger project, involves the construction of a water pipeline to supply the village with filtered and safe water. The majority of the $750 000 cost will be covered by the district government, with the remainder of the money coming from the collective savings of nine villages, UNICEF, the local parliamentarian, and contributions from individual villagers.

Communities such as Bandong have a multitude of problems, but they are working hard to improve their living conditions, and progress is being made.

Securing a safe and reliable water supply is a major concern for families such as this one in Thailand.

Another Approach to Securing a Supply of Clean Water

In 1981, the United Nations proclaimed the objective of "clean water for all by the year 2000." However, projected costs of $600 billion weighed heavily in light of declining foreign aid budgets.

Studies showed that the best solution would be to install hand pumps drawing groundwater, each unit to supply the needs of about 250 people. In the past, foreign agencies had installed thousands of pumps, valued at about $300 each, but had not taught village people how to maintain them. As a result, many people were forced back to polluted water sources when their pumps broke down.

This new water pump in Bangladesh was provided by UNICEF.

The United Nations Development Program decided to test all kinds of pumps before it began the massive task of installation. The World Bank took charge of testing, and 70 different hand pumps from 25 countries were ordered in large numbers and sent for field testing in 20 developing nations. Of the 3000 pumps tested over a three-year period, only 30 models were "recommended" or classified as "satisfactory."

A hydrologist in charge of testing in East Africa, David Grey, was not fully satisfied with any of the pumps that he had tested. He wanted to develop a simple pump that could be made locally and maintained easily. He persuaded DuPont of Switzerland to study the application of plastics in the construction of hand pumps. They came up

with a simple and successful design. The bearings, which would be the parts likely to wear out, could be simply and locally made at a cost of 30 cents per set. The total cost of the pump, which could also be made locally, would be about $10, and the villagers could install it themselves. They could replace worn parts in a few minutes, using a simple wrench.

Currently, 250 000 hand pumps of this kind are being manufactured each year, and it will take another 5 to 7 million units to serve the needs of the rest of the people who need them, with one pump for every 150 to 200 people. DuPont gives its designs for dies, bearings, footvalves, and plungers to anybody. Their aim is to make affordable hand pump technology available throughout the world.

Water shortages and polluted sources are not only a problem of the lesser developed nations. The high standard of living of the more developed world depends on the use of vast quantities of water. This increase in demand is putting a strain on water resources. In addition, many cities such as Boston and Montreal do not have adequate treatment facilities for waste water. Modern technology is also producing dangerous chemical wastes such as dioxins and PCBs (polychlorinated biphenols) which are polluting underground and surface sources, as well as the oceans. The dry Southwest of the United States is experiencing significant water quality and supply problems that are likely to worsen over the next decade.

Question

37. Read the two accounts which illustrate how clean water can be supplied to people in rural areas of lesser developed nations. Explain carefully, using examples wherever you can, why success can only be achieved through co-operative efforts.

The Dry Southwestern United States

California has about the same population as the whole of Canada, with two-thirds of the people living in the arid southern part. To support this large population and its intensive agriculture, an elaborate system of canals, aqueducts, and pipelines has been developed. The Imperial Irrigation District, to the southeast of Los Angeles, is the largest single irrigation district in the western hemisphere, with 2000 km² of irrigated land.

Further to the north are the fruit orchards of the Coachella Valley. Palm Springs is an oasis of mansions, where there are more sprinklers per capita than anywhere else in the United States. On the coast, Los Angeles, with a population of over 3 million, has to import two-thirds of its water supply.

Underground water supplies, or **aquifers**, where water is found in pores of the rock, are being pumped so quickly that they are drying up. Irrigation water is being removed from rivers in increasing quantities. As a result, rivers deprived of their normal flushing capabilities are becoming badly polluted, especially with salts coming from the irrigated lands. Water comes largely from rivers in northern California and from the Colorado River to the east. Resources are only expected to be sufficient for the next ten years.

Arizona is even drier than California yet, in Phoenix, the

Figure 7.31
The Water
Systems of the
Arid Southwest of
the United States

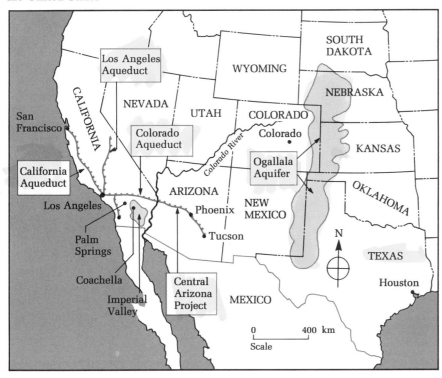

people use three times as much water per head as Canadians, and the city boasts the world's first authentic inland surfing centre. Ninety percent of the water used in the area around Phoenix goes to irrigate crops of cotton, alfalfa, hay, and pecan trees. So much water has been withdrawn from underground sources that the water table has dropped 100 m, and the surface of the ground has sagged by 5 m. This is causing shifts and cracks in the earth, affecting gas lines, rail lines, highways, and buildings.

A huge canal has been built to bring water from the Colorado River, and other dams have been built on local rivers. In return for the help given by the US federal government, Arizona is slowly reducing the area of land which is irrigated. Farms are slowly returning to desert and the water is being diverted for city use. Unfortunately, many of the sources of water, even those 100 m below the surface, have been polluted by chemicals used in agriculture, some of which are known to be carcinogenic.

Texas is facing similar water shortages, with cities like Houston sinking, and farmland going out of production. Texas draws 40 percent of its water from surface sources and the remainder from underground aquifers, the largest of which is the Ogallala Aquifer. There are plans to improve water supplies and sewage treatment systems, but the cost is estimated to be $100 billion. Texas is no longer looking to outside sources to solve its water problems; rather, it is trying to improve the way it uses its own sources. Salt water can be used for irrigation, provided it is trickled along furrows and does not touch the leaves of the plants. In other experiments, attempts are being made to reduce irrigation losses to evaporation by using downward spraying or drip irrigation from pipes in the ground. Engineers who have made much of the Israeli desert green are lending their expertise. In even more sophisticated experiments, attempts are being made to release the tightly-held capillary moisture of the soil for crop growth.

Question

38. (a) Suggest alternatives which might be studied for adoption in the dry parts of the south-western United States. Organize your answer in terms of value and practicality.

(b) What effects would your solutions have on the residents of the areas and on the United States in general, and may be even Canada? (Hint: the NAWAPA proposal)

Scottsdale, Arizona, a suburb of Phoenix. Locate Phoenix on the map on page 277.

Problems and Plans in The Soviet Union

With a long history of food shortages, the USSR developed a plan to use water from northward-flowing rivers to water the Aral-Caspian Basin of the Southwest.

The rivers of the southern USSR, which are currently used to supply water for irrigation, are becoming saltier, and the flow of water has been reduced considerably. Those rivers which flow into the Caspian Sea have experienced a 10 percent drop in the flow of water. Those rivers flowing into the Azov Sea and the Aral Sea have dropped by 25 percent and 30 percent respectively. The level of water in the Aral Sea has dropped by 1.5 m, and water is now draining from the Black Sea into the Azov Sea, threatening the survival of fish with its increasing salinity. Like the Colorado River in the United States, which is little more than a trickle by the time it enters the Gulf of California, the Syr Darya is almost all used up, and the Amu Darya is half depleted before it enters the Aral Sea.

The plan, as shown in Figure 7.32, was to use water pumped from northern rivers to irrigate the South and replenish the rivers and seas. The rivers involved in this plan were to be, first, the Pechora, then the Ob, and possibly the Yenisei. The cost

Figure 7.32 Proposal for the Diversion of Water in the USSR

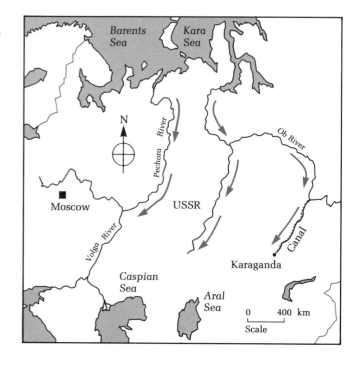

was estimated to be tens of billions of dollars, but the experts were confident that the returns would justify the expense. Others were worried about the effect on migratory wildlife, especially fish, and the possibility that reducing the flow of water to the Arctic Ocean would contribute to a change in climate. Environmentalists staged protests in the Soviet Union which resulted in the proposed plan being put on hold indefinitely.

Questions

39. (a) Attempt to assess the possible impact of the proposed Soviet river diversion scheme on climate, soils, water distribution, and crop yields.

    (b) Speculate on the possible effects of the diversion on navigation along the Arctic coast of the USSR.

40. Suggest other ways in which the Soviet Union could have attempted to improve food production.

Water Pollution

Pollutants in their many forms have spread to all corners of the earth — to the top of the atmosphere and the depths of the oceans. In fact, they have reached everywhere that the circulatory systems of the earth have reached. Some pollutants are biodegradable; that is, they can be rendered harmless by natural processes. But there are so many biodegradable pollutants, such as organic pollutants, entering these circulatory systems that natural processes are unable to keep up with them, and people must intervene to speed up the cleansing process. Other pollutants, especially those from modern industries, do not break down readily. They may persist in the environment and become concentrated as they pass up the food chain. A prime example of this is the insecticide, DDT. It has been banned in many nations for over ten years, but traces of it can still be found in the environment.

Another problem involves the increasing number of chemical pollutants entering the environment. They react with each other to form a potentially hazardous chemical "soup." This soup is mixing with our water supplies and being absorbed by our food.

There have been many recent incidents involving water pollution in Canada.

Some affect a small group of people, such as in 1982, when water in wells in Perkinsfield, Ontario, became unusable due to contamination which seeped in from a local dump. Other problems affect many people. Toxic wastes seeping into the Niagara River, mainly from the USA, are contaminating drinking water for millions of people downstream.

Industry was primarily responsible for the pollution described in these two examples. The other major sources are sewage and agriculture. Inadequate sewage treatment leads to the discharge of insufficiently treated waste that can spread diseases such as dysentery and gastroenteritis. Notices are posted along many beaches, for example in Toronto, to warn swimmers of the dangers. In 1986, tests revealed that 85 percent of rivers in southwestern Ontario were polluted with atrazine, a chemical used by corn growers which can cause genetic defects.

Questions

41. (a) Find detailed maps of British Columbia. Your maps should show the physical features including rivers, economic activities including primary and secondary industries, and the distribution of the population.

    (b) On a large outline map of British Columbia, mark on its principal rivers and communities. Identify those places where you would expect to find pollution problems, and devise a method of depicting the kinds of pollutants involved. You might choose to divide them into the following categories:

    · agricultural pollutants
      - bacterial
      - chemical
    · industrial pollutants
      - forestry
      - paper manufacture
      - mine operations
      - other manufacturing
    · sewage

      On your map you should also indicate the major source points or areas from which the pollutants would be expected to originate.

    (c) What other resource-based industries could be affected downstream?

    (d) Suggest solutions to the identified problems.

42. Below is a map which represents a fictitious lesser developed nation. Suppose you were an engineer, asked to advise this nation on the best strategy for improving the quantity and quality of water supplies. You are also asked to help the people become aware of potential future pollution sources as their country proceeds with the development of its resources and industrial economy. They would appreciate any suggestions for the prevention or reduction of future pollution problems.

    Indicate the order in

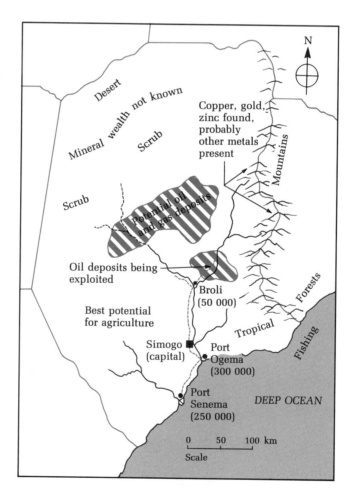

Figure 7.33
The Country for Which You Are to Formulate a Development Strategy

which you would organize your projects, and the benefits which you would expect from each. Bear in mind that this is a nation with limited access to funds. It will be necessary to approach other nations or international organizations for initial and on-going investments, though the development of potential natural and agricultural resources will provide considerable capital. You will not have to estimate the costs of your suggestions, but be aware that loans have to be repaid with interest, and that best results have come where water resource development is coupled with other projects such as health care and education.

Basic information:

Population: 6 000 000

Area: 240 000 km²

Birth rate: 47 per 1000

Death rate: 22 per 1000

Gross National Product Per Capita: US $850

Urban population: 26%

Capital: Simogo, population 1 000 000

For other information, see the map showing the country's present physical and economic resources and activities.

Habitat and Wildlife Destruction

The world is home to an estimated 5 million species of plants and animals. Approximately 1.7 million of these have been identified. Many scientists believe that there may be as many as 10 million species. Some species are distributed widely over the earth's surface, while others are very localized. The osprey, for example, which lives by plunging into the water and catching fish with its sharp talons, is found near rivers, streams, lakes, and the sea, everywhere except the polar regions. In contrast, the El Segundo Blue is a tiny butterfly found only in two small plots of land in Los Angeles, California. One of these plots is about the size of a football field and is surrounded by an oil refinery!

By altering the varied environments which cover the earth, we destroy many of the life forms which depend on those habitats. The tropical forests are home to an enormous variety of species, many of which are potential sources of food and medicines. Yet we are destroying forests at an ever-increasing rate, and our careless use of marginal lands is leading to desertification.

In the search for higher yields from our agricultural

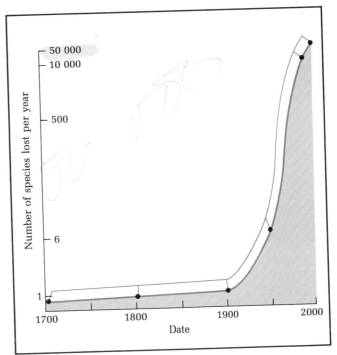

Figure 7.34
The Destruction of Species

crops and animals, we reduce the great variety of natural species and are losing their genetic make-up. Our air, water, and land are being poisoned and built over, destroying the conditions needed to support many species.

Why should we care? Surely we are doing these things so that the human race can progress? There are many reasons for us to be concerned and to act quickly to halt this destruction. Included with these reasons is the fact that wildlife still provides much of the food for humans. Fish, for example, represents a major source of protein for a large part of the world's peoples. In addition, wild vegetation is food for many of the world's domestic animals.

Improvements in the degree of resistance of our crops and animals to diseases and pests depend on our being able to interbreed them with wild varieties. Future genetic engineering experiments will draw heavily on wild sources for the gene pool, so it is essential that we make an effort to preserve these sources now.

There are still more reasons to be considered. Half of our medicines are derived from plants, so the preservation of these plants is vital to the future well-being of the population. Natural forests provide energy, building materials, and the raw materials for valuable timber markets. Wild areas also provide an environment much appreciated by many people as an escape from modern life.

In addition to all of the arguments outlined above, there is one consideration some people find difficult to comprehend. Human beings form just one of the many species which inhabit this earth. Other species have an equal right to exist, yet we have the power to permit or deny their existence. This is an awesome responsibility. Chief Seattle, a Dwamish Indian leader from whom the city of Seattle got its name, acknowledged this responsibility in a speech he made in 1854 to an assembly of tribes who were preparing to sign a treaty with the white man. He said, "The earth does not belong to man, man belongs to the earth . . . .Man did not weave the web of life; he is merely a strand in it."

What is being done to preserve this irreplaceable resource? The idea of preserving this heritage has slowly developed over the past century, but has accelerated during the last 30 years. There are many approaches being taken, such as establishing parks, promoting better management of wildlife, preserving wildlife in protected environments, and creating international laws pertaining to environmental concerns.

Parks like our own National Parks have been set up in many parts of the world. These include Tanzania's Serengeti Park, Australia's Great Barrier Reef Park, and Nepal's Mount Everest Park. Unfortunately, many biogeographical areas are still not protected, and there are real pressures exerted on existing parks by surrounding people. In Indonesia, however, it is encouraging to note that people recognize the value of keeping forested areas as catchment zones for water which will be used by the farmers. In several African parks, dams have been built

to supply water for wild animals, and people are permitted to use the ponds for fish farming. More efforts have to be made to establish such reserves, especially in the sensitive tropical forest areas.

A unique effort to conserve and make people aware of the tropical rain forest environment was carried out at Brisbane's Expo '88. A tropical forest the size of a football field was constructed on the banks of the Brisbane River, in the heart of this city of 1 million people. It includes plants, orchids, and hundreds of birds that were all carefully transported from natural areas of Australian tropical forests as trails were constructed.

Many Australians are concerned about the loss of their rain forests, which have been reduced to half the area covered 200 years ago when settlement started. With the creation of this easily accessible park at a world's fair, people from all over the world, but particularly Australians, were made aware of this very important but threatened habitat.

From their earliest existence, people have depended on wild species for their food.

Extensive hunting has led to the destruction or near-destruction of such species as the passenger pigeon, bison, certain varieties of turtles in Mexico, and the black rhinoceros in Kenya. Controlled hunting, careful restocking, selective culling of protected herds, and stocking ranches with wild animals have helped in the initial recovery of many species, and the preservation of a sustainable source of food, fur, and leather for many people.

Animals in a Kenyan game park

An Australian rain forest similar to the one on display in Brisbane during Expo '88

Zoos, botanical gardens, and rare-breeds centres may not be the best answer for conservation, but by establishing contact between humans and other species, they encourage a greater appreciation for wildlife, and, through admission fees and donations, they generate the revenue that makes their work possible.

A small gene bank where seeds, eggs, and sperm are preserved for future use can protect thousands of species, but the techniques used are not perfect, and human carelessness or a power failure can easily destroy the organisms. In addition, when replaced in the natural world, the organisms may lack resistance to new diseases. A better approach is to establish on-site protection in key areas where there is a great diversity of life. These centres were identified by Nikolay Vavilov and are referred to as **Vavilov Centres**.

International laws have been established to protect endangered species. The most significant of these is the Convention on International Trade in Endangered Species (CITES). Over 80 countries have signed this treaty, which aims to reduce the thriving illegal trade in endangered

**Figure 7.35
Countries That
Have Signed
Wildlife Treaties**

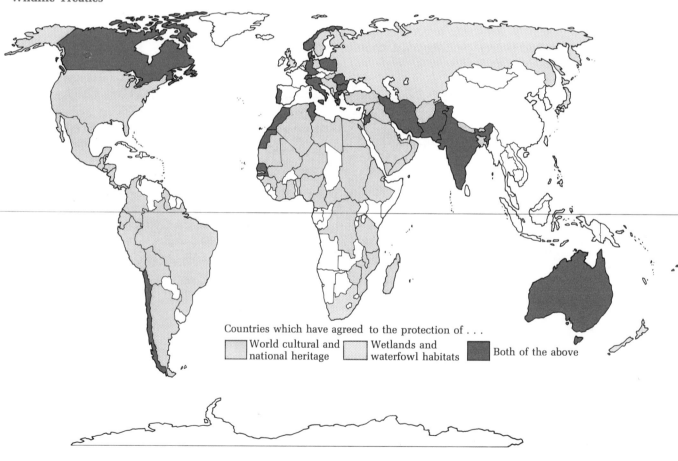

Countries which have agreed to the protection of . . .

World cultural and national heritage

Wetlands and waterfowl habitats

Both of the above

species. Some countries, such as Japan, have signed the agreement while still permitting the importation of such items as tortoise shells and crocodile skins.

Migratory animals, in particular birds, are difficult to protect, because of their natural movement across different countries. Canada, the USA, Mexico, Japan, Australia, and the USSR have signed bilateral treaties of protection for these animals. Migratory species are also protected by the Convention on Migratory Species of Wild Animals which came into effect in 1983.

An ostrich in East Africa

**Figure 7.36
The "Vavilov Centres" of the World**

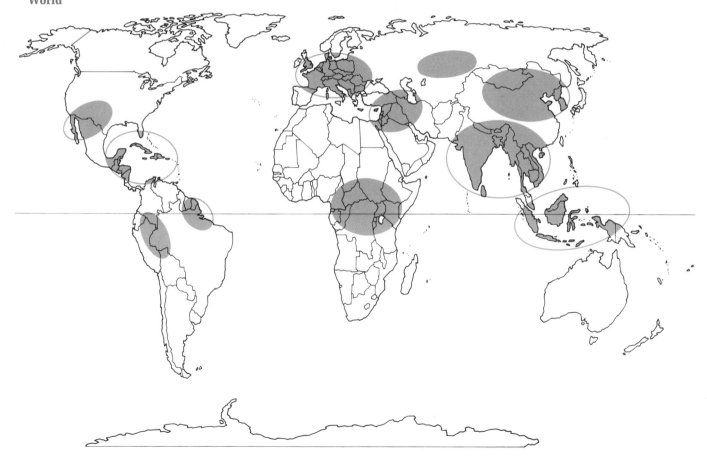

Special places of natural and human interest are protected under the Convention Concerning the Protection of the World Cultural and Natural Heritage. Such areas as the Galapagos Islands, the Pyramids, the Taj Mahal, and the Serengeti are protected by this convention.

Another area of concern is the protection of wetlands upon which so many of the world's species depend, and which have been drained and reclaimed at an alarming rate. The Convention on Wetlands of International Importance Especially as Waterfowl Habitat has been signed by 34 countries. Nearly 300 wetland sites have been preserved under this convention, covering an area of approximately 20 million hectares.

What should we do for the future? Clearly, there is a need to continue the efforts outlined above. More than this, there is a need for careful planning. For this reason, the World Conservation Strategy was launched in 1980, providing a global co-operative approach to the future.

Figure 7.37 Countries Applying the World Conservation Strategies

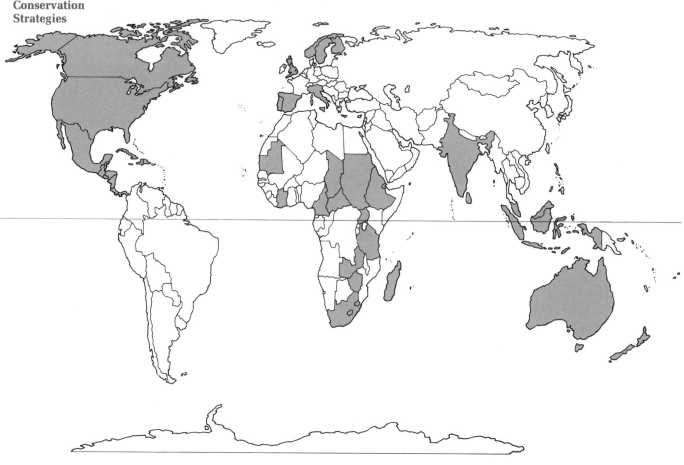

The strategy makes three important proposals:

- plants and animals must be helped to retain their ability to be self-renewing;
- the life support systems of the world, the atmosphere, water, and soil must be conserved to permit life to continue; and
- genetic diversity must be preserved as the key to our future.

Many countries applauded these ideas, but only 30 are applying the policies.

Questions

43. What evidence have you encountered personally which relates to efforts to preserve wildlife and/or habitat? Describe the location for this activity, and explain how these objectives were being achieved and/or what problems were being encountered.

44. (a) Why is the preservation of environment and wildlife considered by many people to be more important than solving more widely reported world problems?

(b) Do you hold this opinion? Justify your answer.

Permafrost Environments

Approximately 50 percent of the land in Canada and the USSR is permafrost. This type of ground is also found in Alaska, Antarctica, and many scattered mountainous regions with constant low temperatures. In permafrost regions, the sub-soil portion of the ground remains frozen throughout the year. Surface thawing takes place in summer, but the depth of this thawing varies, depending on climatic variations, the nature of the materials making up the soil, and its slope and drainage characteristics.

Digging into the permafrost layer requires modern machinery.

Permafrost environments are very fragile. Because plants grow slowly, growth usually cannot repair damage which is done to the surface. When heavy machinery or even small, four-wheeled vehicles travel over the tundra, especially in summer when the active layer is soft, they create tracks into which water drains. Often the water flows along the indentations and creates gullies which destroy the natural drainage of the area. This in turn affects the environment of the small plants. These plants are well adapted to the short summer period of continuous light, during which they have to complete their whole life cycle. To get a "jump" on the following year's growth, some even set their buds before winter returns! A slight change in their growing environment can be devastating.

(a) Area of Permafrost in Canada

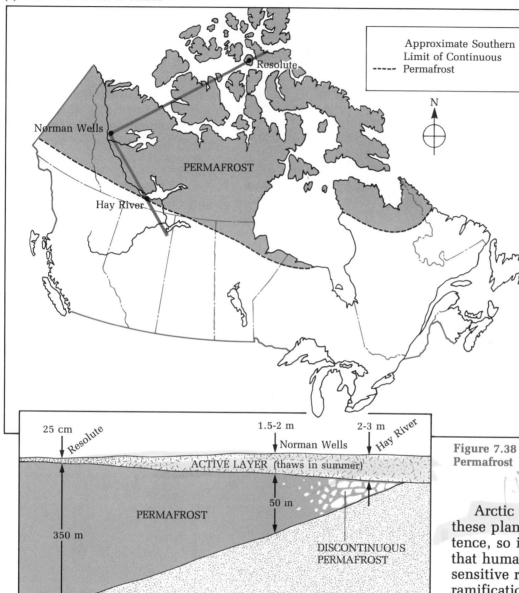

Approximate Southern
Limit of Continuous
----- Permafrost

N

Resolute

Norman Wells

PERMAFROST

Hay River

25 cm
Resolute

1.5-2 m
Norman Wells

2-3 m
Hay River

ACTIVE LAYER (thaws in summer)

50 m

PERMAFROST

350 m

DISCONTINUOUS
PERMAFROST

(b) Depth of the Active and Permafrost Layers

**Figure 7.38
Permafrost**

Arctic animals depend on these plants for their existence, so it can be appreciated that human activities in these sensitive regions can have ramifications for the whole ecosystem. The number of species is more limited than in warmer environments and, as everywhere, plants and animals are highly interdependent. Human activity, even during the winter months, is destructive.

Lemmings are small mammals which are active all through the year in the permafrost environment, usually scampering beneath the snow in burrows, eating the green shoots of grasses and sedges. Their droppings form an important nitrogenous fertilizer in an area where it is scarce, and they are an important food for foxes, many birds of prey, and even wolves. When the snow is compacted by machinery, the lemmings become trapped in a confined area, and may die as a result.

These Arctic permafrost areas are being explored and developed as a source of oil, natural gas, and minerals for use in more densely populated southern areas. Heavy equipment is used to build transportation links across the land and the oceans. Experiments with buried oil pipelines show that they heave (move) as a result of the heat of the oil and the natural freezing and thawing of the ground. This could result in oil or gas leaks which would damage the environment. For this reason, pipelines in these areas are usually supported above the surface. Unfortunately, this interferes with the normal migratory movements of many animals, especially the caribou. When caribou cannot reach their usual pastures, they are forced to overgraze in restricted areas. This damages the ecosystem, and the animals starve. As the numbers of caribou decrease, Inuit hunters suffer, as do the wolves which depend upon the caribou for food.

Another area of concern is the possiblity of an oil spill in the Arctic waters. Protected as these waters are by a thick layer of ice for many months each year, they are still vulnerable. Very little is known about the behaviour of an Arctic oil spill or how to deal with it safely, but oil spills in other waters are known to kill all kinds of aquatic life from algae and plankton to fish, birds, and even polar bears. Such spills could be caused by accidents in undersea drilling or in transportation by submarine pipelines or by tankers.

The future development of large Arctic communities to exploit natural resources would also create serious problems. In particular, metallic mine wastes are often poisonous, and would affect the vegetation and animal life. Large quantities of water are often required for general consumption and sewage systems, which would upset existing drainage patterns. Transportation systems also cause great disruption. Noise and disturbance from additional people, aircraft, and machines would have a considerable effect on wild animals.

As demand for resources increases, people will develop the technology required to make exploitation of these permafrost areas economically feasible. It will be crucial to ensure that this use of the Arctic does not lead to the destruction of an environment which cannot repair itself.

An Arctic lemming

Questions

45. (a) Explain why the environment in tundra areas is described as "fragile."

    (b) Why did traditional Inuit activities not threaten the Arctic environment, whereas present and projected activities do?

46. Suggest suitable strategies for ensuring the future protection of permafrost areas, bearing in mind the need to exploit the resources of these areas.

47. Why is it appropriate that this section on the destruction of wildlife and habitat should be positioned at the end of this chapter?

Conclusion

The systems which permit life to flourish on this earth are complex and interrelated. Without human technological interference, changes would occur, but those changes would be slow, and life forms would be able to adjust.

Our technology and growing numbers exert a strain on the environment's ability to compensate for our careless actions, and it cannot cope. We are not dealing adequately with the poisons that we are creating, and as a result, we are destroying vast areas of land and many species of wildlife. In so doing, we are sentencing ourselves to a risky future, one in which the environment will not be able to bounce back. We can feel some encouragement because of the growing awareness and concern of increasing numbers of people, and because of the success stories, but we are a long way from a satisfactory solution to this problem which will affect us for generations to come.

Vocabulary

biosphere
contour ploughing
desertification
desertization
greenhouse effect
Acid deposition
groundwater
water surplus
water deficiency
aquifers
Vavilov Centres
permafrost

Independent Study

1. Prepare a report on the pollutants which are commonly found in modern airtight buildings. Describe their sources and effects, and explain what can be done to improve the situation.

2. Write a report which outlines the origins of the pollutants listed in Table 7.3. Also, describe what attempts have been made to reduce the problems in a few chosen locations, and the degrees of success or failure which have resulted.

3. Investigate three air pollutants which are not listed in Table 7.3, and which are believed to cause health problems. Describe their sources and health effects. Include any information on the control of these substances which you can find.

4. Research and report on the causes and effects of a dioxin release in Seveso, Italy in 1976.

5. Research and report on the methods used and proposed for the disposal of the waste generated by nuclear reactors.

6. In many areas of Canada and in other nations, much valuable agricultural land is being built over as cities expand. Find statistics and use them to demonstrate the severity of the problem in Canada. What will be the consequences if this trend continues? Use maps and possibly graphs in your answer. Suggest possible alternatives to using this land.

7. Schemes for the diversion of water in North America have been suggested for many years. Describe what is involved in these proposals, and list arguments for and against their implementation.

8. Write a report in the destruction of roads, buildings, monuments, and other such structures, as a result of pollution. Explain the causes of this pollution and use specific examples of results where possible. What efforts are being undertaken to combat the problem, and what degree of success is being achieved? Where possible, estimate the cost of the damage you describe.

9. Within the last few years, there have been reports of toxic wastes being dumped in or turned away from poorer nations. Also, pesticides and drugs which are not considered safe for use in First World nations are sent to other nations. Investigate and report on at least three such incidents. Comment on the morality of such action.

By the end of this chapter, you should be able to:

- explain the meaning of "resource" and the difference between renewable and non-renewable resources;

- explain the influence of politics and business transactions on resource exploitation and marketing;

- describe the major energy issues in the contemporary world;

- describe and evaluate future energy alternatives; and

- assess the importance of technology in resource extraction, and use examples to illustrate how the unwise use of modern technology can threaten our resource base.

8

Impact of Resource Extraction on the World

Friday
Special Needs
6.00 Friday
West End YMCA
931 College
Overcast

Oil in the Persian Gulf

"The Gulf War Goes On and On"..."Gulf War Goes Global." Headlines such as these appear frequently in connection with conflicts near the Persian Gulf. Many nations have been concerned about, or else are directly involved in, the fighting. Others are also cashing in on the sale of arms, ammunition, spare parts, and aircraft to the combatants.

Why the global interest in the Persian Gulf? World oil supplies are the answer. The countries surrounding the Persian Gulf account for 56 percent of the world's oil reserves. Some oil goes via pipeline to the Red Sea and the Mediterranean, but 75 percent of it is taken by tanker out through the Strait of Hermuz. The latest war started when Iraq invaded Iran over territory that Iraq claimed. Iraq attacked Iran's oil installations and Iran retaliated by attacking tankers of Iraq's supporters, especially Kuwait, through which much of Iraq's oil is exported. Ships going through the Strait of Hermuz are within easy range of aircraft from the Iranian naval base at Bandar Abbas or missiles based nearby on Qeshm Island. Figure 8.1 illustrates the locations of the places involved and the extent to which other nations are dependent on Persian Gulf oil supplies.

Forty tankers were sunk in the eight year war which started in 1980. The United States and USSR each tried to protect tankers, in order to keep the area open for commerce, while Britain, France, and West Germany also increased their naval presence.

Supplies for the war came from all over the world. Many countries benefitted greatly from the sale of these

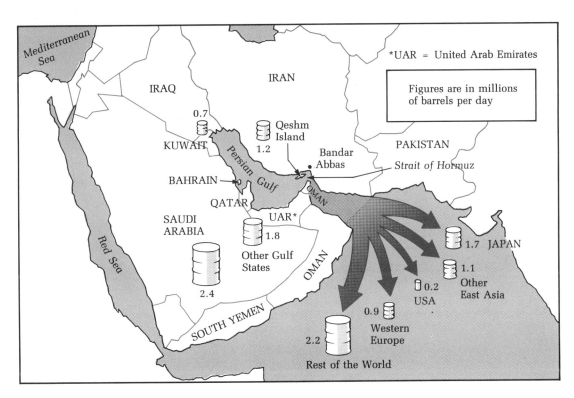

Figure 8.1
Origin and
Destination of
Gulf Oil

*UAR = United Arab Emirates

Figures are in millions of barrels per day

A United States
warship passes
by a Greek oil
tanker which has
been attacked in
the Persian Gulf

supplies, while purchasing
countries went deep in debt.
Iraq, for example, owes US
$50 billion. While it was
mainly the Soviet Union
which supplied Iraq and
western nations which
supplied Iran, several nations
did not hesitate to supply
both sides! As a result, some
unusual incidents occurred.
For example, both Iran and
Iraq bought a certain type of
four-wheeled vehicle from an
East German factory. Convoys
of trucks from the two countries lined up side by side at
the works and then drove
their loads back along the
same highways to their
respective armies. Off-duty
drivers for the two sides slept
in their trucks in the parking
lot, but there was no trouble
between them.

Questions

1. Japan is extremely concerned about events in the
   Persian Gulf. Why should
   Japan be more concerned
   than other nations?

2. Some people describe the
   Persian Gulf area as a
   "powderkeg." What do
   they mean, and why are
   they so worried?

3. The United Nations made
   several attempts to force
   an end to conflict in this
   area.

   (a) In your opinion, what
       factors contributed to
       the longevity of the
       war?

   (b) What suggestions
       would you make for
       restoring long-lasting
       peace among the Gulf
       nations?

Introduction

A **resource** is defined in the
dictionary as "any supply that
will meet a need." Thus,
almost anything that we use
from time to time is a
resource. This textbook, for
example, is a resource to
which you refer. **Natural
resources** are the basis for the
existence of all forms of life,
including our own. Resources
are vital to the simplest
marine organisms and to the
most complex city environment. People have depended
on resources to support their
way of life since humans first
existed. With recent advances
in technology, there has been
a demand for a greater variety
of resources. Fortunately, the
techniques that have developed in association with
improved technology also enable us to find these resources
more easily. These methods
include remote sensing and
geophysical investigations.

The reality is, however,
that for all practical purposes,
many of the earth's resources
are finite. Minerals are created
continuously by geological
processes, but these processes
are too slow to keep pace
with the current demand. It
has been estimated that a significant deposit of iron ore,
for example, will take tens or
hundreds of millions of years

to form, yet such a deposit might be completely exhausted in 25 years. Awareness of the limitations of our non-renewable resources, and the need to nurture our renewable resources, is the first step in ensuring future supplies. It is encouraging to observe increasing awareness of resource issues among the general public, and pressure for conservation being exerted by concerned groups.

No doubt the most valuable resource we possess is our own intelligence. Used to its fullest, it should help us to solve our future problems. We will be able to find new resource deposits, substitute one type of material for another, conserve and recycle those resources which we have already claimed from the environment, and possibly even use resources from the moon or other heavenly bodies. There will be few limits on what we can achieve, provided that we go about the task wisely and with concern about this complex system to which every part, living and non-living, can make a valuable contribution.

The cautiously optimistic statement in the preceding paragraph is in sharp contrast to opinions expressed by a group of international experts calling themselves the "Club of Rome." In 1970, they published a report entitled "Limits to Growth," in which they warned that resources were in danger of becoming exhausted, and that the dangers from pollution would increase exponentially as time passed. To a certain extent, their warnings have proven valid. As described in Chapter 7, pollution and its consequences are a problem of growing concern, and the clearance of tropical forests is having a devastating effect on the environment. However, technology has increased the efficiency with which we find, exploit, and use resources. For example, between 1810 and 1900, the weight-to-power ratio of European steam locomotives increased ten times. By 1950, this ratio had increased an additional four times, and electric locomotives subsequently introduced were 70 times more efficient than 1810 locomotives.

The per capita consumption of certain commodities, such as steel and cement, has been declining in western Europe since 1970, and other commodity use is either declining or stable. The reason for this is improved computer technologies which enable manufacturers to make more efficient designs. Thus, while more people have cars, each car is lighter and more fuel efficient.

It is imperative that we secure a stable resource base for the future. Thus, it is very important that as many people as possible become familiar with the situation and the problems and possibilities that face us all. A most important preliminary step is to learn about the functioning of the dynamic components of the ecosystem, the state of our present and projected resource base, and how people react to each other in connection with the supply and demand for resources.

Dome Petroleum

Dome Petroleum, a Canadian company, came to the attention of Canadians and others during the mid-1980s. A brief outline of its history serves to illustrate that resource development is a complex and risky undertaking, both for those directly involved and for those who invest in the project.

From modest beginnings in 1950, Dome rose to a position of prestige in the early 1980s, and then plunged precipitously toward financial ruin. One hundred shares worth $380 in 1954 were worth $120 000 in May of 1981. At the time of its final takeover by Amoco in June of 1988, its common shares were listed at $1.40 and its preferred shares at $6.93. (**Common shares** are not as secure as preferred shares. Their value goes up or down depending upon the success of the firm. **Preferred shares** have a guaranteed minimum value, unless the company runs into financial trouble, as in the the case of Dome Petroleum.)

Dome was formed by an exploration geologist, Jack Gallagher. He became chairman of the firm and worked for many years with Bill Richards, who became the president. The investments Dome made gave the company total or partial control of various mines and oil and gas deposits, and control of other companies involved in the exploration, transportation, and processing of these products. Figure 8.2 summarizes these holdings.

**Figure 8.2
Dome's Interests as of September 1982**

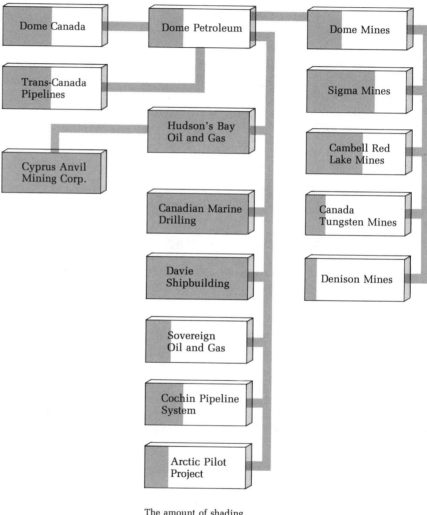

The amount of shading represents the percentage of each organization owned by Dome.

Jack Gallagher's overpowering personal interest lay in frontier exploration and development. He envisioned great potential for the exploitation of oil and gas resources in the Beaufort Sea. The price for world oil had risen sharply in the early 1970s, and many people in Canada (and elsewhere) were concerned about the availability of future supplies. In an environment of anxiety, the Canadian government, under Prime Minister Pierre Trudeau, introduced a system of tax incentives and grants to encourage the exploration and development of Canadian energy resources. It was hoped that Canada would become self-sufficient in oil supplies.

In response to government encouragement, Dome acquired drilling rights to over 5 million hectares of the Arctic. By 1981, it had a giant operation in the Beaufort Sea, with the largest corporate-owned marine fleet and the biggest private air fleet in Canada. To qualify for the tax incentives offered by the government, Dome needed to acquire more Canadian assets. It bought Hudson's Bay Oil and Gas for a colossal sum. This purchase caused Dome to incur debts of $2 billion to four Canadian banks, and US $1.8 billion to 26 US and foreign lenders. It took a long time to complete this deal, and by that time, interest rates on borrowed money had risen to over 20 percent. Dome was not in a position to pay this interest.

The loans from the Canadian banks were not sufficiently secured; that is, they were not backed up by enough equity. **Equity** refers to a valuable asset that could be reclaimed by the lender if the borrower were unable to repay the loan.

There was near panic when an unsubstantiated statement made in the British Columbia Legislature on July 7, 1982 led many people to believe that the Canadian Imperial Bank of Commerce was going to fail as a result of Dome being unable to repay its debts. This rumour alone could have led to a **run** on all banks, particularly the CIBC, whereby people would withdraw their savings, crippling banking operations.

Despite desperate attempts by Dome to renegotiate and re-organize its debts, it was unable to do so. J. Howard Macdonald was appointed chairman and became instrumental in trying to discharge Dome's debts as quickly as possible. The company was eventually acquired by Amoco for the sum of $5.5 billion.

Many investors lost a great deal of money, directly and indirectly, and taxpayers had paid large sums to invest in Dome's Arctic developments. A complex combination of greed, poor timing, government policies, world oil prices, and their consequent influence on the financial climate ultimately led to the demise of what was one of Canada's biggest businesses.

Questions

4. Two factors not mentioned in the case study of Dome, which had considerable influence on the outcome, were that world oil prices did not continue to rise as anticipated (see Figure 8.5), and many nations of the world, including Canada and the United States, went throught a period of recession during which investors were very cautious. Take each of these factors in turn and explain how it would have contributed to Dome's demise. In each case, what might have occurred, had the situation been different?

5. (a) In what ways does the case study of Dome Petroleum illustrate the point that resource development is not just a case of acquiring capital and investing it?

   (b) What additional factors would have needed to be taken into account in order to develop oil and gas resources in the Beaufort Sea? In what ways would each of these factors have added to Dome's problems?

Major Energy Issues

The events which occurred in connection with oil supplies during the last few decades provide us with a view of the relationship between supply, demand, and price structure in a vital commodity. A **vital commodity** is one that is essential to life. From this, we will be able to learn valuable lessons which could certainly be applied to other resources.

The Battle to Control the Supply of Energy in Our World

The year 1973 will stand out in the minds of many people as pivotal to our attitudes about the availability of energy resources. In that year, the world experienced a sudden shortage of oil. This hit industrialized nations such as Japan especially hard, since they depended very heavily on imported sources, but it also affected all nations accustomed to unlimited supplies of inexpensive imports of crude oil.

Shortages had occurred before 1973. During 1917 and 1918 and through most of the 1920s, oil was in short supply. By 1929, however, due to two developments, much more oil became available.

Figure 8.3
Petroleum Basins
of the World

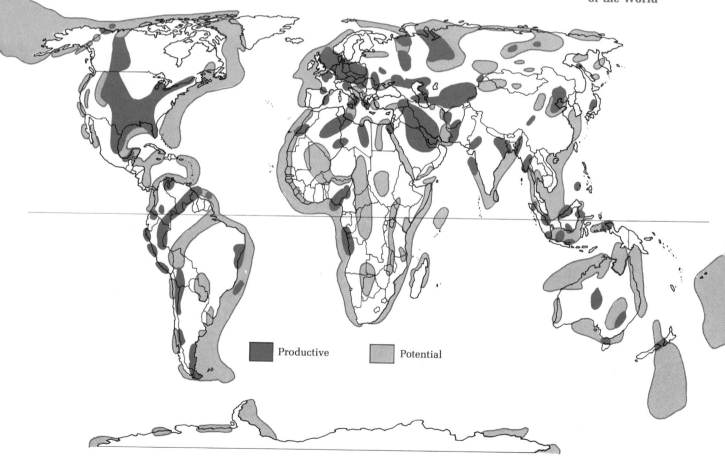

Productive   Potential

One of these developments involved the discovery of huge oil deposits in various parts of the world. The other was the introduction of a technique called **hydrocracking** which enables more gasoline and other useful products to be recovered from each barrel of oil. The enormous increase in production throughout the ten years following World War I saw annual world production climb from 350 million barrels to over 1 billion. This overproduction led to a glut in which prices dropped sharply.

With inexpensive, easily available oil, "gas-guzzling" cars came into fashion in North America, new highways were built and old ones upgraded, poorly insulated houses and office buildings were constructed, and cities sprawled into suburbia as commuting became affordable.

During this period, the oil companies were looking for ways to increase their profits. Pricing and marketing agreements between major companies during the first part of this century made them less vulnerable to changes in supply and demand. In the 1930s, the Texas Railroad Commission set limits to the amount of crude oil that could be produced by its Texas oil wells. This reduction in supply forced the price of domestically produced crude oil in the United States up and resulted in greater profits for the oil industry.

Questions

6. What were people's attitudes toward oil consumption when there was plenty of oil available at very low cost? What would be the consequences in terms of depletion rates?

7. Why was it advisable for major oil companies to come to some agreement about pricing and marketing?

8. Carefully explain why restricting the supply of oil on the market would lead to higher profits for the oil companies.

Some observers, notably Juan Pablo Perez, a statesman of Venezuela, noticed what was going on in the United States. Perez realized that the only way that Venezuela and other oil-exporting nations could make greater profits was to force prices up by creating a shortage of oil. He was instrumental in the founding of a cartel called the **Organization of Petroleum Exporting Countries** (OPEC), which was officially formed in January 1961. A **cartel** is an organization which agrees upon the production and price for a commodity of which they have a major share in the world market. This enables them to force prices to rise. OPEC countries controlled the supply of much of the world's export oil so that

by 1970, when worldwide demand had risen to over 12 billion barrels per year, there was no excess of supply. At that point in history, these nations were in a position to demand whatever price consumers would pay, and they wanted a fair economic return for their resource base.

Beginning in 1973, and coincident with an attack by Israel on Egypt, Syria, and Jordan, the OPEC nations began to cut production. Prices rose abruptly and, as a result, there was an enormous flow of wealth from the consuming countries to the producing countries during the next decade. Although the major international oil companies, commonly referred to as the **Seven Sisters**, lost much of their influence in these OPEC countries, they also reaped greater profits as prices for world crude increased.

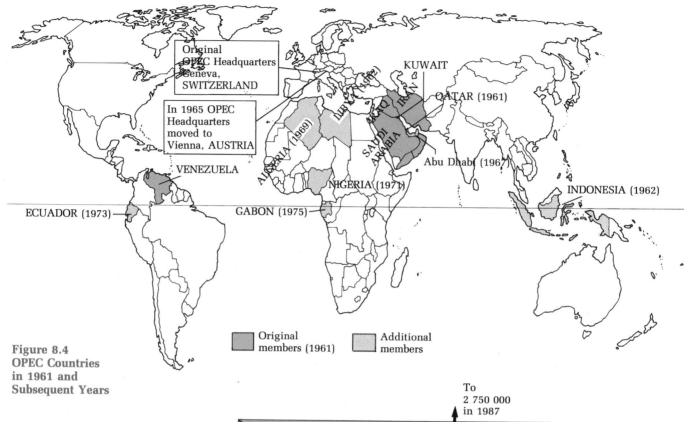

Original
OPEC Headquarters
Geneva,
SWITZERLAND

In 1965 OPEC
Headquarters
moved to
Vienna, AUSTRIA

KUWAIT

QATAR (1961)

ALGERIA (1969)

LIBYA (1962)

IRAQ

IRAN

SAUDI
ARABIA

Abu Dhabi (1967)

VENEZUELA

NIGERIA (1971)

INDONESIA (1962)

ECUADOR (1973)

GABON (1975)

Original
members (1961)

Additional
members

Figure 8.4
OPEC Countries
in 1961 and
Subsequent Years

Question

9. What are the two major
reasons why oil companies
in the consuming nations
would benefit from the
OPEC agreement to restrict
the output of oil? Remem-
ber that they also
produced oil from domes-
tic sources.

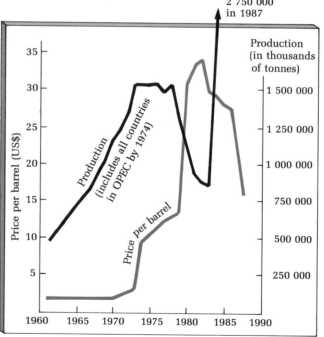

To
2 750 000
in 1987

Production
(in thousands
of tonnes)

Production
(includes all countries
in OPEC by 1974)

Price per barrel

There was a crisis, but only over the supply of high-quality, light crude oil. There were plenty of other energy sources, including heavy oil and oil locked in sand and shale. Reserves or potential reserves of these low-grade oils were estimated to contain several trillion barrels. (A **reserve** is a supply of a natural resource that is not currently being exploited but could be in the future.)

Nations were forced to change their attitudes toward future energy supplies. Two different approaches were developed. The first, referred to as the **heavy metal** approach, involved investing enormous sums of money in the development of these alternative oil sources and the production of energy from other sources such as nuclear reactors. The second approach, the **soft energy path**, advocated moving to more renewable resources, diversifying the methods for power production, and suiting the methods employed to the needs. **Conservation** was an essential part of this latter concept.

Question

10. (a) Graph the statistics given in Table 8.1.

    (b) Describe what your graphs from part (a) are showing. Which countries seemed to be more able to adjust to the shortage of supply, and which countries were less able to make the necessary changes? Using Figure 8.3, which shows the location of oil resources, give reasons for these differences.

In Canada, as in many other industrialized nations, both the ''heavy metal'' and ''soft energy path'' approaches have been used to adapt to the oil shortage. **Megaprojects** such as huge hydro-electric projects and nuclear power stations have been planned, and some have been implemented. While some have met with limited success, others have experienced monetary problems. The development of solar and wind power, among the ''soft'' approaches, is still experimental and expensive. What has been more successful is the move toward conservation.

Table 8.1
Imports of OPEC
Oil into Selected
Countries 1973
and 1984

	OPEC Imports			
	1973		1984	
	millions of barrels per day	% of total crude oil imports	millions of barrels per day	% of total crude oil imports
France	2.49	92	0.85	58
West Germany	2.11	96	0.74	56
Italy	2.35	91	1.03	68
Japan	4.70	96	2.83	78
USA	2.04	63	1.74	42

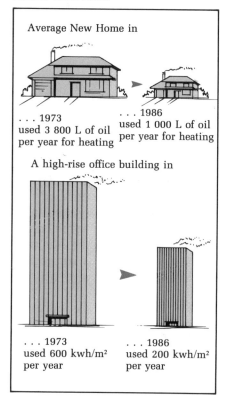

**Figure 8.6
The Results of
Conservation
Efforts 1973-1986**

Average New Home in

. . . 1973
used 3 800 L of oil
per year for heating

. . . 1986
used 1 000 L of oil
per year for heating

A high-rise office building in

. . . 1973
used 600 kwh/m²
per year

. . . 1986
used 200 kwh/m²
per year

The countries which are still hurting from the enormous increases in oil costs are those which have been unable to take either of the approaches described above to develop and conserve new energy supplies and which do not have their own oil resources. These include many lesser developed countries whose international debts have increased due to their dependence on oil-producing nations. Building a better transportation network and industrial base in a developing country requires the consumption of greater quantities of energy. Many modern agricultural practices introduced into developing nations also depend on oil-based fertilizers.

Some of the developing nations, such as Nigeria, also export oil. In order to acquire more foreign currency, they may increase production, yet this puts pressure on other OPEC members to lower prices in order to sell their oil. The oil-producing countries have felt the effects of the consuming nations' efforts to reduce imports of crude oil. The strength of the OPEC alliance has been challenged, and it will take constant vigilance and discipline by member countries to keep this cartel from disintegrating.

In the short run, the industrial nations of the world suffered inconvenience and damaged economies as a result of the sudden jump in oil prices. When looked at in perspective, however, there has been a greater sharing of the world's wealth and, as a result, an appreciation for the irreplaceable resources upon which modern life depends.

Questions

11. In what ways, if any, could the members of a cartel like OPEC influence another member country to keep production in line?

12. Write down arguments for and against joining OPEC. Do this for 1960, 1973, and the present year.

Members of the OPEC nations have experienced considerable change in situation since 1973. The various measures adopted by importing nations to combat the effects of high oil prices have led to a significant decline in OPEC oil exports. The value of oil exports from these countries in 1980, the peak year, was $281 586 millions. By 1986, it had dropped to $77 100 millions.

Between 1973 and 1980, many of these nations had come to depend more and more on this revenue, and were affected very adversely by the subsequent lowering of prices. In 1988, OPEC members met with other producing countries to prevent a drastic drop in international oil prices.

Country	Oil as % of Exports		GNP per capita (US$)	
	1973	1983	1973	1983
Algeria	80.6	80.1	504	2 400
Ecuador	53.0	63.3	371	1 086
Gabon	51.5	82.5	1 248	4 250
Indonesia	50.1	63.7	115	560
Iran	90.8	97.8	762	*1 621
Iraq	94.5	98.6	645	2 150
Kuwait	92.4	79.6	8 449	18 180
Libya	98.8	100.0	2 984	7 500
Nigeria	83.4	92.4	250	760
Qatar	97.3	91.9	5 938	21 170
Saudi Arabia	100.0	100.0	1 299	8 000
United Arab Emirates (UAE)	96.6	90.2	6 736	21 360
Venezuela	88.6	90.2	1 357	4 100
Total/Average	**88.6**	**90.2**	**2 358**	**7 164**

Table 8.2
OPEC's Oil as a Percentage of Total Exports

*1982

Questions

13. Plot a graph using the statistics in Table 8.2. Use this sketch as a guide to setting up your axes.

    Against the Y-axis, you will be plotting the rise or fall of the dependence of each country on the revenues received from imported oil. To get this value, you will need to find the difference between the figures in the first and second columns. Against the X-axis, you will be plotting the positive or negative change in GNP over the same time period.

14. Does there seem to be any relationship between the two factors you have plotted on your graph in question 13? Answer (a) or (b) below.

    (a) If you think there is a relationship between these factors, draw a line to illustrate it on your graph. Explain why there might be a relationship.

    (b) Explain why there is no relationship, if that is your opinion.

15. A country has had a sudden rise in income due to enormous increases in the value of a resource it exports.

    (a) What policies should its government follow, if the resource is renewable or if it is non-renewable?

    (b) What difference should be made in policies when a resource is non-renewable with very limited reserves, or non-renewable with very large reserves?

    (c) How are policies likely to be affected according to whether the country's government is communist, a dictatorship, or democratic? Not only quantities and prices for exports should be considered, but also plans for an increase in revenues.

16. Do you consider that any group of countries is justified in creating a cartel involving a vital commodity? What risks do they run in protecting their own interests?

The Importance of Energy Supply and Demand Today

The thirteen member countries of OPEC produce one-third of the world's oil. One-half of all the exported oil in the world comes from these countries. It is evident that they are in a position to exert a great deal of pressure on the industrialized world. Between January and July of 1986, however, the price of oil on the international market fell from US $28.33 to less than US $10 per barrel. To recover, OPEC nations have attempted to reduce supply in order to force prices up once more. But alternative sources of oil, other forms of energy, and effective conservation methods had been developed during the previous decade. The world demand for oil was 14 percent less in 1985 than in 1979, and was even 2.5 percent less than in 1973! Due to this decline, decisions made by OPEC nations have less impact now.

Many factors have produced this situation. Capital has become readily available for exploration and development of new oil fields. For example, the communist world expanded its oil production by 65 percent between 1973 and 1986. The USSR is now the world's largest producer, and China's production has also expanded rapidly. The sale of oil brings desirable western currency into these communist countries. If we exclude increases in production in the USA, output from non-OPEC oil producers increased 2.5 times between 1973 and 1986.

Directly and indirectly, international politics have an enormous influence on the oil situation. Both the USA and the USSR have a keen interest in the Middle East, and it has become important for each of these countries to exercise some influence in the area. The Soviet Union's occupation of Afghanistan between 1979 and 1988 and the Soviet interests in Libya, Iraq, the People's Democratic Republic of Yemen, and Ethiopia have been balanced by an Ameri-

Figure 8.7
Political Map of the Middle East and Adjacent Countries

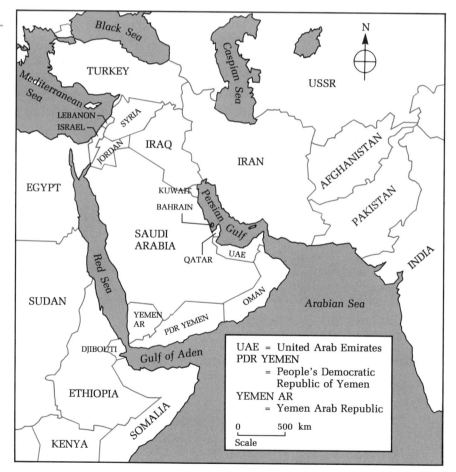

UAE = United Arab Emirates
PDR YEMEN
   = People's Democratic Republic of Yemen
YEMEN AR
   = Yemen Arab Republic

0   500 km
Scale

can interest in Saudi Arabia, the Yemen Arab Republic, Somalia, Pakistan, and Iran.

Other disputes which have a considerable influence on the situation include the Arab-Israeli conflict, differences arising amongst the oil producing countries themselves, and diversity of religious and ethnic beliefs and traditions. Obviously also, consumers have a different view of the situation compared to producers.

Question

17. (a) In what way would the views of the oil-consuming nations differ from those of the oil-producing nations?

(b) Under what circumstance of supply and demand would each of the above groups be able to exert the greatest influence on the other?

Oil-drilling rig platform in the Middle East

Simulation

The major oil-producing nations, A, are becoming increasingly discontented with the low price that is being paid for their oil. They are determined to force their customers, the international oil companies, to pay much more.

The oil companies, B, are worried about the possibility of higher costs cutting into their profits, although they could reap benefits from a higher price for their own oil if the increases were passed on to their customers.

The governments of the consuming nations are concerned about the effects that rising prices would have on the economy of each of their countries. These countries can be divided into the following categories: industrialized nations with some oil resources of their own, C; industrialized nations with no oil resources, D; developing nations with some oil resources but not in the major A group, E; and developing nations with no oil resources, F.

Instructions

Divide the class into six groups, each group representing one of the interested parties A to F described above.

Group A starts the discussion by making this statement to the other groups: "We believe that the price paid to

us for oil is too low. We are going to raise our prices." Each group should then consider its reactions and subsequently take part in a discussion with all of the other groups in the room, in an attempt to protect their own best interests.

Group A, frustrated by the lack of progress from its own point of view, further declares that it is cutting production significantly so that there will be a shortage of oil available in the world. All groups, including the major oil producers, are to write down how they think this will affect their nations and how best they can prepare for it or use the revenues that result. This is to be followed by a discussion of the conclusions.

Group E decide that they are going to produce more oil in order to benefit from the rise in prices. Each group should decide on its reaction, and group E should explain what it would do with the increased revenue. The conclusions should be presented to the class.

Each student should then write an account to demonstrate the effectiveness of organizations such as OPEC, and explain their vulnerability. This explanation should show how the control of a vital resource such as oil can affect people's lives in all corners of the world.

The Concept of Energy Security

All activities depend on a supply of energy in some form. For a secure future, we must be able to rely on the availability of energy to meet our needs. Without this availability, the maintenance and growth of our economy will be threatened, as will be our well-being and way of life.

The word "energy" does not just encompass petroleum and the products derived from it. One source of energy can often be substituted for another. In particular, renewable sources can replace nonrenewable ones. Domestic production of energy can be used to replace imported sources, although these home sources may be more expensive to produce. New approaches to the use of energy can lead to conservation, thus reducing energy demands.

When income from their oil exports increased dramatically, many non-industrialized oil-producing nations greatly increased their own consumption of oil. Saudi Arabia's consumption increased by a factor of 11 and Libya's increased by a factor of 13, between 1970 and 1983. This increase enabled these countries to industrialize. At the same time, however, increased prices led to a decline in consumption in many industrialized countries such as the United States, where consumption decreased by two percent. A decrease in consumption of energy occur-

Figure 8.8
The World's
Reserves of Coal,
Oil, Gas, and
Uranium

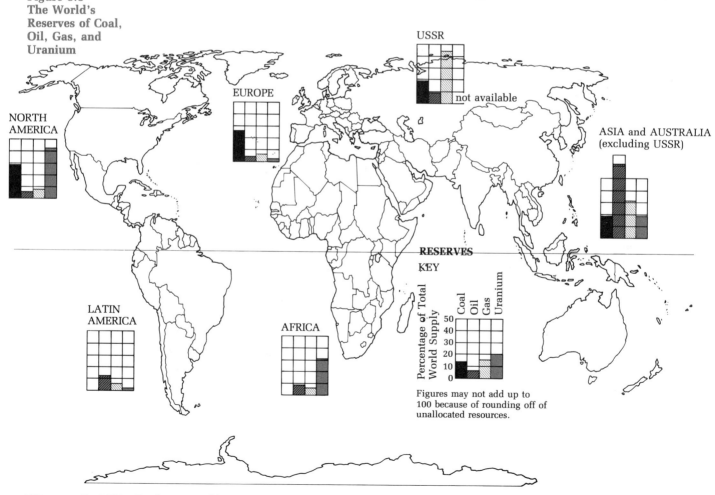

ring simultaneously with an increase in population, economic activity, and wealth depends upon the development and use of conservation technologies.

As the lesser developed nations begin to industrialize, there will be an even greater demand for energy supplies worldwide. This demand depends, of course, upon the ability of these lesser developed nations to pay for industrialization and the energy required for its operation, or on the help which they may receive from other sources. It is important that we realize the demands that development makes on energy supplies. Figure 8.9, showing the energy involved in making, using, and disposing of a single tin can, illustrates the point well.

Energy use has become a vital ingredient in the activities of our modern society. We are aware that some of our energy sources are finite, so it is essential that we turn to alternative sources to replace conventional sources as this becomes necessary. If this is not accomplished, there will be a disastrous decline in the world's economy.

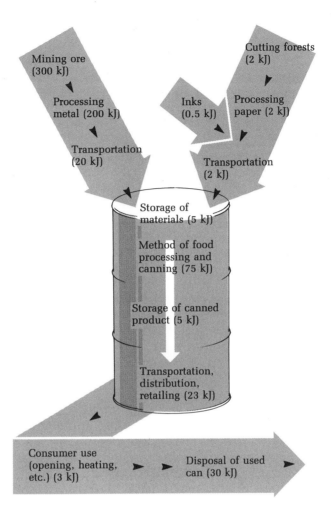

Figure 8.9
The Energy Cycle of a Tin Can

Energy Alternatives for the Future

What are the alternative energy sources? All substances contain energy, but the problem is how to release it so that we can make use of it. Many processes involve the transformation of energy from one form to another. Are there some ways in which we can take advantage of these processes?

Renewable energy sources such as those contained in wood, wind, and falling water have been harnessed directly or indirectly for thousands of years. These sources are still very important, and research is enabling us to realize the alternative ways to use them.

In order to predict our reserves of energy, experts attempt to measure the quantities of known and possible resources, balancing them against projected consumption rates in future years. Coal, with reserves that might last 200 years, has its drawbacks, but also could have possibilities, according to the latest research.

The comparatively new technology using nuclear fuels was greeted at first with great enthusiasm, but it is viewed with much more apprehension and caution today. (See the section on nuclear power, later in this chapter.) Then there are the myriad of other sources, from the ultimate in energy — our sun — to that derived from soybeans or sewage sludge.

Interest in other alternative energy sources increases when conventional sources are in short supply or very expensive. It will remain to be seen whether interest and investment turn some of these projects into commercial reality. For now, we will concentrate on a few of these which look as though they will be important in the foreseeable future.

Coal

Coal was a vital energy source between 1870 and 1960. In the years preceding 1960, oil as a source of energy had grown steadily in importance and eventually eclipsed coal. However, many people would be surprised to discover that coal still provides one-quarter of the world's fuel, and about 20 times as much energy as all of the nuclear reactors of the world put together!

The drawbacks to using coal include the difficulty of moving a bulk solid when compared to a liquid or gas, the products of its combustion (which are partly responsible for acid precipitation), and the ash residue.

Technology recently developed in Europe enables us to overcome each of these problems. The coal is pulverized at the mine. Water and some chemicals which remove the pollutants are added to the coal, giving the mixture a consistency very much like that of oil. It is called **fluid-carbon** (also **carbogel**) and has the same appearance, colour, flowing, and burning properties as oil. Malmo, a city in Sweden, uses fluid-carbon to power a boiler which heats most of the buildings in the city, including a hospital.

Experiments have been conducted in New Brunswick to explore future applications of carbogel. If the technology that results from these experiments is adopted, it could increase demand for coal from mines which had been abandoned or which are currently working below capacity because of poor world markets. World coal reserves are vast, and the technology involved in their development could restore coal to its previous position of importance as oil supplies dwindle.

Nuclear Energy

People's ideas about nuclear energy have changed. In the early 1970s, many people held the view that nuclear power was the answer to our future needs. Reactors were designed and many were built. During the time of the oil crisis, the nuclear alternative looked very attractive, especially for countries like Canada that had the necessary resources. Yet in the United States today, nuclear power only delivers half as much power as wood, and one-fifth of the power produced from coal. The graphs in Figure 8.11 illustrate how official projections regarding the importance of nuclear reactors in the year 2000 have been modified.

Approximately one-seventh of world energy production comes from nuclear sources, and some nations depend very heavily on it. Sixty-five per-

Figure 8.10
World Coal
Deposits

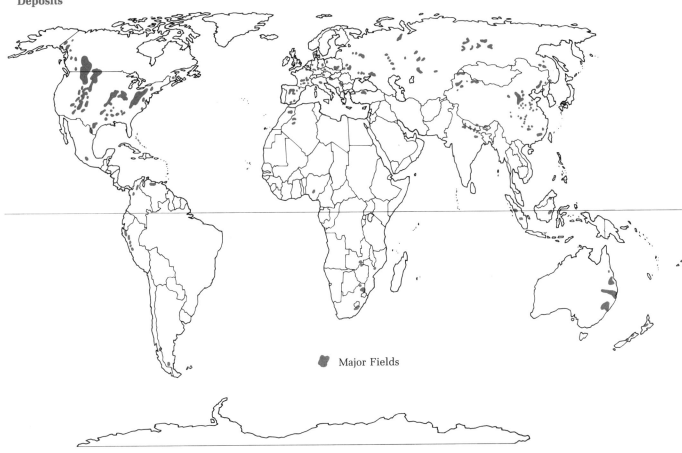

Major Fields

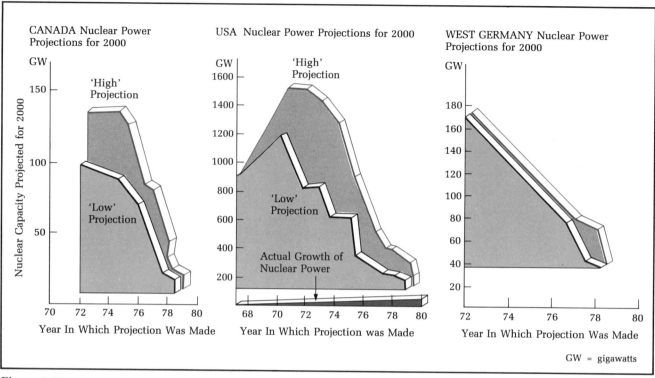

CANADA Nuclear Power Projections for 2000

USA Nuclear Power Projections for 2000

WEST GERMANY Nuclear Power Projections for 2000

GW = gigawatts

**Figure 8.11
Nuclear Power
Projections for
the Year 2000 in
Canada, the USA,
and West Germany**

cent of France's electricity comes from nuclear reactors; in Canada, nuclear power plants generate ten percent of the total production of electricity.

As you are probably well aware, nuclear reactors are very expensive to build, and even more expensive to shut down at the end of their useful existence. Radioactive wastes are produced, and we are faced with making provision for their safe storage. Then there is always the danger from mishaps such as the one that occurred at Three Mile Island, USA, in 1979 and Chernobyl, USSR, in 1986. Negative official and public attitudes toward nuclear power stations will result in their relegation to a minor though still vital component of the total energy picture.

Biomass

Energy can, of course, be extracted from plant or animal residues such as wood or dung (referred to as **biomass**), by burning it to produce heat. Whereas, in North America, wood supplies only three to four percent of our primary energy, in the lesser developed nations it is the primary energy source for about 2.5 billion people. The great demand for wood in these nations is contributing to the destruction of their forests and the spread of the deserts. Burning dung as a fuel deprives the soil of much needed fertilizers and humus which retains moisture and improves soil structure. Despite the fact that biomass is renewable, it still has to be carefully managed.

One source of biomass energy used for thousands of years, but little-known in North America, is peat. A form of immature coal, peat forms from plant material in a water-logged environment. In the traditional method, peat was cut into brick-shaped pieces and allowed to dry before it was burned. Today, scientists are looking into the possibilities of large-scale peat harvesting, processing, and use. The most extensive peat resources, 170 million hectares, are in Canada, with 150 million hectares in the USSR and 40 million hectares in the USA. The removal of vast

Collecting wood
in Ethiopia

areas of peat would, however, destroy and damage the wetlands upon which so many species of life depend. It would also have negative effects on the regulation and control of surface run-off, resulting in floods and intervening periods of inadequate water supply.

Another form of biomass energy uses any vegetable oil. Sunflower and soybean oils, and oil left over from frying potatoes, have been used successfully on an experimental basis to power engines.

Any vegetable material, when mixed with sugar and suitable enzymes, under the right conditions of temperature, will form alcohol. When this alcohol is distilled, it forms a fuel suitable for use in engines. Ethanol and methanol are the two main alcohol fuels used in transportation. Ethanol usually comes from plant materials such as corn, and methanol comes from natural gas. Both of these forms of alcohol are often mixed with gasoline to produce gasohol.

The cost of producing fuel alcohol is currently more than the cost of imported crude oil, but it does have some distinct advantages. It is a renewable resource and can be made from crops which can be grown on marginal land. When grain crops are used to produce alcohol, only the carbohydrates are used, leaving crop protein to be used as animal feed. Alcohol is a cleaner burning fuel, so it is better for the environment and for the engine than gasoline. Any surplus farm crop could be used to produce the alcohol, thereby improving farmers' incomes and making the producing country more self-sufficient in energy resources. In Brazil, where gasoline prices are significantly higher than in Canada, 80 percent of motor vehicles use ethanol (ethyl alcohol) derived from sugar cane. Such use of potential food supplies should be questioned, however. In Brazil, for example, many people starve, yet sugar cane, in this case a non-food crop, is grown on potential foodland.

Other ways of converting energy to a useful form involve the conversion of plant and animal material in garbage to methane gas, which can be used as a substitute for natural gas. Combustible components can create heat and possibly electricity, and recycling can dispose of much of the remainder. The sludge produced as a product of sewage treatment can be processed into a heavy oil suitable for use in diesel engines.

Question

18. Re-read the paragraph outlining the use of garbage and sewage sludge as a source of energy.

   (a) Explain how these techniques would benefit the inhabitants of a major city. Be specific in your answer.

   (b) Why are most cities so slow at adopting such measures?

Solar Power

For decades, people have conducted experiments aimed at harnessing the sun's rays, with limited success. The techniques developed cannot compete economically with conventional methods of producing electricity, but the dream still drives many to experiment. The most innovative method being investigated involves the use of a satellite. The Solar Powered Satellite (SPS), with a large array of solar cells, will be located above the equator in **geosynchronous orbit**. This means that the satellite will stay above one spot on the earth's equator, and orbit the earth from west to east once every 24 h. In this orbit, the satellite will be bathed in sunlight which has not been weakened by passing through the earth's atmosphere. It will

A geothermal power station in New Zealand

convert this energy to microwaves which penetrate easily through clouds to a receiver on the earth's surface.

The material for an SPS's construction would be taken from the moon. Removing material from the moon would be much cheaper than taking material from the earth because of the moon's lower gravitational force. Obviously, this is a technology for the future, but it is one in which many nations have expressed an interest, in particular Japan, the USA, and the USSR. The level of interest indicates that these nations have some measure of concern about future energy supplies. The development of such a scheme depends on the same criteria by which we measure today's innovations — is it technologically possible, and would it be economically feasible?

Nuclear Fusion

Nuclear fusion is a reaction in which the nuclei of lightweight atoms combine, releasing large quantities of energy. The energy that this process could release from 1 g of heavy water (deuterium) is equivalent to burning 1.25 t of oil. Thus, a glass of water could provide enough energy for a city. Energy produced in this manner would generate no atmospheric pollutants, hazardous chemicals, or radioactive by-products, although there would eventually be small quantities of radioactive hardware for disposal. The raw materials required to produce the reaction, deuterium or tritium, can be extracted from seawater. The technology required, however, is difficult and exceedingly expensive, although some progress has been made.

Hundreds of millions of dollars have been invested in several countries, including Canada, for developing the necessary technology. So far, the required reaction has only been sustained for a fraction of a second. Ideally, the reaction should continue indefinitely. The investment in research, plus the $2 billion estimated to be needed for the first commercial fusion plant, must be offset by potential returns from the sale of energy. As a possible future energy source, with unlimited resources, perhaps the economic risk is warranted.

Geothermal Power

Beneath the earth's surface, the temperature of the rocks increases with depth. In some areas, often associated with past or present volcanic activity, very hot areas are close to the surface. We can use this heat if it is accessible. Groundwater coming in contact with this natural heat source forms steam and can be used directly or indirectly to turn turbines or heat water for use in heating homes, swimming pools, and greenhouses. Water can be introduced artificially, if it does not occur naturally. Often the water contains dissolved minerals and gases which corrode turbines and pipes, and which can also create an unpleasant and overpowering odour. For this reason, the steam is usually used first to heat fresh water which is then used for the purposes described. (Many people bathe at spas in the mineral-laden waters, to alleviate a medical condition, especially skin disorders.)

Sources of geothermal power are often located far from the centres of population, making them uneconomical to develop. Yet the technology for their development is currently in use. In Iceland, geothermal power contributes over one-third of the energy used, and there is much more available. It is used to heat 80 percent of all of the houses and produces one-third of the electricity used. It is currently heating over 100 000 m² under glass and helps in the raising of fish in low temperature water and the recovery of salt and other chemicals from the hot water solutions in geothermal areas.

Hydro-electric Power

There are few suitable hydro-electric sites remaining to be developed in the industrialized nations. Locations remote from their markets can only be economically developed if the potential for production is large enough to offset the enormous investment in the construction of generating stations, lengthy transmission lines, and the loss of electrical power as it is transported. Developments like James Bay, Churchill Falls, and Nelson River meet these criteria. The ecological effects of such megaprojects are another matter, and are discussed in Chapter 7.

In the lesser developed nations, there is still potential for hydro-electric projects. Yet the experience of megaprojects such as the High Aswan Dam in Egypt and the

Figure 8.12
Geothermal Sites

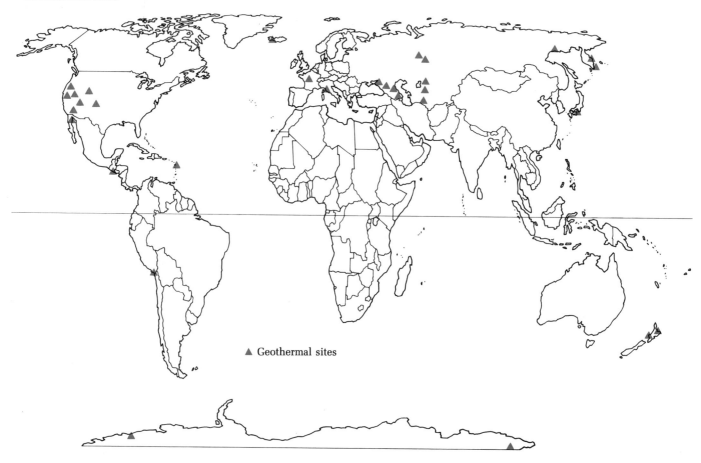

▲ Geothermal sites

A hydro-electric
station in Canada

Itaipu project on the Parana River of the Brazil-Paraguay border has shown that there are environmental as well as social drawbacks. The valley lands which would be flooded represent the loss of scarce, fertile, agricultural land.

A trend advocated for both more and lesser developed areas is to introduce additional small-scale projects, each to supply the requirements of a small market. However, the trend toward large projects continues to be evident in China, where the three gorges through which the Yangtze River flows will be the sites of megaprojects in which Hydro Quebec and BC Hydro are collaborating.

Tidal Power

In certain localities, the tidal range is sufficient to turn turbines installed in a dam at the mouth of a bay. Suitable sites are limited, although there are tidal power stations in operation in France and Nova Scotia. Using salt water to generate electricity creates materials problems such as corrosion. Tides can also cause problems because they have a cycle which changes the time of peak power production, and a period of high and low tide when little water flow takes place.

Other Forms of Oil

Most of the oil that has been extracted so far in the world has flowed or been pumped to the surface with little difficulty. This is referred to as **conventional oil**. Known global reserves of conventional oil are expected to last for about another 30 years, and it is anticipated that resources yet to be discovered will provide oil for an additional 30 years, at the current rate of consumption.

These reserves are dwarfed in volume by **oil** or **tar sands and shales**, from which oil is more difficult and expensive to extract, because they are so viscous. Reserves in Canada, the USA, and Venezuela, for example, exceed those of the conventional resources in the Middle East by 1.7, 4.7, and 4.3 times respectively. Apart from the expense, which makes unconventional oil uncompetitive on world markets, the extraction of this oil also creates environmental problems not usually associated with conventional sources. The deposits are extracted using strip mining techniques which affect the landscape and vegetative and animal life, as well as the movement of water on and below the surface.

Question

19. In this account of alternative energy sources, the emphasis has been on the technology rather than on where these techniques could be best applied. Consider each of the topics discussed and comment on the possible use of these ideas in industrialized and lesser developed nations. In each case, give reasons for your assessment. Consider first the next decade, then a period from 10 to 50 years in the future.

The Promise and Threat of Technology

The previous section, dealing with alternative energy sources, illustrates the point that improvements and progress in supplying energy depend on advancements in technology. These in turn depend on economics, supply and demand, and political inclination. Such is also the case in the fields of other extractive industries.

Agricultural research over the last 50 years has led to the introduction of new farming methods, the use of chemicals, and genetic manipulation. Where such techniques have been used, there have been enormous returns in increased food production. The sudden increase in agricultural productivity, which came to the industrialized world in the 1940s and to lesser developed countries 20 years later, is referred to as the "Green Revolution," and has been discussed in Chapter 5. These improvements have to be balanced against the environmental impact on soils and the results of chemical accumulation in the enviroment. These topics have been discussed in more detail in Chapter 7.

Fishing

Fish form a very important source of protein. The annual world harvest of fish exceeds that of beef. On average, each person in the world consumes 16 kg of fish per year, and this provides 23 percent of all the animal protein consumed. In many Asiatic countries such as Indonesia, the Philippines, and Bangladesh, fish forms over 50 percent of the animal protein intake. Fish is growing in popularity in industrialized countries, but in the lesser developed nations, it forms a much more important part of the diet. In such countries, it can make the difference between a poor and an adequate intake of protein.

Improved technology led to a tripling of the world fish catch between 1950 and 1970. During that period, it was believed that harvests would continue to increase and would eventually provide the answer for protein-deficient diets.

This was not to be, however. Huge fishing fleets, especially those with factory ships, ravaged the fish stocks so badly that they were unable to sustain their numbers. For example, the haddock catch from the northwestern Atlantic fell from 250 000 t in 1956 to 20 000 t in 1974.

It is essential that the fish left behind form a sufficient

A fishing trawler off Canada's East Coast

breeding stock to ensure future supplies. Many of the primary fishing nations such as Japan and the USSR are now taking very small fish as well as using scraps from fish processing to produce feed for animals and fertilizers for use in industrialized countries. When fed to animals, 1 t of fish meal produces less than 0.5 t of pork or poultry, and even less if it is used to grow feed grain. To remove this as a source of direct protein for people in developing nations is morally questionable. If, for example, foreign nations did not remove fish from the ocean around the west coast of Africa, there would be enough protein available to double the amount consumed by the average African.

Question

20. Why is international co-operation necessary in attempting to make fish and whale stocks sustainable? Which other resources require this kind of international agreement? Give reasons for your answers.

Mineral Resources

Known reserves of most minerals are large, and with the increased use of recycling and more efficient mining and processing, few shortages are foreseen on a worldwide basis for the next 25 years. The table below lists the years of supply believed to exist, assuming 1981 consumption rates. Resource potential has been assessed using geological, geophysical, and economic evaluation. Consumption rates continue to rise, and therefore the longevity of these resources is shrinking.

Table 8.3
Years of Mineral Reserves Based on 1981 Consumption Rates

Bauxite (aluminum ore)	260	Tin	40
Copper	65	Uranium	large
Diamond	20	Zinc	41
Gold	30	Antimony	70
Iron Ore	410	Cadmium	39
Lead	48	Chromium	374
Manganese	186	Cobalt	116
Nickel	76	Germanium	large
Platinum	176	Molybdenum	97
Silver	24	Titanium	138

Of course, these deposits are not spread evenly among the nations of the world, and trading between countries will become increasingly important. Certain commodities are absolutely vital, and for this reason, some countries stockpile them for fear of being cut off, perhaps in time of war.

Recycling and substitution will become an increasingly

Figure 8.13
United States' Stockpiles of Vital Minerals

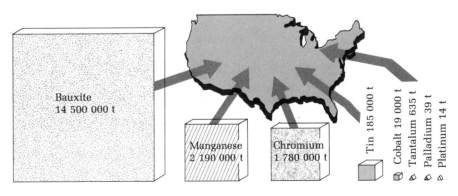

important part of the future mineral supply picture. The recycling process not only conserves our valuable resources but also saves a considerable quantity of energy. Today, almost one-half of our steel and one-third of our aluminum come from scrap. Metals can sometimes be substituted for each other or be replaced by glass and plastics. Plastics come from fossil fuels, however, which may make them a less desirable alternative. There are also some minerals which at present cannot be replaced. These include platinum, which is a catalyst, and chromium, which is used in making stainless steel.

Question

21. South Africa supplies many important minerals to other nations, in particular, chromium, gold, and diamonds. How might this advantage affect the attitudes of its trading partners, with respect to its apartheid policy?

The Importance of the Theory of Plate Tectonics

The development of the **theory of plate tectonics**, particularly the ideas and new knowledge gained in the last two decades, is proving to be of great benefit now, and holds much promise for the future. The theory embodies the concept that the earth's crust is supported on rigid plates, some large and some small, and that these plates are moving. The reason for this movement has not yet been proven, but it is probably due to the convection currents in the earth's upper mantle dragging the plates. The convection currents are believed to be caused by heat released during radioactive decay in the earth's interior.

Where convection currents diverge at the surface, new crust material is formed and new minerals are created. This process is usually accompanied by volcanic and earthquake activity. With a few exceptions, this divergence takes place beneath the oceans. Thus, we are able to conclude that such zones are potentially valuable for mineral extraction when the necessary technology is developed.

Where there is a convergence between plates, heavier rock, usually that beneath the ocean, is forced under the less dense rock of the continents. This movement and friction lead to the occurrence of volcanoes and earthquakes, as mentioned above. In addition, the fault zone becomes the site of metamorphic activity whereby rocks are transformed, often into valuable metals such as gold and silver. Similar transformations also take place along plate edges where one plate is sliding horizontally past another. Folding of the sedimentary rock layers above the zone of convergence leads to other forms of metamorphism and the creation of different forms of valuable minerals. Oil is often trapped in these folds or in contact with faults created by such earth movements. Mineralization also occurs where two plates of a similar density come together and crumple.

The upheaval caused by earth movements forces formerly deep-seated rocks to be exposed at the surface. Thus, valuable coal deposits are

**Figure 8.14
The Plates of the World**

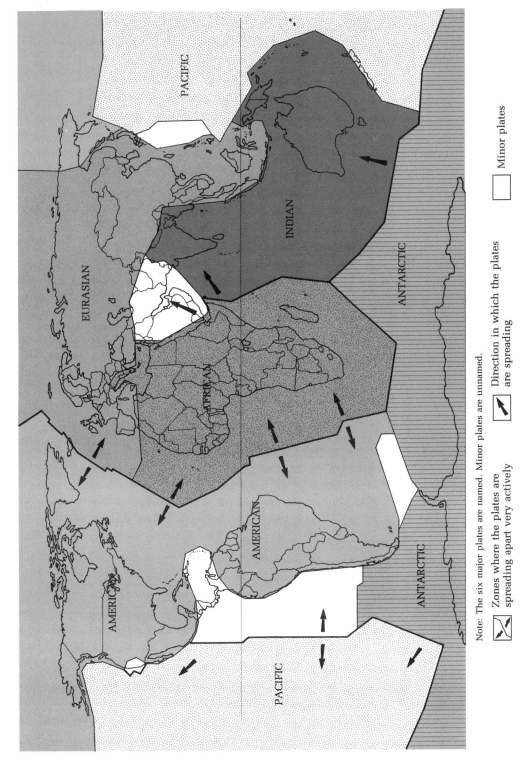

Note: The six major plates are named. Minor plates are unnamed.

Zones where the plates are spreading apart very actively

Direction in which the plates are spreading

Minor plates

exposed for surface mining, or come close enough to the surface for exploitation. Minerals that were formed deep down in the crust also come within our reach.

Through the study of plate tectonics, geologists and geophysicists have been able to make great strides forward in their quest for resources. This progress is largely based on a better understanding of the conditions in which the resources form and become concentrated into economically viable deposits. The theory of plate tectonics, coupled with better mapping, remote sensing, and other sensing techniques, provides us with the potential for filling our future mineral resource requirements.

Resource Development and Native People

We are well aware in Canada of the conflict between those who wish to develop resources, especially in remote northern areas, and the native inhabitants whose traditional way of life depends on an environment suitable for hunting and fishing. Native groups are exerting influence on governments to compensate them for their losses, and pressure from environmental organizations is having some influence in ensuring that any development has as little harmful effect as possible on the indigenous people.

Kahnawake Indians involved in a protest of government action in Quebec

Case Study

The Yanomami Indians of Brazil

There are areas of the world where the native people and the environment have a more precarious relationship than exists in Canada. One such area, occupied by Yanomami Indians, straddles the Brazilian-Venezuelan border.

In this border area, the Brazilian government intends to establish four military outposts to protect its territory against guerillas and drug traffickers. These outposts are also intended to lead the way for highways, electrification, and an influx of tax-paying Brazilians. No doubt it will also lead to the exploitation of the forests and minerals.

The Brazilian government has promised to provide the Indians with a reserve twice the size of Nova Scotia, but native leaders as well as other concerned groups do not trust the government to keep its promises. The Waimiri-Atroari Indians were given a reserve in 1971, only to have it broken up less than ten years later to allow for the development of a tin mine. There is also a concern that the Yanomami Indians have little resistance to diseases that would be brought by the new workers and settlers.

The Brazilian government is facing an enormous international debt situation, approximately $134 billion in 1987. It is anxious to develop the resources of the area in which the Yanomami people live, and the native people have little influence in protecting their own interests.

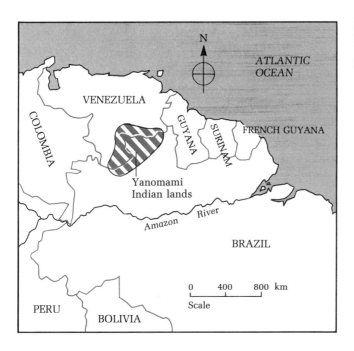

Figure 8.15
Homeland of the
Yanomami
Indians

However, there are many people in other countries concerned about their plight. Their influence has been exerted in the past through the withholding of grants and loans from such agencies as the World Bank and the Inter-American Development Bank until sufficient safeguards are in place.

Yanomami children playing in the forest

Question

22. Assume that you are one of the following people: a mine developer; an anthropologist; a Brazilian politician concerned with the national economy; or an ecologist. Decide what your attitude would be toward the situation of the Yanomami Indians, and defend your position. Your account should be about 500 words in length.

Development of world resources must be done with regard to the future. We must strive to make sure that our renewable resources give us a sustained yield in perpetuity. We must conserve our non-renewable resources until the technology is developed to harness other substitutes economically. Another very large concern must be that the exploitation of one resource does not destroy another, as when the pollutants from mining operations destroy the fish in nearby waters. Thus, we must have a constant regard for the environment upon which we depend.

Conclusion

There are plenty of resources in the world. Some of these are easily accessible while others would be prohibitively expensive to develop in today's market. Control of a vital commodity such as oil can allow a country to have a greater influence on the marketplace under the right circumstances.

The wise use of technology is the result of the wise use of our greatest resource— the human brain — and can lead us to a bright tomorrow. Inappropriate use of this technology due to greed or short-sightedness could destroy many of the renewable resources upon which we depend so heavily. For the human race to prosper requires determination to make wise decisions. Such decisions, in turn, depend on knowledge, understanding, and concern for others and for all components of the environment.

A large open-pit copper mine in Arizona

Vocabulary

resource

natural resource

common shares

preferred shares

reserve (of a resource)

equity

run (on a bank)

vital commodity

hydrocracking

Organization of Petroleum Exporting Countries (OPEC)

cartel

Seven Sisters

heavy metal (approach to energy development)

soft energy path

conservation

megaprojects

fluidcarbon

carbogel

biomass

geosynchronous orbit

nuclear fusion

conventional oil

(tar) sands and shales

theory of plate tectonics

Independent Study

1. Investigate the history, development, and effects of the exploitation of oil in the North Sea.

2. Using charts to illustrate your answer, describe and compare in detail five modern methods currently used in the search for new mineral deposits.

3. When the reserves of oil in a field become reduced, certain techniques are employed to recover more oil.
   (a) Describe these techniques.
   (b) Consider the effects that these techniques will have on future energy supplies.

4. Investigate and report on the effects that oil revenues have had in an oil-exporting developing world country of your choice. Use graphs and tables to illustrate your answer wherever possible.

5. Research in detail the mechanics, costs, and applications of your choice of an alternate energy source.

6. Select an alternate energy source which might be valuable for the world in the future.

7. (a) Using newspapers and periodicals, select two examples of large-scale resource extraction or energy development in Canada for your study. These might include mining, logging, oil sands extraction, or hydro-electric development.
   (b) Research the impact that each development has had on the following:
   - the local and national economy
   - the environment of that area, including waterways, natural vegetation cover, local landscape, etc.; and
   - the native people, if applicable.

9

Gaining a Perspective

You

Some of what you learned as you read this book and took part in related activities should have left a deep impression. Maybe you were sickened by the way in which our environment is being defiled. Your deepest memories might be of the dreadful living conditions of the world's poor, or frightening images of nuclear destruction.

Overwhelmed as you may be, do not forget the achievements. Some of the heartening success stories result from the efforts of large organizations such as the UN and CIDA. Others are due to the efforts of small groups, such as the Alberta farmers who help to repair farm machinery and teach these skills in Nicaragua. Individuals can also help, as local volunteers or lobbyists, for example.

Progress toward a better world can be made in many ways. The first step is to know what needs to be done, and the reasons for the success or failure of past efforts. You should now be aware of many of the world's problems, and have a general appreciation of their causes. As a result, you are in a much better position to contribute in the future. It is important that each of us accepts that we can help and that the challenge will always be passed on to the next generation. Your actions can make a difference.

Questions

1. (a) List five occupations in which people have the opportunity to improve conditions in the world. Explain the reasons for choosing each occupation.

   (b) Explain five ways that volunteers help in Canada or abroad.

2. In what ways do your present, or could your future plans contribute to a better world? Consider employment and/or voluntary activities.

Introduction

Because this book makes use of many statistics, graphs, and theories, there is a danger that the world could be seen as an abstraction. But this world is very real, with billions of people affected by a multitude of interacting factors. We hope that after reading this book, you are able to view world events with a clearer perspective.

Canadians have greater opportunities than many other people to influence the future course of events. As individuals, or through groups or political organizations, our voices and actions can help in places where small contributions, in a variety of forms, can enable people to prosper, both physically and mentally. Through concerned action, we can influence governments to act on matters which they might prefer to ignore.

Canada's international involvement has brought us considerable respect, but there is still much that we could do, at home and abroad, to contribute to the well-being of people. The interplay of environment and people is worldwide, and is no longer restricted by boundaries and oceans. By helping others today, we ensure a brighter future for ourselves and for our children.

Prospects for The Environment

There can be no doubt that we have created many environmental problems. We also observe, however, an increasing worldwide awareness of these problems which is resulting in action to reduce pollution and to conserve our precious resources.

In 1987, under the leadership of Norway's Prime Minister, Gro Harlem Bruntland, a report called *Our Common Future*, commissioned by the United Nations, was published. It warned of environmental damage resulting from the continual growth of the global economy. It states that we do not give sufficient regard to the needs of the other components of the biosphere, and that we seem obsessed with increasing our material wealth. The report warns of the long-lasting and little-known effects of technology, and urges a return to smaller-scale activities with an emphasis on local self-sufficiency.

Many birds and animals throughout the world are threatened with extinction.

Despite some shortcomings in its treatment of the environment, Canada is in the forefront of the environmental protection movement. This country is a signatory to many international treaties which are helping to protect and preserve endangered and rare species. One recent success story involves the whooping crane which has been pulled back from the edge of extinction. Other birds can find refuge in the hemispheric shorebird reserve at Shepody Bay, New Brunswick, the first of its kind in Canada. This reserve is modelled on one already established in Surinam. These two reserves are linked by the semipalmated sandpiper which travels the 4000 km between them in three or four days each spring and fall.

We are also working with, and trying to influence, the United States to improve air and water quality, in particular in those areas where pollutants pass over international boundaries. We have presented proposals for international co-operation before the United Nations General Assembly. We have hosted international gatherings, such as the Montreal Protocol of 1987, where important agreements were made to reduce damage to the protective ozone layer. The first North American meeting of the Convention On International Trade in Endangered Species (CITES) was held in Ottawa in 1987.

Within our own country, we are toughening pollution control laws and applying stricter penalties for offenders.

We have established many parks which will preserve much natural habitat, so that animals and plants indigenous to these areas can survive and so that we can observe and learn from them.

One important national park was created in 1987 in the Bruce Peninsula, about 300 km northwest of Toronto, Ontario. Steps were also taken to establish another park in South Moresby, in the Queen Charlotte Islands, British Columbia. The Bruce Peninsula park will help to preserve the unique environment of the

One action against the type of pollution shown in the photograph to the left is the establishment of national parks such as Georgian Bay Islands National Park, Ontario, shown above.

Niagara Escarpment in an area of urban encroachment. The proposal for a South Moresby park was in response to the concern of native and non-native groups who are desperately trying to preserve the special environment, which has been called "the Galapagos of Canada." The park would also help to preserve artifacts from the Haida culture. The Ninstints Haida site has already been designated as a World Heritage Site by UNESCO.

The impact of concerned citizens has led to another significant development. In 1986, a Guelph, Ontario, subscriber to *Equinox* magazine wrote to express her concern about a report on the destruction of Costa Rica's Monteverde Cloud Forest Reserve. That letter sparked a nation-wide effort, backed by the World Wildlife Fund (WWF), to purchase and protect 12 000 ha of the rain forest. A small group of landowners, farmers, and biologists had already bought land adjacent to the forest to protect it from logging, and the WWF of Canada granted them enough money to stop the logging until the land could be purchased. The necessary amount was estimated to be $500 000.

Slide shows presented by visitors to the forest inspired the interest of many others. Steven Price of the WWF worked with a naturalist group at the University of Toronto to present a "Monteverde Night," emceed by David Suzuki. The Ontario government donated $21 000 and, by August of 1987, about $70 000 had been raised without any large-scale efforts. Encouraged by the response, the WWF of Canada initiated a media blitz. The message relayed was that for $25 (tax deductible), people could buy an honorary deed to one acre (0.4 ha) of the rain forest. The campaign had an immediate response, but was even more successful when two grade 12 students from Richmond Hill, Ontario prepared a 30-second advertisement which was aired on a popular radio show. Enough money was collected by mid-1988 to complete the purchase of the land, a little more than two years after the letter in *Equinox* was written. This provides a wonderful example of what co-operative effort can accomplish.

Question

3. Re-read the story about the Monteverde Cloud Forest Reserve.

   (a) Identify the people, organizations, and activities participating in this project. Design a flowchart to show the connections between them.

   (b) Do the research necessary to name one other environmental problem, large or small, which might respond to citizen involvement. Explain how people, organizations, and government could take part, and what your own contribution might be.

Haida Indians and their supporters confront the RCMP at a roadblock on Lyell Island. The result of this and other protests was the establishment of a national park reserve which preserved the Haida homeland and the unique rain forest ecosystem.

Future Frontiers

Young people today are probably better informed about world conditions than any previous generation, so it is very important that they have as much input as possible in the decisions made by governments and international organizations. It is also crucial that those in a position of economic, political, and military power do not exploit people lacking the advantages of education, access to employment, and a voice in political affairs; rather, they should attempt to raise up the disadvantaged so that all can benefit from new developments.

What are our future frontiers, and how might they benefit us? Geographically speaking, the polar regions form a relatively unknown frontier. Geologists believe that, because Antarctica, South America, India, and South Africa were connected at one time, Antarctica probably contains the same vast mineral reserves as these other areas. Mining companies in the northern polar regions are already exploiting oil, gas, lead, silver, and zinc.

Moral judgements come into play, however, in connection with present and future territorial claims and resource development. Disputes concerning control of certain segments of Antarctica and the "Canadian" Arctic

already exist, and many other countries, not yet involved, would like to have some control of, and benefit from, Antarctic resources. We must also be concerned about preserving these fragile environments. It should still be possible to act responsibly in Antarctica, because of its insignificant level of development.

The ocean provides us with another comparatively unknown frontier which, unfortunately, is already suffering significant damage. International co-operation has allowed some fish and whale stocks to recover, and has

The oceans of the world hold significant resources such as fish and oil. The human-created island in the Beaufort Sea is an example of recent efforts to tap underwater resources.

helped to reduce oceanic pollution. Well-managed oceans could provide us with sustainable sources of protein and enormous amounts of minerals. Some of these minerals, especially oil and gas, are already being exploited. It will be important for countries to collaborate to ensure that any mineral exploitation will not endanger the living resources of the sea.

Space exploration has provided us with a new frontier of knowledge about the universe and our own earth. In the distant future, we may be able to extract resources from other heavenly bodies, and maybe even inhabit them.

For the moment, though, our chief benefits have come from observations of the earth from space, and spinoffs from the technology involved. Progress in space exploration has depended upon the development of miniaturized computer technology.

This, in turn, is having beneficial effects in many fields, from research and medicine to retail operations and automobile design. New materials and equipment, such as the components of artificial arteries, and new, smaller heart pacemakers, have been developed using technology from the space program.

Satellite technology, which also depends on the space program, permits widespread and reliable instant communication, at decreasing cost.

This has revolutionized world stock market operations and will permit more people to have access to information from around the world. Using satellite imagery together with computer processing, we are improving our ability to locate mineral deposits and assess crop yields and areas of crop failure.

If nations would cooperate, knowledge of crop failure in one part of the world would prompt nations in the other hemisphere to plant additional crop areas to ensure sufficient world supplies.

Satellite information helps us to conduct food and forest inventories, and to detect damage by insects and dis-

Satellite imagery is used to assess crop yields and areas of crop failure.

eases. Measures can then be taken to prevent further losses. Satellites are also used extensively in weather forecasting, navigation, and search-and-rescue. By revealing military manoeuvres, satellites may play an important role in maintaining peace between the superpowers.

Questions

4. Other fields of investigation which might be considered frontiers because of the rapid changes occurring in them include medicine, the mind, the workplace, transportation, leisure, and education.

   (a) Choose two of the fields listed in the above statement, and explain how they offer a frontier for human progress.

   (b) What potential dangers or problems are inherent in their development? How might these be avoided?

5. Suggest one frontier other than those included in the preceding text, or in question 2. Justify your choice.

Migrations

As we explore new frontiers, we must remember that the world in which we live is an ever-changing entity. As change occurs, it effects more change, like waves radiating from a stone thrown into a pond.

One of the major changes evident in today's world is the way in which people are moving. This is truer today than in any other comparable time in human history. In the developed world, people are travelling more widely than in the past; in 1987, passengers on international airlines travelled an estimated 685 million kilometres. Some of this movement is only short-term, but significant internal migrations occur within countries like Canada for a number of different reasons. A family may decide to move closer to friends or relatives or in search of employment or better pay. Whatever the reason, Canadians are very mobile and move from one home to another every three to five years, on average.

As indicated in Chapter 4, there is also a trend for Canadians to move into urban centres. As a result, there has been a significant growth in the largest Canadian cities, especially since World War II. Whatever the nature of the moves, there are push and pull factors to explain them. Push factors account for a

move from a certain area and pull factors are the attractions of a specfic location.

There is also massive international migration. Since colonization, 45 million Europeans have settled in the Americas, and many of the countries of the world are still receiving immigrants in large numbers. In 1987, for example, the United States received over 1 million legal immigrants.

There is a large-scale movement to western Europe of people from the poorer countries of southern Europe, northern Africa, and the Middle East. A large labour force has thus been assembled for the industries of Europe, but social and political problems have been created as well. The presence of "Gast Werkers" (migrant workers from another country who have come to work, usually in industry) has produced some resentment, and there has been little mixing of these immigrants with the local population. In a crisis like the West German mine disaster of June 1988, however, families of German miners and guest-worker Turkish miners reached out to console each other. Significant movements of migrant workers include those listed in Table 9.1.

Questions

6. Obtain a base map of the world. Examine Table 9.1 and then illustrate the information shown there on your world map.

7. (a) What is the direction of most work-related international migrations?

   (b) What attitudes, both positive and negative, might develop in the countries which have received migrant workers? Explain your answer.

Refugees

Although there have been major refugee movements in the past, the coverage by the mass media as well as the scale of refugee suffering in the 1980s has alerted the world to the severity of the problem. When refugees move, the push factors are extremely strong, while the pull factors may be almost non-existent. A refugee may have no plan other than to escape from a country ravaged by starvation or war, and no concern or knowledge about the nature of the country of refuge.

Approximately 80 percent of refugees, worldwide, are women and their dependent children.[1] Altogether , as determined by the United Nations, there were over 15 million refugees in the world in 1988. Those regions which

Table 9.1
Source Countries
and Recipient
Countries of
Migrant Workers

Source Country	Recipient Country
Tunisia, Algeria, Morocco, Portugal, Spain	France
Turkey, Spain, Greece, Yugoslavia, Italy	West Germany
Finland	Sweden
Turkey	The Netherlands, Austria, Sweden
Yugoslavia	Austria, Switzerland
Italy	Switzerland
Sri Lanka	Middle East
Thailand, India, Bangladesh, Pakistan, Sri Lanka, Malaysia	Western Europe
Central America, Malaysia, India, Bangladesh, Pakistan, Sri Lanka, Caribbean	United States, Canada
Mexico, Puerto Rico	United States
Chile, Bolivia, Uruguay, Paraguay	Argentina
Colombia	Venezuela, Ecuador

Refugees board buses in Woods Harbour, Nova Scotia, after arriving there in lifeboats.

Sri Lankan refugees line the deck of a tugboat after being rescued off the coast of Newfoundland.

have produced most of the refugees in recent times include Africa, Southwest Asia, Central America, and Southeast Asia. For the most part, the countries which receive the refugees are in the same regions as those which send them. In many cases, the refugees are as poor in their new home as they were in the old.

A small percentage of refugees are able to enter a developed country such as Canada, the United States, or Australia. Canada has had a tradition of accepting victims of war or extreme distress, yet the Canadian government, among others, has found it difficult to distinguish between legitimate refugees and those who are really immigrants wanting fast admission into the country.

Questions

8. Describe your general impressions of refugees and the countries from which they come. What sources of information have helped most to create the image you have of refugees?

9. In general, what is the relationship between the source regions of migrant workers and refugees? Suggest reasons for the pattern you see.

10. What difficulties might a refugee from the developing world have in adapting to Canadian life?

**Figure 9.1
The Location of
Refugees Around
the World in 1988**

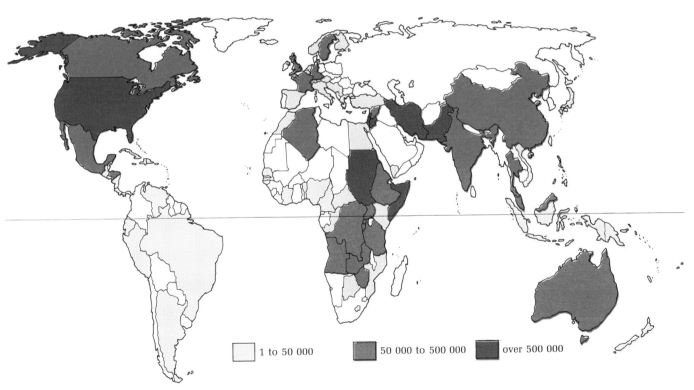

| | 1 to 50 000 | | 50 000 to 500 000 | | over 500 000 |

Changes and Changing Values

With the movement of large numbers of people and their subsequent interaction with other cultures, traditional values are changing rapidly. In addition, the influence exerted by western nations via the expanding network of mass media (largely due to the development of satellite technology) is having an enormous worldwide impact.

The amount of information in the world is said to double every three to five years.[3] At times, it threatens to overwhelm us. This is beginning to have a significant impact on the way of life in both the developing and the developed world.

Many of the traditional values which societies have held for centuries are beginning to break down under the impact of the information explosion and the changes which accompany it.

For example, the television shows, music, and movies which originate in the English-speaking world are beginning to change the attitudes that millions of people in the world have toward marriage, divorce, family, education, success, and women's roles. In India, for example, where most marriages have been arranged by the families of the bride and groom, there is today a small but growing trend toward North American dating practices. The impact of large numbers of people has led to the breakdown of traditional family units.

At the same time, there has been a widespread resurgence in traditional values elsewhere. The countries of eastern Europe and the Soviet Union have been experiencing a revival of Christianity during the 1980s. There has also been a rise in Islamic fundamentalism in the countries of the Middle East and Southwest Asia.

Many of the changes which we can see in the world are positive, and reflect the growing awareness of crucial issues such as the environment, the quality of life, and individual rights.

Across most of the industrialized world, organizations have sprung up whose main focus has been the quality of the environment. Concern about acid precipitation, toxic wastes, and the general pollution of the environment have spurred citizens' groups into action. The rise of the Green Party in West Germany, which is dedicated to the protection of the environment, illustrates how new values are being put forth for public discussion.

Worldwide concern has also been raised about the abuse of human rights in certain nations. The speed of communication has opened up the possibility of people from all over the world learning about such abuses quickly; this publicity has resulted in some governments becoming more sensitive to individual human rights. Organizations such as Amnesty International and the Red Cross have been instrumental in exposing human rights abuses and trying to reduce or eliminate them.

In general, we are seeing the values in our world changing, sometimes for the better and sometimes for the worse. What is particularly noteworthy is that the change is rapid and that each individual has an opportunity to affect the types of changes which are occurring.

Question

11. (a) What do you consider "traditional values?"

    (b) Do your family values seem traditional to you, or are they undergoing social change?

    (c) What are the strongest forces affecting your own sense of values?

    (d) Do the mass media, including television, movies, and videos represent the life you lead? Explain whether the values represented to the world in American entertainment match or are at odds with your personal outlook.

The Pacific Rim

With our growing awareness of worldwide events, the increased movement of people, and our interdependency in trade, politics, economics, and defence, it is important that we develop a new world perspective. Our view of the world is not only shaped by our experience of it but is also very much influenced by images or projections. For generations, students' impressions of the oceans and continents bore a close resemblance to Mercator's projection of the world, a classic of atlases.

The Mercator projection, however, may distort proportion. In particular, it cannot do justice to relationships between countries bordering the Pacific. There, an outward view is into the ocean's breadth and across and on either hand to Pacific neighbours. It is a natural outlook for Canada, since, originally, this country seems to have been peopled in a migration from Siberia, possibly over a land bridge north of the Pacific.

This country has been only intermittently hospitable to immigration from the East: the Chinese were wanted as labourers but were discouraged as settlers; we refused to allow the *Komogata*

Maru to dock when it arrived with Sikh refugees in 1914; and we turned on Japanese-Canadians in a spasm of anxiety about loyalty in World War II. But in the long run, the need for trade and commerce may make us a more rational member of the Pacific community, a community of which we are geographically a part.

Canada has had an extended, though irregular, trading history with countries on the Pacific Rim. Wheat, lumber, iron ore, and coal have been exported, and a great variety of manufactured articles, from teacups to automobiles, have been imported in turn. Now, for British Columbia especially, the Pacific Rim stimulates and

promises to reward regional initiative.

Centuries ago, great civilizations thrived on the rim of the Pacific Ocean. From Peru, where the Inca empire rose, to the empires of ancient China and Thailand, there have been periods of remarkable cultural, political, and economic development in this region. During much of the twentieth century, however, many of the countries of the Pacific Rim have been excluded from the economic and social progress of Europe and North America. Recently, great economic, political, and social developments have begun to stir this whole Pacific region, and several countries have emerged as major regional and world economic powers.

A ship loading grain in Surabaya Harbour, Indonesia

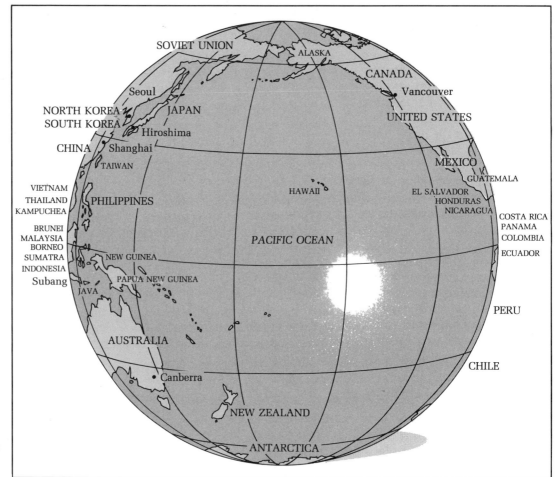

Figure 9.2
This map of the Pacific Rim brings a different perspective to the study of the region which surrounds the Pacific Ocean. Most of the maps of the world centre on Europe, with the Pacific Ocean cut into two parts; by contrast, this map focusses on the Pacific itself.

Japan, South Korea, Taiwan, Singapore, and Hong Kong have become part of the "economic miracle" of the Pacific.

Since the end of World War II, the presence of US naval fleets in the Pacific as well as a string of military bases have kept a strong American influence alive in the region. This presence has helped to contain the perceived communist expansion into the Pacific, but it extends beyond the military. Heavy American investment in the countries of this region has been a major factor in their rapid economic growth, and the United States is their best market. The US has also maintained close economic and political ties with Canada, Japan, Australia, New Zealand, the countries of the Association of Southeast Asian Nations (ASEAN) and, more recently, with China.

The Soviet Union has become interested in the new developments within the Pacific Rim. It has strong economic interests in the products coming from countries such as Japan and Taiwan, and sees the potential of new markets in the booming economies there.

The impact of the US in the region has also been cultural and political. From Coca-Cola and rock and roll to the demands of the young people in China and South Korea for democratic reforms, the US has significantly altered the direction of change in the region. It should be noted, however, that other developed nations have influenced the region as well. Britain and France, for example, both maintained colonies throughout the South Pacific and left a social, cultural, and political legacy which is still identifiable today.

Only Japan, however, can equal the United States in its impact. In fact, during the last decade, Japan has outdistanced the United States in economic growth. Gradually, there has been a shift in

	Real growth rate of GNP (%) 1973-1986	Change in life expectancy		Average annual growth rate (%) for industry		Average annual growth rate (%) for exports	
		1970	1985	1965-1980	1980-1986	1965-1980	1980-1986
Australia	2.7	71	78	2.9	2.0	6.0	5.5
Canada	2.4	73	76	3.4	2.9	6.2	7.2
China	7.6	61	69	10.0	12.5	5.5	11.7
Ecuador	3.8	58	66	13.7	3.5	15.2	8.4
Hong Kong	8.5	69	76	-	-	9.5	10.7
Indonesia	6.1	47	55	11.9	1.8	9.6	2.0
Japan	4.3	72	77	8.5	5.0	11.5	6.4
S. Korea	7.2	60	69	16.5	10.2	27.3	13.1
Malaysia	6.3	61	68	-	6.0	4.4	10.2
Peru	1.4	54	59	4.4	-1.1	2.3	0.1
Philippines	3.3	57	63	8.0	-3.5	4.7	-1.7
Singapore	7.8	68	73	12.2	4.4	4.7	6.1
Thailand	5.9	58	64	9.5	5.0	8.5	9.2
USA	2.5	71	76	1.9	3.2	6.9	-2.7

Table 9.2
Economic Changes in Selected Pacific Rim Countries and the United States since 1965

A modern pulp plant in Japan

power from the Americans to the Japanese and, to a lesser extent, to other countries such as Taiwan.

Despite US influence since 1945 especially, there still remains considerable diversity within the region. This diversity provides some of the dynamism, but also some of the challenges for the future. Laos and Kampuchea, for example, are still struggling to recover from the devastation of years of war and the loss of millions of their people. Singapore has established itself as a major world centre for trading and commerce. Hong Kong faces an uncertain future, as its territory will be returned to China in 1997. Taiwan has changed from a quiet tropical island to an industrial dynamo within the last 40 years. Slowly emerging from isolation, China could become a world power, by virtue of its population and armed forces.

The nations lying along the Pacific coast of Central and South America still languish in poverty, unable to share the prosperity found in other areas of the region. Civil strife wracks much of Central America, and Peru, Ecuador and Chile have grown little economically in the last decade. In Peru, for example, the economy has shrunk in size despite the country's population growth.

The decline in the relative strength of the United States in the Pacific Rim raises many questions. Will the Soviet Union attempt to fill the gap left by the retreat of the United States? Will Japan's geopolitical role in the Pacific match its economic power? These and other questions reflect the fascinating interplay of politics and economics in the Pacific Rim region.

These pictures of the Hong Kong Harbour (top) and a shipyard in Singapore (bottom) illustrate the growing economic power in the Asia Pacific region.

Questions

12. (a) What advantages does the United States gain from a strong military presence in the Pacific Rim area?

    (b) What forces might act on the United States to limit or reduce its role in this region?

13. What geopolitical disadvantages does the Soviet Union have in its attempts to enter the Pacific region?

14. Although, by the terms of the peace treaty that ended World War II, Japan is not to undertake a major military buildup, there is some temptation for it to do so. Explain why.

15. In what ways can the Pacific Rim be considered a microcosm (miniature representation) of the world as a whole?

16. (a) Traditionally, Canada has been oriented toward Europe and the United States. With the rise of a number of countries in the Pacific Rim, what benefits might there be for Canada in establishing links with the Pacific region?

    (b) What could western provinces such as British Columbia and Alberta do to foster the growth of ties with the Pacific Rim countries? Think in terms of economic policies, educational curricula, and political decisions.

A Letter From Venezuela

These extracts, taken from a letter written by Linda Hannell, a 30-year-old Canadian, illustrate the differences in living conditions, lifestyle, and culture which she is encountering in her daily life in Venezuela. For the past few years, she and her husband, François, have been sailing an old wooden schooner around the Caribbean islands, supporting themselves by conducting day charters for tourists. They will be living in Cumana, Venezuela for about a year while they remodel the interior of their boat.

Dear Chris,

Hola! Nice quiet Monday here today. I'm lazing around writing letters, reading a few good poems, enjoying the solitude that might be a little quieter if those pups in the cockpit would stop screaming their heads off!

Yes, Nellie had her pups, two little fat fur balls. With only two to share all those nipples, they're getting to look like little piglets. The people on a couple of boats around here say that

they may want puppies, so hopefully this happy story will have a happy ending.

François is in Canada for a month. He'll be visiting his brothers and sisters and their families in Montreal and Havre St Pierre. He'll also be buying some things we cannot find down here, which we need to redo the interior of the boat. These include special epoxy resins and glues and good quality screws. He's also getting his shots for hepatitis, yellow fever and typhoid, while I get mine down here. That's one thing I never thought about before we got here. But lately, some friends of ours have come back from Peru with hepatitis, and the local people are saying it's a particularly bad year for malaria in the Amazon River area, which we hope to visit. There's no such thing as a malaria shot, so if you know you're going into malaria-infested areas, you take special pills for months before, during and after you've left the area.

Thank you for the present. When I saw which book you'd sent me, I got really excited! Margaret Atwood is one of my favourite authors, and you certainly can't get her books here. In fact, in Cumana you can't find any books in English unless they're traded with other boat people.

I bought myself a bicycle today! An old-fashioned one-speed model, with a basket at

the front and a rack behind. It's great! Before, I had to walk everywhere I wanted to go in town, or wait up to 20 minutes for a bus — and even then it often happened I'd get myself on the wrong bus and end up farther away from where I wanted to go than when I started out! It was great riding the two kilometres down to the grocer this afternoon — all independent — passing the barrio, with the little children calling out the only word they know in English: "Hello!" Then they laugh when you say "Hello!" back. I'm still not sure whether they're being friendly or if they just like to laugh at the way gringos [foreigners] speak. And now, when they gather in groups with their hands out asking for money, I just ride by, out of their grasp. That may sound callous, but there are so many.

At the grocer, the Chinese family that runs the place all came out to admire my golden machine. I've gotten to know them well because they deliver groceries to us in the marina every other day or so. Lately, with François still gone, the deliveries have consisted mainly of puppy food and long-life milk!

I fasted for two days after François left. It was supposed to be a week's fast, but I felt so terrible after two days that I quit early. I had thought of meditating, like the fasting monks. Ha! I don't know how they can think about God with their stomachs screaming from a very physical level.

The puppies are still with me. They will be six weeks old this Monday. I'm still optimistic that I will find them homes, so

optimistic in fact that I refused to give them to one local man who wanted to take both of them a few days ago. He was anxious to have them right away, and by the look in his eyes, I thought that he might have wanted to take them home for dinner.

I want to Caracas for four days with a girlfriend and her son and saw my first bullfight. I could stand it for only five minutes, and then the three of us left in a hurry. Six-year-old Zachary was crying his eyes out while all the local children his age were screaming with delight, and those outside who couldn't afford tickets were cramming against us as we tried to push out throught the gates.

I'm loving Venezuela, despite its dark side. I now have a tutor who comes to the boat three times a week to help me sound less like a gringo. It's neat going into town now and I'm beginning to understand what I hear. It's a fascinating culture here and I want to know more and more about it.

Love from Linda

Questions

17. (a) When you had finished reading the letter from Linda, what one part stood out in your memory?

(b) Why did you remember it so vividly, and in what way, if any, do you feel that it illustrates the difference in lifestyle, attitudes, or culture between Canada and Venezuela?

18. (a) Many people in Canada and other industrialized nations consider that the citizens of poorer nations are always unhappy. In what ways is this conclusion inaccurate? Use examples from the letter to illustrate your answer.

(b) Why do you think that we have developed this attitude?

19. Venezuela has a much higher GNP than many other lesser developed nations largely because of revenues from exported oil.

(a) Refer to the tables in the Appendix and compare and contrast other key indicators such as infant mortality and population doubling times with two other countries of the Third, Fourth, or Fifth Worlds. Refer to Figure 1.1 to identify these nations.

(b) Use an atlas and other parts of this book to account for differences and similarities that you observe.

20. Write an essay of 1500 to 2000 words on the impact of present trends and developments upon the lives of the people of Venezuela or another country suggested by your teacher. You should refer to an atlas, to earlier sections and the Appendix in this book, and to other sources at your disposal. Include the following topics:
   - the environment; industrialization; the provision of basic needs such as housing, employment, food, education, and health care;
   - the impact of expansion and exploitation of future frontiers including the spinoff technology involved;
   - the causes, nature, and impact of internal and international migrations;
   - the changing values of society;
   - and the effects, if any, of the changing pattern of worldwide trade, especially as a result of the increasing importance of many Pacific Rim countries.

Conclusion

As you have read through and studied this book, you have had an opportunity to explore a wide variety of issues which affect the world. Beyond the factual data presented and the skills you have been asked to apply are the values and attitudes which are considered as well.

The authors of *World Issues* have set out to show, from as many perspectives as possible, the "interdependent web of all existence." It is for readers to decide for themselves whether troubling issues can best be settled through negotiation, say, or technology, and if technology, then whether it should be implemented on a large or small scale. And when the scope of the problem seems to go beyond all of these options, what then? That is why the book has emphasized the importance of gathering data and using the knowledge and skills of geography for prevention of problems, as well as for their solution.

The questions following invite you to explore some of the issues raised in this book, as well as to analyze the relationships between them.

Questions

21. Select four examples from the book of each of the following:
   - the importance of the contribution of one person to tackling an issue;
   - the potential of self-help groups of programs where people are encouraged to solve their own problems;
   - appropriate or innovative technology which has been used in dealing with a particular issue.

22. Look back through this book and select four key issues. For each one, select at least one other which is related to it. Explain what the relationship between these issues is and why it is of significance.

Independent Study

1. Select four countries from the Pacific Rim as well as Canada. Include countries which are on opposite sides of the Pacific.

   (a) Give a brief economic and political sketch of each country. Include GNP per capita and literacy rate as well as statistics reflecting some of the changes which have been taking place over the last 20 years.

   (b) What are the key differences among these countries? For example, which are mired in serious economic and political problems and which are experiencing rapid economic growth?

   (c) Considering the issues which have been discussed in this book, which ones are reflected in the countries which you have selected?

   (d) What importance will this region of the world have for the political and economic concerns of the two superpowers — the United States and the Soviet Union?

2. (a) Describe Canada's historic attitude to refugees and how the number of refugee claimants has changed over the last 20 years.

   (b) What countries have produced the greatest number of refugees during the time period that you have used? Describe the kinds of push factors which have affected them. If possible, include one or two specific case studies or an interview with someone who has entered Canada as a refugee.

   (c) Construct a series of questions which could be used as the basis of a questionnaire and interview five people to obtain their point of view on Canada accepting refugees.

   (d) What criteria should be used to evaluate claimants who apply to Canada as refugees? Use your answer here as the basis for a policy paper in which you would present your recommendations to your local M.P.

3. Many people have become acutely aware of environmental hazards which are developing as a result of our lifestyles.

   (a) Report on the findings of one modern investigation, such as the Bruntland Report referred to on page 326.

   (b) Investigate other writings that deal with the same issues. You might consider reading *Silent Spring* by Rachel Carson (Houghton Mifflin, 1982), and an address given by Chief Seattle in 1854, which is published in its translated form in *Fellowship*, Vol. 42, No. 11, a bulletin published by the Fellowship of Reconciliation, 523 N. Broadway, Nyack, New York, 10960. Summarize the contents of these writings, quoting significant passages.

   (c) Such works and speeches may be very moving, but are they strong enough to convince people to take action? Is there any point in investing money in them? Support your answer with examples.

4. At the beginning of this book, you had an opportunity to reflect on some of the issues which you believed to be the most crucial ones facing the world today. Having spent some time studying these issues, take time to read over your first list once again. Has your point of view changed about which are the key world issues and how they can be dealt with, or is your outlook much the same as it was? Outline the rationale for your choice of issues.

Karen Flynn
Canadian Student from Jamaica

Karen is in her last year at high school. She left Jamaica five years ago, when she was 14. Following her parents' separation, her father headed for Canada, in hopes of making a better life for himself and his family. Her mother went to the USA, and Karen and her younger sister lived with her great-grandmother in St. Andrew, Jamaica.

Karen attended local schools where, she said, the discipline was much stricter than here; they had no choice in the subjects they studied, and they had to wear uniforms. There was not enough space in the high schools, so the schools operated in shifts, with one group of students attending from 7:30 a.m. to 12:30 p.m. and the next from 12:30 p.m. to 5:30 p.m. Job prospects, even for those with a good education, were poor, and Karen attributes many of the problems plaguing Jamaica to unemployed youths with time on their hands.

At home, Karen and her sister shared the chores of cleaning, cooking, and gardening. She spent a lot of time reading and only rarely watched television because of the expense of electricity. She enjoyed going to church on Saturday, and bathing in the river, washing clothes, and getting ready for school on Sunday.

Karen's worst memory of Jamaica is of the violence associated with the election of

1981. "People were shooting, stabbing, and killing each other . . . . At night, I would not go to sleep, for fear that I'd be killed. I would lay in bed at night, and listen to the gunshots on the streets. I was really scared because our house was on the main road, and the gunmen had easy access. Each passing day, I would thank God for protecting us. People would ask the kids who their parents were voting for. Many parents were murdered because they were going to vote for the wrong party."

Karen could hardly believe it when her father finally told her and her sister to join him in Canada. When she arrived, she was struck by the beauty of

Canada, and how clean it was. She had trouble adjusting to a new family situation, and, two years later, moved into her own apartment, with the help of her part-time job and government assistance.

Canada gave Karen her first taste of prejudice. "There are times when it really hurt me; I got really angry to the point that I would hit someone for calling me a racial name. I have changed, and now I will actually laugh at a bigot.

"The first day at school, I had the jitters. I was so scared, the school was so big, and there were so many people. The first day it snowed, I stayed in bed. My dad told me I just had to get used to it. It seemed no matter how warm I dressed, I was always cold. Now I have accepted winter.

"Here in Canada, my future is a lot brighter than in Jamaica. I have a chance to further my education, and have better job opportunities. I have met the most wonderful people anyone could ever meet. I really love being here."

Karen offers a bit of advice, first to parents who have brought their children to Canada: "Spend time with them to help them adjust." To the young people, she says, "Take advantage of the many opportunities Canada has to offer, especially in education. Education, after all, is the key to success."

Questions

1. Identify three ways in which Karen's life in Jamaica is different to your own. Speculate on how these differences might affect your outlook on life in each country.

2. Why was it that Karen did not experience prejudice until she reached Canada? Why is she now able to laugh at bigotry? In what ways can each of us reduce prejudice and bigotry?

3. Comment on Karen's final statement, that education is the key to success. Your answer should encompass many parts of the world, and many forms of education.

Appendix

Table of Selected World Statistics (1988)

Region or Country	Population Estimate mid-1988 (millions)	Crude Birth Rate	Crude Death Rate	Natural Increase (annual, %)	Population "Doubling Time" in Years (at current rate)	Population Projected to 2000 (millions)	Population Projected to 2020 (millions)	Infant Mortality Rate [a]	%Population Under Age 15/65+	Life Expectancy at Birth (years)	Urban Population (%)	Government View of Fertility Level (H = too high, S = satisfactory, L = too low)	Per Capita GNP, 1986 (US$)
World	5,128	28	10	1.7	40	6,178	8,053	77	33/6	63	45	-/-	$3,010
More Developed	1,198	15	9	0.6	120	1,266	1,337	15	22/11	73	73		10,700
Lesser Developed	3,931	31	10	2.1	33	4,911	6,716	86	37/4	60	37		640
Lesser Developed (Excl. China)	2,844	35	12	2.4	29	3,699	5,312	96	40/4	57	35		780
Africa	623	44	15	2.9	24	886	1,497	110	45/3	52	30	-/-	620
Northern Africa	138	39	11	2.8	25	187	279	92	42/4	58	41		1,000
Algeria	24.2	42	10	3.2	22	33.7	49.4	81	46/4	61	43	H	2,570
Egypt	53.3	38	9	2.8	24	71.2	103.0	93	40/4	59	45	H	760
Libya	4.0	39	8	3.1	22	5.6	8.4	74	45/3	65	76	S	-
Morocco	25.0	36	10	2.6	27	33.3	48.5	90	42/4	61	43	H	590
Sudan	24.0	45	16	2.8	24	33.4	55.6	112	45/3	49	20	S	320
Tunisia	7.7	31	9	2.2	31	9.9	13.6	71	40/4	63	53	H	1,140
Western Sahara	0.2	49	23	2.5	28	0.2	0.4	-	-/-	-	-	-	-
Western Africa	194	47	18	2.9	24	279	479	125	45/2	47	28		530
Benin	4.5	51	20	3.0	23	7.1	14.2	115	49/5	45	39	H	270
Burkina Faso	8.5	48	19	2.8	24	11.8	20.6	145	44/3	46	8	S	150
Cape Verde	0.3	35	8	2.6	26	0.5	0.7	77	46/5	60	27	S	460
Côte d'Ivoire	11.2	46	15	3.1	22	17.3	32.1	105	46/3	52	43	S	740
Gambia	0.8	49	28	2.1	34	1.1	1.8	169	44/4	36	21	H	230
Ghana	14.4	42	11	3.1	22	20.5	33.9	72	44/3	58	31	H	390

Guinea	6.9	47	23	2.4	29	9.2	14.4	153	43/3	41	22	H	-
Guinea-Bissau	0.9	44	20	2.4	29	1.2	1.8	132	44/3	45	27	S	170
Liberia	2.5	48	16	3.1	22	3.6	6.2	127	47/3	50	42	H	450
Mali	8.7	50	22	2.9	24	12.3	21.1	175	46/3	43	18	S	170
Mauritania	2.1	50	20	3.0	23	3.0	5.2	132	46/3	45	35	S	440
Niger	7.2	51	22	2.9	24	10.6	18.9	141	47/3	44	16	H	260
Nigeria	111.9	46	17	2.9	24	160.9	273.6	122	45/2	47	28	H	640
Senegal	7.0	46	20	2.6	26	9.8	16.3	137	44/3	44	36	H	420
Sierra Leone	4.0	47	29	1.8	38	5.4	8.9	175	43/3	35	28	H	310
Togo	3.3	47	14	3.3	21	4.9	8.9	117	45/3	54	22	H	250
Eastern Africa	**186**	**48**	**15**	**3.3**	**21**	**278**	**512**	**109**	**47/3**	**51**	**17**		**220**
Burundi	5.2	47	18	2.9	24	7.3	12.4	119	45/3	48	5	H	240
Comoros	0.4	47	14	3.4	21	0.7	1.3	96	47/4	55	23	H	280
Djibouti	0.3	43	18	2.5	28	0.4	0.7	132	46/3	47	74	S	-
Ethiopia	48.3	46	15	3.0	23	71.1	127.6	118	46/3	50	10	H	120
Kenya	23.3	54	13	4.1	17	38.3	79.2	76	51/2	54	19	H	300
Madagascar	10.9	44	16	2.8	25	15.6	25.8	63	44/3	51	22	H	230
Malawi	7.7	53	21	3.2	21	11.4	21.1	157	47/3	46	12	H	160
Mauritius	1.1	19	7	1.2	58	1.3	1.6	27.2	31/5	68	42	H	1,200
Mozambique	15.1	45	19	2.6	27	21.1	34.2	147	45/3	46	19	S	210
Reunion	0.6	24	6	1.8	38	0.7	0.8	12	33/5	70	60	-	3,940
Rwanda	7.1	53	16	3.7	19	11.2	21.8	122	48/2	49	6	H	290
Seychelles	0.1	26	8	1.9	37	0.1	0.1	17.4	36/6	70	37	H	-
Somalia	8.0	48	17	3.1	23	10.4	18.6	147	45/3	41	34	S	280
Tanzania	24.3	50	15	3.6	19	36.6	68.6	111	48/3	52	18	H	240
Uganda	16.4	50	16	3.4	20	24.7	46.4	108	48/3	50	10	H	-
Zambia	7.5	47	13	3.4	21	11.6	22.0	87	47/3	55	43	H	300
Zimbabwe	9.7	47	12	3.5	20	15.1	29.4	76	48/3	57	24	H	620
Middle Africa	**64**	**44**	**17**	**2.7**	**25**	**89**	**152**	**118**	**44/3**	**49**	**34**	**H**	**440**
Angola	8.2	47	21	2.6	27	11.5	19.1	143	45/3	43	25	S	-
Cameroon	10.5	43	16	2.6	26	14.5	23.5	126	43/4	50	42	H	910
Central African Republic	2.8	44	19	2.5	28	3.8	5.9	148	43/4	45	35	H	290
Chad	4.8	43	23	2.0	35	6.3	9.5	143	42/4	39	27	S	-
Congo	2.2	47	13	3.4	21	3.2	5.9	112	45/3	55	48	L	1,040
Equatorial Guinea	0.3	38	20	1.9	37	0.4	0.7	130	40/5	45	60	L	-
Gabon	1.3	34	18	1.6	44	1.6	2.2	112	35/6	49	41	L	3,020
Sao Tome and Principe	0.1	36	9	2.7	25	0.2	0.3	61.7	46/5	65	35	S	340
Zaire	33.3	45	15	3.0	23	47.9	84.7	103	46/3	51	34	H	160
Southern Africa	**40**	**34**	**10**	**2.3**	**30**	**53**	**76**	**72**	**39/4**	**59**	**53**		**1,620**
Botswana	1.3	48	14	3.4	20	1.8	3.3	67	48/4	58	22	H	840
Lesotho	1.6	41	16	2.6	27	2.3	3.6	106	42/4	50	17	H	410
Namibia	1.7	45	17	2.8	24	2.4	4.1	111	44/5	49	51	-	1,020
South Africa	35.1	32	10	2.3	31	45.3	63.5	66	38/4	60	56	H	1,800
Swaziland	0.7	47	17	3.1	23	1.0	1.9	124	46/3	50	26	H	600

(continued)

Region or Country	Population Estimate mid-1988 (millions)	Crude Birth Rate	Crude Death Rate	Natural Increase (annual, %)	Population "Doubling Time" in Years (at current rate)	Population Projected to 2000 (millions)	Population Projected to 2020 (millions)	Infant Mortality Rate[a]	%Population Under Age 15/65+	Life Expectancy at Birth (years)	Urban Population (%)	Government View of Fertility Level (H = too high, S = satisfactory, L = too low)	Per Capita GNP, 1986 (US$)
Asia	2,995	28	10	1.8	38	3,611	4,629	82	35/5	61	36		1,020
Asia (Excl. China)	1,908	32	11	2.1	33	2,399	3,225	96	38/4	58	33		1,480
Western Asia	124	37	9	2.8	25	169	257	89	41/4	62	57		2,750
Bahrain	0.5	32	5	2.8	25	0.8	1.1	32	32/2	67	81	S	8,530
Cyprus	0.7	20	8	1.1	62	0.8	0.9	12	25/11	75	62	L	4,360
Gaza	0.6	48	7	4.1	17	0.8	1.4	58	49/2	64	-	-	-
Iraq	17.6	45	10	3.5	20	26.5	43.8	86	48/3	62	68	L	-
Israel	4.4	23	7	1.6	42	5.4	6.2	11.2	32/9	75	89	L	6,210
Jordan	3.8	42	6	3.6	19	5.7	9.6	56	46/3	69	59	S	1,540
Kuwait	2.0	32	3	2.9	24	2.7	4.0	18.4	37/1	72	80	L	13,890
Lebanon	3.3	28	7	2.0	34	4.1	5.8	51	42/5	67	80	S	-
Oman	1.4	47	14	3.3	21	2.0	3.2	117	44/3	52	9	S	4,990
Qatar	0.4	30	2	2.7	25	0.5	0.8	42	34/1	69	86	S	12,520
Saudi Arabia	14.2	42	9	3.3	21	21.7	35.9	85	45/3	61	72	S	6,930
Syria	11.3	47	9	3.8	18	17.2	28.0	59	49/4	64	49	S	1,560
Turkey	52.9	31	9	2.2	32	65.9	87.5	95	36/4	63	53	H	1,110
United Arab Emirates	1.5	30	4	2.6	27	1.9	2.6	38	30/1	68	81	S	14,410
Yemen, North	6.7	55	22	3.3	21	10.0	19.5	175	47/3	45	15	H	550
Yemen, South	2.4	48	15	3.3	21	3.6	6.3	116	48/3	51	40	H	480
Southern Asia	1,137	35	13	2.2	31	1,448	1,987	111	39/4	54	25		270
Afghanistan	14.5	48	24	2.4	29	24.5	39.1	183	46/4	39	15	H	-
Bangladesh	109.5	43	17	2.7	26	145.8	206.0	135	46/3	50	16	H	160
Bhutan	1.5	38	18	2.0	34	1.9	2.7	139	40/3	46	5	S	160
India	816.8	33	13	2.0	35	1,013.3	1,308.8	104	38/4	54	25	H	270
Iran	51.9	45	13	3.2	21	73.9	130.6	113	44/3	57	51	S	-
Maldives	0.2	47	10	3.7	19	0.3	0.6	83	45/2	60	26	S	310
Nepal	18.3	42	17	2.5	28	23.8	33.1	112	41/3	52	7	H	160
Pakistan	107.5	43	15	2.9	24	145.3	242.2	121	43/4	54	28	H	350
Sri Lanka	16.6	24	6	1.8	38	19.4	24.2	30.5	35/4	70	22	H	400
Southeast Asia	433	31	9	2.1	33	542	720	72	39/3	61	25	S	650
Brunei	0.3	31	3	2.7	25	0.4	0.4	11	38/3	71	64	S	15,400

Burma	41.1	34	13	2.1	33	51.6	70.1	103	39/4	53	24	S	200
East Timor	0.7	44	22	2.2	31	0.9	1.1	166	35/3	43	12	-	-
Indonesia	177.4	27	10	1.7	40	213.7	264.7	88	40/3	58	22	H	500
Kampuchea	6.7	40	17	2.3	31	8.5	12.0	134	35/3	48	11	L	-
Laos	3.8	41	16	2.5	28	5.0	6.9	122	43/3	50	16	S	-
Malaysia	17.0	31	7	2.4	28	20.9	26.4	30	37/4	67	35	S	1,850
Philippines	63.2	35	7	2.8	25	85.5	130.7	51	39/3	66	41	H	570
Singapore	2.6	15	5	1.0	71	2.9	3.0	9.4	24/5	73	100	L	7,410
Thailand	54.7	29	8	2.1	33	66.4	83.6	52	36/3	64	17	H	810
Vietnam	65.2	34	8	2.6	27	86.0	121.2	53	40/4	63	19	H	-
East Asia	**1,302**	**20**	**7**	**1.3**	**52**	**1,451**	**1,665**	**41**	**28/6**	**67**	**47**		**1,620**
China	1,087.0	21	7	1.4	49	1,212.0	1,404.0	44	29/6	66	41	H	300
Hong Kong	5.7	13	5	0.8	83	6.3	6.9	7.7	23/8	76	93	-	6,720
Japan	122.7	11	6	0.5	133	130.0	131.7	5.2	21/11	78	77	S	12,850
Korea, North	21.9	31	6	2.5	28	28.2	37.6	33	39/4	68	64	S	-
Korea, South	42.6	19	6	1.3	52	48.8	54.7	30	30/4	68	65	H	2,370
Macao	0.4	23	6	1.7	41	0.5	0.6	12	23/8	68	97	-	-
Mongolia	2.0	37	11	2.6	26	2.8	4.4	53	42/4	62	52	L	-
Taiwan	19.8	16	5	1.1	63	22.4	24.9	6.9	29/5	73	67	S	-
North America	**272**	**16**	**9**	**0.7**	**98**	**296**	**327**	**10**	**21/12**	**75**	**74**	**S**	**17,170**
Canada	26.1	15	7	0.7	94	28.4	30.2	7.9	21/11	76	76	S	14,100
United States	246.1	16	9	0.7	99	268.0	296.6	10.0	22/12	75	74	S	17,500
Latin America	**429**	**29**	**8**	**2.2**	**32**	**537**	**711**	**57**	**38/5**	**66**	**68**		**1,720**
Central America	**111**	**32**	**7**	**2.5**	**27**	**143**	**197**	**53**	**43/4**	**66**	**63**		**1,640**
Belize	0.2	36	6	3.0	23	0.2	0.3	36	47/4	69	50	S	1,170
Costa Rica	2.9	34	5	2.9	24	3.7	5.0	18.9	37/5	74	45	S	1,420
El Salvador	5.4	35	7	2.8	25	7.2	10.3	65	46/4	66	43	H	820
Guatemala	8.7	41	9	3.2	21	12.2	19.7	65	46/3	61	33	S	930
Honduras	4.8	39	8	3.1	22	7.0	12.0	69	47/3	63	40	H	740
Mexico	83.5	30	6	2.4	29	104.5	137.8	50	42/4	66	70	H	1,850
Nicargaua	3.6	43	8	3.5	20	5.1	7.7	69	47/3	62	57	S	790
Panama	2.3	27	5	2.2	32	2.9	3.7	25	38/4	71	51	S	2,330
Caribbean	**33**	**26**	**8**	**1.8**	**38**	**38**	**47**	**60**	**33/7**	**68**	**54**		**-**
Antigua and Barbuda	0.1	15	5	1.0	71	0.1	0.1	10	27/6	72	31	H	2,380
Bahamas	0.2	24	5	1.9	37	0.3	0.4	26.4	38/4	70	75	S	7,190
Barbados	0.3	16	8	0.8	88	0.3	0.3	10.8	30/11	74	32	H	5,140
Cuba	10.4	16	6	1.0	69	11.4	12.5	13.6	26/8	74	71	S	-
Dominica	0.1	21	5	1.6	44	0.1	0.2	23.9	40/7	75	-	H	1,210
Dominican Republic	6.9	32	8	2.4	28	8.6	11.0	70	39/3	65	52	H	710
Grenada	0.1	26	7	1.9	36	0.1	0.1	22	39/7	72	-	H	1,240
Guadeloupe	0.3	20	7	1.3	52	0.4	0.5	17.0	31/7	72	46	-	-
Haiti	6.3	41	13	2.8	25	7.7	10.1	117	40/5	54	25	H	330

(continued)

Region or Country	Population Estimate mid-1988 (millions)	Crude Birth Rate	Crude Death Rate	Natural Increase (annual, %)	Population "Doubling Time" in Years (at current rate)	Population Projected to 2000 (millions)	Population Projected to 2020 (millions)	Infant Mortality Rate[a]	%Population Under Age 15/65+	Life Expectancy at Birth (years)	Urban Population (%)	Government View of Fertility Level (H = too high, S = satisfactory, L = too low)	Per Capita GNP, 1986 (US$)
Jamaica	2.5	23	6	1.7	41	2.9	4.1	20	37/6	73	54	H	880
Martinique	0.3	18	6	1.2	59	0.3	0.4	13	28/8	74	71	-	-
Netherlands Antilles	0.2	19	6	1.4	51	0.2	0.2	10	30/7	76	-	-	-
Puerto Rico	3.4	19	7	1.2	56	3.7	4.1	14.9	28/10	75	67	-	5,190
St. Kitts-Nevis	0.04	24	11	1.4	51	0.04	0.05	27.8	34/9	67	45	H	1,700
Saint Lucia	0.1	28	6	2.2	31	0.2	0.3	21.5	41/5	69	40	H	1,320
St. Vincent and the Grenadines	0.1	26	7	2.0	35	0.1	0.1	26.5	44/6	69	-	H	960
Trinidad and Tobago	1.3	29	7	2.2	31	1.6	2.2	12.7	34/6	70	34	H	5,120
Tropical South America	**238**	**30**	**8**	**2.2**	**32**	**300**	**401**	**63**	**37/4**	**65**	**69**	**L**	**1,680**
Bolivia	6.9	40	14	2.6	27	9.2	13.2	110	43/3	53	49	L	540
Brazil	144.4	28	8	2.0	34	179.5	233.8	63	36/4	65	71	S	1,810
Colombia	30.6	28	7	2.1	34	38.0	49.3	48	36/4	64	65	S	1,230
Ecuador	10.2	36	8	2.8	25	13.6	19.7	66	42/4	65	52	S	1,160
Guyana	0.8	26	6	2.0	34	0.8	1.1	36	38/4	68	32	S	500
Paraguay	4.4	36	7	2.9	24	6.0	8.8	45	41/4	66	43	S	880
Peru	21.3	34	9	2.5	28	28.0	38.6	88	41/4	61	69	H	1,130
Suriname	0.4	27	7	2.1	33	0.5	0.6	33	37/4	69	66	S	2,510
Venezuela	18.8	29	5	2.4	28	24.7	35.4	36	39/4	70	82	S	2,930
Temperate South America	**48**	**23**	**8**	**1.5**	**46**	**55**	**67**	**31**	**31/8**	**70**	**84**	**S**	**2,050**
Argentina	32.0	24	9	1.5	45	37.2	45.6	35.3	31/9	70	85	S	2,350
Chile	12.6	22	6	1.6	45	14.8	17.7	19.5	31/6	71	82	L	1,320
Uruguay	3.0	18	10	0.8	83	3.2	3.5	29.5	27/11	71	84	L	1,860
Europe	**497**	**13**	**10**	**0.3**	**266**	**506**	**499**	**13**	**21/13**	**74**	**75**		**8,170**
Northern Europe	**84**	**13**	**11**	**0.2**	**373**	**85**	**84**	**9**	**19/15**	**75**	**86**		**9,950**
Denmark	5.1	11	11	-0.1	(-)	5.1	4.8	8.4	18/15	75	84	S	12,640
Finland	4.9	12	10	0.3	247	5.0	4.9	5.8	19/13	74	62	S	12,180
Iceland	0.2	16	7	0.9	79	0.3	0.3	5.4	26/10	77	90	S	13,370
Ireland	3.5	17	10	0.8	88	4.1	4.8	8.7	29/11	73	56	S	5,080
Norway	4.2	13	11	0.2	330	4.3	4.3	8.5	19/16	76	71	S	15,480
Sweden	8.4	12	11	0.1	673	8.3	7.9	5.9	18/18	77	83	L	13,170
United Kingdom	57.1	13	12	0.2	408	57.3	56.6	9.5	19/15	75	91	S	8,920

Region / Country												
Western Europe	156	12	10	0.2	398	157	148	8	18/14	75	83	11,380
Austria	7.6	12	12	0.0	(-)	7.3	7.1	10.3	18/14	75	55	S	10,000
Belgium	9.9	12	11	0.1	1,034	9.7	9.1	9.7	19/14	75	95	S	9,230
France	55.9	14	10	0.4	166	57.9	58.7	8.0	21/13	75	73	L	10,740
Germany, West	61.2	10	11	-0.1	(-)	59.6	51.5	8.6	15/15	75	94	L	12,080
Luxemburg	0.4	12	11	0.1	770	0.4	0.4	7.9	17/13	74	78	L	15,920
Netherlands	14.7	13	9	0.4	169	15.2	14.7	7.7	19/12	76	89	S	10,050
Switzerland	6.6	12	9	0.3	277	6.6	6.1	6.8	17/14	77	61	S	17,840
Eastern Europe	113	15	11	0.4	190	117	122	18	24/11	71	63		-
Bulgaria	9.0	13	11	0.2	385	9.4	9.5	14.5	21/11	72	65	L	-
Czechoslovakia	15.6	14	12	0.2	289	16.2	16.8	13.9	24/11	71	74	S	-
Germany, East	16.6	13	13	0.0	(-)	16.5	16.3	9.2	19/14	72	77	L	-
Hungary	10.6	12	14	-0.2	(-)	10.6	10.5	19.0	21/13	70	58	L	2,010
Poland	38.0	17	10	0.7	100	39.9	42.4	17.5	26/9	71	61	S	2,070
Romania	23.0	16	11	0.5	141	24.5	26.6	25.6	25/9	70	49	L	—
Southern Europe	144	12	9	0.3	219	148	145	16	22/12	74	68		5,660
Albania	3.1	27	6	2.1	33	3.8	4.6	43	35/5	71	34	S	-
Greece	10.1	11	9	0.2	330	10.3	10.1	12.3	21/13	74	58	L	3,680
Italy	57.3	10	10	0.0	3,465	57.2	52.6	10.1	19/13	75	72	S	8,570
Malta	0.4	15	8	0.7	99	0.4	0.4	13.0	24/10	75	85	S	3,470
Portugal	10.3	12	9	0.3	231	10.5	10.5	15.8	23/12	73	30	S	2,230
Spain	39.0	12	8	0.4	154	40.7	40.7	9.0	23/12	76	91	S	4,840
Yugoslavia	23.6	15	9	0.6	110	25.0	25.9	27.1	24/8	70	47	S	2,300
USSR	286	20	10	1.0	68	311	354	25	26/9	69	65	S	7,400
Oceania	26	20	8	1.2	59	30	36	36	28/9	72	70		9,050
Australia	16.5	15	7	0.8	88	18.7	21.9	9.8	23/10	76	86	S	11,910
Fiji	0.7	28	5	2.3	31	0.8	1.0	21	38/3	67	37	H	1,810
French Polynesia	0.2	28	4	2.4	29	0.3	0.3	23	37/3	71	57	-	-
New Caledonia	0.2	24	6	1.8	38	0.2	0.2	36	36/4	68	60	-	-
New Zealand	3.3	16	8	0.8	87	3.6	4.0	10.8	25/10	74	84	S	7,110
The Pacific Islands[d]	0.2	34	5	2.9	24	0.2	0.3	33	47/4	71	29	-	-
Papua-New Guinea	3.7	36	12	2.4	29	4.8	6.8	100	42/2	54	13	H	690
Solomon Islands	0.3	41	6	3.6	19	0.5	0.8	42	48/3	68	9	H	530
Vanuatu	0.2	38	5	3.3	21	0.2	0.3	38	46/3	69	18	S	-
Western Samoa	0.2	37	8	2.9	24	0.2	0.3	50	42/5	65	21	H	680

(-) data unavailable or inapplicable

a Infant deaths per 1000 live births

b Average number of children born to a woman during her lifetime

c A = complete data . . D = little or no data

d Comprising the Federated States of Micronesia, Palau, and the Marshall and N. Mariana Islands

Glossary of Terms

A

Acid deposition
Acidic deposits in rain, snow, or solid form, usually the result of pollution

Alternate energy sources
Energy sources that are not commonly used, and the development of which is in the formative stages. Nuclear fusion, wind, and tidal power are examples.

Antiballistic Missile (ABM) System
Interceptor missiles, radar, and other equipment used to intercept and destroy enemy ballistic missiles

Appropriate technology
Technology which is well-suited to the recipient country and is generally labour intensive. The machines are ones which can be used and repaired with ease in the country.

Aquifer
An underground routeway along which water flows relatively easily. A layer of sandstone sandwiched between layers of shale often forms an aquifer.

Assured destruction
The ability to destroy enemy cities and military installations, even after having been attacked

Automation
Occurs when machinery is introduced to perform tasks which would otherwise be carried out by human labour

B

Balfour Declaration
A statement by Arthur Balfour, British Secretary of State for Foreign Affairs, in 1917, promising British support for a Jewish homeland

Ballistic missile
A missile propelled by a rocket for the first part of its journey. It travels in an arc.

Barefoot doctors
The lay people trained to do specific medical tasks where no doctor is available

Barrios
See **Shanty towns**

Bartering
A system of trade where one object is exchanged for one or more others of equivalent value

Bilateral aid
Aid sent directly from the donor country to the recipient country

Biomass
The energy contained in plant material such as wood or peat

Biosphere
The part of the earth's surface where living organisms can maintain themselves

Birth rate
The number of live births per 1000 people in a population, per year

Black market
Supplies a country with goods or currency that are illegal or difficult to obtain any other way

Blockade
The isolation of a place to prevent, for example, the passage of troops or supplies

Boundary line
The geographical limit of state sovereignty where it intersects the land or water surface

Bourgeoisie
The middle class which dominates an economy, according to Marxian philosophy

Bureaucracy
The people employed in the administration of an organization

Bustee
A registered community of the very poor in an Indian city

C

Canadian International Development Agency (CIDA)
An agency which oversees the use of Canadian tax money for foreign aid projects

Canadian University Services Overseas (CUSO)
An organization which provides opportunities for students in Canadian universities to help out in other countries by planting crops, digging wells, etc.

Capital
Money which is to be invested or used to develop an area economically

Capital-intensive
Describes an industry or other economic activity that requires a great deal of capital

Capitalism
An economic system in which individuals can own and operate businesses and keep the profits generated

Carbogel
See **Fluidcarbon**

Cartel
An agreement concerning pricing and production, between major producing countries of a particular commodity. OPEC is a cartel having considerable influence on world oil production and pricing.

Cash crop
A crop, such as coffee, bananas, or cocoa, grown mainly for its export value

Central Treaty Organization (CENTO)
A pact (originally called SEATO) between Iraq, Turkey, the United Kingdom, Pakistan, and Iran, mainly involving co-operation in the fields of culture, agriculture, health, communications, and transportation

City states
An area of political influence that developed around a city. City states were common until the development of the "modern state" during the last few centuries.

Colonies
Territories which are dominated politically and economically by a foreign power

Common market
A customs union with an additional agreement to permit capital and labour to move freely across international boundaries

Common shares
Shares in a company, each of which entitles the holder to a vote. The value of these shares goes up or down depending upon the success of the firm.

Communism
An economic and political system in which the people or the government owns the property as well as the economic means of production. In theory, wealth is shared with everyone in society according to their needs. Communism is based on the writings of Karl Marx.

Conservation
Reducing the loss of energy, thus decreasing demand for more energy supplies

Contour ploughing
Ploughing horizontally across a slope to reduce surface erosion

Conventional oil
Oil that flows fairly freely through the pores of rock

Conventional war
A war fought without the use of nuclear weapons

Cottage industry
The household manufacture of goods

Council for Mutual Economic Assistance (COMECON)
An economic union between the USSR and nations of eastern Europe

Cradle of civilization
An area where food surpluses made it possible for complex societies to emerge thousands of years ago

Cross-breed
The process whereby two plants or animals with desired characteristics are used to parent a new offspring with more desirable features than the parents

Cruise missile
A guided missile, the engine of which burns throughout flight. It is not usually detected by low-level radar, and is controlled by computer.

Cultural diversity
A place where there are groups of people with different cultural backgrounds

Culture
The way of life of a person or a group of people

Customs union
Countries practising free trade and also applying the same tariffs to goods imported from elsewhere

D

Death rate
The number of deaths per 1000 people in a population, per year

Demography
The study of population and its changes and patterns

Dependency load
The percentage of a population below 15 and over 65 years of age

Desertification
The destruction of biological activity on the land, eventually leading to desert-like conditions

Desertization
The spread of deserts due to natural changes only, not involving mankind's activities

Deterrent
Weapons capable of retaliation that will make an enemy hesitate before attacking, or refrain. (Deterrence is the policy which advocates this approach.)

Developed world
Those countries which have a relatively high standard of living and are highly industrialized

Developing world
Those countries which are relatively poor and are not highly industrialized

Doubling time
The amount of time needed for a population to double in size

E

Economic Commission for Africa (ECA)
A United Nations organization which encourages multinational co-operation between many poor nations

Economic Community of West African States (ECOWAS)
An organization founded in 1975 by 15 West African countries. Its objective is to achieve co-operation in agriculture, industry, transportation, resources, etc. It is hoped that such co-operation will lead to an economic union.

Economic union
A group of countries which are essentially organized as one

Entrepreneurs
Business people who invest money with the hope of making a profit

Equity
The value of a property or business. Equity is used to back most loan applications.

European Economic Community (EEC)
Several countries in western Europe which have agreed to eliminate tariff barriers and other restrictive economic practices. The EEC is also referred to as the Common Market.

Exclusive Economic Zone (EEZ)
An area of water over which a nation has absolute control. Around Canada, the EEZ is normally 370 km wide.

F

Fall-out
Radioactive particles created by a nuclear explosion and returned to earth downwind, usually in precipitation

Favelas
See **Shanty towns**

Fifth column
A group of people who live in a given country but act against it because they sympathize with an enemy

Fifth World
The poorest countries of the world where there is little sign of development, few known resources, and the standard of living for the population is very low

First strike (pre-emptive strike)
The first attack of a nuclear war

First World
The most economically developed countries in the world. They are highly industrialized countries such as Canada.

Flashpoint
A location where tensions are high and war might break out at any moment

Fluidcarbon
An oil-like substance made from coal

Food and Agricultural Organization (FAO)
A United Nations agency whose main goal is to reduce hunger in the developing world through improved farming techniques and crop management

Fourth World
Countries where there is widespread poverty but where there are also signs of economic growth. With time and technology, significant economic growth can take place.

Free enterprise
See **capitalism**

Free trade
An agreement between two or more countries to remove tariffs on goods traded between them

Frontier
A zone of exploration and expansion

G

Gastroenteritis
A serious upset of the digestive system which can lead to severe diarrhea, dehydration, or even death

Geopolitics
The spatial (territorial) claims of nations and their orbit of influence beyond their political boundaries

Geosynchronous orbit
The orbit traced by a satellite which remains constantly above one location on the earth's surface

Grass-roots medicine
The practice whereby lay people are taught to do basic medical procedures. This enables basic health care to be offered where no doctors are available.

Green Revolution
The agricultural research and resultant changes in grain crops which began in the 1950s and 1960s. New high-yielding varieties of crops were introduced which were more productive but required more inputs such as fertilizers and irrigation.

Greenhouse effect
The slow warming of the earth which is attributed to a buildup of carbon dioxide in the atmosphere. The carbon dioxide acts like the glass in a greenhouse, allowing short-wave radiation from the sun to penetrate to the earth's surface, but preventing the long waves, or heat waves, from escaping.

Ground zero
The point on the earth where a nuclear weapon is detonated (or the point directly below an airburst)

Groundwater
Water that is held or flows beneath the surface of the ground. It is usually in the pores of soil and rocks.

H

Hard target
A structure protected against the effects of nuclear attack, for example, a missile silo

Heartland
An enlarged pivot area. (See **Pivot Area**.)

Heavy metal (approach to energy development)
The construction of major energy production sources such as nuclear reactors

Hierarchy
A pattern in which there are a number of classes or levels such as in a society which has high and low classes

High-tech
Sophisticated forms of technology such as computers that are able to perform many functions with great speed and ease

High-Yielding Varieties (HYVs)
Varieties of cereal crops such as wheat or rice that produce much higher yields of food than older varieties, but require more fertilizer, water, etc.

Hiroshima and **Nagasaki**
Two Japanese cities devastated in 1945 when atomic bombs were dropped on them

Hunger
The painful sensation or state of weakness caused by the need for food

Hydrocracking
A technique developed in the 1920s which enabled more gasoline and other products to be extracted from a barrel of oil

I

ICBM
Intercontinental ballistic missile

Industrial revolution
A period of time in Europe when new technologies were introduced into industrial production. It signalled the beginning of mass production

Industrialization
A process in which industry introduces modern, larger-scale technology to manufacture products

Infant Mortality Rate (IMR)
The number of deaths per 1000 live births per year

Information explosion
The rapid increase in the amount of knowledge and its communication throughout the world

Infrastructure
The economic skeleton of an economy, such as roads, schools, and banks

Insurrection
The political overthrow of a government

K

Kilotonne
The amount of energy that would be released by the simultaneous explosion of approximately one thousand tonnes of TNT, a way of measuring the explosive power of a nuclear blast. The ''Little Boy'' bomb which destroyed Hiroshima was 13 kt, or 0.013 Mt.

L

Labour-intensive
Describes an economic activity in which a great deal of labour is needed

Laser (Light Amplification by Stimulated Emission of Radiation)
A beam of light that could be used (from a satellite) to destroy enemy installations

Latin American Economic System (SELA)

An organization which includes many Latin American countries and whose goal is to integrate self-sustained and independent development of the area

Launch on warning (launch under attack)

A strategy of launching nuclear weapons when warning systems indicate that enemy missiles are going to attack

Lesser developed countries

Those countries which are the poorer nations of the world and have not yet fully industrialized. Widespread poverty is commonly found in these countries.

Limited nuclear war

A nuclear war in which a limited number of nuclear weapons (possibly 10 or 100) are used

M

Malnutrition

Occurs when an individual experiences hunger over a long period of time or has major inadequacies in diet

Malthusian checks

Events which cause widespread death and keep a population from growing beyond the food supply available to it

Mandate (League of Nations)

Permission given by the League of Nations to administer a conquered nation

Maritime states

Countries adjacent to oceans or seas

Marshall Plan

A plan funded by the USA to help Europe recover after World War II

Mass production

The use of machines to produce large quantities of goods relatively quickly

Megaprojects

Projects designed on a huge scale. An example is the Itaipu hydro-electric dam in South America or the proposal to divert water over great distances in North America.

Megatonne

The amount of energy that would be released by the explosion of approximately 1 million tonnes of TNT, a way of measuring the explosive power of a nuclear blast. Eighty bombs like the one exploded at Hiroshima equals 1 Mt.

Mixed economy

An economic system in which there is some free enterprise or private ownership of companies as well as government ownership and regulation

Money economy

An economic system in which currency is used to purchase goods rather than the use of bartering

Multilateral aid

Aid that comes from many countries and is channelled through an international agency such as the Red Cross

Multinational corporation

A company with its headquarters in one country and branch plants elsewhere

Multiple Independently Targetal Re-entry Vehicle (MIRV)

Multiple re-entry vehicles (many warheads) carried to enemy territory by a ballistic missile. Each of them has a mechanism to guide it to a separate target.

Mutually Assured Destruction (MAD)

A strategy to prevent nuclear war based on the assumption that each side is capable of destroying the other. Missiles involved are usually targeted at cities.

N

Nation

A political entity which has sovereign political control over a piece of territory

Natural decrease

The rate at which a population decreases, not including emigration. This occurs when the death rate exceeds the birth rate.

Natural increase

The rate at which a population increases, not including immigration. This occurs when the birth rate exceeds the death rate.

Natural resource

A naturally occurring resource such as a mineral or fish

Neo-colonialism

Occurs when a corporation uses or exploits a country for its own interests in ways which are against that country's national interest

Neo-Malthusianism

A modern philosophy which basically follows the teaching of Malthus and outlines the dangers of population growing too quickly and outgrowing the food-producing capacity of a country

Non-governmental organization (NGO)

Such organizations use private donations in aid projects.

North
A term used to describe those countries of the world which have a comparatively high standard of living. Most of these countries are in the northern part of the world, with the exception of Australia and New Zealand.

North Atlantic Treaty Organization (NATO)
A military agreement between several European and North American countries. In particular, its goal is to prevent the further spread of communism into western Europe.

Nuclear club
Members are countries possessing one or more nuclear weapons. (USA, 1945; USSR, 1949; UK, 1952; France, 1960; China, 1964; Israel, late 1960s; India, 1974. Pakistan is believed to have joined in 1987.)

Nuclear family
A family composed of just the father, mother, and children

Nuclear-free zone
An area in which nuclear weapons are not permitted, for any reason

Nuclear fusion
A technique still in the experimental stages, involving the release of huge quantities of energy from water

Nuclear winter
The theory that multiple nuclear explosions will alter the atmosphere very severely and that temperatures in the succeeding year(s) will be so low that crops will not grow. Any people who survive the initial nuclear effects may freeze to death.

O

Oil (tar) sands and shales
Oil deposits which do not flow readily and which are held tightly in the pores of sands or shales

Oral Rehydration Therapy (ORT)
A mixture of salt, sugar, and clean water fed to children in order to stop diarrhea and the resultant dehydration

Organization for European Economic Co-operation (OEEC)
An organization comprising 18 European countries. It was formed in 1948 to administer the funds of the Marshall Plan. (It is the predecessor of the modern EEC.)

Organization of Petroleum Producing Countries (OPEC)
An organization which includes many oil-producing countries. These countries make decisions on production levels and prices so that they have some control over the income from their exports.

P

Permafrost
Ground which is permanently frozen, except for the near-surface "active layer" which thaws for a brief period each summer

Pershing II
A US intermediate-range missile. It has a 1600 km range and, from bases in western Europe, could reach its target in 5 min with pinpoint accuracy.

Pivot Area
An area which, because of its geographical characteristics, has the potential to become a powerful state (suggested by Sir Halford Mackinder)

Population density
The average number of people per square kilometre for a certain country or area

Population growth rate
The rate at which a population increases each year. It is expressed as a percentage.

Population pyramid
Composed of two bar graphs back to back and constructed vertically. Each age group of 5 years is represented by 2 bars, one for the male population and one for the female population, starting with the youngest at the bottom.

Populationist
Describes a philosophy which proposes that population is generally beneficial to a country

Preferred shares
Shares in a company which do not entitle the holder to a vote, but which earn dividends. These shares have a guaranteed minimum value unless the company experiences financial trouble.

Pre-industrial economy
An economic system based on small-scale production from cottage industry

Prejudice
An unfavourable opinion that is formed without any basis in fact

Primary health care
Involves the training of many local health workers in a basic way to work in their own villages to diagnose simple health problems, attempt to cure them, and educate the local people in health matters.

Proliferation
The process which leads to more and more nations possessing nuclear weapons, or an increase in the number of nuclear weapons in one country

R

Racism
The generalized, permanent exploitation of real or biological differences, to the advantage of the accusor and to the detriment of the victim, for the purpose of justifying aggression

Reserve (of a resource)
A deposit that has potential value but which is not yet developed

Resource
Something in reserve of which we make profitable use

Rule of 72
A simple method of calculating the number of years necessary for a population to double in size. This is found by dividing 72 by the annual percentage rate of population increase.

Run (on a bank)
Occurs when insecurity leads many depositors to withdraw their money from a bank

S

Second World
The communist countries of the world

Seven Sisters
The major international oil companies

Shanty towns
The shacks that are built around the edges of many Third World cities, by families who have moved there in search of a better life

Sharecropping
A system of land rental where a farmer pays the owner of the land a certain percentage of the crop yield

Socialist economy
An economic system in which there is both private and public ownership of corporations as well as extensive government regulation of the economy

Soft energy path
Satisfying energy requirements through small-scale local production coupled with conservation

Soft target
A target not protected against the effects of nuclear attack, for example, a city

South
A term used to describe those countries of the world which have a comparatively low standard of living. Most of these countries are in the southern part of the world. Australia and New Zealand are included in the "North" because of their high standards of living.

Southeast Asian Collective Defence Treaty (SEATO)
An organization which existed from 1954 to 1975 to provide collective defence against communist aggression in Southeast Asia

SS20
The NATO way of describing a Soviet intermediate-range nuclear missile. From bases inside Warsaw Pact countries, this missile can reach its target in 10 to 15 min.

Strategic Defence Initiative — SDI (Star Wars)
In theory, an impenetrable shield over the United States which would keep out enemy missiles. It depends largely on satellites equipped with laser beams.

Superpowers
The two dominant nations in the world, USA and USSR

Supranationalism
Agreements made between countries which, in effect, reduce or remove normal barriers between them

Synthesis
A process whereby information is taken from a number of different sources and blended together to produce conclusions

T

Tax holiday
An exemption from tax extended to a corporation as an incentive to locate in a certain country

Terrorism
The threat of violence to intimidate or coerce

Theory of plate tectonics
The movement of the rigid plates which are believed to support the earth's surface. This movement is used to explain the formation of many geological structures, and the occurrence of earthquakes and volcanoes.

Third World
This term has two meanings. The first meaning is a group of non-communist countries which make up the developing world. If the world is divided into five worlds instead of three, the Third World means the group of developing countries which are relatively affluent, have significant natural resources which are being developed and/or are well into the process of industrialization.

Triad
A combination of submarine-launched ballistic missiles, ICBMs, and intercontinental bombers. Defence against simultaneous attack by all three would be difficult.

U

Underemployment
Occurs when a person works at a job which requires fewer qualifications than that person has acquired

Undernutrition
Occurs when a person has a diet deficient in quantity of food intake

Urbanization
The growth in the proportion of people living in large settlements compared to rural areas

V

Vavilov Centres
Areas on the surface of the earth, as identified by Nikolay Vavilov, which contain a great variety of life, and within which areas should be set aside for protection

Verification
Determination of whether the potential combatants are complying with arms control agreements

Vital commodity
A commodity, such as food, which is vital to life

W

Warsaw Pact
A defensive alliance between USSR and nations of eastern Europe

Water deficit
Occurs when the water supplied by precipitation and other sources is less than that lost through evaporation, transpiration and run-off, etc.

Water-related diseases
Diseases that are associated with the consumption of, or contact with, polluted water, for example, malaria and cholera

Water surplus
Occurs when the water supplied by precipitation and other sources is greater than that lost through evaporation, transpiration and run-off, etc.

World Health Organization (WHO)
An organization within the United Nations which studies the incidence and cause of diseases, and organizes relief efforts

World Bank
A bank established in 1944 to administer the receipt and distribution of money for aid projects around the world

Y

Yield
The amount of energy released in a nuclear explosion

Yield
The amount of a crop which is grown in a given area in a year

Z

Zero-Option
A proposal for the scrapping of all intermediate-range Soviet and American nuclear missiles in Europe

Index

A

Acid deposition, 263
Acid precipitation, 259-64
 aquatic environment, and, 263-64
 results, 259
 snowmelt, 264
 solutions, 261-64
 sources, 259
Acid rain, see Acid precipitation
Africa
 national boundaries, 104-105
 superpowers' interest in, 106
Aging population, 217-18
AIDS, 43
Alliances, 89
 Canada's role in, military, 93-94
 common market, 95
 customs union, 95
 Economic Commission for Africa
  (ECA), 97
 Economic Community of West
  African States (ECOWAS), 97
 economic union, 95
 European Economic Community
  (EEC), 96
 free trade, 95
 Latin America Economic System
  (SELA), 96
 major economic, 95-98
 major military, 90-91
Amaranth, 192
Amin, Idi, 108
Apartheid, 80
Aquifers, 276
Arabs, and Israel, 110-12
Arctic environmental concerns,
 287-89
Armed conflict, 108
 causes, 108-10
 religious causes, 108
Atmosphere
 state of, 253-59
 urban pollution, 253-54, 256-58
Automation, 150-51

B

Bakery in Nairobi, 63
Balfour Declaration, 111
Bandong, Thailand, water supplies,
 274-75
Bangladesh, 109, 176
 historical background, 177-78

Barefoot doctors, 43
Barrios, 32
Bartering, 132-33
Bhopal, India, 257-58
Bilateral foreign aid, 6
Biomass, 311-12
Biosphere, 235
Birth rate, 207
Black market, 133
Blocs, 89
Blockade, 114
Boundaries
 changes in, 101-102
 establishment of, 101
 national, within Africa, 104-105
 political, evolution of, 100-101
Boundary line, 100
Bourgeoisie, 142
Breast feeding, 181
 vs. bottle feeding, 182-83
Bretton Woods Conference, 58
British Empire, 84-85, 134
Bruce Peninsula Park, 327-28
Bruntland, Gro Harlem, 326
Brussels, 113
Bustee, 169

C

Canadian International Development
 Agency (CIDA), 64-67
 bureaucracy of, 67
Canadian University Students
 Overseas (CUSO), 44
Cancer, and sulphur dioxide
 emissions, 260-61
Capital, 134
Capital intensive (automation), 150
Capitalism, 141
Carbogel, 308
Carbon dioxide, 267
Cartel, 299
Case studies
 Agripina, 19
 Bangladesh, 176-78
 Canadian International
  Development Agency (CIDA),
  64-67
 cancer, and sulphur dioxide
  emissions, 260-61
 Chernobyl nuclear reactor
  explosion, 265-66
 Cuban Missile crisis, 114-115
 desertification in Mali, 251-52
 Dome Petroleum, 296-97

Francis family, Waterford, ON,
 248-49
Hungary, 143-44
Israel, and Arabs, 110-12
Nairobi bakery, 63
Penen of Sarawak, 47-48
pollution in Mexico City, 254-55
population control in China,
 221-23
profiles of hunger, 169-70
Sudan, 106-107
Venezuela, letter from, 339-40
water shortages in Southwestern
 U.S., 276-77
water supplies in Bandong,
 Thailand, 274-75
Yanomani Indians, Brazil, 320-21
Cash crops, 184-85
Cattle-grazing, Botswana, 62
Central Treaty Organization
 (CENTO), 90
Chernobyl nuclear reactor explosion,
 265-66
Chief Seattle, 282
Child labour, 55-56, 152
Children
 organizations aiding, 68
 solutions to malnutrition-disease,
  167
China, population control, 221-23
Chisholm, Alex, 233
Cholera, incidence of, T38-41
Churches, foreign aid, 68
CITES, 284-85, 327
City state, 104
Climatic regions of the world, major,
 F11
Club of Rome, 295
Coal, 308-309
Colonialism
 benefits of, 137
 legacy of, 136-37
Colonies, 136
Common market, 95
Common shares, 296
Communism, 141-42
Communist Manifesto, The, 142
Conservation
 CITES, 284-85
 habitats/wildlife, 282-87
 international laws, 284-86
 National Parks, 282-83
 oil supplies, 301
 tropical rain forests, 282-83
 Vavilov Centres, 284

Genetic engineering, 190-91
Geography, role of, 8
Geopolitics, 79
    British Empire, 84-85
    heartland, 83
    Japanese Empire, 83-84
    nature of, 82-85
    pivot area, 82-83
Geostationary orbit, 35
Geosynchronous orbit, 312-13
Geothermal power, 313-14
Giles, Paul, 52
Grass-roots dentistry, 74-75
Grass-roots medicine, 43
Greenhouse effect, 267-69
Green Revolution, 187-88, 189-90
Groundnut, 192-93
Groundwater, 269

H

Habitat destruction, 281-89
Hannell, Linda, 339
Haushofer, Karl, 82
Haves vs. have-nots, 28-29
Health, effect on population, 204
Heartland, 83
Herzl, Theodor, 111
Hierarchy, 144
High tech, 156
High-yielding varieties (HYV),
    187-88
Human rights organizations, 68
Human Suffering Index, 78
Hungary, 143
Hunger
    contributing factors, 172-75
    defined, 163
    forgotten crops, 192-93
    genetic engineering, 190-91
    government policy on, 170-71
    Green Revolution, 187-88, 189-90
    land ownership, 184-85
    pest control, 174-75
    pests, 171
    possible solutions to, 181-83
    profiles of, 169-70
    statistical analysis, 179
    synthetic foods, 191
Hydrocracking, 299
Hydro-electric power, 314-15

I

Immigration, 20
Industrialization
    automation, 150-51
    child labour, 152
    defined, 130
    desirability of, 132-33
    and economy type, 132-33
    education, 132
    historical perspective, 134-35
    and technology, 133
    entrepreneurs, 152
    environmental damage, 152-53
    how accomplished, 144-45
    industrial accidents, 153
    infrastructure, 148-49
    problems with, 152-53
    urbanization, 152
Industrial Revolution, 134-35
Infant Mortality Rate (IMR), 208
Information explosion, 156
Information gap, 35
Infrastructure, 148-49
Inquiry model, 20-21
    apply and communicate, 20, 21
    come to a conclusion, 20, 21
    evaluate, 20, 21
    focus and identify, 20
    organize, 20
    plan, 20, 21
    record, 20, 21
International Monetary Fund, 58, 59
Israel, and Arabs, 110-12
Insurrections, 137
Issues, major world, 4

J

Japan, geopolitics of, 83-84

K

Kennedy, John F., 114
Kenya, working in, 24-25
Khomeini, Ayatollah, 108
King, Martin Luther, 45
Korean War, 128
Kruschev, Nikita, 114

L

Labour intensive technology, 133
Land ownership, 184-85
Land reform, 185, T186
Latin America Economic System
    (SELA), 96

League of Nations, 89, 101
Lemmings, 289
Less developed countries (LDCs), 7
    causes of underdevelopment, 146
    diseases, fighting, 43-44
    industrialization, 132-33
    obstacles to economic growth, 151
"Limits to Growth" (Club of Rome),
    295
Locusts, 172, 174

M

Mackinder, Sir Halford, 82-83
Macro-state, 15
Malaria, incidence of, T38-41
Malnutrition, 163
Malthusian checks, 214-15
Malthusianism, 214-15
Malthus, Thomas Robert, 214
Mandate, 111
Maritime states, 100
Marx, Karl, 142, 215
Marshall Plan, 96
Mass production, 134
Measles, 37
Megaprojects, 301
Mercator projection, 335
Mexico City, pollution in, 255
Micro-state, 15
Migration, 331
Military expenditure, 119, F120
Mineral resources, 317-18
Minority groups, 44-46
    blacks, 44-46
    children, 55-56
    native groups, N.A., 46-47
    women, 48-53
Mixed economy, 142
Money economy, 132
Monnet, Jean, 96
Montreal Protocol, 1987, 327
Mozambican National Resistance
    (MNR), 79-80
Mozambique, 78-81
    Canadian aid to, 81
    McLean Report, 80-81
    Portuguese, effect on, 79
Multinational corporations, 139-40
Multilateral foreign aid, 61
Munn, Ted, 254

Photo Credits

Helena te Bokkel, 283 right, 285 right; Canapress Photo Service, 4, 45, 47 left, 52 right, 95, 102, 110 bottom, 112 left, 112 right, 117, 122, 128 top, 128 bottom, 199 mid-right, 156 bottom, 201 left, 201 right, 202, 254 top, 254 bottom right, 258, 266, 316, 320, 321, 328, 329 top, 329 bottom, 332 top, 332 bottom; CIDA, 32, 34 left, 52 left, 56 right, 59, 61 top, 64 both, 65, 66 all, 132, 133, 178, 226, 241; FAO Photo/S. Bunnag, 151; Government of South Korea, 129 top left, 129 bottom left, 129 bottom right; Christine Hannell, 24, 30 top, 49 bottom, 68, 69, 74, 118, 198, 230, 247 bottom, 287, 289, 339, 344; Robert Harshman, 7 bottom left, 7 bottom right, 22 bottom left, 27, 28, 32 right, 135, 137, 156 top, 174, 184, 216/217, 256, 278, 322; Robert Haskett, 2 bottom left, 2 bottom right, 3 bottom left, 3 bottom right, 3 top left, 3 top right, 5, 9, 14, 15, 17, 18 bottom left, 18 bottom right, 18 top, 19, 22 top right, 22 bottom right, 29 bottom right, 36, 47 bottom right, 50 top left, 51, 55 top, 110 top, 130, 140, 147 bottom, 148, 149, 153, 175, 207, 214 top, 221 top, 221 bottom, 222 top, 222 bottom, 223, 237, 242/243, 254/255 (middle), 313, 335, 337, 338 top, 338 bottom; Imperial Oil, 305; Kai Slide Bank/Toronto, 325; NASA, 330; National Parks-Parks Canada, 327 top, 326; Nyasaland Government and Information Department, 49 top right; Ontario Ministry of Agriculture and Food, 327 bottom, 248 top, 248 bottom, 249 top, 249 bottom; Ontario Ministry of Lands and Forests, 247 top; Ontario Ministry of Natural Resources, 315; Population Reference Bureau, 243 bottom; Tourism Australia, 282/283; UNESCO, 29, 30 bottom, 246; UNICEF Photo, 29 top right, 43, 48, 50 bottom, 53, 55 bottom, 57 both, 61 bottom, 78, 81, 107, 146, 147 top, 154 top, 154 bottom, 162, 165, 168 left, 168 right, 183, 185, 208, 211 top, 211 bottom, 214 bottom, 252 left, 252 right, 274, 275, 311; U.S. Army Photo/Oswald Butler, 93, 117; U.S. Department of Defence, 114, 115, 294; WHO Photo/D. Henrioud, 42; World Bank/Tomas Sennett, 150.

Sources

Chapter 1

Page 10 Figure 1.2

Adapted from *The New Jacaranda Atlas*,
3rd ed. (Brisbane: Jacaranda Wiley Ltd., 1987)
pp. 2-3.

Page 11 Figure 1.3

Adapted from *The New Jacaranda Atlas*,
3rd ed. (Brisbane: Jacaranda Wiley Ltd., 1987),
p. 6.

Page 13 Figure 1.5

Adapted from *The New Jacaranda Atlas*,
3rd ed. (Brisbane: Jacaranda Wiley Ltd., 1987),
p. 7.

Page 16 Figure 1.6

Adapted from *The New Jacaranda Atlas*,
3rd ed. (Brisbane: Jacaranda Wiley Ltd., 1987),
pp. 12-13.

Chapter 2

Page 27 Note 1

R. Harshman, eyewitness account.

Page 30 Table 2.1

*United Nations Compendium of Human
Settlement Statistics 1983* (New York, 1985),
pp. 264-282.

Page 33 Table 2.2

United Nations. *Estimates and Projections of
Urban, Rural and City Population, 1950-2025:
The 1986 Assessment* (New York, 1986).

Pages 39-41 Table 2.4

World Health Organization (WHO). *World
Health Statistics* (Geneva, 1984), *Weekly
Epidemiological Record* (Geneva), Vol. 59
(1984), pp. 141-148, and Vol. 50 (1985),
pp. 149-156; *World Health Statistics Quarterly*
(Geneva), Vol. 37 (1984), No. 2, Vol. 38 (1985),
No. 2, and Vol. 39 (1986), No. 2. As quoted in
*World Resources 1987: A Report by The
International Institute for Environment and
Development and The World Resources
Institute* (New York: Basic Books Inc., 1987).
Director: J. Alan Brewster.

Page 45 Figure 2.2

US Census Bureau; National Center for
Education Statistics.

Page 51 Note 2

Joni Seager and Ann Olson, *Women in the
World: An International Atlas* (London: Pan
Books, 1986).

Page 53 Note 3

Material taken from all articles in *The New
Internationalist* (March 1988).

Page 56 Table 2.5

Population Reference Bureau. *The World's
Youth: A Profile* (Washington, July 1985).

Page 58 Table 2.6

World Development Report. As quoted in *The
Globe and Mail*, 5 Oct. 1987.

Page 65 Table 2.7

Ministry of Supply and Services Canada. *CIDA
Annual Report 1986-1987*, p. 12.

Page 66 Table 2.8

Adapted from *CIDA Annual Report 1986-1987*,
p. 12.

Chapter 3

Page 79 Figure 3.1

*Notes on the Visit to Canada of the Delegation
of the Christian Council of Mozambique 1988.*

Page 83 Figure 3.2

Harm J. De Blij and Peter O. Muller, *Human
Geography: Culture, Society, and Space*,
3rd ed. (New York: John Wiley & Sons, Inc.,
1986), p. 459.

Page 84 Figure 3.3

Modified from Harm J. De Blij and Peter O.
Muller, *Human Geography: Culture, Society,
and Space*, 3rd ed. (New York: John Wiley &
Sons, Inc., 1986), p. 461.

Page 86 Figure 3.4

Harm J. De Blij and Peter O. Muller, *Human
Geography: Culture, Society, and Space*,
3rd ed. (New York: John Wiley & Sons, Inc.,
1986), p. 436.

Page 89 Figure 3.6

Modified from Harm J. De Blij and Peter O.
Muller, *Human Geography: Culture, Society,
and Space*, 3rd ed. (New York: John Wiley &
Sons, Inc., 1986), pp. 470-471.

Page 91 Figure 3.7

Adapted from Harm J. De Blij and Peter O.
Muller, *Human Geography: Culture, Society,
and Space*, 3rd ed. (New York: John Wiley &
Sons, Inc., 1986), pp. 472.

Page 94 Figure 3.8

Ministry of National Defence. *Challenge and
Commitment: A Defence Policy for Canada*
(Ottawa, 1987), p. 47.

Page 96 Figure 3.9

Harm J. De Blij and Peter O. Muller, *Human
Geography: Culture, Society, and Space*, 3rd
ed. (New York: John Wiley & Sons, Inc., 1986),
p. 472.

Page 97 Figure 3.10

Martin I. Glassner and Harm J. De Blij,
Systematic Political Geography, 3rd ed. (New
York: John Wiley & Sons, Inc., 1980), p. 379.

Page 98 Figure 3.11

Martin I. Glassner and Harm J. De Blij,
Systematic Political Geography, 3rd ed. (New
York: John Wiley & Sons, Inc., 1980), p. 383.

Page 103 Figure 3.14

Harm J. De Blij and Peter O. Muller, *Human Geography: Culture, Society, and Space*, 3rd ed. (New York: John Wiley & Sons, Inc., 1986), pp. 426-428; Martin I. Glassner and Harm J. De Blij, *Systematic Political Geography*, 3rd ed. (New York: John Wiley & Sons, Inc., 1980), pp. 307, 309, 319-320.

Page 104 Figure 3.15

Martin I. Glassner and Harm J. De Blij, *Systematic Political Geography*, 3rd ed. (New York: John Wiley & Sons, Inc., 1980), p. 58.

Page 105 Figure 3.16

Glenn Frankel, ''Boundaries drawn 100 years ago haunt Africa,'' *The Toronto Star*, 15 Jan. 1985, p. H4.

Page 106 Figure 3.17

A.M. Lesch, ''A View from Khartoum,'' *Foreign Affairs* (Spring 1987), Vol. 68, pp. 807-826.

Page 109 Figure 3.18

Based on Norman Myers, ed., *Gaia: An Atlas of Planet Management* (New York: Anchor Books, 1984), p. 244.

Page 110 Note 1

''Ten Minutes of Horror,'' *Time*, January 6, 1986, pp. 60-62.

Page 113 Note 2

R.Z. Chesnoff, ''When a war needs guns, try Brussels,'' *U.S. News and World Report*, 101:32-33, Di '86.

Page 119 Table 3.4

Ministry of National Defence. *Challenge and Commitment: A Defence Policy for Canada* (Ottawa, 1987), p. 83.

Page 121 Figure 3.2

Ruth Leger Sivard, *World Military and Social Expenditures 1987-88* (Washington: World Priorities, 1987). As quoted in *The New Internationalist*, 1985, p. 17.

Chapter 4

Page 131 Figure 4.1

Harm J. De Blij and Peter O. Muller, *Human Geography: Culture, Society, and Space*, 3rd ed. (New York: John Wiley & Sons, Inc., 1986), p. 307.

Page 139 Note 1

R. Haskett, eyewitness account.

Page 139 Note 2

R. Harshman, eyewitness account.

Page 140 Table 4.2

''The Top 1000 U.S. Companies Ranked by Stock-market Value,'' *Business Week*, April 15, 1988, pp. 174, 176, 178; ''The 25 largest companies outside the U.S.,'' *Forbes*, July 25, 1988, p. 208.

Page 144 Table 4.3

The World Bank. *World Development Report 1988* (Washington, D.C., 1988); *The 1988 Update of the 1987 World Bank Atlas* (Washington, D.C., 1988).

Page 152 Note 3

Latin American Evangelist, July/September 1985.

Chapter 5

Page 176 Table 5.2

Kaleidoscope, 1988.

Pages 180-181 Table 5.3

The World Bank. *Social Indicators of Development 1987* (Washington, D.C.).

Page 189 Table 5.6

U.S. Agency for International Development. As cited in Lester Brown, *State of the World* (Worldwatch Institute, 1987).

Page 189 Table 5.7

U.S. Agency for International Development. As cited in Lester Brown, *State of the World* (Worldwatch Institute, 1987).

Pages 194-195 Table 5.8

The World Bank. *Social Indicators of Development 1987* (Washington, D.C.).

Chapter 6

Page 206 Figure 6.1

Harm J. De Blij and Peter O. Muller, *Geography: Regions and Concepts*, 4th ed. (New York: John Wiley & Sons, Inc., 1985), pp. 26-27.

Page 207 Table 6.2

United Nations Global Estimates and Projections of Population by Sex and Age: The 1984 Assessment (New York, 1984).

Page 208 Table 6.3

Population Reference Bureau. *1988 World Population Data Sheet* (Washington, D.C., 1988).

Page 212 Table 6.4

Population Reference Bureau. *Population Data Sheet 1987*.

Page 212 Table 6.5

Population Reference Bureau. *Population Data Sheet 1987*.

Page 212 Table 6.6

Statistics Canada. *Historical Statistics of Canada Series B100-107* (Ottawa, 1965); *Canada Year Book 1980-81* (Ottawa: Statistics Canada, 1981), pp. 5, 7; Central Statistical Office. *Annual Abstract of Statistics* (London, England, 1981), pp. 35-36; Bureau of Census. *Statistical Abstract of the U.S.* (Washington, D.C., 1988), Table No. 82.

Page 213 Table 6.7

East-West Population Institute. As quoted in *Global Issues: Viewpoints in General Studies* (Australia: The Jacaranda Press, 1987), p. 52, Fig. 3.2.

Chapter 7

Page 231 Figure 7.1

U.S. National Cancer Institute, 1988.

Page 232 Figure 7.3

Christian Science Monitor, October 7, 1987.

Page 236 Figure 7.5

UN Food and Agricultural Organization (FAO). *Unasylva*, Vol. 28 (1976), No. 112-113. As reported in *World Resources 1986: A Report by The World Resources Institute and The International Institute for Environment and Development* (New York: Basic Books Inc., 1986), Director: Jessica Tuchman Mathews.

Page 238 Figure 7.7

Earthspan Briefing Documents: The Global 2000 Report to the President (Penguin Books, 1982). World Conservation Strategy; World Wildlife Fund data; Fuelwood and industrial wood projections from Norman Myers and *World Forest Products Demand and Supply 1990 and 2000* (FAO, 1982). Adapted from Norman Meyers, ed., *Gaia: An Atlas of Planet Management* (New York: Anchor Books, 1984).

Page 241 Figure 7.10

Sara Southey, ''Cooking with waste: Indian ingenuity makes bio-gas viable,'' *The Globe and Mail*, 2 April 1988, p. D4.

Page 245 Figure 7.12

Based on Norman Myers, ed., *Gaia: An Atlas of Planet Management* (New York: Anchor Books, 1984), p. 41.

Page 252 Table 7.2

J.A. Mabbutt, ''A New Global Assessment of the Status and Trends of Desertification,'' *Environmental Conservation*, Vol. II (1984), No. 3, p. 106.

Page 257 Table 7.4

U.S. Environmental Protection Agency. *National Air Pollution Emission Estimates, 1940-1984* (Washington, D.C., 1984). As quoted in *World Resources 1987: A Report by The International Institute for Environment and Development and The World Resources Institute* (New York: Basic Books Inc., 1987), p. 147, Table 3. Director: J. Alan Brewster.

Page 260 Figure 7.15

National Cancer Institute. *Atlas of U.S. Cancer Mortality Among Whites: 1950-1980*. Washington, D.C.: U.S.D.H.H.S., National Institute of Health Publication No. 87-2900, 1987.

Page 265 Figure 7.22

World Resources 1987: A Report by The International Institute for Environment and Development and The World Resources Institute (New York: Basic Books Inc., 1987). Director: J. Alan Brewster.

Page 269 Figure 7.26

World Resources 1987: A Report by The International Institute for Environment and Development and The World Resources Institute (New York: Basic Books Inc., 1987). Director: J. Alan Brewster.

Page 270 Figure 7.27

World Resources 1987: A Report by The International Institute for Environment and Development and The World Resources Institute (New York: Basic Books Inc., 1987). Director: J. Alan Brewster.

Page 271 Figure 7.28

Michael Keating, "Canada: one of the world's great guzzlers," *The Globe and Mail*, 18 Oct. 1986, p. D5.

Page 272 Figure 7.29

Based on Norman Myers, ed. *Gaia: An Atlas of Planet Management* (New York: Anchor Books, 1984), pp. 108-109.

Page 273 Figure 7.30

Christie McLaren, "Billions wasted on irrigation think-tank reports," *The Globe and Mail*, 12 Feb. 1987, p. A1.

Page 277 Figure 7.31

Michael Keating, "Water overuse haunts U.S. West," *The Globe and Mail*, 21. Aug. 1985, p. 9.

Page 278 Figure 7.32

Michael Keating, "Soviets look to diversion," *The Globe and Mail*, 22 Aug. 1985, p. 10.

Page 284 Figure 7.35

Adapted from Norman Myers, ed., *Gaia: An Atlas of Planet Management* (New York: Anchor Books, 1984), p. 165.

Page 285 Figure 7.36

Based on Norman Myers, ed., *Gaia: An Atlas of Planet Management* (New York: Anchor Books, 1984), pp. 166-167.

Page 286 Figure 7.37

Based on Norman Myers, ed., *Gaia: An Atlas of Planet Management* (New York: Anchor Books, 1984), p. 111.

Chapter 8

Page 293 Figure 8.1

Charles A. White, "Gulf War Goes Global," *Canada and the World 1987*, September 1987, pp. 6-7.

Page 296 Figure 8.2

Jim Lyons, *Dome: The Rise and Fall of the House That Jack Built* (Toronto: Macmillan of Canada, 1983), plates following p. 120.

Page 298 Figure 8.3

Financial Times of London.

Page 301 Table 8.1

Paris International Energy Agency. *Quarterly Oil Statistics 1974 and 1985.*

Page 303 Table 8.2

OPEC Annual Statistical Bulletin 1984; World Almanac 1977; Statesman's Yearbook 1986-1987 (London: Macmillan Press, 1987).

Page 306 Figure 8.8

The Jacaranda Atlas of the World (Brisbane: The Jacaranda Press, 1986), pp. 20-23.

Page 307 Figure 8.9

Compiled by Dr. Prem Nanda, Energy Educators of Ontario, as part of *Energy Starter Kit #7* (Toronto, June 1984), p. 60.

Page 310 Figure 8.11

From diagrams based on many sources and published in *Energy — Search for an Answer* (TVOntario, 1984), pp. 105-107.

Page 314 Figure 8.12

World Energy, CLS Graphics Open House (Edenbridge, Kent).

Page 317 Table 8.3

Norman Myers, ed. *Gaia: An Atlas of Planet Management* (New York: Anchor Books, 1984), pp. 110-111.

Page 317 Figure 8.13

Norman Myers, ed., *Gaia: An Atlas of Planet Management* (New York: Anchor Books, 1984).

Chapter 9

Page 332 Table 9.1

Joni Seager and Ann Olson, *Women in the World: An International Atlas* (London: Pan Books, 1986).